missions in creative tension

MISSIONS IN CREATIVE TENSION

THE GREEN LAKE '71 COMPENDIUM

Edited by Dr. Vergil Gerber

William Carey Library
CHRISTIAN MISSION BOOKS
South Pasadena, California

Library of Congress Catalog Number: 74-184218
International Standard Book Number: 0-87808-114-3

Published by the William Carey Library
533 Hermosa Street
South Pasadena, Calif. 91030
Telephone: 213-682-2047

PRINTED IN THE UNITED STATES OF AMERICA

To

concerned
mission colleagues
who are sensitive
to the tensions
created by the success
of the Church worldwide
and are searching
for practical guidelines
to effective
church/mission/church relations
which will facilitate
fulfillment of
the Church's mandate
and hasten
her Lord's return

contents

Part 3: The Conference Handbook

Part 4: A Sampling of Early Response

(Edited by *Frank A. Ineson*)

APPENDIX

acronyms

ACCC	American Council of Christian Churches
AIC	Africa Inland Church
AIM	Africa Inland Mission
C&MA	Christian and Missionary Alliance
CMS	Church Missionary Society (Anglican)
CNEC	Christian Nationals Evangelism Commission
DOM	Division of Overseas Ministries
EFMA	Evangelical Foreign Missions Association
EMIS	Evangelical Missions Information Service
EMQ	Evangelical Missions Quarterly
FEGC	Far Eastern Gospel Crusade
GEM	Greater Europe Mission
GL'71	Green Lake EFMA-IFMA Retreat-Study Conference
ICCC	International Council of Christian Churches
IFCA	Independent Fundamental Churches of America
IFMA	Interdenominational Foreign Mission Association
LAM	Latin America Mission
MARC	Missions Advanced Research and Communication Center
MK's	Missionary Kids
NAE	National Association of Evangelicals
NCCC	National Council of the Churches of Christ
OMF	Overseas Missionary Fellowship
SIM	Sudan Interior Mission
TAM	The Associated Missions (of the ICCC)
TEAM	The Evangelical Alliance Mission
UBS	United Bible Societies
UFM	Unevangelized Fields Mission
WCC	World Council of Churches
WEF	World Evangelical Fellowship
WIM	West Indies Mission

contributors

EDMUND P. CLOWNEY, *President*
Westminster Theological Seminary, Philadelphia, Pennsylvania

RAYMOND J. DAVIS, *General Director*
Sudan Interior Mission

HECTOR ESPINOZA, *President*
Mexican Evangelistic Institute, Mexico City

HORACE L. FENTON, JR., *General Director*
Latin America Mission

WALTER FRANK, *General Director*
Greater Europe Mission

EDWIN L. FRIZEN, JR., *Executive Secretary*
Interdenominational Foreign Mission Association

VERGIL GERBER, *Executive Director*
Evangelical Missions Information Service

IAN M. HAY, *North American Director*
Sudan Interior Mission

FRANK A. INESON, *Research Analyst/Writer*
World Vision International;
Missionary Information Bureau, Brazil

BRUCE KER, *Assistant Professor of Missions*
Western Conservative Baptist Theological Seminary
Portland, Oregon

LOUIS L. KING, *Foreign Secretary*
The Christian and Missionary Alliance

SIDNEY LANGFORD, *Home Director*
Africa Inland Mission

ALFRED LARSON, *General Director*
Unevangelized Fields Mission

GEORGE LINHART, *Pastor*
Grace Chapel, Havertown, Pennsylvania

GORDON MACDONALD, *Pastor*
First Baptist Church, Collinsville, Illinois

JOSEPH S. MCCULLOUGH, *General Director*
Andes Evangelical Mission

CHARLES J. MELLIS, *President*
Missionary Aviation Fellowship

GEORGE W. PETERS, *Professor of World Missions*
Dallas Theological Seminary, Dallas, Texas

DONALD G. PETERSON, *Cataloger/Bibliographer*
Wheaton College Library, Wheaton, Illinois

PAUL W. SHEA, *Student*
Trinity Evangelical Divinity School, Deerfield, Illinois

JACK F. SHEPHERD, *Education Secretary*
The Christian and Missionary Alliance

PETER STAM, *Canadian Home Director*
Africa Inland Mission

WILLIAM H. TAYLOR, *General Secretary*
Central American Mission

J. ALLEN THOMPSON, *General Director*
West Indies Mission

preface

GL '71 was really a "rap session" for evangelical mission leaders. It was convened September 27 through October 1, 1971 at Green Lake, Wisconsin under the aegis of the Evangelical Missions Information Service. It was jointly sponsored by the Evangelical Foreign Missions Association and the Interdenominational Foreign Mission Association taking the place of their triennial Mission Executives Retreat. It was attended by nearly 400 carefully selected participants -- administrators, professors, pastors, students and some outstanding national churchmen from overseas. One single subject occupied their attention: MISSIONS IN CREATIVE TENSION.

To speak of tensions as creative may on the surface seem like a contradiction. Generally we think of them as negative rather than positive. It is precisely at this point -- where the two are in conflict -- that the need for calling the Green Lake '71 Conference arose.

Missions in the 70's find themselves at the very heart of severe tensions swirling around church/mission/church relations. They spring largely from a fact unique to our times: A VIRILE, DYNAMIC CHURCH WORLDWIDE. Firmly rooted in national soil. Maturing in uneven patterns and at varying stages. But experiencing unprecedented growth. Struggling for national identity. Assuming forms compatible with indigenous cultures. Independent yet interdependent.

This new eschatological phenomenon of the church worldwide brings into sharp focus the changing role of missions and missionaries in the 70's and creates tensions of new magnitude. The "home base" now is everywhere and the "receiving church" now is also the "sending church." Missions and missionaries instrumental in part at least in bringing about this phenomenon now face new problems of relationship and dimension of mission growing in part out of their past successes.

Though tensions can be positive resulting in strength and stability, they also can be negative and divisive, stifling growth of the church and hindering fulfillment of her missionary calling.

The GL'71 "400" met at Green Lake to take a hard look at themselves and the missionary role committed to them. They recognized the sins of attitude and action which have produced misunderstanding and magnified tensions in the past and in the present. The need for confession and change was obvious and uppermost in their minds.

At the same time there was a positive realization of the Lordship of Christ as Head of His church, the unity of His body overseas and at home, the sovereign fulfillment of His missionary purposes, the solid foundations which have been laid for His church worldwide, and the glorious anticipation of His return and the consummation of all things.

> "He purposes in His sovereign will
> that all history shall be consummated
> in Christ." Ephesians 1:10 (Phillips)

MISSIONS IN CREATIVE TENSION is a documentary report of what happened at Green Lake. The component parts of this book were not prepared originally for publication nor do they necessarily represent polished or final forms of the author's ideas. They were presented for discussion and interaction. For the same purpose we share them with missionary colleagues who were not at Green Lake hoping that the study of these pages will result in the same heart searching, heart warming change and interchange which we experienced.

VERGIL GERBER

Part 1

studies from a preliminary retreat

founded in 1917

AFRICA EVANGELICAL FELLOWSHIP · AFRICA INLAND MISSION · ANDES EVANGELICAL MISSION · ARCTIC MISSIONS · BELGIAN GOSPEL MISSION · BEREAN MISSION · BIBLE CHRISTIAN UNION · BIBLE CLUB MOVEMENT · BIBLE & MEDICAL MISSIONARY FELLOWSHIP · CENTRAL AMERICAN MISSION · EVANGELICAL LITERATURE OVERSEAS · EVANGELICAL UNION OF SOUTH AMERICA · FAR EAST BROADCASTING COMPANY · FAR EASTERN GOSPEL CRUSADE · GOSPEL FURTHERING FELLOWSHIP · GOSPEL MISSIONARY UNION · GOSPEL MISSION OF SOUTH AMERICA · GOSPEL RECORDINGS · GREATER EUROPE MISSION · HOME OF ONESIPHORUS · INTERNATIONAL CHRISTIAN FELLOWSHIP · INTERNATIONAL MISSIONS · JAPAN EVANGELICAL MISSION · LATIN AMERICA MISSION · MEXICAN INDIAN MISSION · MISSIONARY AVIATION FELLOWSHIP · MISSIONARY SERVICES, INC. · NORTH AFRICA MISSION · NORTHERN CANADA EVANGELICAL MISSION · ORINOCO RIVER MISSION · OVERSEAS CHRISTIAN SERVICEMEN'S CENTERS · OVERSEAS MISSIONARY FELLOWSHIP · POCKET TESTAMENT LEAGUE · RAMABAI MUKTI MISSION · REGIONS BEYOND MISSIONARY UNION · SLAVIC GOSPEL ASSOCIATION · SOUTH AMERICA INDIAN MISSION · SUDAN INTERIOR MISSION · SUDAN UNITED MISSION · THE EVANGELICAL ALLIANCE MISSION · TRANS WORLD RADIO · UNEVANGELIZED FIELDS MISSION · WEST INDIES MISSION · WOMAN'S UNION MISSIONARY SOCIETY · WORLD MISSIONS TO CHILDREN · WORLD RADIO MISSIONARY FELLOWSHIP · WORLDWIDE EUROPEAN FELLOWSHIP

INTERDENOMINATIONAL FOREIGN MISSION ASSOCIATION *of North America*

54 Bergen Avenue, Ridgefield Park, New Jersey 07660 *Telephone: (Code 201) 641-1070*

EDWIN L. (JACK) FRIZEN, JR., EXECUTIVE SECRETARY

June 18, 1971

Dear IFMA member:

Greetings from the IFMA Board Retreat held at Africa Inland Mission's lovely headquarters in Pearl River. We have just concluded three days together. For the last five years the Board Retreat has been filling the gap between the busy business meetings and the annual meetings of the IFMA membership. Each year we have taken a topic; this year it was "The Mission and the Church" in preparation for Green Lake '71, the joint IFMA/EFMA Retreat.

In a sense this retreat was a "mini-GL '71" Vergil Gerber was with us. We tried to predict what to expect at Green Lake. The subject is "The Sending Church and the Mission Church Overseas." In some ways it is more important to interdenominational missions than it is to the EFMA. In order to prepare ourselves, the Board tried to face the questions we felt you would want to consider.

In church growth around the world, there appear to be many variable but universal factors: <u>first</u>, attitudes, both current and past, of missionaries toward nationals are a major influence. <u>Second</u>, the basic concept of the church we want to achieve is important; the clearer our goal the more flexible our patterns can be to the changing climate overseas. <u>Three</u>, the sympathetic relationship of the mission to the church rather than the structure itself.

For your own preparation let me make a few suggestions:

1. Have the right representatives at GL '71; what one Board Member called "the opinion formers" of your mission.
2. Read widely: EMIS is furnishing each delegate to Green Lake with a special issue of EMQ and preparatory papers. Get your people exposed before they come so they can get the most out of it.
3. Understand your own church/mission/church relationships.
4. In one sense, GL '71 is a workshop; what you get out of it will depend on the work you put into it. The structure of the program is to provide each delegate with the best possible circumstance for analyzing his own needs and plotting a course of action to see that they are met.

Prayed for people grow. Whether it's our growth as individual missionaries or the growth of the church, the most consistent factor is prayer. Let us pray!

Come believing!
Your brother in Christ,

Philip E. Armstrong
President

I. QUESTIONS TO CONSIDER IN DETERMINING CHURCH/MISSION RELATIONSHIPS

The following questions have been compiled from the "feedback" participation during the 1971 IFMA Board Retreat after the presentation of the prepared background papers and discussion.

For the best preparation for GL '71 these questions could be profitably answered by each IFMA mission delegate from the perspective of his experience. (Eventually each mission should consider, for future overseas and homeland conferences, having a number of position papers written by its staff and involved representatives of its constituency on these and other questions which may be raised at GL '71.)

A. Church/Mission Relations in the Sending Country

1. Recruitment

a. Has consideration been given to the wide variety of churches, pastors and officers with which IFMA missions deal?
   1) Has the mission classified the different church groupings and developed coping strategies?
   2) Should the mission represent these classifications on mission councils?
   3) Should mission leadership expose itself to a greater extent to pastors and leaders of all these classifications?

b. What problem is presented by the mobility of students and consequent limited adequate contacts with any one church?
   1) Should the mission suggest a plan for the pastor to maintain contact with absentee students?
   2) Should the mission ask representative pastors including mission council members to formulate such a plan?
   3) Does the mission strongly stress the need for candidates to have strong personal ties with a local church?
   4) What should the mission do to help candidates work more closely with their home or supporting church or churches?

c. How should the largely impersonal relationship between mission and churches regarding recruits be improved?
   1) Should the full mission file be shared with the pastor or church missionary committee?
   2) Should a special reference form be prepared for pastors?
   3) Should the mission make an immediate phone call to the pastor upon receipt of preliminary questionnaire from a candidate?
   4) Should mission personnel arrange for personal visits with the pastor concerning prospective candidates?
   5) Should the pastor meet with the mission board when the candidate is interviewed?
   6) Should meetings be arranged for a representative of the mission with the church missionary committee?

d. How can the mission help the many candidates who apparently fail to demonstrate in their home churches qualifying gifts for missionary service?
   1) Should the mission encourage churches to institute a program of service for prospective candidates, even during their school years?
   2) Does the mission encourage prospective candidates to gain experience in different phases of church service?

3) Could the mission help churches relate to potential candidates who are more involved with outside organizations than with the local church?

2. Mission Structure

a. How can the mission increase the voice of a local church in mission affairs?
   1) Should delegates from churches be invited to the mission annual meeting?
   2) Should a member from a church grouping which has significant support in the mission be represented on the mission board on a term basis?

b. How can communications between the church and mission on official matters be improved?
   1) Should the mission arrange for seminars for pastors in different cities or areas?
   2) Should more effort be made for mission representatives to meet with the pastor of a supporting church and the responsible missionary committee or officers?
   3) Should a standard presentation be prepared for pastors on the nature and strategy of IFMA missions?
   4) Should policy papers dealing with the matters of finances, structure and strategy of the mission be shared with supporting churches and updated regularly?
   5) Should special comprehensive mission reports be made available to supporting churches each year in addition to the regular financial statement?
   6) Should reports regarding individual missionaries and their performance be shared regularly with supporting churches?
   7) Should mission leaders send an occasional "Memo to Pastors" to give some detailed information which would help to involve the pastor in mission concerns?

c. How can meaningful involvement of churches or pastors in mission affairs be secured considering the diversity of structures in churches and missions?
   1) Has the mission attempted to declare its policies and any distinctives to supporting churches?
   2) How can missions encourage churches to declare their basis of missionary support and to recommend what reports and involvement in the mission would be desirable?

3. Finances and Publication.

a. Has the mission defined the responsibility of the church and the mission in the securing of support for missionaries, candidatesand administrative expenses?
   1) Is partnership and mutuality possible in the light of differing situations and churches?
   2) Should the mission take initiative in sending information and giving inspiration?
   3) Should the church take initiative in the actual raising of missionary support?
   4) Should mission administration expenses be included in the support structure?
   5) In these matters how can sensitivity to the direction of the Holy Spirit best be maintained?

b) How can communications be improved between home churches and mission boards?
   1) Should more pastors and key laymen be involved in mission councils and committees?
   2) Should mission executives give priority to consult with pastors and church missionary committees regarding applicants?
   3) What creative forms can mission executives use to keep pastors and missionary committees informed regarding mission policy and missionaries supported by the church?
   4) Should the mission sponsor pastors' conferences?
   5) Should arrangements be made for furlough missionaries to spend extended time ministering in the home church?

c) How can help be given to meet the support needs of nationals who replace missionaries in overseas service functions?
   1) Should the mission initiate re-education of supporting churches to contribute toward this need?
   2) Should key national leaders be brought to minister in North American churches?
   3) Should salaries and expenses for key national workers be included in the mission administrative budget?
   4) Should organizations such as Christian Nationals' Evangelism Committee be used to raise support of key nationals with the mission serving as the "introducing agent"?

d) How can IFMA missions adequately project a favorable contemporary image to supporting churches?
   1) Does the mission report to home churches regarding church planting, church growth, results of evangelism, numbers of national pastors and national missionaries?
   2) Is training given for deputation secretaries and furlough missionaries regarding the current scene in North American churches as well as overseas concerns?
   3) Are mission representatives urged to use current films and literature only?
   4) Does the mission encourage overseas trips for involved pastors and Christian business men?

Mission Personnel

a. How can local churches receive from mission agencies an accounting of the stewardship of missionary manpower?
   1) Would a standard church or mission questionnaire help provide needed information?
   2) Is it easier for a mission to frankly answer a church questionnaire concerning the life and work of a missionary than to initiate a report for a sending church which may not be favorable in all respects?
   3) Should the Field Council pre-furlough evaluation of the missionary be shared with the home pastor or church?
   4) Should a written missionary self-evaluation sheet be shared in person with the pastor and/or the church mission chairman or committee?
   5) What steps should be taken to arrange for a scheduled meeting between the sending church/pastor/mission committee and the missionary on furlough and/or an executive representative of the mission?
   6) Should the mission help pastors recognize and accept a counseling responsibility for furlough missionaries?

7) Does the mission recognize and accept the responsibility to take the pastor into confidence on matters concerning the missionary, even extreme matters which could result in possible severance from mission service?

b. How can the missionary on furlough best serve within the program of a local church?
   1) What responsibility does the mission administration have to help establish for missionaries a program of furlough service in coordination with supporting or sending churches?
   2) Should a missionary family supported by several local churches concentrate their service mainly in one church each furlough?
   3) What proportion of furlough time should be spent in service in a local church, rest, family obligations, continued study opportunities, general mission representation, etc.?
   4) What is the best expenditure of time, finances, and physical energy of the missionary during his furlough service?
   5) Does a missionary on furlough have a responsibility to offer to serve for a definite period of time within the program of witness and outreach of a local supporting church?
   6) Should the home church plan short-term assignments and invite or require missionary participation in coordination with the mission?
   7) Should the mission communicate with the church to learn about opportunities for furlough missionary involvement in local ministry?
   8) Should the mission initiate recommendations to churches for furlough activity which could enhance evangelistic and other church ministries?

c. How can the church exercise a spiritual ministry to the children of missionaries in North America in post high school training?
   1) Should the mission help the pastor recognize the problems of adjustment and testings which these young people face?
   2) Should the mission encourage the church to appoint a missionary secretary (perhaps a former missionary) to maintain a counseling correspondence with MKs (even when there appears to be open rebellion)?

d. How can the mission and the local sending church cooperate to minister to the specific pastoral care needs of the missionary family during furlough?
   1) With the missionary having a relationship with several or perhaps many churches, should he relate to one for pastoral care?
   2) Does the mission require the missionary to maintain membership in an evangelical church which is willing to exercise spiritual responsibility?
   3) Does the mission emphasize to the missionary the necessity of recognizing the spiritual authority of a local church?

4) If a deeper relationship were maintained through interest and service in a major supporting church, is it possible that it may not be necessary to have such a wide circle of additional supporting churches?

B. Church/Mission Relations Overseas

1. What is the mission view of the centrality of the local church in the New Testament?

2. Has extensive study been given to the cultural history of the people and country?

3. What are the present political pressures and climate affecting the mission and missionaries?

4. What does a study of the age and growth of the church and the mission in a particular area reveal?

5. What has been the history and experience of other ministries in the area?

6. What is the mission and the church definition of the church, both local and regional, as to function, authority and polity

7. What is the present development of the church and her desires concerning:
   a) Availability of maturing leadership?
   b) Administrative and financial autonomy?
   c) Ability to assume responsibility for institutional development?

8. What are the long range plans of the mission and church regarding future opportunities for evangelism in unreached areas and in untouched segments of the population?

9. What is the church growth climate in the area? (resistant/non-resistant)

10. What practical steps have the mission and church taken that continued faith and prayer will be exercised to see God build His church in resistant fields?

11. Have the details of the role, profile and stragegy of the mission been worked out for the area?

12. What steps have been taken by the mission leadership to help the individual missionary develop positive attitudes toward his calling to serve the Lord in the mission and church during possible changing roles and assignments?

13. What are the policies of other missions (denominational, interdenominational, or service agencies) which will affect missions and church members in the area?

14. What are the mission's plans for turning institutions over to the church?

15. What is the mission's plan in regard to personnel and financial assistance to the church in the future?

16. What studies have been made concerning the problems, costs, etc. of transferring ownership of properties?

17. Has the mission seriously considered withdrawal from the area?
    a) If so, what timetable and plan will most contribute to the strengthening of the church?
    b) Does the mission desire to retain control of as much as possible, or does it desire to turn over control to the church as soon as possible?
    c) After control of a particular work has been given to the church, is there danger of continued control by missionaries through influence and/or dominance?
    d) Are the missionaries convinced that the Holy Spirit can and will work pragmatically in and through the church apart from the mission?

II. RETREAT IMPRESSIONS

On the last morning Board members were asked to submit their personal impressions of the Retreat and how it had been of help in preparation for GL '71. These impressions were noted on the overhead projector and further discussed and amplified. Following is a compilation of these impressions.

- We are social creatures and need relationship. The informal attitude more important than the formal structure.
- Need clear principles (presuppositions) on which to make decisions for differing situations.

A deeper impression of the inexorable changes in the church-mission scene which require alertness, faith, flexibility, courage and humility.

- I recognize that there are missions that have successfully wrestled with the problems we face in our mission and I want to learn from them.
- I recognize the diversity of the Holy Spirit's work, therefore I am not looking for a formula but for an accurate insight into our needs so that we may correct present deficiencies which are keeping us from our goal for the church.

We must be activist, not reactionary. Relationship attitudes tend to become set and if not anticipated and foreseen. are difficult if not impossible to alter or change.

- A new awareness of the worldwide oneness of the Church of Christ. We dare not think or talk in terms of we-they.
- Need for closer liaison with the home churches in candidate screening, orientation, and in the service of their missionaries.
- Need for complete flexibility in organization, methodology, etc. Diversity of the answers.

These sessions have been a measuring rod of evaluation of:
- Where we are in church-mission relationships,
- Of where we want to go,
- And what corrections need to be made in order to enable us to get there.

- Rapid breathtaking advance toward the leadership of the national church - Our relationship to it.
- Flexibility needed in our mission - Goals - Time schedule.
- Importance of helping the home church and the receiving church.

- I feel GL '71 really began this week for me.
- In returning to my office I sense
  (a) the benefit of clarification of issues on several levels.
  (b) Stimulation and anticipation in view of the cross-pollination that will be involved.
  (c) Renewed confidence in the ministry of the Holy Spirit as He leads many diverse agencies under many varied circumstances to move forward the purpose of our Lord to build His church.

A clearer understanding of complexity of problems faced by missions working for years in emerging nations. -- Helpful to be exposed to terminology and to go into these concepts in depth. -- A new awakening to realize that we have reached a new plateau. Withdrawal, cross pollination necessary. "Younger" churches now becoming sending churches.

I expected
- Less or shorter papers.
- More true brainstorming - trying to come up with some truly key, yet undiscovered ideas.
- Less defensiveness.
- Less "covering ourselves." Oh, that we had the security and confidence in one another to realize that the Holy Spirit is not being crowded out because we use our minds.

I got
- A thrill out of what real interaction did take place. Group dynamics is the key! Group members need to be prepared so they will speak up.
- Several pin-pointed concepts
  a) Regarding our relation to sending churches,
     - Classify them - they are not homogenous.
     - More personal contact needed.
  b) Regarding our work abroad,
     - Consider service agencies developing into private national corporations or boards.

- Stimulus to push harder for church establishment and growth.
- There is no one answer to this tension - no synthesis.
- Great help to evaluate present position of church/mission relationship in our areas.
- Rapidity of maturation of national church.
- Need for missions to help home churches.

III. GREEN LAKE '71 PREPARATION

The following three questions concerning further preparations for GL '71 were answered in small discussion groups:

A. What objectives should GL '71 seek to accomplish for each delegate?

1. a) Awareness of the problem in its diversity.
   b) Desire to contribute to its solution.
   c) Renewed understanding and appreciation of the nature of the Church as set forth in the Scripture.

2. a) Defining principles and guidelines.
   b) Exposure to the diversities and complexities of situations and solutions.
   c) Improved attitudes of missions and missionaries toward the Church and Christians.
   d) Provide information leading to the above.

3. a) Presentation of a definite framework (skeletal base) for Biblical, social, and psychological principles that will help us to be able to apply these to our particular situation.
   b) Development of universal principles that will apply everywhere though the outworking may be different in each place.
   c) Realization of the unity of the Body and the diversity of the organizational expression of that unity.

4. a) Become teachable.
   b) Attain flexibility.
   c) Appreciate the place of the Church in God's plan.

B. What steps should EMIS take to prepare the delegates?

1. a) Recommended reading: The Twenty-Five Unbelievable Years, by Ralph Winter

2. a) Definition of program.
   b) Send pre-Conference information to delegates.

3. a) Inform delegates that God is a God of variety. The church is at various stages of development; national and political circumstances affect the church-mission relationship; God is at work in various ways.
   b) The three papers to be circulated to discussion and group leaders before GL '71.
   c) Recommend articles by evangelicals to be read to prepare for GL '71.

C. How can IFMA missions be better prepared for GL '71

1. a) Send precis of Retreat conclusions.
   b) Encourage delegates to program time to read study materials.
   c) Recommend that each delegate prepare a statement of the mission/church relationship in his area.

2. a) Regional seminars led by IFMA Board members.

3. a) Make available a copy of Retreat papers to missions not represented on Board.
   b) Compile brief resume of group discussion with an emphasis on variety of expressions.

Interdenominational Foreign Mission Association
54 Bergen Avenue
Ridgefield Park, New Jersey 07660
June 18, 1971

THE PARTNER RELATIONSHIP OF CHURCH AND MISSION

By Raymond J. Davis

The coming into being of churches through the faithful witness of messengers of the Gospel has generated urgent questions concerning church-mission relationships. It is cause for great gratitude to God, to quote the late Kenneth Scott Latourette, that the church has been established in every country of the world save one. The very fact that it has become necessary to consider the nature of the relationship of church and mission is indicative of progress in the fulfillment of God's purpose in the world. We welcome its necessity and its urgency.

There are two major positions in the relationship of churches and missions, with numerous modifications within each.

One is the union of church and mission which eliminates any distinction between the two. The other is a dichotomy whereby both sides maintain separate organizational structures. Supporters of union cite Christ's desire that all believers "may be one"; proponents of separation argue the Headship of Christ and His purpose for the Church.

Our acceptance of one or the other of these structures will depend upon our concept of the Church and its role in the world. If the concept of church/mission organizational relatedness in order to conform properly to our Lord's purpose "that they all may be one" is believed essential; if administrative union is considered necessary that the world may believe in Christ; the fusion of church and mission follows as the most likely procedure.

If, on the other hand, the church is conceived of as the body of Christ, composed of all regenerate believers in the Lord Jesus, alive and dead, without reference to geography, race or ecclesiastical affiliation; if existence as a true church is demonstrated by being rightly related to and properly regulated by the Head of the Church; and if the unity of John 17;21 is a spiritual unity, both complete and indestructible and such unity is evidently demonstrated in concrete situations such as worship, fellowship, suffering and witness; then there is no issue in keeping church and mission separate.

Is there scriptural warrant for one view rather than the other? Are there theological reasons to undergird one and not the other? We think not. Although organization of some sort is involved, scripture does not delineate any particular organizational pattern as the one to follow. No blueprint of church-mission relationship is found therein. We conclude therefore that the life of the Body, the Church, and its relationship to the Head, rather than details of administration, is the concern of the New Testament. The New Testament leaves the Church free to adopt that structure that will enable it to approximate most nearly the New Testament ideal of life in Christ, its Head.

The criterion by which the church-mission relationship should be judged is therefore functional and practical rather than theological. It should be a relationship that allows the Church as church to develop and express its life in Christ.

What, then, are the characteristics of the church's life in Christ? Without doubt Christ Jesus pervades the church by His presence, emanates it by His Spirit, fills it with His life, beautifies it with

His grace, governs it by His authority and uses it as His instrument to bring other men to salvation. As the church's vital Head, He provides the church with all that is necessary for its life and health. As the church's vital Head, His will must govern the church's action. His voice must speak supremely. No church-mission administrative structure must be allowed to restrict the life-giving channels from the Head to the members, nor paralyze the obedient response of members to their Head.

We believe, therefore that the partner relationship is that attitude which offers the church overseas a more favorable climate for development toward maturity in Christ. By a partner relationship we mean the association together of two entities which by nature are not and cannot be one but who for purposes of common interest and concern agree to share their strengths and resources to complement one another and work together in a dual relationship as in a yoke.

In a church/mission partner relationship the participants recognize three categories of activity and concern:

(1) That which pertains to the church only.
(2) That which pertains to the mission only.
(3) That which pertains to both church and mission

In the church/mission partner-relationship each respects the sphere of responsibility of the other by nature, and maintains an attitude of interest short of involvement. In the area of responsibility which is common to both church and mission, there remains an organizational separation but with the clasping of hands together in mutually agreed endeavor in pursuit of common goals. For the accomplishment of work together bridges of mutual understanding are built.

Careful description of the functions which are distinctive to each in the partnership are drawn, understood and respected. Where common concerns bring church and mission together, responsibilities are committed to individuals and committees representative of both parties for the accomplishment of work. Here, too, detailed guidelines and job descriptions are essential to understanding and fulfillment of responsibility. It is recognized that such a partnership committee cannot legitimately originate action or exercise authority for either church or mission. It fulfills a working relationship under the direction of the representatives of the partnership who of necessity exercise individual prerogative in the implementation of recommendations, guidelines and policy.

The considerations which in part lead us to believe the partner relationship is the most suitable for church and mission are:

(1) <u>Obedience</u>: The partner relationship enables the church to achieve the Biblical standard in obedience to scriptural injunction. The Lordship of Christ in the church provides through direct access to Him and from Him all His church requires to obey His commands and to fulfill His purposes. The pooling or fusion of resources in personnel, time and finance inevitably produce dependence upon other than Christ who commanded that His people look to Him. (Matthew 23:23; I Cor. 9:14; 16:1-2; Gal. 6:6-10)

(2) Nature: The distinctive nature of church and mission demands separate roles. The mission is not a church in the true sense of that word and exercises no ecclesiastical powers. The mission is composed of believers who are representatives of a church or community and who operate as agents in process of fulfillment of a commanded personal and group function. The church is the authoritative body to which God has committed the task of world evangelization. The mission is governed directly or indirectly by those whom it represents. A church is autonomous, self-governing. The mission's life and ministry is temporary and transient, having a specific objective in mind which when achieved permits its withdrawal or redeployment. The church is permanent and presumably continuing indefinitely.

(3) Individuality: The partner relationship preserves the right of the church to exercise its independence and assume the character, within Biblical limits, which its own culture and societal norms demand. History reveals that although missions have been used of God to inaugurate great movements, it is only as the people involved recognize the church as indigenous to their way of life and distinctly their own, that they maintained steady growth. The church, in the absence of restraint from without, finds opportunity for exercise of independence.

In order to grow strong, a living organism must stand upon its own base, be free to make up its own mind on the issues, make its own mistakes and discover directly how to correct its weaknesses.

Churches in the West often conceive of missionary work in terms of their own members who have gone overseas to proclaim the gospel to the "heathen." The great response of the recipients of the gospel in many places has enabled them to see that it is not just a question of the over-burdened Western missionary seeking the cooperation of local workers for the growing work of the church. There is a theological necessity, too, which makes it not only expedient but right to build up the church, both in power and in responsibility.

(4) Recognition of Self-Concept: Persons, groups, tribes, churches all possess the common need of finding an identity distinctive of their own self-concept. While the Church of Christ in the world is complete only when all true believers in all churches are gathered up in one, yet the local church is complete in itself in a very real sense. Thus in each church there resides the necessity of possibility of fulfillment, according to its own limitation, of the purpose of God in the world, namely the extension of the Gospel.

Scripture nowhere supports an initial period when younger churches need not comply, or when peculiar economic circumstances automatically cancel out obedience or call for a delay until educational and living standards are met. It is God's will that all believers actively participate in carrying the Gospel to all the world. The injunctions of the Apostle Paul in the Epistles of I and II Corinthians and Galatians were written to newly started mission churches. God planted them as He implants in every believer, the necessary motivating forces of love, mercy and Holy Spirit enablement to accomplish this assignment. The church possesses the full resources of God's grace to do it.

Not to be actively missionary, therefore, is to be disobedient to the Head of the Church, to grieve the Holy Spirit and to cause atrophy of spiritual faculties. Such disobedience saps spiritual vitality and makes for permanent weakness. Where non-indigenous people and resources are integrated into the church, there is a tendency to produce such a condition, thus delaying, if not destroying, the possibility of attainment of the Biblical standard. Failure to measure up to the standard of maturity in such matters produces a consciousness of inadequacy, incompleteness, weakness and dependence on the part of the church and resultant discouragement.

(5) Stamped with Stigma of Colonialism: Most of the younger churches live in an atmosphere of massive reaction against the West and the Western missionary. Especially is this true of the newer nations. They instinctively feel that missions are a form of Western aggression and no matter what the missionary says or does, he is considered to be a part of it. This attitude is shown to be transferrable to the church.

In Clark's recent book, The Church in China, it is stated, "And so ... another considerable missionary exodus. Another Christian outreach to China seemingly tottered with the murder of more than 200 missionaries and the temporary departure of others. Again the reason lay, not so much in Chinese opposition to Christ Himself, as in their indignation at Western political, economic and cultural frustration which engulfed them. The great weakness had been that in the popular mind Christianity in China had been identified with Western culture and Western exploitation."

Prime Minister Nehru in explaining the Indian government's restriction on foreign missionaries entering India said, "As far as possible the Indian church should be independent..."

Separation of church and mission reassures the newly independent governments and non-Christian nations that wait to see how well Christianity will root in their own soil before committing themselves.

A prominent Indian church leader has written: "Mission boards should not only be mentors, bankers or recruiting agencies, nor should they withdraw into just being detached observers. They have to discover the happy medium where they know the extent which they should help with advice, consultation or substance and when to withhold. During the process of its growth to maturity, the church would benefit greatly if it could find in its related mission board a catalyst, a creative critic and a responsible donor. The mission boards have to learn the discipline of restraint in their funding of the indigenous churches--just as they have learned the gracious art of generous giving."

(6) Freedom of Initiative: The presence of one visitor within the family circle puts restraint upon family conversation and activity. So in the younger churches the presence of one foreigner causes constraint. The missionary, however gracious, and tactful, produces by his presence the experience in his national brethren of a feeling of inferiority and seldom do they do as well as they are capable of doing. Their initiative, the very characteristic that needs developing and expression, is otherwise retarded.

Lyall writes: "The main objective of missionary work is to have strong local autonomous and independent churches with their own leadership and responsibility for their own support. Any other situation justifies the criticism the church is a foreign accretion and when the parent disappears, the dependent child disappears as well."

Ralph Winters points out in his book, The Twenty-Five Unbelievable Years - 1945-1969 that whereas the pundits and prophets predicted the demise of the world-wide missionary enterprise as the political imperialism of that period collapsed, rather the exact opposite proved to be true. He shows that whereas a heightened economic imperialism displaced the political imperialism of the period, and though this was not a part of a deliberately planned scheme whereby control over liberated people could be maintained, nevertheless, inevitably a residue of domination remained, since whatever the relationship may be, such is there as long as foreign influence is present.

Concerning the non-Western world at the close of this period, Winters continues, "great expectations of freedom were compromised since there is an element of imperialism in any continued force that takes initiative from indigenous national leadership, no matter how beneficial that force might be in a material sense."

It is unlikely that in any arrangement other than that where the parties concerned are removed from the restraints of extra-personal participation in group activity that initiative will thrive. It is certainly possible that continued close organizational association of church and mission will result in domination on the part of one upon the other and control consciously and planned, or sub-consciously. Such unhealthy potential must be avoided.

(7) Recognition of the church for what it is: The genius of the Gospel is that it possesses the ability to adapt and fit into any and every culture and social system. In doing so, it does not remove the possibility of conflict or domination by a diverse force. It is important to have a reliable means of true evaluation of the relative maturity of the church. Missionaries intimately involved in the church tend to underestimate the maturity of the church. Nationals tend to overestimate the maturity of the church. There is the human tendency for idealism to replace realism. The same is true in a family where children and parents disagree on the matter of relative maturity in the younger generation.

We have a tendency to equate Western Christianity with Biblical norms. Christianity, however, is not a Western entity. Born in the first century, it has steadily moved westward through the centuries. The basic skeletal configuration of Christianity in our times however has acquired Western contours as the white and English-speaking nations absorbed the basic tenets of the Christian faith and formed around them a body composed of Western cultural and social acquisitions.

Success here, in the search for a right relationship between church and mission, is dependent upon the preservation of the culture and social structures of the community in which the church is being born, insofar as it does not run counter to clearly recognized Biblical norms.

Tippett has shown that the church may be born indigenous and that it is not age that produces indigeneity. Most mission agencies today have conformed to the belief that the new churches established in non-Western lands must be New Testament churches rather than Western, where unfortunately in many instances Christian church movements resultant from missionary work of the past century were established in deeply-set patterns imported from the West.

The question here is actually determination of when a church can be called indigenous. The three self-concept of Venn as revised by Allen is an over-simplification.

There is a steadily growing conviction among Christians, partly as a result of the deeper understanding of the Bible and partly as a result of experience gained in actual working situations, but the word "autonomy" cannot be used of the individual believer or his Church without qualification. The same is true of the classic concepts of modern missionary policy: self-government, self-support and self-propagation. For one thing, the New Testament speaks of "self" only as something to be denied, or at least as something to be discovered only through being set aside and forgotten. The secular use of these expressions has no relation to the Christian life. It is as far away from the Bible as is the idea of a church in bondage to foreign powers and cultures -- or even to other churches.

The secular meaning of phrases such as "self-government," "self-support," and "self-propagation" is altogether different from that understood by evangelicals like Henry Venn. He and others like him assumed they were dealing with the converted, both missionaries and local Christians. They assumed the rule of Christ before they spoke of self-rule. Without Christ's Lordship, there was no theological significance in either dependence or autonomy. The danger is that we should use these concepts without relation to the Lordship of Christ, a danger abundantly realized in the history of modern missions. We are not called to abandon them altogether. A church is not mature, it has not grown up into the full stature of Christian humanity, and is therefore not really a church at all, if it is not self-governing, self-supporting, self-propagating, but it is true for churches and for individuals that he who would seek to save his soul or self, shall lose it.

It matters that a church should be self-governing, but this "autonomy" is not the most vital principle of its being; the vital thing is, we might say, Christonomy, the "rule of Christ." Where Christ rules there is the true self, and where His Spirit is there is true liberty. True liberty demands the existence of autonomy in relation to others. But both we ourselves and the "others" are under the rule of Christ. That is the only liberty, the only autonomy which we are concerned to define in our study of church/mission relationships in the modern world.

Perhaps autonomy is an unsatisfactory word to use in this connection; it has become debased in secular use. The expression "responsible self-hood has been suggested as a better rendering. Perhaps the word "responsible" by itself would be sufficient. But the "responsible church" is really too wide a term. It is a much deeper thing than mere independence.

There are three ideas which pertain to the church in this context and these will always be found in a church which is truly indigenous. First, there is the unquestioned concept of divine direction and the realization of the immediacy of Christ's presence and Headship. Secondly, is the realization that every church exists in a particular environment, that it must be related to the soil and permeate the society in which it is seeking to witness to Christ. Thirdly, there will be the awareness of an actual exercise of freedom from outside influences and control from whatever source.

Winter points out, "the very phrase younger church is part of the problem in the discussion of the indigenous church overseas. It may be better than daughter church, but a church is a community and therefore corresponds much more to the whole society than to an individual. True, it is possible to speak of older and younger societies, but many churches that have been started fairly recently by Western missionary endeavors, are not young societies, but rather old societies with a new faith."

(8) Its Validity in Practice: Illustrations abound that portray the viability of the church/mission partner relationship. Others here could relate the manner in which the practice of a true partner-relationship is working well. Let me speak of our experience where in seven of the ten countries in S.I.M. Africa is found a church organization. Here the church in varying stages of development is recognized in a partner relationship with the mission. The timetable differs, but the policy is the same, the plan is there. It is not to be understood that the ideal has been or is always attained. There are shortcomings and failures on the part of both mission and church to be sure. We experience the inability to rightly measure maturity, to fully and completely trust the Holy Spirit to empower and guide the church without our help. There is too often the application of dual standards of discipline. There is sometimes the failure of or incomplete understanding and appreciation of cultural and social forms in the Christian community. There may be lack of complete understanding of our manner of living and method of working on the part of the church. There is that which yet hinders on a man-to-man basis the closest fellowship. But more than ever, the shape of tomorrow will be the result of the conscious design and the remodeling of structure rather than of gradual haphazard unplanned development. Such changes and revisions are necessary for both church and mission. Where there is understanding in basic essentials and a full and complete desire on the part of both parties to succeed in our life and work together, it finds fruition. Thus today more than 3,300 churches with 900,900 in the Christian community are living happily and working closely together with hundreds of missionaries in a clearly-defined, carefully followed plan of church/mission partner relationship.

In conclusion, we re-state that the primary objective of ascertaining and maintaining the proper relationship of church and mission as separate organizations is the recognition of Christ as the Head of the Church. When looking to Him as the progenitor, sustainer, and ultimate glory of the church, there is not only no need for the church to look to any other for complete provision of all that she may need, but in the measure in which she does look to another is the Holy Spirit ignored and grieved. Therefore, the church will best look to Christ for her spiritual life, her guidance, her material resources. The freedom and liberty of oneness in fellowship and separation in organization, releases both men and material possessions for the continual expansion of Christ's kingdom in obedience to the Head of the Church.

SOURCE MATERIAL

SIM Publications
SIM Study Papers - Cotterell - Crouch - Fuller - Pickering
Mission with Integrity in India, by Renuka Mukerji Somasekhor
Who Controls the Missionary? - Louis King
The Responsible Church and the Foreign Mission - by Peter Beyerhaus and Henry Lefever
An Introduction to the Science of Missions - by J. H. Bavinck
The Twenty-Five Unbelievable Years - 1945-1969 - by Ralph Winter

IFMA Official Board Retreat
May 24-27, 1971
Pearl River, New York

IFMA MISSIONS AND CHURCH PLANTING IN AREAS WHERE OLD CHURCHES ARE ESTABLISHED

By Walter Frank

Why should any missionary society squander valuable manpower and money endeavoring to start Christian churches in traditionally "Christian countries" where a national church exists?

It appears that Missions are always justified, either where no church exists or where the church is in such a weak and apostatized anemic condition that it cannot evangelize its area.

Since World War II, a steady flow of missionaries has entered Europe. Today there are 1,615 Protestant missionaries in Europe, in lands where the Protestant church has existed in a greater or lesser degree for more than 400 years. This number has quadrupled within the past ten years. After 400 years, it is helpful to observe that there are still 250,000 towns, villages and cities without a Protestant church.

In the more predominatly Protestant country of Germany, however, in most every fair sized town or city, one is greeted by two great steeples representing the Protestant and Catholic churches.

Is it then enough to say..."There is a church here, we must move on to more pagan lands?"

What we should be saying is, "There is the steeple, but where is the Church?" There is the 'church', but "where is the Church?" Dr. Herbert Butterfield, Professor of Modern History at Cambridge University, said, "The spiritual effect of the Reformation was largely nullified some 50 to 100 years after Luther nailed his theses to the church door at Wittenberg."

STERN, one of Germany's leading weekly pictorials, carried the following questions on its cover in September, 1962:

> 94.6% of all the people in the German Federal Republic call themselves Christians. Do they really believe on God? Or do they call themselves Christians because they were once baptized, or because it has advantages, because it is the accepted thing, because it can't hurt anything, because there might be something to it after all? Or do they call themselves Christians because they believe that Jesus Christ is God's Son, that He was crucified and rose again? Do they believe on the resurrection of the flesh and the afterlife? How many believe on that for which they pay tax?

STERN further illustrated the impotency of Protestantism by adding that less than five percent of all church members worship weekly. In large metropolitan areas attendance at Sunday services slides to nine-tenths of one percent. The men who attend average 53.8 years of age, while the women average 55.5 years. TIME candidly defines the Christians' task in Europe with these dismal words: "In Western Europe, church leaders wonder how to evangelize post-Christian pagans for whom towering cathedrals are museums rather than centers of living faith."

If the traditional church in European countries is the Body of Christ in these lands, then it could be argued that we are spiritually and ethically responsible to work with them to evangelize their area. This position, however, needs to be examined in the light of a number of additional factors.

Is the traditional church the Body of Christ or does it merely contain the Body of Christ?

Does the traditional church possess the spiritual vitality necessary to evangelize its area?

Is the theology of the traditional church true to the Scriptures?

It is important to note that in the early days of the free church movement, free church leaders of the English-speaking worlds did not plan an evangelistic campaign to conquer ground from state and national churches in Europe. Emigrants from these churches by tens of thousands were converted and won to active participation in the burgeoning free church movement in USA. It was these who felt called to a work of evangelism in their homeland with its static, legally bound church life and its masses of nominal Christians. The emigrants especially felt led to establish the religious freedom which was characteristic of the policies in the European countries. Thus it was that Swedes, Norwegians, Danes, and Germans, after a visit and conversion in the United States, returned to their native countries glowing with zeal to preach revival and establish groups of believers.

Gunner Westin, the Swedish author of "The Free Church through the Ages," calls attention to the fact that "from the European point of view it is interesting that the American statistical reports considered Europe as a mission field. They published information about the mission stations, missionary workers, and communicant members. It was especially the Baptists and the Methodists who in this way made known their concern about the modern European free church movement. However, Congregationalists, Episcopals and Seventh Day Adventists also actively approached European countries with aggressive missionary zeal.

In the middle of the 1890's, the number of missionary workers in Europe in the American missions was 2,745 and there were 153,500 communicants. Within 40 years from 1850 the number of communicants had increased from 5,400 to 153,500. These 2,745 American missionaries considered Europe a major mission challenge and were not deterred by the fact that almost every European belonged to a so-called Christian church. They considered that whether Catholic or Protestant, if they don't know the Gospel, they are lost, and if there is no vigorous Bible-believing, Bible-preaching church, we must do all possible to plant one and risk the stigma of being viewed as a sect.

Today, the need to plant vigorous evangelical churches is far more acute, illustrated by the pathetically humorous statement of the State Church pastor in Germany who declared, "We are all Christians here without having the least suspicion as to what Christianity is." Since the turn of the century, theology in Europe has experienced the ebbs and flows of higher criticism, modernism, liberalism, neo-orthodoxy, existentialism, restorationalism and endless perversions of scriptural interpretation replacing simple acceptance of the inspiration of Scripture.

Do we agree that our responsibility is not primarily that of the past generation or of the next generation, but for this generation of Europeans?

Inasmuch as it is easier to hear the Gospel in the French-speaking countries of Africa than in the mother countries in Europe, and since one will much more likely run across a born-again believer in Spanish-speaking lands of Latin America than in Spain, we should not become discouraged by the critics who point to the great piles of stone called churches, nor should we succumb to those who hark back to the Reformation and cry, "Europe had the Gospel." These are hangups that develop from an ignorance of history and/or a misunderstanding of the true nature of the church.

The Church is the Body of Christ on earth, a depository of the Truth. A missionary church is a spiritually alive church, vigorously holding forth by life and by lip the Word of Life. There can be no easy answers to the subject before us. Sweeping generalities are out of order. Careful and prayerful studies must be made before new churches are launched in areas where the Body of Christ existed in one form or another for centuries.

Church planting in European lands constitutes a major challenge but with multiplied problems:

1. Traditional problem
2. Social problem
3. Theological problem
4. Financial problem

1. Traditional Problem. In Europe there exists no comity agreement between Christian missions or churches, yet the strongest comity of almost any field of the world is there. Almost no area exists where one can feel free to plant a church wihout firm opposition from local Protestants or Catholics. In America one can establish a church almost anywhere that you can secure a few people. In the minds of traditionally Christian Europe, however, only two churches are accepted as proper: Protestant (Lutheran-Reformed) Church or the Catholic Church. Even the existing tiny free church movement is viewed with contempt by the traditional church and her people, even though very few are faithful adherents.

Considering the fact that the people of these countries have identified their religion with a large stone edifice for generations and that from generation to generation each new baby was automatically ushered into the church on the assembly line of infant baptism followed by the rite of confirmation, it is of little wonder that any intrusion into this formula and establishment creates domestic and social foment.

2. Social Problem. Evangelistic endeavors in Germany and other European countries have proved fruitful but the real hangup follows in church relations. When a German becomes a Christian through the regenerative work of the Holy Spirit he has three options:

a) Remain where he is in the State Church. In most cases this proves spiritually disastrous for obvious reasons.

b) Remain officially a member of the State Church, but meet with a fellowship group or one of the free churches to receive spiritual food and fellowship.

c) Make a clean break with the State Church, Catholic or Protestant, through the proper legal process recognized for those who desire to break these ties. Papers must be filled out and properly notarized declaring the believer free from the State Church and no longer responsible to pay church tax. (Many are reluctant to take this step and find it the path of least resistance just to remain in the church, attend the morning worship there, and then fellowship with a free group or one of the "gemeinshaft" groups in the afternoon or evening.) It is our experience that the most rapid spiritual growth is evident in the lives of those who boldly make a clean break with any religious structure which compromises the fundamentals of the evangelical

In view of the above, it is not difficult to understand why church planting and development has not flourished in lands of a traditional Christian culture. It is only as people break completely with the old that they can become a living and effective member of a New Testament self-supporting, self-governing and self-propagating church.

3. Spiritual Problem. When a mission or missionary launches into a program of pioneer church planting, let him first be aware of his body of belief. Greater than any of the above road blocks to church planting will be the deeply imbedded theological concepts of infant baptismal regeneration, the sacrament of consubstantiation in the communion and the belief that these mystic forms carry some merit that may be forfeited by separation from the traditional church. For many it requires much careful counselling and Bible study before they are ready to throw their entire future spiritual experience in with this tiny group of nondescript foreigners.

4. Financial Problem. Neither Protestants or Catholics in these countries have been taught the scriptural grace of giving and Christian stewardship. Tithing is foreign to them and free will happy giving is almost without example. It is easy to see how this would be so in countries where the church is state-supported, where spiritual life is at a low ebb, and where the teaching of the Lordship of Christ is unknown.

Care must be taken from the very beginning of the infant church to teach Christian stewardship. As in every mission field, a plan must be early adopted to challenge the young church to assume responsibility for the operation of the church. Two major financial undertakings lie ahead and require wisdom, sacrifice and sensitive timing:

a) The phasing out of the missionary leadership requiring appointment and support of their own pastor;

b) and the securing of a suitable permanent facility for the growing church.

Suggestions for those considering a major ministry of evangelism and church planting:

1. Prayerfully study the religious situation of the country and choose an area where little or no Gospel witness exists. There are thousands of such areas in Europe.

2. Make it clear from the beginning that you are not a sect, nor desire to start a new denomination.

3. Where there exists a struggling evangelical group, seriously consider assisting in the encouraging and strengthening of this group through a cooperative effort rather than confusing the situation by starting another group. Most will appreciate your help.

4. Through evangelistic efforts, door-to-door surveys or other means, discover a responsible area or an area where a number of Christians live constituting a nucleus for the beginning of a church through Bible study groups, etc.

5. Always team up with a national, or several, who share your burden in a Paul-Timothy relation which will both play down the American image and at the same time train national leadership.

6. Realize that you are engaging in the hardest type of missionary work in the world and dig in for the long pull. Be prepared for opposition but expect God to faithfull give the increase. It will likely take six to eight years before a church is established so unless you have conviction that God has called you to this work, you will capitulate short of your goal.

7. There are no short cuts to success. Get to the people, door-to-door, man-to-man, market places, campaigns, literature distribution, home Bible studies, holy consisten Christian living and a testimony without reproach.

8. Be more committed to your task than the Mormans, the Jehovah's Witnesses, or the Communists. Believe that you have the Living Water so desperately needed, the Word of Life, the only remedy for the lostness of men.

9. Believe that when people are won to Christ the work has only begun. Go and make disciples, bring men to maturity in Christ and from the very first handful of that infant church be sure they know that God expects them to be spiritual reproducers.

10. Ask the Lord Jesus Christ to endow you with great faith. In each new area into which he leads, you will need to hear His words, "I have much people in this city." even though they are presently invisible.

The Church of our Lord and Saviour Jesus Christ does exist on the Continent, scattere weak and often obscured within the giant ecclesiastical structure. Here and there an occasional State Church with a believing pastor, and again, almost by surprise, one will be greeted by a small but sometimes a vigorous free church as an oasis in the desert longing for fellowship. Examples of significant, live and impressive testimonies, however, are minimal. I pray that many dedicated young people will step into the European scene to work together with God at this crucial time to build His Church

IFMA Official Board Retreat
May 24-27, 1971
Pearl River, New York

WHAT ABOUT INSTITUTIONS?

by Sidney Langford

The question of the place of institutions in modern missions is a subject that has been brought to our attention rather forcefully in recent months. Dr. Donald McGavran charges that "interdenominational and faith missionary societies, while theoretically devoted to carrying out the Great Commission, often in practice have become as institutional and evangelistically ineffective as the denominational agencies."[1] Many missions have drifted into a situation where their chief emphasis is on institutions as over against evangelism and church growth.

The comment of Dr. George Peters concerning the African scene reinforces this. He states,

> Most of Africa is a field white unto harvest. Evangelism is a most urgent need. Missions and churches who place evangelism first are reaping abundantly, doubling every three or four years. The tragedy of the situation is that most evangelical missions are so overloaded with institutionalism that it becomes practically impossible to free personnel for the ministry of evangelism.[2]

Institutions have hindered evangelism in another way also. In Church/Mission relations the tensions which have built up have often arisen over the handling of institutional work. Church growth studies indicate that where there is tension between church and mission there is a loss of energy and effectiveness in growth. Hence it is imperative that we address ourselves to the subject of institutions.

This is a rather broad topic and impossible of just treatment in a paper of this size. I want to direct attention to one aspect of it. In the words of the one who assigned this topic to me, my purpose is "to explore what happens to institutions which missions have run as the churches emerge... outlining the tension areas and the problems and then give an approach to solution to some of these problems."

. Historical Perspective of Institutions

In many instances historically Christian missions have been forced to initiate institutional work in various countries of the world. As the early colonial governments generally lacked personnel, they therefore were limited to the extent of being involved solely in the maintenance of government to keep law and order. It was the spiritual motivation of missionaries that instituted church-related medical and educational programs. In actuality missions in sub-Sahara Africa have been forerunners in the field of education. They have been responsible for educating the masses for more than 65 years during the approximate period of time between 1880 and 1945. This time element would of course vary in different areas of Africa.

The same can be said for the mission medical programs. However, the colonial governments did move into this sphere of activity much sooner than they did into education. Even today the gigantic medical needs of the continent still demand much in the way of specialized personnel to meet physical needs and to train nationals for medical ministries.

As emerging national governments are prepared to assume full responsibility for the educational and medical programs, they should by all means do so. Already this is being done in many countries in the sphere of education. All primary schools are being supervised and taught by nationals, and now the high schools are fast moving into that category as qualified teaching staff is available. Does this mean that missions should withdraw completely from the field of general education? I do not think so, especially where governments look favorably upon the establishment of Christian high schools. These should be maintained as truly Christian institutions as it must be recognized that many of the government-controlled schools are deteriorating spiritually. The products of church-controlled schools will continue to produce strong Christian leadership which will make its impact upon the church and nation.

Involvement in certain types of institutional work gives prestige with national governments and in turn has created a climate that is favorable to the testimony of the church and mission.

For example, medical work has been used to open up remote areas and in turn people have responded to the Gospel more readily.

The unified effort of several missions in establishing a medical center to treat the local population and those at a distance by a flying doctor service and also in training national medical personnel professionally and spiritually to meet the need of the masses does not go unnoticed by the government. In fact on several occasions the President of the country has visited such institutional ministries and has given special commendation to those responsible for the development of such a program.

Even the enemies of the Gospel, such as the Muslim government officials in the Sudan, recognized the effectiveness of institutional ministries. In their plan to eliminate Christianity they forbode missionaries to do educational and medical work as the government testified that these brought the missionaries into too close a relationship with the people and thus gained their favor and response to the message they had come to bring.

II. Institutions and the Emerging Church

Viewed from the historical perspective, we discover a seeming paradox. On the one hand we have present day missions and churches which have gotten bogged down by institutions and are limited in their evangelism, whereas on the other hand we have a church whose very existence is due, to some degree,

› institutions such as schools and hospitals.

ı dealing with this very important matter of the national church and its elationship to institutions there are several viewpoints that must be given ı order to assist missions and the church in arriving at a balanced opinion s to how these should or should not be employed by the church in the ccomplishing of its goals. The following are suggestions for our onsideration:

. A clear definition of the theology of the church needs to be outlined for the national leadership.

ı many cases missions have allowed various types of institutional programs › become so interwoven with functions which are biblically assigned to the hurch. For instance, the organizational format for the ministries of our ıstitutions and the church are basically the same and consequently the hurch leaders will consider one to be just as important as the other.

ven though missions might endeavor to give clearcut instructions as to the ınctions of the church, in reality the church leadership observes the impor- ınce and priority that has been placed on institutional work and also the fact ıat missions find it difficult to withdraw from such. Therefore the autonomous hurch will follow our example and express reluctance in giving up work which ıey consider to be part of the church's responsibility.

he national church in many cases does not have a clear view of the position r nature of the mission, which is an agency of the sending churches, as istinct from the nature of the Church of Christ itself and has chosen to attern itself after the mission instead of reflecting the Scriptural pattern f the church. Unfortunately the national church has had opportunity of only bserving the ministries of missions which of course has included both church nd institutional functions rather than just the functions of the church. This as resulted in confusing the functions of the mission with the functions of the hurch so that institutional work has become equated with church work.

is not uncommon to find that many African leaders, both church and govern- ıent, consider press work as an educational program to be just as much a art of the church's functions as evangelism. Some of the commissions of frican governments on Africanization have even made inquiry of the church adership as to whether the church has complete autonomy and in their ıinking this includes every department of the work that has been carried on y the mission. Because of such pressures, the national churches felt onstrained to demand control of all the institutional work as well. Any uggestion to separate such ministries from the church's responsibility is onsidered to savor of colonialism and hence a desire to hold onto the reins f the work which they feel should be turned over to the church.

In trying to reason with church leadership concerning separating institutional work from the functions of the church, it has been pointed out to Kenya church leaders that such separation has already taken place in the general education program. For years the mission was completely in control of all of the primar and secondary schools, and in the mind of the church leaders these were though of as the mission's Christian education program that would eventually come under the church. However, as the government acquired qualified national staff, they have gradually assumed the responsibility for these schools and at present the mission has no control. Thus the church is aware of the fact that institutional work has been separated from that which they thought would be under their supervision. In Tanzania the mission's Department of Educatior was actually transferred to the church before the government had assumed responsibility for all of the subsidized schools and when the government effecte a change the church had to turn over this responsibility to the government. Th church of course did this without a question, but in some measure they feel that they have lost a function that belonged to the church.

The church needs to be alerted to the fact that other areas of institutional work such as medical, presses, and industrial schools might all have to be turned over to government. In some areas the government has already made known its plans to eventually assume full control of mission or church medical institutions. The church needs to realize that the Scriptural functions of the church, such as evangelism, church growth programs, and Christian education can never be turned over to the government. However, it should also be noted at this juncture in the process of Africanization that institutions under the supervision of the national church may have a greater possibility of being preserved as a testimony than if they were under the control of the mission.

In order to encourage the church to be relieved of the responsibilities of institutional functions, it might be suggested that the facilities of the press be sold in shares to various African Christians and that an independent Christian company be formed, similar to Scripture Press or Gospel Light, as a profit or non-profit organization. Perhaps if the church had been instructed along these lines years ago, such a proposal might have been accepted. But the present reaction is that we are taking something away that is rightfully theirs and to this they will not agree. To sum up this point, the failure of missions to teach the national church the difference between the functions of a mission society and the Biblical functions of the church has made it difficult for the church to understand why we should encourage them to be separated from institutional work.

2. The national church does not understand all that is involved in institutional ministries.

Missions for the most part have not instructed the church concerning the institutional work in the same manner in which we have taught them concerning the functions of the church. Therefore they have a dim view of what happens in this area. The church is greatly impressed with all the income coming into the coffers of the mission through the specialized ministries of hospitals, press and bookshops, but they are unaware of how these funds are administered and therefore assume that the mission is in the money-making business.

For instance, in a mission hospital situation the church knows that the missionaries' salaries are not paid by the institution and also that the hospital charges a fee, while in government dispensaries the dispensers receive a salary and they do not charge for their services or medicine. Therefore the conclusion is that the mission must certainly be making a good profit.

If missions would have instructed the church leadership years ago of all that was involved and that the receivable income to care for overhead and expansion is minimal, perhaps they would not have been ready to assume the administrative responsibilities. However, in most cases the time for educating them is past, and at this juncture words of warning are listened to with suspicion.

3. Institutions and the non-profit basis.

Missions have endeavored to carry out their work on a non-profit basis and the church does not understand this concept as they have never had it explained to them until it became evident that the institutional work was to be turned over to them. The fact that missions are administering institutions as a means of propagating the Gospel and as a service to the people and not for the purpose of making an income is something that has been difficult for them to understand. The church has made known that it would be expecting to make a substantial income from the press, literature, and medical work in order to obtain additional income for pastors and church projects. Although they have been alerted to the pitfalls concerning this, it is still one of their goals. Perhaps the fact that a large income is not to be realized hastily might cause a measure of disillusionment on the part of the church, and hence disenchantment with institutional work. This might prove to be a blessing but it could result in the curtailment of some Christian testimony and service.

The church that is interested in obtaining large amounts of income from its institutions for the preservation of the church as an organization will not be vibrant in the propagation of the Gospel nor increase in church growth or stewardship because they will have reduced the church program to a business enterprise. Churches following this pattern need to be warned and instructed where they should place their priorities.

With the emergence of the church and its growth to maturity very often the very institutions which contributed so much to the growth of the church have become points of tension between church and mission.

Some illustrations of problems in the financial area that have occurred are as follows:

In the case of the administration of a large city bookshop which was in the process of being transferred to the church, the mission tried to encourage the postponement of the complete transfer until all outstanding bills were paid, so that the church might start with a clean slate. Such a suggestion was interpreted as delaying tactics in order to enable the mission to obtain more of the income. In view of this the mission had no other alternative than to acquiesce to the church's desires. Now they are complaining because they find themselves in the bind of the payment of these bills and are not receiving the income that was anticipated. The transfer of administration to the national church has likewise made some of the suppliers reluctant to grant credit on book orders. Such matters create tension and destroy confidence.

There is also the case of the national hospital administrator who felt that invoices did not need to be paid immediately and therefore brought disrepute on the name of the hospital, and even a threatened law suit. This did not become known until court action seemed evident. This same administrator finally had to be removed from his position by the church because of mishandling and hence disappearance of hospital funds. The failure of the church to deal with this matter within a reasonable time was also a cause for tension between the church and the mission until the church took action.

4. Personnel and Institutions.

Within the last 25 years missions have assigned the larger part of its missionary staff to institutional ministries, and our reason for doing so would no doubt be because of the demand in the spheres of education, literature, and medical work. However the church has been aware that we have given priority to these areas rather than to evangelism, Christian education, and church growth programs, and now they are following in the pattern of the mission. The best trained, even theologically, are being assigned to institutional programs rather than to strictly church ministries. One of the reasons is because of substantial and secure salaries that are available to them. We are creating a problem where institutions are going to be more important to them than the real functions of the church. Study by both the church and mission are urgently needed to rectify this.

To summarize the viewpoints expressed in the previous points that have been outlined, the ministry of missions in the past through the various types of institutional programs for the purpose of the furtherance of the Gospel and as a service to people has played an important part in the accomplishment of the goals that were projected and in many respects still do. However it must be recognized that the importance of these being maintained by the church is greatly diminishing, especially wherein they do not fit into the right perspective as related to divine priorities outlined in the Scriptures. Wherein possible, we should be careful about turning all institutions over to the church. Some would be best operated by the government, others by private Christian companies, and some perhaps not at all.

The main tension areas are in the suspicion generated when the mission tries to help the church understand the relationship of the church to institutions, the functions of the church, and the difficulties in operating an institution. There is a lack of understanding on the part of the church as to the premise on which we both stand. The mission has one definition of what it wants to accomplish through institutions and the church has another. In that missions have failed to communicate to the church the real purpose for institutional work, the church has established its own purpose. Even though the church and mission may talk about these together, we are not communicating with each other because our purposes are different. To solve the problem, both the church and mission must agree on one common purpose as to what institutions and their functions really are in contrast to the God-given functions of the church, and to place full priority where it belongs -- upon the church.

I think we as interdenominational missions are at a very important juncture in history. We need to do some in depth thinking on the role of institutions. The past effectiveness of certain institutions does not necessarily mean present effectiveness in building the church. Times have brought tremendous changes in the emerging countries of the world. With these changes the need in the areas of education, medicine, etc., have changed.

Careful investigation and research need to be done on all of our institutional work to determine which contribute to the growth of the church and how much. In the light of such investigations, it should be decided where man power and money power would be best used to advance the cause of Christ. Such investigation would prevent "the tail from wagging the dog" as seems to be the case so often today. Instead, institutions should be allowed to exist only as they contribute significantly to the growth of the church.

In a day, then, when the national church is emerging and taking leadership in the evangelistic task, it may be the right time, after careful investigation, to permit some institutions to die gracefully. This will undoubtedly eliminate certain present points of tension in mission/church relations.

Now what about those institutions which are making a significant contribution to the growth of the church? How can we maintain a healthy, cooperative relationship between church and mission in the administration of these institutions?

I do believe that the need of the hour is to get our priorities straightened out. Have we placed too much importance upon much of our institutional work with the results that the national church has often fallen into the same pitfall and the institution has often become the battlefield to determine who will control? I am convinced that if we began to re-emphasize evangelism and church growth -- where we put the majority of our man and money power -- many of our present tensions over institutions would disappear.

5. The Other Side of the Institutional Coin

More than a decade of years ago we spoke of missions at the crossroads. By this term we meant that the whole survival of missions depended on unavoidable changes in structure and relationships toward the established churches. We also meant that the indigenous churches had emerged to take over the leadership role in the developing nations of Africa.

The indigenous principle of church planting has been achieved in many local areas. There are literally thousands of churches which govern, support, and propagate themselves. In most major tribes and nations the church has been planted, the Scriptures are printed, and effective leadership has emerged. Now the question is, what place remains for missions?

The first answer is to be found in the "institutions" which missions established for the furtherance of their witness. It is here that generally speaking the indigenous principle was not pursued from the beginning. Hospitals, high schools, publishing houses, theological schools, printing presses, and book stores were seldom structured to become indigenous.

Few institutions have become self-governing. In practice, any sincere Christian can become an evangelist or a pastor if his motivation is such. However, we certainly do not believe or practice that any sincere Christian can run a hospital, publish a book, run a press, or edit a magazine. We all admit that skill, training and experience are required to govern this kind of work. Few moves have been made to create African Christian managers, supervisors, publishers, executives, officers of our institutions.

Fewer still of our institutions are self-supporting. The local revenue required to make a viable business out of any institution generally ran afoul of the mission's financial policy which permitted such institutions to be run on a non-profit basis. Seemingly it is almost a cardinal sin for any mission or missionary to run anything that looks like a healthy business. This so-called bias has been passed on to the mission-established church. But quite frankly, the church has not bought this idea.

In view of the non-profit aspect of our institutions, they therefore never become self-propagating. Book shops operating on marginal costs cannot give birth to book shops. Publishing houses which sell with a "give-away price mentality" cannot make enough profit from one good publication in order to produce a second needed publication. Revolving funds often do not revolve.

In order to adequately meet the need in church-related institutional programs a crash course must be provided in order to Africanize the institutions. The principle of Africanization is correct, necessary, and urgent. Institutionalization requires the selection of highly qualified African Christians. The provision of first class training for their jobs, and a guaranteed wage and opportunity for advancement equal to the expatriates they will replace are also required.

But how shall we adequately Africanize unless we heavily subsidize? Here again we are faced with no other alternative. If Africanization is the right policy then subsidization is the only way to achieve it within the immediate future. None of our institutions can become self supporting until we begin to operate them on sound business principles. Unless we are prepared to move the institutions into a sound management structure we have no other choices but to subsidize or shut down. We must prepare ourselves and the church in Africa to run sound businesses and help them to do so. There is no other way out of the institutional dilemma except to watch them erode and collapse. Strongly established institutions could well continue to be the major voice in the Christian witness across Africa. I speak of those institutions that government will not ultimately take over, such as the publishing houses, printing presses, book stores, etc.

Such proposals as indicated above are provocative and stimulating and need to be given serious and prayerful consideration by all mission leaders.

IFMA Official Board Retreat
May 24-27, 1971
Pearl River, New York

---

[1] Donald McGavran, "Crisis of Identity for Some Missionary Societies," Christianity Today, May 8, 1970, p. 724.

[2] George Peters, "To Those That Labor in Behalf of Africa," Africa Pulse, Vol. 1, No. 2, March 1970, p. 2.

CHURCH-MISSION RELATIONSHIP - A FUSED PARTNERSHIP

By Alfred Larson

In the Bible we have a sovereign declaration, "I will build my church and the gates of hell shall not prevail against it." (Matt. 16:18) No specific location was indicated by the Lord Jesus, nor were any qualifying limitations placed on this statement.

This emphasis on the church was predominant in the writings of the New Testament.

As interdenominational mission organizations, we ask ourselves: What is the most effective and God-honoring way to relate our programs to the national churches which have been brought into being through our ministries?

In our strategy for the years before us, we recognize that the national church is in the forefront, not the mission. It is the church, not the mission, which is the abiding body and which must dominate in the church-mission relationship.

There are a number of questions before us: Acknowledging that the mission societies are accidents of history rather than Biblical ideals, what is the place today of the interdenominational mission society? When is a national church truly autonomous? Is there a particular pattern of church-mission relationship which would serve as an ideal for all fields of the world? Is the program of church-mission cooperation conditioned by cultural, political, psychological and other factors?

The interdenominational mission relates to the sending church, in a sense, as a service agency while maintaining a separate administration and organizational structure. Generally speaking, this relationship to the sending church has been acceptable, whereas the relationship to the receiving church has become increasingly more complex through the years.

In an article on mission-church relationships, Dr. Peters indicates that there are being advocated these four patterns of relationship with the receiving church:

1) The pattern of complete organizational disassociation of mission and church.

2) The pattern of fraternal partnership and obedience.

3) The pattern of mission partnership and missionary servantship.

4) The pattern of partnership of equality and mutuality.[1]

Let us define briefly these patterns of mission-church relationship:

1) The pattern of complete organizational disassociation of mission and church: Here the mission and church are two autonomous bodies

---

1 - George W. Peters, Mission-Church Relationship I, Bibliotheca Sacra, CXXV (July 1968) 499, p. 205-215

with separate administrations cooperating together. The mission carries the responsibility of evangelizing and establishing churches, and these churches become a part of the national church organization. The missionary, then, does not come under the jurisdiction of the national church; rather, the church and mission programs are set up in cooperation one with the other.

2) The second pattern of fraternal partnership and obedience is similar to the preceding one. Both groups remain distinctive and autonomous entities with each group having its own organization, personnel, budget, and program. However, the difference in this pattern is that here the mission functions more or less as a service agency to the national church, loaning workers to the churches for specific projects and also promoting certain projects for the benefit of the church, such as educational institutions, etc.

3) The third pattern is often referred to as Fusion. The Rev. Jean B. Bokeleale, General Secretary of the Churches of Christ in Congo, is a strong advocate of fusion of church and mission. A summary of his presentation of fusion follows:[2]

a) Disappearance of legal status of the mission in favor of the church.

b) A missionary becomes a full member of the church and is available to serve in any office of the church.

c) All equipment and properties come under the ownership of the church, the missionary having priority in certain areas such as a missionary residence.

d) All finances controlled by the church.

e) Direct relations, without an intermediary, between the home board of the mission organization and the young church.

In this program of fusion, as advocated by Mr. Bokeleale, the national church becomes responsible for total administration on the field of both church and mission. Therefore, the missionary program as well as the missionaries are integrated into the national structure. Ownership of property, placement of personnel, and all finances come under the administration of the national church.

The missionary in this type of program is usually referred to as a fraternal worker who is assigned to his ministry by the national church and is responsible to the national church. Usually he would still receive his support from home churches through the mission organization, to the national church, and then to him. Dr. Peters, in referring to this pattern, states: "While the mission considers itself a partner of the national church, the missionary becomes a servant of the national church. The missionary partnership has been converted into servantship."[3]

2 - Minutes of National Executive Committee of the Congo Protestant Council, June 1-4, 1969, IV Resolutions.

3 - George W. Peters, Ibid p. 214.

4) The pattern of partnership of equality and mutuality: Dr. Peters writes on this relationship: "Missions must be related to the churches and must become an integral part of the churches, fully involving the national churches. The missionary's ministry must be rendered through the church, but not mainly to the church. Principally, he works neither in the church nor for the church, but with the church. His service is mainly to the unevangelized world. Whatever his official membership may be, he is a full-fledged member of the board of missions and the national church with rights, privileges, and responsibilities, serving in the missionary expansion of the church. This assignment is his by divine calling and mutual agreement between him and his mission and the national church, and cannot be altered by unilateral action either by the mission or the church. Only in this manner is true partnership possible and equality and mutuality evident."[4]

In seeking to establish the recommended pattern for church-mission relationships, certain factors must be kept in mind. Much is said these years on the theme, "From Missions to Mission." The emphasis seems to be that all the church is and does is mission. One could ask the question: If then everything is mission, is anything mission? It seems to be easy to speak of total mission and lose the thrust of missions. It is the concern of missions to press forward, reaching out to the unevangelized. It is our desire and hope to see churches established and growing. Therefore, of necessity, we are deeply involved in training programs in order to establish the younger churches in the Word. In light of our calling to missions, do we continue to be chiefly engaged in outreach to unsaved people or are we becoming largely institutional-minded and more absorbed with the church than the world? Are an increasing portion of our energies being directed to the maintenance of churches and institutions for Christians, when the cutting edge of the church should be reaching out to new frontiers with the Gospel? Has this institutional-mindedness contributed to our lack of mobility and the building of what is termed as the mission-station mind?[5]

In considering the church-mission pattern, we must also give real thought to the question of mutual confidence and trust. As interdenominational mission boards, we draw our support from across the spectrum of Protestant churches in our home countries; yet we invariably form a fellowship of churches in the countries in which we serve. It is our earnest desire to see a burden for missions in these young churches and the pattern of church-mission relationships ought to be one which will encourage the church to send out its own missionaries to other areas.

Our goal is world evangelization. In this goal we see three major areas of thrust: (1) The proclamation of the Gospel to the unevangelized, (2) the establishing of local churches, and (3) the training of national leadership in the Word.

Accepting the fact that the church is dominant in the church-mission pattern, our desire is that the church-mission relationship would result in the coming to fruition of strong, developing, evangelistic,

---

4 - George W. Peters, Mission-Church Relationship II, Bibliotheca Sacra, CXXV (Oct., 1968) 500, p. 302-303.

5 - T. Watson Street, On the Growing Edge of the Church, John Knox Press, p. 25 - 38.

mission-minded local churches. The missionary involvement should strengthen a local church by:

- Understanding its needs.
- Working alongside its leaders.
- Identifying with its goals.
- Instructing its congregation.
- Exemplifying its potential in personal life and service.
- Appreciating its spiritual gifts and work.
- Recognizing its desire for fellowship.
- Joining in its ministry.
- Interceding for its problems.
- Counseling its leaders.

Dr. George Peters writes in Africa Pulse: "It should be realized that the church-mission relationship is an organizational and not a theological issue. It, therefore, does not affect our theological position nor our fellowship in the Lord. It is my impression that ecumenism makes its appeal to the evangelical churches on the organizational level and thereby will win indirectly the victory on the theological and ecclesiastical levels. It is my opinion that evangelical missions can well afford, if need be, to operate (as some consider it) on a sub-ideal level organizationally in order to win the battle theologically. Let us not weaken our impact in relationship and influence because of organizational differences. Much wisdom, grace and humility will be required to know the way of the Lord on this critical issue which can easily estrange us from our brethren and the churches."[6]

It would seem that basically the pattern of partnership of equality and mutuality is the strongest presentation for church-mission relationships. I would see the outworking of this pattern within the framework of submersion of the mission into the church, with the following suggestions for implementation:

The missionary's role: He is sent out to serve with the church. Therefore, it is advisable for him to come under the administration of the church. He would be integrated into the church's program. His assignment would then be made by the church and he would be under the discipline of the church.

This is the point at which mutual confidence is so essential. The missionary has been sent of God to serve His Lord. The receiving church assigns the missionary to his place of service after prayerful consideration of his calling, his gifts, and in light of the short-range as well as long-range plan for the work of the Lord in that field.

In the area of finances, it would seem that the church-mission relationship would be strengthened if all funds contributed toward a project or program be sent directly to the church, whereas the salary and work support of the missionary be sent directly to him.

The church would have the *ownership of most of the property*, with the exception of the missionary's housing and specific areas such as radio stations, printing presses, etc., as agreed by the church and mission organizations.

6-George W. Peters, An Analysis from Africa, Africa Pulse, I (March 1970) 2, p. 3.

The administration of these institutions, which do not come directly under church ownership, would be by a board of nationals and missionaries for each institution. The membership of the board should always have a minimum of an equal number of national and missionary members. If a balance were to be placed in favor of one group, it would always be to the national group. The board should be responsible to the church or mission as agreed.

Educational and medical institutions may or may not be administered directly through the church program. These institutions could have an organization similar to that stated above.

The recommendation is that there be one program--that is, the church's program. There would no longer be a need for a mission governing body to discuss the administration of the work, for the church's annual meeting would care for this. The missionary field council would handle areas of responsibility assigned to it by the church and mission. These areas would include education of missionaries' children and others as specified.

The basic principle is that the missionary serves the Lord within the framework of the receiving church.

It is our conviction that the missionary may be temporary; therefore, we always keep in mind the reduction of his activities. Strategic withdrawal of missionary personnel, transfer to other assignments locally or to other countries, should always be included in the planning of the program of the church with which the mission is associated.

We are reminded by G. Watson Street: "Aggressive evangelism can be lost through ecclesiastical machinery. The national church can develop a mind-set of 'squatter's rights' in a territory white unto the harvest. Some national churches have fallen into the bondage of clericalism which establishes an ecclesiastical domain and looks after it rather than after the evangelistic opportunities. If such a situation develops, the sending churches must say, 'Here we stand. We must obey God rather than man. Our evangelistic duty must take precedence over inter-church relations.' Such things must be said at times. Perhaps it would be helpful if they were said more often. We must not move from a dictatorship of the mission only to succumb to a dictatorship of the national church, but it must be said that all the dangers of repressing aggressive evangelism are not on one side. American missions have also succumbed to ecclesiasticism. There appears as much evangelistic zeal among some national pastors as among missionaries. The national church is not seeking to deny the freedom and initiative of the missionary. This freedom and initiative have been allowed and guaranteed in every arrangement. What is insisted upon is the freedom and initiative which does not create a missionary empire but fulfills what has been the great goal of the missionaries--that they may decrease and the church in that land increase."[7]

Again we remind ourselves that different areas of the world have different emphases in church-mission relationships. This is true in UFM. Our prayer is that we will ever look to the Lord to direct us and that we will ever be sensitive to the leading of the Holy Spirit.

Perhaps a strategy for UFM could be outlined as follows: (Attached)

7 - T. Watson Street, Ibid, p. 61-62

IFMA Official Board Retreat
May 24-27, 1971, Pearl River, New York

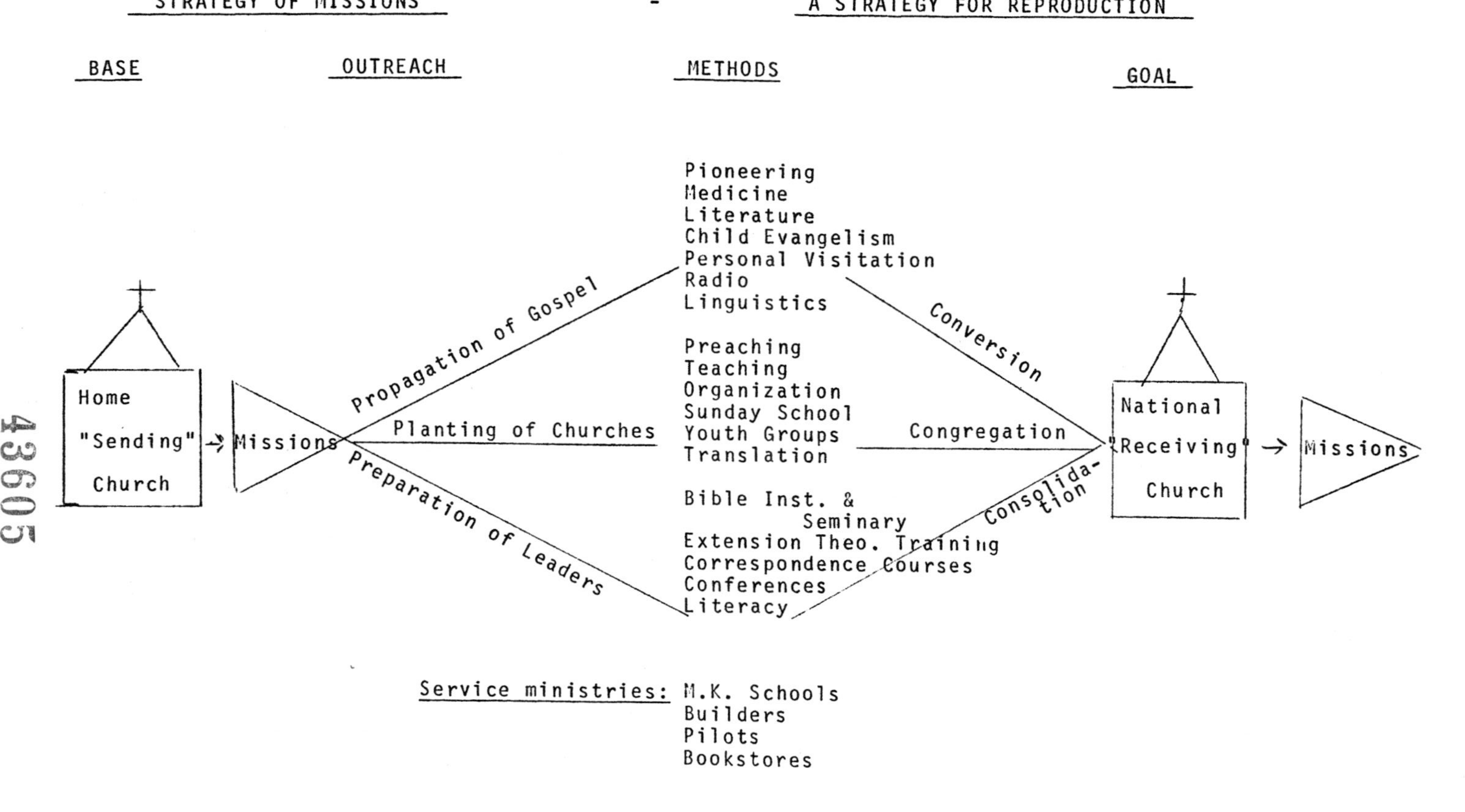

Charles E. Piepgrass
U. F. M.

IFMA MISSIONS AND SENDING (Supporting) CHURCHES --- A Pastor's Viewpoint

By George Linhart

Introduction

1- This is A pastor's Viewpoint!

2- Nothing written about this relationship except for a recent Africa Now (Nov.-Dec., 1970) article entitled: "The Missionary: Do You Know Who Sends Him," by Kerry Lovering.

3- We could conclude at the beginning that Mission Boards are to assist local churches... and not to present crises in our local churches.

4- Churches are asking questions today of Mission Boards. Right or wrong, they have been informed from various sources of potential dangers and problems.

5- The Theological Spectrum of Protestantism
Radicalism-Liberalism-Confessionalism-New Evangelicalism-Fundamentalism.

6- The Ecclesiastical Spectrum of Protestantism

WCC — DOM-NCCC

WEF — NAE-EFMA

ICCC — ACCC--TAM

IFMA

IFCA

Independents — Churches, Missions

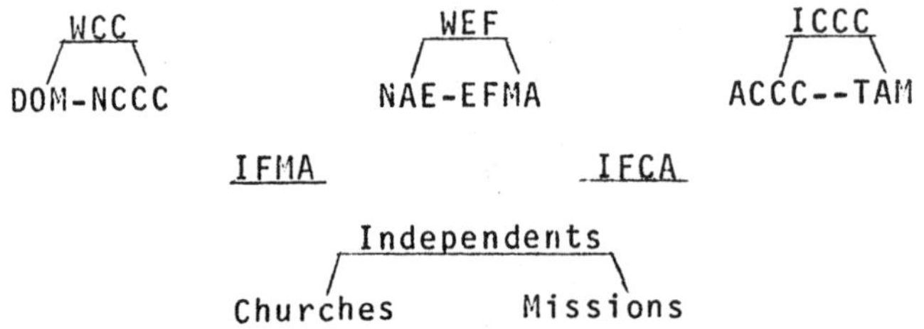

7- At the present time IFMA Boards are servicing a limited constituency. And it would appear as though this will become more limited in the future.

I. BIBLICAL RESPONSIBILITY

1- Need to emphasize the importance of the Local Church.

2- The Local Church has Biblical warrant.

3- Mission Boards--though without Biblical authority, are an extension arm of local churches.

4- God is not by-passing the Church today!

5- Actually Team Work is necessary here.

6- Team Work involves:
   a- Prayer Support - cf. 2 Cor. 1:11

   b- Fellowship - Phil. 1:3, 5

   c- Finances - Phil. 4:13-16

7- Nature of what we have makes it difficult to have a close Church-Mission sense of Responsibility

A. EARLY CHURCH

1- Missions in Acts was under Apostolic Authority and under the liberty of the Holy Spirit.

2- Preached the Gospel - Acts 14:21

   Taught Disciples - 14:21, 22

   Established Churches - 14:23

3- Reports were made:
   To Sending Churches - i.e. Antioch - Acts 13:3; 14:25-7
   To Other Churches - Acts 15:3, 4, 6, 12; 21:19
   To Others by Letter - Rom. 15:18, 19; I Cor. 15:10

4- At End of Term - Checked Churches - Acts 15:36, 41

5- Reports told
Successes - Acts 14:22, 29

Soundness - Gal. 2:1-8; Acts 11:1-4

Strategy - Rom. 15:24; Rom. 1:10

B. TODAY

1- Denominational Missions set up the policy, practices, goals and support structures.

2- IFMA Missions do the same....
But they answer to no one church or churches,
Yet - They offer their services to the churches.
Relieve churches of detail work

3- But with this service comes problems.

II. MUTUAL RELATIONSHIPS

1- It seems as though the nature of our system and arrangement makes it difficult to have a close Church-Mission Relationship.

2- Through high school the church has taken the initiative with youth.

3- During college there is little contact.

4- Contact for Missions is made usually during the final year or semester. And Missions offer the specific place of service.

5- It would appear as though Church and Mission Board would be aware and in concord in the following areas for a happy relationship:

A. ADEQUATE BIBLICAL PREPARATION

Class Room Academics: Working knowledge of Bible. Ability for expressing Bible Truths.

B. <u>EFFECTIVENESS IN PERSONAL SOUL-WINNING</u>
Knowledge of the Gospel. Ability to lead others to Christ. Success in soul-winning.

C. <u>UNDERSTANDING OF THE CHURCH</u>
Nature of the Church
Identification with a Local Church
General functions of a Local Church

D. <u>RECOGNITION OF THE CALL</u>
Who takes the initiative here?
Holy Spirit, Church, Mission Board

E. <u>THOROUGH CANDIDATE EVALUATION</u>
From a local church and pastor's viewpoint.

F. <u>STRATEGY and GOALS OF MISSION BOARD</u>

G. <u>AVAILABLE USE OF CANDIDATE</u>

H. <u>MISSION BOARD'S POSITION & ATTITUDE</u>
Officially and in practice.
Attitudes toward: WCC, Dialogue, Cooperation, Separation

I. <u>GENERAL INFORMATION ABOUT MISSION BOARD</u>
Support policy, term of service and furlough, etc.

III. ACTUAL RECIPROCITY

1- "...a mutual exchange of privilege, a recognition of licenses or privileges granted by others."

2- For the exchange of privilege, here are a few thoughts from a pastor's viewpoint.

A. RELINQUISH TO CHURCHES...areas that rightly belong to them. What are some of these areas?

1- Prime source of counsel.

2- Evaluate Qualifications.

3- Place of/to serve.

B. REPORT FACTUALLY TO CHURCHES

i.e. 1- Yearly or quarterly standardized report form.

2- Evaluation of missionaries' effectiveness.

C. RESPONSE TO CHURCHES

1- Delegate Option - i.e. as stockholders to annual meeting.

2- Representation from National Evangelical Groups on Boards.

Conclusion:

1- Alternatives to Action:

Establishment of a denominational approach.

Growth of a number of independent mission agencies.

Local Churches or Schools establish their own boards.

2- Could it be that that which was a necessary product of the times (while denominations were sound or tottering) may be outliving itself and its usefulness.

3- As IFMA MISSIONS are pressured by the National Churches of foreign lands, and adjustments have been made, it appears that we face the same today from the Sending Church.

4- As I see it then, this is the problem. We will either seek to service those churches that have sent and supported appointees to IFMA Missions, or we will seek to precipitate crises (unintentionally) that will force decisions against a continued close working relationship.

RELATIONSHIPS IN IFMA MISSIONS WITH NON-EVANGELICAL CHURCHES
or
Tension Points Which Arise in Latin America with the Catholic Church
and
Particular Problems Which We Face in Latin America with the Emerging Pentecostal Churches

By J. S. McCullough

For centuries it was stated that "Rome never changes," meaning the Roman Catholic Church. That is no longer true as many changes are taking place such as a new openness, friendliness, Scripture distribution, lay participation, liturgical change, a program of social concerns and many others. This has been described as "A changed face, but not essentially a changed nature" as no fundamental doctrines or dogmas have been changed. Nevertheless there is a new climate that presents to evangelicals the greatest opportunities in history to win Catholics to a saving knowledge of Christ.

There has also been a change of attitude toward the Catholic Church among evangelicals in Latin America. Outright persecution of evangelicals has virtually ceased except for isolated pockets here and there. This in itself brings a more wholesome atmosphere and improved relationships.

Roman Catholicism is still the official state religion in most Latin American countries, but religious freedom is given to other groups to propagate their message. Some of the best customers in our bookstores are now nuns and priests anxious to purchase Bibles and New Testaments in every available language.

There are tension points, however, and many are still searching for a right attitude and relationship toward the Roman Catholic Church in this rapidly changing climate.

1. Political
   a) It is felt that the Catholic party in Venezuela has been a factor in the government's reluctance, if not denial, of visas to new evangelical missionaries. No regular visas for missionaries have been issued since last July.

   b) The continued claim of the Catholics to a virtual monopoly on missionary work in jungle and indigenous areas of Venezuela, while they push their missionary work in similar areas where evangelicals are ministering.

Solution

This can best be handled by prayer followed by an effort to get the ear of government officials when the Lord opens the way.

2. New Openness

   We are thankful for this and it gives us a great opportunity to have personal contact with Catholics and to witness to them. There is much confusion caused by the statement that "Catholics and Protestants are now one, and it is only a matter of time until there will be one church." This is said frequently by Catholics and perhaps by liberal ecumenical Protestants who work diligently to that end. This can cause the real thrust of evangelism to be blunted. We must recognize that a great problem is the fact that many people do not know the difference between the Protestant and Catholic, and Catholic or Christian.

Dr. William H. Taylor has said, "The climate that is being produced in some circles is militating against conversions. As Dr. Emilio Antonio Nunez says, 'If the Roman Catholic Church has the truth, why did I ever leave it to become an evangelical?' He further asks, 'If Roman Catholics are already the sheep of God's fold, what need is there of evangelizing them?'"

a) Invitations from Catholic leaders to join meetings, etc.

We welcome opportunities that are opening to us on every side and we should take advantage of them. Dr. Kenneth Kantzer stated "At the same time it was pointed out that acceptance of treatment as 'Brethren' and consequent identification with the traditional Roman Catholic position could put the evangelical worker in a position of compromise that could cause not only questions but some very real problems regarding the validity of his Biblical position."

One IFMA leader wrote, "There is a difference of opinion as to how far we should go in the matter of accepting invitations to speak in seminaries, etc." Dr. Delbert Kuehl said about public meetings, "Our counsel is that we be extremely careful in relationship to any public intercourse, for example, a converted priest coming in his priestly robes to attend services at the evangelical church. We feel the danger here is that such may be misconstrued to leave the impression that we are really one and eliminate the sharp edge of our opportunities in evangelism among Catholic people."

There are opportunities for exchange of pulpits with priests. We don't think the priest should be invited to occupy an evangelical pulpit and while there can be confusion in the mind of the man on the street when the evangelical pastor preaches in the Catholic church, we can probably live with this.

Solution

While we are in disagreement with the Catholic system we are not enemies of Catholics, but should love them and seek to win them to a personal experience of salvation through Christ. We ought to take advantage of every opportunity for personal contact and friendship with no limitations set.

We do not encourage group contacts and meetings. We do not feel that joint services can be considered. We do not encourage ecumenical or public prayer meetings although there is no objection to private prayer with anyone.

3. Welfare and Social Concerns

The new program of the Catholic Church in welfare service, education, medical, cooperatives, efforts to correct social injustices and other areas of helpfulness to the people is indeed commendable. This is a contrast to the system that previously seemed to thrive on ignorance, superstition and poverty. The Catholics are far ahead of evangelicals in getting help through government and other organizations, so that we can't always do for our believers what they can.

Solution

In matters of social service where cooperation can be for the good of the public, we see no problem as long as we have no organizational relationship. In times of disaster such as in the Peruvian earthquake, cooperation is imperative and helpful. Some social projects may permit cooperation and others might not so that we will have to make some decisions as we come to them.

4. Dialogue

William H. Taylor has summed this up very well. "What I can't see, under any circumstances whatsoever, is the Roman Catholic-Protestant dialogue which seems to take as a starting point that both bodies are essentially Christian but do not know each other, hence the eagerness to emphasize the areas of agreement and to de-emphasize the areas of difference. When Evangelicals allow themselves to be drawn into ecumenical relations and activities that convey the idea of unity (even a growing one) I think that they are on dangerous ground and I think that the Evangelicals will consciously or unconsciously be making concessions to the other side."

Solution

Dialogue can be a waste of time that might better be spent more profitably. We are stewards of our time as well as message.

5. Attitude Toward Catholic Converts

There are really two points of view as to what position the converted Catholic should take. (1) The convert would do well to stay within the church and try to reform it internally. (2) The convert should join an evangelical church and use this as a base for further witness to Catholic friends and relatives.

The first position seems to be untenable because of their continued identification with and participation in the Roman Catholic Church which as a system is corrupt. It seems imperative that there be a break with the Roman system and a fellowship with God's children who love and study the Word of God.

Solution

We recommend that Catholic converts make a clean break with the Roman system and align themselves with evangelical churches.

6. Scripture Translations

C. Peter Wagner has written, "The most significant sign of the times in the Protestant church in Latin America has been the debate on the 'common Bible.' In its consultation in Oaxtepec, Mexico in 1968, the United Bible Societies set out to promote among the churches a joint Protestant-Catholic translation of the Scriptures. In the ensuing two years, however, the grass roots reaction from the churches was so strong against this policy that now the UBS has given it up in Latin America."

If the above is true then this solves some of the problems that have been building up among evangelicals.

Solution

The Bible Society proposals seem wise to some and unwise to others. Certainly the national churches should be very much involved in all decisions pertaining to translation. Circumstances will vary from country to country and one will have to be guided to the right decision in each situation. Translations will always be available to Protestants without the imprint of the Roman Catholic Church and without the Apocryphal books.

Problems Faced in Latin America with the Emerging Pentecostal Churches

The growth of Pentecostal churches and groups in Latin America has been phenomenal. Out of some twenty million evangelicals about 66% are related to some form of Pentecostalism. It is estimated that by the turn of the century their growth will reach about 90% of the believers in Latin America. In Chile alone there are between 100-120 distinct Pentecostal groups.

Hubert Cook wrote "Regarding the Pentecostal churches, these have historically been the thorn in the flesh, because they engage strongly in proselytizing and we have always declined to cooperate with them, and the line of demarcation has been fairly clear. The Charismatic movements have invaded our churches--some have been split and fellowship has been disrupted and we have lost workers. It has created a real problem area."

Another IFMA leader wrote - "In recent years we have not had difficulties from the more moderate Pentecostal groups such as the Assemblies. It is from the radical groups such as the New Wave and others that have come into our areas where we have had churches established and have taken away some church members. Sometimes after a period of time the people become disillusioned and return to us. When large campaigns are held by Pentecostals it puts the evangelical churches in a difficult position. If they do not cooperate in any way, the church people even though they may be quite well indoctrinated will often go and some are led away from the evangelical church. If they do cooperate, they have to be careful that they do not identify themselves with the extremes in some of the positions of Pentecostalism to which we do not adhere. One of our pastors was invited by the Foursquare leaders to such a campaign, and after carefully considering it and praying about it decided to attend. This church did not lose any of its own members and gained a number who were brought to Christ or became interested during the campaign and yet did not find that their own people were led away or enticed by the special Pentecostal emphasis regarding the Holy Spirit and the tongues matter."

The tension points specifically are:

1. Insistence of Pentecostals that non-Pentecostals preach only a partial gospel, leaving out essential elements--"healing," tongues, etc., and this creates tension among believers. It is a kind of pride that says unless you have experienced these "signs and wonders" you haven't arrived.

2. Divisions in local congregations promoted by Pentecostal elements continue though not as frequent as in past years.

3. Proselytizing by Pentecostals.

Solution

Evangelicals have a dynamic in personal witness and great campaigns that is entirely apart from the forms of witness used by Pentecostals and this should be maintained.

Local churches must teach believers according to their doctrinal standards and we should continue to root and ground believers in the Word of God as we understand it.

We can do better work if we go about things as we understand them and we believe that by the same token the Pentecostals find this to be true in their case. To force groups together with different doctrinal points of view only brings confusion.

Often Pentecostal members become completely disillusioned and then attend an evangelical church.

William H. Taylor has summarized this very well. "Let us get on with the work of the Lord as He has made His will clear to us as to what we should believe and how we should act and serve. Let us pray for all members of the Body of Christ everywhere, thanking God for all who have come out of darkness into His marvelous light. But let each march according to the music that he hears."

BIBLIOGRAPHY

Great help has been received in correspondence from -

LEWIS, Alvin T., Acting Director - The Orinoco River Mission

COOK, J. Hubert, General Director - Evangelical Union of South America

KUEHL, Delbert, Executive Assistant Director - The Evangelical Alliance Mission

TAYLOR, William H., General Secretary - The Central American Mission

KANTZER, Kenneth, Dean, Trinity Evangelical Divinity School Mimeographed paper - Roman Catholicism and the Ecumenical Movement

WAGNER,C. Peter - Mimeographed paper - Winning Roman Catholics in the Post Vatican II Era

IFMA Official Board Retreat
May 24-27, 1971
Pearl River, New York

MISSIONS AS "ORDERS"

By Charles J. Mellis

his presentation is primarily an attempt to distill the writings of r. Ralph Winter on the validity of non-churchly structures as the ost dynamic means of carrying out the mission of the Church. Re-ources used are:

1. "The Anatomy of the Christian Mission," EMQ, Winter, 1969 (reprinted as an appendix in #3 below).

2. "The New Missions and the Mission of the Church," pamphlet, William Carey Library, South Pasadena.

3. <u>The Twenty-Five Unbelievable Years: 1945-1969</u>, William Carey Library, South Pasadena. *

he two articles are primary sources. The book provides helpful ackground; direct reference to the subject is found at pp. 64-73 nd 77-84.

r. Winter's background

His discipline

His method

His titles--significance

ertical & horizontal structures

Internal/external expressions

Examples

So what? Look at . . .

See also <u>The Warp and the Woof</u> by Ralph D. Winter, William Carey Library, South Pasadena, California, 1971.

History

Roman hierarchy and orders

How Protestantism developed

The American pattern unique

Comparative nature of V/H structures

Advantages/disadvantages of V/H structures

Two crucial tasks:

1. Avoid a repetition of the American experience in the churches we found.

   Encourage Orders

2. Resolve the tensions between V/H structures in America.

   Types of tensions

   Possible solutions

Continuing study needed

Concluding remarks

RELATIONSHIP OF IFMA MISSIONS TO NATIONAL CHURCHES IN THE EMERGING COUNTRIES

By Peter Stam

ithin the past fifty to one hundred years God has used IFMA missions o bring into being a significant number of large, strong and mature ational churches in the emerging nations of the world. Recent trends re towards a much closer relationship between the missions and the hurches, with increasing domination of the work within each nation by he church. There are inevitably tensions which have developed as a re- ult of this movement, some of them serious enough to endanger the very xistence of the missions involved. This paper explores some of these ension points, and suggests possible solutions.

. HISTORICAL DEVELOPMENT

hough burdened with undesirable connotations today, the word PATERNAL- SM rather accurately describes early relationships between mission ocieties and infant churches in what are today called emerging coun- ries. New converts could neither read nor write, and even when a be- inning was made in reducing languages to writing, preparing primers, ranslating Scriptures, teaching elementary reading, the young church as still an infant in need of parental guidance, discipline, training. hat day has long since passed in many countries, and for some years he relationship has more accurately been described as FRATERNAL, with ission and church existing side-by-side, cooperating closely in a con- inuing discharge of the missionary mandate, but maintaining a distinct rganizational and legal identity.

ust within the last decade or so, pressures toward further changes ave been increasing rapidly, with demands from national churches in any areas for complete merger, or absorption of the mission by the hurch. Nationalism has undoubtedly been the strongest factor in this ressure, with churches in newly independent countries being subject to ressure from political and governmental sources, and they themselves lso wishing to exert their own identity and their independence of for- ign domination. This pressure has been further intensified by the xample of many of the denominational missions, which, looking on their ounger churches as an extension of the homeland organization, and ex- eriencing a decreasing number of missionary candidates, have rapidly urned over authority and assets to these younger churches, with the elatively few remaining missionaries continuing their service as "fra- ernal workers" under national direction. With the realization that ational churches could be more easily influenced than foreign mission ocieties, ecumenists have utilized and encouraged this trend towards hurch take-over of missions in their fostering of the church unity ovement.

ut regardless of the various factors explaining this trend today, we ust come to grips with the situation as it is, and seek God's direc- ion in bringing into being such a happy and fruitful relationship be- ween church and mission as shall glorify the Name of our Lord and peed to completion the task He has given us.

II. POSSIBLE ALTERNATIVES FOR THE FUTURE

There are five possible alternatives before us as we seek the answer to this dilemma.

1. A continuing parallelism which retains the organizational autonomy of both church and mission with informal cooperation in the continuing ministry, but with each determining its own policies, assigning its own workers, and handling its own finances. This may well be a viable option in some countries, and is the course which has been followed by many of our societies until the present time.

But in many countries, and particularly in Central Africa, parallelism is no longer an acceptable alternative. In the ears of Africans it has the same connotation as apartheid, or separateness, and this they will not tolerate--nor will their governments for very long. (Africanization"(or Latinization) is not only a politically potent concept, but an emotion-laden word. It means much more than training nationals to take over the foreigner's job--it means national leadership in every realm of life and in every organization. In recent years large business corporations have had to appoint nationals to their top posts, like it or not, and it is now time for missions to bow to the same edicts.

2. The other extreme is that of complete merger, or absorption of the mission by the church, with total loss of identity and authority by the mission, and total control by the church. This is the course followed by many of the denominational missions, as indicated above, though many of them have lived with it long enough to admit that it is not the answer either. In the September 1970 issue of the Missionary Research Library's Occasional Bulletin, page 7, under a heading "Partnership in Mission," we read:

> "For many years, at least one of the Commission's boards had vigorously emphasized dissolving of mission structure and integrating fraternal workers into the life of the national church. With this, there had been a tacit assumption that anything the related church desired should be determinative of our response. In recent years, there has been a growing understanding that autonomy is a mutual matter, and that neither partner in a relationship of equal churches is called upon to deny its own integrity or calling to mission in the world.
>
> "It needs to be reasserted continually, without pomposity or irritation, that the Commission is more than a servicing agency for indigenous churches. It is an instrumental expression of the United Presbyterian Church's fulfillment of its mission to the world, and to assume that the ecumenical era demands a total subordination in program and the use of personnel to the individual determination of indigenous churches would be a restrictive error.
>
> "For personal questions, this implies that both sharing and receiving bodies need to establish with each other the kind of open relationships and related procedures that will make certain they fulfill their mutual stewardship of the human resources of both churches."

Dr. George Peters of Dallas Seminary recently pointed out that the ecumenically popular course of complete fusion of mission and church simply does not work. Statistics show that when missionaries go as fraternal workers seconded to the church, and with no mission organization o represent their interests, almost two-thirds leave before their first erm is over. The church has told the fraternal worker that it wants im, but he finds that either

1. The Church has no job for him, or

2. The Church wants to exploit him by giving him a job that any national could do, but for which the Church has no funds.

e quickly becomes dissatisfied and quits.

3. A third alternative which has been considered valid in some parts f the world has been that of the recruitment of outstanding nationals nto the mission organization. LAM and OMF have both followed this path n recent years, and they can best testify to its present validity or therwise. Dennis Clark in his recently published, The Third World and ission asks, "In the present climate of opinion in most Third World ations, is it credible to imagine nationals serving within the strucure of Western missionary societies?" This is confirmed in a memo by r. Horace Fenton, General Director of LAM, dated November 1970, in hich he says:

> "We have been greatly blessed and strengthened by the acquisition of gifted and consecrated Latins into full membership in the Mission. But the proportion of them is still relatively small... The rate of accession of competent Latins might be accelerated by the setting up of a recruitment and screening program for Latin America. But this wouldn't meet the real situation; it would still be hard--too hard--for many competent Latins to commit themselves, for short terms or for life, to an organization which is still, governmentally, so North American oriented."

lark then observes, "Despite the present climate of opinion, however, here is a scramble by many societies for "key nationals," and this harsses many receiving churches, preyed on by the 'servant covetor'." He uggests that "the more likely pattern of development will be the trengthening of existing missionary societies in Third World nations nd proliferation of others."

4. The fourth possible alternative we mention is that currently beng developed by the LAM. In a news release dated January 22, 1971 hey stated:

> "Delegates to the consultation reached a consensus that the ministries which comprise the Latin America Mission's work should constitute themselves as a community or fellowship of autonomous units--some of them international in scope such as Evangelism-in-Depth, and others grouped geographically. Latin Americans will bear major responsibilities."

his "spinning-off" of the various ministries of LAM into autonomous nits loosely bound together in an international family would seem to it the service-mission character of LAM but could hardly be the answer or a church-planting mission with close ties with a national church.

5. The fifth, and most likely alternative, for most of our societies ould be a middle path between Parallelism (No. 1) and complete fusion No. 2). According to Dr. Peters, this has been tried in many countries nd has been successful in most. He states that "There is no uniform

answer, no sacred pattern, no right or wrong." Each society and church must work out the pattern best suited to the culture and circumstances. "That pattern is best which leads to the deepest relationship and fellowship between Church and Mission." After a study of many such relationships, he stated that "With partial fusion, in most cases the work goes on better than ever, with tensions gone, and mutual confidence and fellowship."

III. There are of course many OBSTACLES to be overcome in working out such an arrangement.

1. Fear of Missionaries

a) that they might be assigned to a position they don't want or for which they do not feel qualified,

b) that national leadership will be poor in quality, and that projects built up through the years will soon "go down the drain" as a result,

c) that nationals might try to control the missionary's personal finance,

d) that the national church will become involved with ecumenical bodies and thus cause embarrassment with the home constituency,

e) that because of lack of understanding of African thinking, aspirations, viewpoints, wrong motives are often imputed.

2. Suspicion on the part of national church leaders of the motives of the mission and missionaries. Such suspicion is largely due to ignorance, since for the most part they have not been invited to sit in on Mission Council sessions, and not knowing what happens, suspect the worst. A climate of mutual respect and trust must be built up, and complete frankness and openness is essential for this.

3. Unspiritual attitudes on the part of either church or mission leaders can constitute formidable obstacles to the working out of partial fusion. Extreme nationalism, self-assertiveness, pride, desire for power, all these erect barriers. Peter Beyerhaus, in an article entitled "The Three Selves Formula" in the International Review of Missions brings this out effectively.

"It is possible for a church to affirm its human 'self' against God, and so to become odious to both God and man. The Church should therefore hesitate to apply to itself an ideal that stresses the affirmation of the self... It is possible for a church to manage its own affairs, maintain its own economy and win quite a number of new members, without any of these activities meeting with God's approval. They could be nothing more than collective self-assertion for the sake of power, self-satisfaction, self-sufficiency, and self-extension, and this is the very opposite of what Christ meant the Church to be."

4. Racial prejudice on the part of some missionaries. This is not as common as it once was, but there are still those who are unwilling to accept a national Christian on an equal

basis, to welcome them into their homes, to acknowledge their right to control their own churches, destinies, etc. Such individuals should no longer be permitted to poison the atmosphere of missionary work in emerging nations. Their presence is a formidable obstacle.

ut by prayer, sympathetic consultation, and an unselfish willingness to ive up personal rights for the sake of the work and the glory of hrist, such an arrangement CAN be worked out which will fit into the olitical and cultural situation in most countries. The foresight to eep ahead of such pressure build-ups and thus forestall unnecessary onfrontations is exceedingly important.

V. TENSION POINTS IN CHURCH/MISSION RELATIONS, AND SOME SUGGESTED SOLUTIONS

ension points frequently encountered in working out closer relations ith national churches can be divided into two groups: Organizational nd Financial.

A. ORGANIZATIONAL

1. The question of ULTIMATE AUTHORITY is basic to everything lse, the real key to many of the tension points. It must be considered n two areas: national, or authority for work and personnel within a ountry where the mission ministers; and international, or the overall inistry, organization and personnel of the mission. In Central Africa oday, and probably in other sections of the Third World as well, there s little question that authority for the work and direction of personel on a national level must sooner or later rest with the national hurch. Governments are increasingly insisting on this, and church eaders are relaying the pressures they feel on to the mission. Demands or ONE HEAD, and he a national, are heard with increasing frequency. here such authority can be vested in a joint board or council with some issionary representation, the extreme of total capitulation is avoided. hen nationals know that they have a clear majority, counting noses no onger seems important, and generally the presence, advice and viewpoint f the missionary is desired and appreciated.

nternationally, there appear to be many reasons to retain ultimate uthority within the ranks of the mission organization. Conditions vary o greatly from one country to another that nationals of one country nderstand with difficulty the challenges and problems of another. Furher, on the international level, it would seem strongly advisable for he mission to retain its status as an outreach organization rather than eing tied down organizationally with the church in any one country.

2. How far to go in merger, or fusion? Inevitably a tension oint, and a basic one, with nationals generally pushing for total aborption of the mission by the church, and the mission and missionaries esisting, holding the line, attempting to retain identity and authorty. This is a useless and needless struggle, resulting only in bitteress, fear and frustration. Mutual trust and understanding are essenial, and a willingness to give up much (but not all) when the national hurch is mature enough to accept it. The time element here is a ouchy one, with nationals frequently considering themselves ready beore the missionary is prepared to agree. The answer, as already ointed out, will vary with the country and the culture, with the maturty of the church and the character of the mission. AIM's Kenya field

may perhaps be considered a typical example, and a copy of the agreement which was worked out with the A.I.C. Kenya in June, 1970 is appended to this paper. In general, it calls for placing AIM church-related departments including evangelism, education, literature, medical, radio, under the Africa Inland Church, seconding missionaries to the church for assignment and direction, turning over all church-relate properties, including missionary residences, to the church, but retaining a minimal mission organizational structure, with mission committees chosen by the missionaries, a secretary, treasurer, and necessary offices. Also retained are jurisdiction over the school for M.K.'s, tele communications system, title to certain urban properties purchased outright by the mission, mission guest houses, and legal registration.

3. Preservation of legal status by the mission has been a sore point in some countries. Legal implications in any given country should be thoroughly investigated, with professional advice if possible In AIM's experience, the churches in Tanzania and Kenya were ready to grant to the Mission the right of continuing legal existence, but in Congo it has become an emotion-laden issue due to ecumenical pressures for total fusion. Thus far the legal status, (personalite civile) has been retained, but this is interpreted as a lack of trust, and it seems evident that this request will be acceded to, perhaps with a compromise the two legal identities are merged into one new one, including both, and with one legal representative for the church, and another to care for mission interests. Here, too, decisions must be made in the light of specific situations, with consideration being given to both emotional and rational factors, and in the light of both cultural and political realities.

4. Assignment of personnel is one of the greatest tension points. It seems inevitable that responsibility for such assignment must pass from mission to church, though preferably to joint committees of some kind with minority missionary representation. But there are inevitably problems. Church leaders facing pressures from family, members, community and government naturally have difficulty in objectively assessing alternatives, and their priorities often differ from those of the mission. Once authority is in their hands, they tend to exercise it rather forcibly, at least for a time, with little regard for the training, experience or preferences of the missionaries being assigned. AIM's experience in Tanzania, the first of our fields to turn this authority over to the church, was for a period of several years very difficult, with nearly half of the missionary force requesting transfer to other fields because of unwillingness to accept specific assignments made by the church staffing board. After such heavy losses, the African Church finally realized that if they wanted the help of the missionaries, they would have to consider individual training and preferences to a greater extent. Relations, and assignments, have been much happier during the past several years. There seems to be no easy solution to this tension point, and the national church often insists on learning the hard way, and paying the price in loss of missionary personnel. On the other hand, there have been many examples of missionaries demonstrating the fruit of the Spirit to an unusual degree in accepting irrational assignments, with resulting unusual blessing from God because of such submission and patience. For a continuing effective ministry among our national brethren, we must be prepared to stand by them sympathetically and patiently, allowing them to make mistakes where they insist, making the best of resulting difficult situations, and accepting as from God's sovereign hand the decisions He permits them to make.

5. The exercise of initiative in beginning or expanding various ministries. This too can be a sore point, with a national church determined to exercise newly acquired authority to the point of stifling evangelistic initiative. A burden for church extension or outreach into a new area may have to battle a church committee that is more concerned with starting a high school for children of the Christian community. Admittedly a legitimate desire, but a totally different priority. If at all possible, the initiative of the mission and missionary should be safeguarded, though it should be exercised independently only when the church proves completely unwilling to go along with the projected advance. In our recent Kenya agreement this freedom was preserved in the following words:

> "In order to carry out the objectives and functions of the Africa Inland Mission, it needs... (a) to be free to initiate, in consultation with the Church, and carry on work which is not directly related to the Africa Inland Church, and to sponsor or second missionaries for other works."

But it is essential to consult with the church at every point. to seek to challenge the leadership and to involve them in the new project as much as possible, listening to their advice, and following it where practical, in order that the project development may be as acceptable to them as possible.

6. Pressure to turn institutions over to the church. This will be dealt with at length in another paper, but is included here for the sake of completeness. The national churches frequently consider institutions such as hospitals, schools, printing presses, and bookshops which have been carried on by the mission for years as potential sources of financial income, or as status symbols, and therefore want to take control, sometimes before they are really prepared to do so, and without realizing the complexities of the project. The inevitable result in such cases is maladministration by poorly-trained men, financial loss, and the gradual disintegration of a fruitful project built up through years of effort and investment.

There are several possible solutions to this problem. If eventual turnover to nationals appears inevitable, preparation should include the placing of a few capable nationals in key places sometime prior to the turnover so that they might become thoroughly familiar with the financial status and operation, the problems to be faced, and the goals and priorities of the institution. If, on the other hand, an institution is of such a complex or specialized nature that transfer to the church is NOT the answer, the possibility of setting up independent corporations, perhaps interdenominational or inter-mission in character, should be investigated. Bookshops and publishing enterprises might well be reconstituted as commercial profit-making organizations, such as has been beautifully exemplified by the SIM's turning over of their Niger-Challenge Press to a Nigerian concern, Associated Press of Nigeria,now carrying on in a profitable and businesslike manner.

7. Operation of mission projects and institutions by the mission alone can frequently cause bitterness and misunderstanding. Schools for missionary children are typical of this problem. These sometimes run afoul of government policies to integrate all schools, and church leaders tend to look longingly on such an institution as a possible answer to their own teenager's desire for more education. A token integration by acceptance of a limited number of national

students sometimes relieves such pressure. Including one or two church leaders in the board or committee operating such a school helps tremendously, since bringing such representatives into the operation effectively dispels any mystery and resulting misunderstanding. One or more nationals should be included in the directing bodies of every institution if suspicion and nationalistic pressures are to be avoided.

8. Pressure for representation on Mission Councils at all levels. This tension point is obviously open to debate, and some will undoubtedly argue that there ought to be national representation at every level. In an interdenominational organization, however, particularly one devoted to OUTREACH, I believe there are solid reasons for limiting membership to the mission itself. This has already been touched on in our consideration of possible alternatives. The national churches need a top mission body with which they can negotiate, and missions certainly need to consult with national church leaders. Both of these needs are met if the relationship is maintained on a consultative or negotiating level, rather than actual membership. The partial merger or fusion should be limited to the national level only.

9. Ecumenical Involvement. Tension arises in this area where national churches do not recognize the same dangers and compromise as does the mission. This is often the case in emerging countries where ecumenists have played their hands carefully and their long-range objectives (for example, union with Rome) and short-range methods, frequently unscrupulous, are not fully understood by national churches because contact in the past has been very limited.

Congo is a pertinent example of this at present, with the newly-formed Eglise du Christ au Congo (E.C.C., Church of Christ in Congo) having been set up as a unified church for the whole nation. Some churches and missions have already withdrawn because of ecumenical involvement, but others profess not to see any real difference between this new development and the old Congo Protestant Council - as long as the E.C.C. abides by its guarantees not to join the World Council of Churches, and not to infringe on the autonomy of regional groups. Tensions here are aggravated by pressures from supporting churches in homelands, which tend to see such issues in black and white and interpret them in terms of the situation in the West with which they are familiar.

Such tensions need to be resolved with sympathy and understanding, and lots of patience, with teaching from the Scriptures, and perhaps a clear statement that if such entanglements are persisted in, the church might have to choose between the mission and these ecumenical involvements.

10. Lack of missionary vision of the national church. Not universally true, thank God, it is nevertheless all too common a problem that the national church does not completely share the missionary's vision to reach out into the unevangelized areas of a country or segments of a society. For example, there is relatively little real interest in the Africa Inland Church, Kenya, to reach out into the deserts of northern Kenya in behalf of the 500,000 nomads following their herds of camels around from one water hole to another. To the existing church it seems that establishment of more secondary schools, dispensaries and hospitals is definitely a higher priority, though a few African missionaries have gone, and have received some support from the Church. One solution to this tension point, aside from Scriptural teaching of our God-given responsibility, would be to take some of the church leaders on survey trips through such areas, that the very sight of completely unreached men and women might be used by the Spirit of God to challenge them to share their faith.

IV. B. FINANCIAL TENSION POINTS. Inevitably and universally the handling of money causes problems, and this is one area where church-mission relationships can become very sticky indeed.

1. The SECURING OF FUNDS is the first problem area here. Most churches in emerging lands are relatively poor, with undersupported clergy and no money for anything but support of the local pastor. A regional or field-wide church organization, with officials to support, appears to them to be an insuperable burden. Teachers in a theological seminary, or radio preachers, are still not pastoring a local church, and as far as giving is concerned, out of sight, out of mind. On the other hand, the missionary has a private pipeline to those wealthy Christians in his homeland and if he truly, genuinely wants to help the national church, why doesn't he cut that church into the gravy line?

This is all aggravated by the fact that ecumenical interests are all the while dangling offers of generous cash grants, and scholarships for overseas study before the dazzled eyes of church leaders and promising young men within their congregations. It is not easy to point out the dangerous strings attached to such offers, for they are invisible strings for the most part.

Nationalization intensifies the problem (whether it be Africanization or Latinization). When, after years of training under the missionary an African is ready to take over that bookshop, or dispensary, or administrative post, why is not the missionary's house and salary available with the job? The complexities of our personalized support system elude them. Don't the Christians in the homeland want that job continued effectively?

Solutions are difficult to find. Most of our societies are just not set up to raise or solicit funds for national churches, and besides, the very thought of such an activity would appear to run counter to both the traditional "faith principle" and the sacrosanct "indigenous church policy." Perhaps we need to rethink both! The ideal answer would seem to be help for the national church THROUGH or FROM the mission responsible for having brought it into existence. But most interdenominational missions have a difficult enough time financially without this further burden.

One possible answer is the use of the facilities of an outside organization such as Christian Nationals Evangelism Commission (C.N.E.C), which proposes to raise funds for the support of national workers in various parts of the world. In discussing this possibility with Dr. George Peters, he pointed out the desirability of the mission society involved serving as the "introducing body" in bringing such an organization into contact with the national church, but urged that from that point on, negotiations be carried out directly between the two, so that the church could never hold the mission responsible for shortage or diminishing funds. Such support would be arranged only for non-pastoral personnel, and on a planned basis of diminishing proportions over a period of, say, ten years, with the national church gradually getting under the burden as they were able.

We may, of course, see the day when national churches will send their own representatives to visit churches in Western nations in order to raise money for their own programs. Such a development would leave churches here in a real quandary as to who to trust, and who to support.

Government subsidies for education and medicine have frequently been a tension point. Some societies have on principle refused to accept such subsidies, and more than one society has been forced out of their field of service by the national Christians because of such refusal. Such a position would seem unwarranted in many countries, in the light of the fact that there is no choice of educational or medical facilities in many places, and taxes collected from the nationals can thus provide benefits for them only if the missions accept such subsidies and use them in behalf of the local population.

2. The HANDLING OF FUNDS inevitably results in tension when it is cared for by poorly trained nationals, or, obviously, by men with flexible ideas regarding the use of designated funds! There have been instances in East Africa where the church has asked missionaries to care for church funds because they did not trust the capabilities or judgment of their own men for the job. In one such case the missionary wisely agreed to accept only on condition that the church assign to him a capable national assistant to learn the job and eventually take over.

There ARE capable, well-trained nationals in many countries, some of them with university training in business, who would be more than equal to carrying such responsibilities. The problem is that such men can and do command a salary beyond the ability of most national churches to pay. This is the type of situation where outside financial help would probably enable the national churches to break out of the vicious circl of poor pay--poorly-equipped men. A really capable man, adequately trained, and adequately supported, perhaps from overseas sources, would gradually command the respect and confidence of the church, and increased giving would then hopefully enable that church to gradually undertake his support.

One tension point in the handling of funds is that resulting from undue control of funds from overseas by missionaries. Funds designated for church projects should be turned over to the church to use as designated, but without further missionary control or manipulation. When the location of a Bible school, for example, is determined by the missionary through whom funds are available, simply because he is the pipeline for those funds, and regardless of other more strategic factors, bitterness is bound to result.

3. Costs of transfering properties. To a national church, the news that the mission has agreed to turn over properties, houses, lands, schools, hospitals to that church is music in a joyful major key - until they suddenly receive an exhorbitant bill for legal fees and government assessments involved in such a transfer. If at all possible, the churches should pay such costs, but they should be completely informed as to all that is involved BEFORE such proceedings are begun. In cases where such fees are beyond the ability of the church to handle, an assist from the mission will result in gratitude and confidence in the mission's motivation and genuine desire to help. But arrangements must be thoroughly understood in advance by all parties.

4. Maintenance and use of buildings and properties. In any arrangements worked out between national churches and mission, the use and maintenance of buildings should be clearly understood by all. When properties are turned over to the church for their exclusive use, they should understand that from that point on all maintenance costs are theirs. Where missionary homes are involved, perhaps with an understanding that these are reserved for missionary use as long as the

church desires missionaries at that place, the agreement should be that the mission or missionaries maintain that property or building as long as they are using it.

5. Missionary salaries. The handling or amount of missionary salaries has not generally proven to be a point of tension with the church. There are in many countries a sprinkling of well-educated nationals getting considerably higher salaries than missionaries, and though the latter are considered wealthy by local standards, this is usually recognized as a concomitant of Western civilization. The handling of missionary salaries and allowances could become a source of friction, however, if cared for in field offices with nationals gradually taking over. Problems in this area can be generally avoided if missionary allowances are handled directly between the home office and the individual, perhaps by deposit of funds in the missionary's personal bank account in the homeland. He is then notified by statement, and draws on that account by check. No field or church office is then involved.

Conclusion. The above are only some of the many tension points which could be cited, and undoubtedly there are other, and perhaps better, solutions to many of them. Flexibility is essential and the answers will vary with each mission and each country. Our God has exhorted us to be as "wise as serpents and harmless as doves," - and has promised to give us the wisdom we need.

By assignment, this paper has dealt with "tension points" - inevitably somewhat negative. But I am convinced that there are rich dividends and an abundant spiritual harvest still awaiting us if we are prepared to accord to national churches raised up, called out, by God Himself, their rightful identity and authority. Patience and love are needed in abundance. We must be prepared to stand by and see them make mistakes, learn the hard way if they insist. The grace of God will prove more than sufficient for us to accept their decisions, even when they seem to affect us adversely. And an open door of opportunity to witness and bear fruit will result, where unnecessary confrontations on essentially unimportant points would close that door.

IFMA Official Board Retreat
May 24-27, 1971
Pearl River, New York

RESOLUTIONS AGREED TO BY THE AFRICA INLAND MISSION, KENYA FIELD COUNCIL at its meeting 26th June 1970 for presentation to THE AFRICA INLAND CHURCH

The Africa Inland Mission has presented the Africa Inland Church document of 28 January 1970 on Church-Mission Relationships to its missionary body and to its Councils and as a result now presents the following resolutions in the spirit of Christian love and brotherly fellowship for carrying on the work which God has given us to do.

The Africa Inland Mission accepts the position that the Africa Inland Church should govern itself and so be responsible for all of its activities. The Africa Inland Mission is prepared to take the position of a department of the Africa Inland Church in all Africa Inland Church-related matters with the following provisions:

1. To place all Africa Inland Mission Church-related departments under the Africa Inland Church (Ref. JSE Min. 1/1/70), details to be negotiated through the departments concerned.

2. To second missionaries, by their consent, to work in any Africa Inland Church department.

3. To give to the Africa Inland Church the responsibility of assigning missionaries in Church-related work according to their call and terms of service under which they have come to Kenya.

4. To turn over to the Africa Inland Church, under mutually agreed terms, all Church-related property--both moveable and immoveable--these to be done by transfer title by title, department by department, and by inventory lists to the Africa Inland Church Kenya Trustees Registered. Thus "Africa Inland Mission stations" will be turned over to the Church and called "Africa Inland Church stations."

5. To do all it can to help the Africa Inland Church establish new and adequate Central Offices in Nairobi.

6. Missionaries of the Africa Inland Mission, while serving in Kenya, will accept corporate membership in the Africa Inland Church.

7. In order to look after the support, housing and welfare of missionaries (see No. 8b of Africa Inland Church document 28/1/70), the Africa Inland Mission needs:

    a. to have a committee of missionaries with appropriate officers to represent the missionaries and the Home Councils,

    b. to hold township and other properties such as Rift Valley Academy, etc. which are not related to the Africa Inland Church (Ref. C.F.C.Min. 30/70).

8. In order to carry out the objectives and functions of the Africa Inland Mission, it needs:

    a. to be free to initiate in consultation with the Church, and carry on work which is not directly related to the Africa Inland Church and to sponsor or second missionaries for other works (Ref. C.F.C. Min. 24/70),

    b. to be responsible for Africa Inland Mission departments such as Rift Valley Academy, missionary children's hostel at Eldoret, Mission guest houses, Mission telecommunications, etc.

    c. to have its Government registration in Kenya for legal purposes.

9. The Africa Inland Mission declares its intention of putting the above actions into operation immediately after they are accepted by the Africa Inland Church and the Africa Inland Mission International Conference.

MISSIONS-CHURCH RELATIONSHIPS VIEWED FROM THE MISSION'S STANDPOINT

By William H. Taylor

I sincerely regret that I am unable to attend the meeting of the Executive Board planned for May 24-27. However, I trust that my thoughts on the topic assigned to me may contribute in some small way to the discussion that will be held around this general theme.

We who serve in the world of missions are constantly in contact with churches through their pastors, leaders and membership. It has been assumed that certain tensions exist between missions and churches and based on this assumption, we are asked to address ourselves to the subject and seek to find answers for the problems that exist.

Actually I am amazed that in my experience there is almost total absence of tensions. Perhaps they are there and I am not fully aware of them. I find that churches are generous with the Lord's money and show great confidence in missions. They count on mission organizations to carry out their end of the bargain by conducting their affairs in a businesslike way at home and through a proper supervision of activities on the field. They do not always know how well they are performing but they believe the best and hope for the best. To be truthful, I find that churches ask less of missions than missions ask of churches. It is this almost total reliance on our word that we are getting the job done that makes me believe we should take the initiative in approaching supporting churches and their pastors to find out what they are thinking, what questions do they have about the work and if they are really satisfied that missionaries accomplish in the world what they have been sent out to do or claim that they are doing.

One of the best ways to find out what is not known is by means of a survey. Of course the questions have to be properly asked and sent to the people who are in a position to speak for themselves and for the churches or organizations whom they represent. As far as I know, no survey in depth has been conducted that would bring to light what people really think about the subject of missions and missionaries. I fear that we are guessing too much and that we are taking certain things for granted. I am almost positive that the world of missions has changed so drastically in the last ten years that Christians in the pew do not know about it. This lack of information may be due to the fact that they are not reading mission publications or hearing mission leaders speak on these subjects from the pulpit. What may be even worse is that our publications and pulpit presentations are not touching on this vital subject.

Now I come to the main point which is nothing more or less than a suggested list of subjects that need to be explored as a partial solution toward bringing churches and missions closer together.

1. How are missions constituted and how do they operate? The average Christian understands very little about this. What avenues are open, if any, by which the people who are giving money could express themselves to the individuals who are charged with the responsibility of leading missionary organizations? How profitable an hour's discussion could be involving a mission leader and the official board of a church in openness concerning any facet of the

mission's work! Particularly would this be true if it had to do with the work of a missionary supported by that church.

2. How many churches make a yearly review of their missionary commitments? What could be done to determine whether certain projects or individuals enjoying a place on the budget might be found to be either unnecessary or undesirable? By the same token, what new increases in support might be considered proper due to the constantly rising cost of living, additions to the family or new work undertaken by a missionary?

3. What can be done that will bring the missionary on furlough closer in touch with the supporting church? I have heard of a few cases in which the missionary has been asked to help for a month or more in connection with visitation or other fixed responsibilities. Precious time and hard-earned money is sometimes wasted in idleness or meaningless activities on the part of furloughing missionaries. Missionaries need guidance and many of them might be indeed grateful if they had something more specific to do than "just visit around."

4. How can we get a better picture of the prospective missionary when he is making application to serve? As we in the CAM are now doing it, the pastor's referee form is identical to the one sent to any other person. Despite the fact that college and seminary days imply a separation from home and the church, I still believe that the man most qualified to judge as to the suitability of an applicant is the pastor himself. Would it be worth the time and money involved for the Candidate Secretary to interview the pastor, and even better yet, to interview the applicant himself rather than rely upon referee forms and other correspondence?

5. How can we improve the promotion of missions? This would touch on the area of literature, films or slides, displays, formal and informal presentations. With television bringing the best (and the worst) into almost every home, how do missions' presentations stack up by way of comparison? Has the time come for the production of films on missions that present on a broader scale what is being done and what needs to be done by the church in general rather than by a specific mission to feature its own work and having to bear the expense alone of a costly production.

6. With travel now so relatively inexpensive and with millions of tourists going to so many parts of the world with pleasure as the chief motivation, why cannot churches send their pastors on meaningful visits to see what God is doing in other parts of the world? A two-week exposure to the situation in a foreign country would be worth a year's reading on the subject.

7. How can we stop talking to ourselves and widen our circle of contact and friendship with those from whom we can learn so much that we do not now know? They in turn might get some answers to their questions through the information we could make available to them.

If I seem critical, it is because I am critical of myself. I see so much that is lacking and I see changes that should be brought about which we must initiate. If not, in all probability the changes will never come. Could I assume that other missions and their leaders are in the same boat? If this is true, then perhaps the answer is to work toward some kind of strategy which is so frightfully lacking. At the same time, admittedly there are almost insurmountable barriers to be overcome if anything substantial is to be done collectively in the world of missions. Doctrinal distinctives, organizational inclusions and exclusions, the availability or unavailability of money when the item of expense comes up - any one or all of these could discourage us from attempting to do anything. Whether we like it or not, the world moves on and I fear that the world of missions moves at a slower pace than the one at which the world moves.

In summary, yes, there are tensions, but I do not think the church creates the tensions. I think missions, missionaries and mission leaders are responsible and that we should take the initiative to streamline our own operations for the rest of the 70's and on into the future.

IFMA Official Board Retreat
May 24-27, 1971
Pearl River, New York

Part 2

advance study papers for delegates

GL'71
Mailing No.1
to delegates

INSTRUCTION SHEET #1

GL'71 is different
from other conferences you have attended.
It actually begins now...with you...
long before we convene at Green Lake.
The program is geared to delegate participation and interaction, rather than platform and positional presentation.
And the value of GL'71 will depend to a large degree on the preparation you make now!

ENCLOSED: Participants Study Paper #1
Feedback Questionnaire #1
An exclusive MULTIBOOK offer

UNDER SEPARATE COVER you will also receive in this first mailing two basic study books:*

The summer issue of EVANGELICAL MISSIONS QUARTERLY

The Third World and Mission by Dennis Clark

(*copies for overseas personnel will be sent to your North American headquarters or held for you at Green Lake.)

INSTRUCTIONS:

READ these study materials thoroughly

RESPOND 1. Fill in and return feedback questionnaire. Only those who do will receive Study Paper #2

2. Enclose your check and order for CROSSROADS IN MISSIONS. Only those who do will receive the MULTIBOOK study materials.

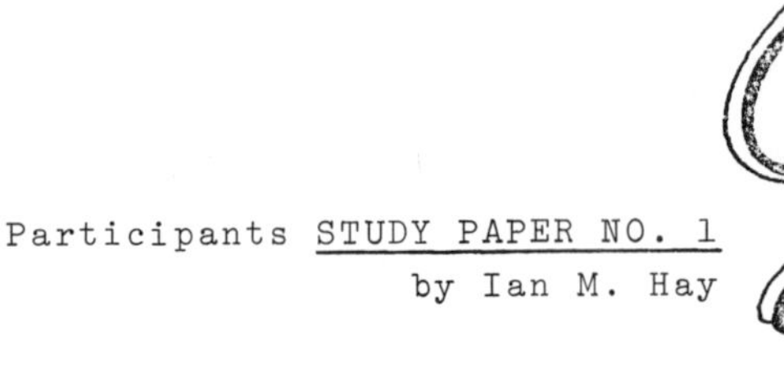

Participants STUDY PAPER NO. 1

by Ian M. Hay

Church/Missionary/Mission Relationships

AN OVERVIEW

MISSIONARIES, like Ulyses, find themselves charting a course through dangerous waters with a Scylla on one side and a Charybdis on the other. All too often, they cannot either identify the dangers or grasp the reason for their dilemma. Mission Boards are a composite of the missionaries. They face the same dilemma. The purpose of GL'71 is to try to identify these areas of tension, to bring together the thinking of our various missions in regard to the church to help each to relate to his own situation in a better way. In this preliminary paper I would like to give an overview. Nothing I say is really new but it may be helpful to look at the whole picture before we zero in on particular areas of tension.

GOD AND THE WORLD

Fig. 1

We must begin with God. The Bible does not argue His being, it simply states it. The whole thrust of the Bible message is God's concern and dealing with the World. His care and desire that the people who inhabit this globe might know Him; that they might be true men as they find their identity realized in a right relationship with Him. That is why we were made and, as Augustine said "our hearts are restless until they find their repose in Him."

So, the Bible declares God's purpose in all the ages. It shows us His heart of love, a love so great that He gave His Son:[1] The theme of the Bible is summed up in Paul's words "God was in Christ, reconciling the world to Himself."[2] Before the foundation of the world in the eternal councils of the trinity this reconciliation was planned. And in "the fullness of time God sent forth His Son, made of a woman, made under the law, to redeem them that were under the law, that we might receive the adoption of sons."[3]

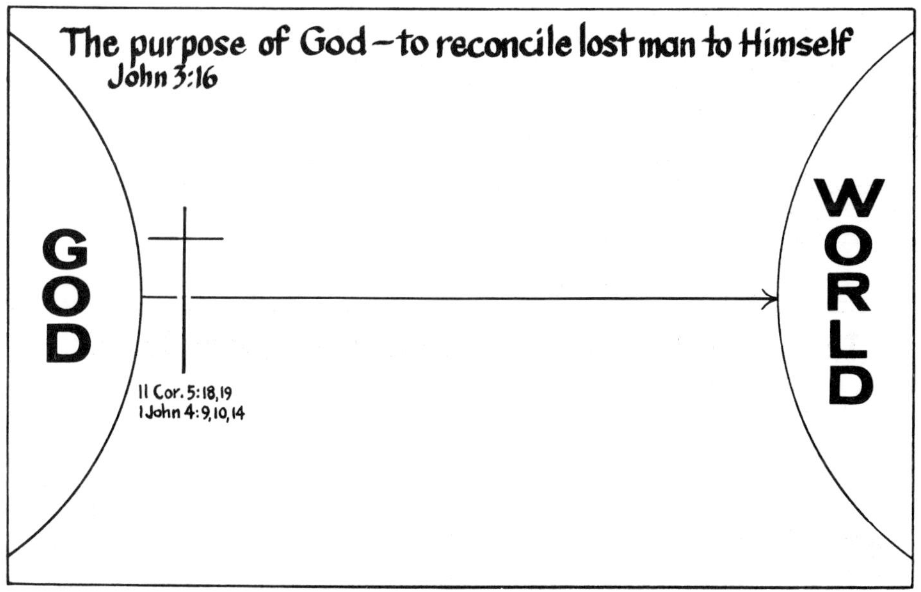

Fig. 2

The purpose of God for the world is centered in the person of His Son who was sent into the world. He came stripping Himself of His Godly prerogatives in order to become flesh and dwell amongst us.[4] Because of His pity for the world; because of His compassionate heart - God sent. Because of His obedience to the will of the Father, Jesus came.

"In this was manifested the love of God toward us, because that God sent His only begotten Son into the world, that we might live through Him. Herein is love, not that we loved God, but that He loved us, and sent His Son to be the propitiation for our sins. ...And we have seen and do testify that the Father sent the Son to be the Saviour of the World."[5]

THE PURPOSE OF GOD NOW

Jesus came. At the end of His time on earth He could say to His Father, "I have finished the work which thou gavest me to do."[6] In His death, burial, resurrection and ascension He completed the purpose of God in reconciling the world to Himself. That work was finished. He said so on the cross.

What then did Jesus mean when, in commissioning His disciples, He said, "As my Father hath sent me, EVEN SO send I you."?[7] There is the heart of the missionary enterprise. The purpose of God then is the purpose of God now, God is concerned with each generation. He loves NOW and the people alive NOW are to know of that love. We can never lose sight of the fact that the only way God could communicate with us was for the Eternal Word to become Flesh and dwell amongst us so that as John says we could perceive God -- we could feel, taste, touch, hear and know Him.[8] As Ken Strachan said, "The foreign word became indigenous flesh." That has to happen in the 1970's and God chooses to do this through His children. The Scriptures teach that each child of God is to go as Jesus came. Paul completes the thought -- "We stand in Christ's stead and beseech men to be reconciled to God."[9]

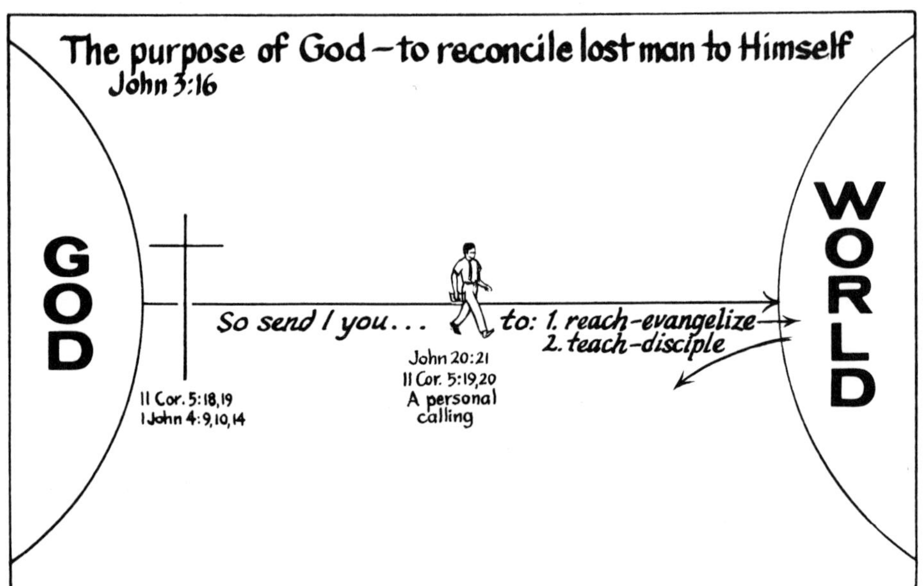

Fig. 3

Every believer is a witness. The normal result of the infilling of the Spirit of God is "Ye SHALL be witnesses unto me."[10] Does this mean then that every believer is a missionary? There have been some trite cliches thrown around in recent years which have tended to blur the distinctions between being a witness (which everybody should be) and being a missionary (which is a personal calling from God). R. Pierce Beaver in his book, "The Missionary Between the Times" makes a distinction between Evangelism (or local witness) and Sending (or Mission.) For our purposes we are talking about the foreign-ness which includes the crossing of cultural barriers to take the message of Jesus Christ into the world. The missionary is one who is overmastered by his knowledge of what Christ has done for him, he is one who also senses a personal directive and calling by the Holy Spirit to reach out into the world in a special way. He thus becomes a sent one -- sent by God for a specific purpose. This of course in no way denigrates the one who is not thus sent. Take Antioch as an example. The fact that Paul and Barnabas were to be foreign in their witness did not make them superior in any sense to Lucius, Simeon of Manaen who stayed at home.[11] It created no hierarchy. Their tasks were nevertheless different, for to be an apostle -- a sent one -- is a distinct calling demanding spiritual gifts separate from those of the pastor-teacher.

In the purpose of God then, chosen ones are Spirit Directed into different areas of the World. They are to fulfill, there, the commission which Christ gave. That commission is two-fold. We are to reach and teach; to preach (or evangelize) and to Disciple. The task then is more than just a proclamation of the Gospel.It must include the discipling of those who respond and therefore it must lead to the development of a church which itself becomes missionary in outreach. Douglas Webster said:

> "The surest sign that the gospel has taken root in a new culture is the throwing up of missionaries from that culture to reach out further still. The gospel is received in order to be retransmitted. Missions are integral to genuine Christianity, like all its other scandals."[12]

NO INDIVIDUALISM

I have emphasized the personal calling of the individual missionary. This emphasis has been quite strong in the past years. It is traditional. It is also Scriptural. God does deal with individuals in a special way. There is a personal intimate vertical relationship between the individual and His God in terms of Missionary service. This truth cannot be neglected. On the other hand it should not be emphasized to the neglect of other truths which are equally Scriptural.

Dr. Francis Schaeffer has emphasized this point in his new book,

> "We have looked carefully at the individual as he stands in relationship to God. The community stands in the same place. I think we have failed here. We have had a fixed, static concept of the church, that somehow or other the church is not a breathing reality. But even though Christianity is individual, it is not individualistic. (emphasis mine) he must come to God as an individual, but after we have come one at a time, God does not make us to be horizontally alone."[13]

Dr. George Peters has said the same thing,

"The church is in the line of apostolic succession, not office or officebearer. The office and officebearer receive their significance, authority and value from the church, not vice-versa. The church is God's authoritative, responsible and mediatorial agency and creation.

"I emphasize this for two reasons. First, to correct the sense of independence of some evangelists and evangelistic organizations. They must keep in mind that they are God's agencies only as part of the church of Jesus Christ, the body of Christ and the temple of God. The church never exists for the evangelist or the evangelistic organization. The reverse is always true. It is well to keep in mind that we as individuals are never the whole, nor can an organization claim primacy. Such prerogatives belong to the church of Jesus Christ under its Head, the Lord Himself."[14]

This points out the strong Scriptural emphasis that the church must labor with God in sending out missionaries. The individuals do have a very vital relationship to the local church which sends them out. The Biblical pattern for this is set for us.

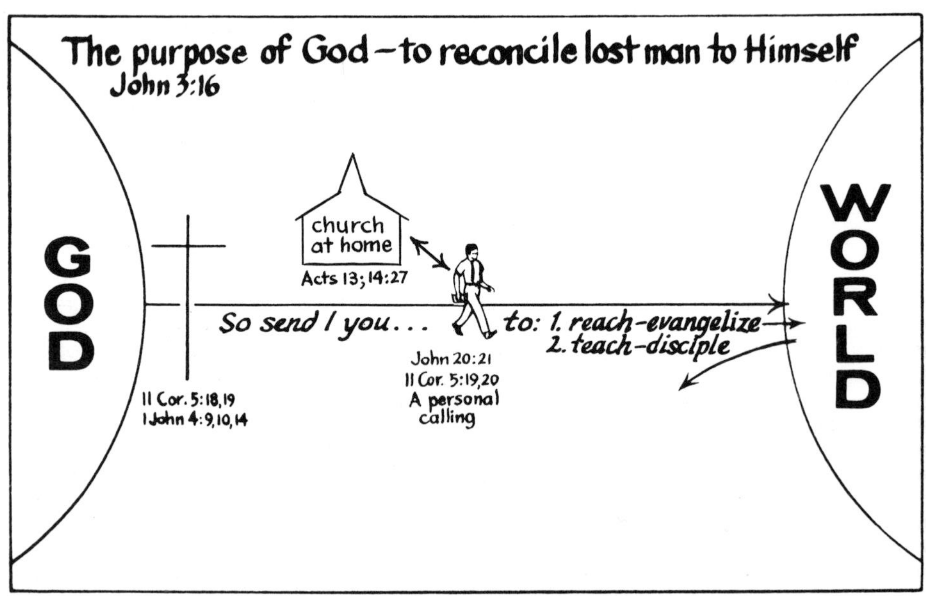

Fig. 4

"Now there were in the church that was at Antioch certain prophets and teachers; as Barnabas and Simeon that was called Niger, and Lucius of Cyrene, and Manaen, which had been brought up with Herod the tetrarch, and Saul. As they ministered to the Lord, and fasted, the Holy Ghost said, Separate me Barnabas and Saul for the work whereunto I have called them (there was a personal calling) And when they had fasted and prayed, and laid hands on them they sent them away."[15]

Paul and Barnabas, knowing themselves what God wanted to do found themselves chosen and released by the local church which was also sensitive to the Spirit's direction. The body of believers in Antioch participated in the recognition of their personal calling. This Biblical pattern ought to be true today as well. We even find these first century missionaries returning to their home church for a deputation ministry.

"And thence said to Antioch, from whence they had be recommended to the grace of God for the work which they fulfilled. And when they were come and had gathered the church together, they rehearsed all that God had done with them and how he had opened the door of faith unto the Gentiles."[16]

There is no reason to think that God has changed His basic plan for the church. It is still His agency in the world. It is still responsible for the evangelism of the lost and for the instruction of His children. Regardless of those changes in procedure and organization that the contemporary world has forced upon us, the local church remains as the sending authority for missions.

"This swings the spotlight back to the local church as source of missionary personnel. Hopefully, the church works closely with mission boards, seminaries, and Bible Colleges, but it should not rely on them to inspire its members to missionary service."[17]

THE PLACE OF THE MISSION SOCIETY

Where does the Mission Board fit into all of this. Try as I may I cannot find mission societies <u>per se</u> in the Bible. Of course there are many other things we do that aren't mentioned specifically in the Bible. The Bible gives us the principles and God guides us in each generation how best to apply them. It should be noted that the traces of a missionary agency can be found among the Apostles. Paul and Barnabas, Barnabas and Mark, Paul, Silas, Timothy and Luke are combinations which are at least similar to today's missionary agencies. Missionary work today is a far more complex thing than it was in the first century. Times are different and so are governments. We do not have a unit like the Roman Empire to work in today. In fact, the world is so complex that it would be a rare local church that could effectively work directly with missionaries, governments, travel agencies and so on. Here then is the place for the Mission Board. It answers the logistical problems and helps overcome the complications of the twentieth century. It does for the local church what it cannot do for itself.[18] It thus becomes the "thing", the "mechanics" to get the job done.

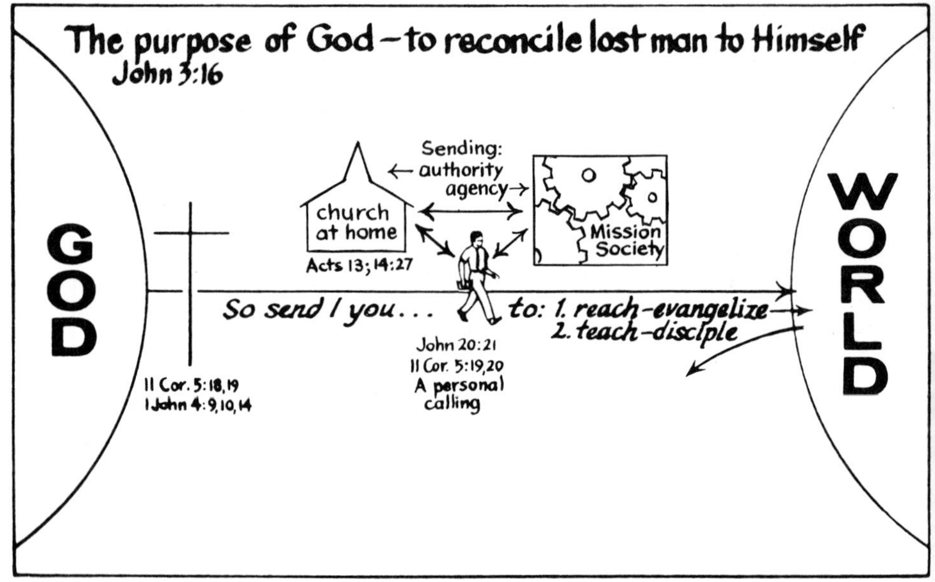

Fig. 5

The Mission Society, whether denominational or interdenominational really performs the same function. In each case the local church has delegated to the society the authority and the responsibility of the church to get the job done. The Mission therefore is the Agency through which the local church exercises its sending authority. In each case, however, there must be accountability on the part of the Mission to the local church. There must be openness of communication and understanding.

The Mission Society does have a valid raison d'etre. It is a channel outwards to help the local churches accomplish their responsibilities in foreign lands. It should also serve to stimulate the local church by providing creative tension between churches here and there. Dr. Peters raises this question: "What if the Church fails? What if the Church does not sense the urgency? What if the Church loses its divine message of evangelism?"[19] These are not hypothetical questions. It has happened. The reason Mission agencies may have usurped the place of the local church is by default. All too often the Church has not accepted its responsibility.

On the other hand, historically, the pattern has always been that the major thrust of evangelism and missions has come through para-ecclesiastical groups such as mission agencies. Charles Troutman of LAM, drawing from Latourette and Winters, has put this thought in perspective when he says,

> "From the fifth century the Christian Church has grown, not through its parish-diocesan structure, but through certain monastic orders, ready to dedicate themselves to their special tasks. This

was particularly true in Germany, Scandinavia and Russia until the time of the Reformation. It is interesting to note that when the monastic orders were destroyed in Protestant countries, for almost three centuries there was no missionary movement. This did not change until the time of Zinzendorf and William Carey. With the formation of special missionary boards, the era of modern expansion began, making it possible for Latourette to speak of missionary societies as Protestant monastic orders.

"These two movements - ecclesiastical and para-ecclesiastical - can be seen at the present time. Those denominations which concentrate on bringing their various agencies under central control and that have worked toward unification, have a dwindling interest in missions and evangelism. As their efforts and thoughts have concentrated on the 'theology of the Church', they have turned inward. It is from this group that we have heard so much of the 'end of missions'. On the other hand, those churches and denominations which have either encouraged their own missionary societies or permitted the support of interdenominational agencies have seen a remarkable growth and success in their outreach, seldom paralleled in church history.

Structurally only the Roman Catholic Church has maintained the double thrust of maintaining its basic structure and providing for extension. In the hierarchy of priests-bishops-pope, it provides for the spiritual life of its own members. By its encouragement of specialized orders it provides for its geographical expansion and religious growth. It appears that the normal processes of congregational life do not produce the Lord's full vision for His Body. In Protestantism, with its very different doctrine of the Church, a fragmentation and proliferation of societies has resulted. Outwardly, there appears no resemblance to the Roman Catholic structure, but, in actual practice, Protestantism has produced the same thing -- churchly and para-ecclesiastical bodies."[20]

THE CHURCH OVERSEAS

There is yet another area of relationship. This perhaps is the biggest question facing all of us in the 70's. The relationship between the mission/missionary and the local church in the receiving countries.

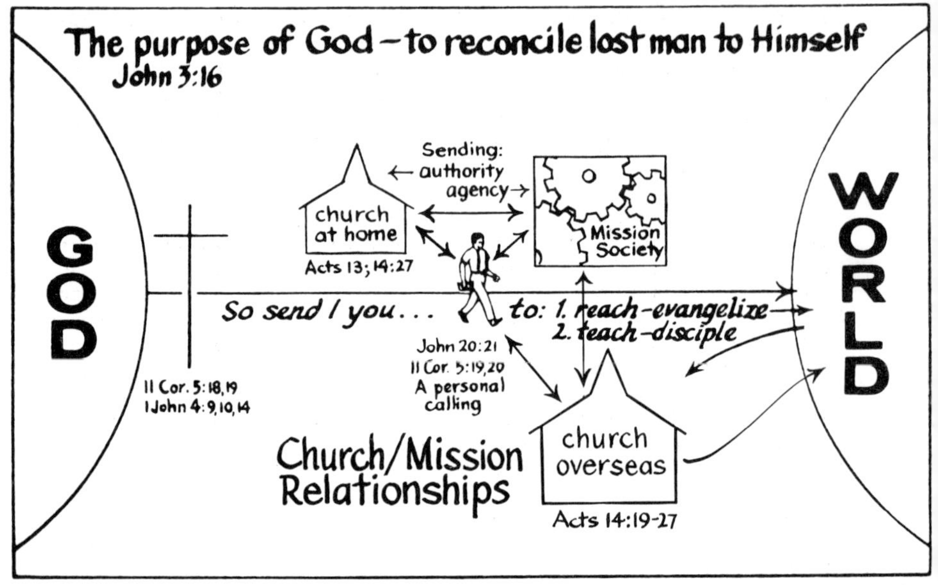

Fig. 6

Much of what has been said above applies to these relationships too. Careful and prayerful thought must be given to these relationships. What guidelines can we draw up that will help missions and individual missionaries to find the right solution in each situation? For certainly there will be no one answer -- no pat solution for every country.

If we mean what we say that we are there to see a church born and discipled, are we big enough to plan for changes in relationships and not look on them as defeat? The criticism which is so rampant of missions in the South Pacific (Hawaii in particular) should largely be criticism, not of the missionaries themselves (although there may be room for that too), but of their descendants. In other words, they didn't plan to leave. In our discussions of types of relationships let us not lose sight of the decided value of strategic withdrawal or altered relations. Do we not come to a place where as a church planting Mission, we say with Paul and Barnabas that we have completed the work to which we were appointed.[21] For those of us who think of ourselves in these terms, there should be a sense of timing so that we know when we have finished it. We should plan strategic withdrawal, leaving only a skeletal force, as needed, turning ourselves in that locality into a "service" mission.

TENSIONS

These, then, are the relationships which exist. There stands the missionary right in the middle, with relationships in all directions. These relationships create tensions. Let us strive to identify those tensions and make sure that they are creative. What problems are there that the missionary has because he must relate in three directions -- (1) to his home church, (2) his mission society, and (3) in the receiving countries? When the Mission has worked out its relationships properly in the receiving country, what tension does that create with its supporting constituency? How can these sending churches be educated to what is really happening in church/mission relationships overseas?

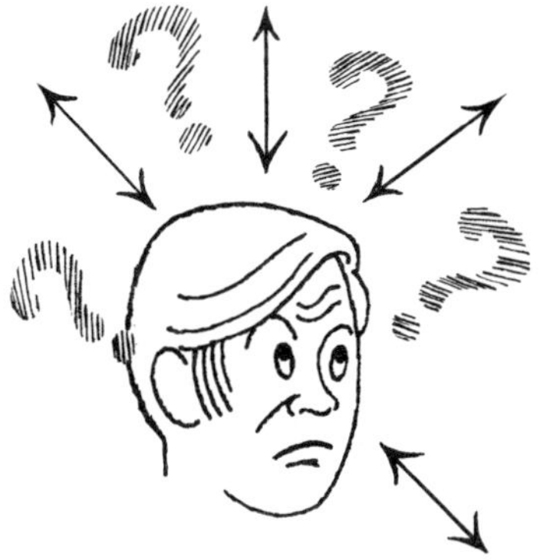

Fig. 7

CONCLUSION

We must never forget that in all of this we are talking about the Body of Christ -- The Church which He loved and for which He gave Himself.

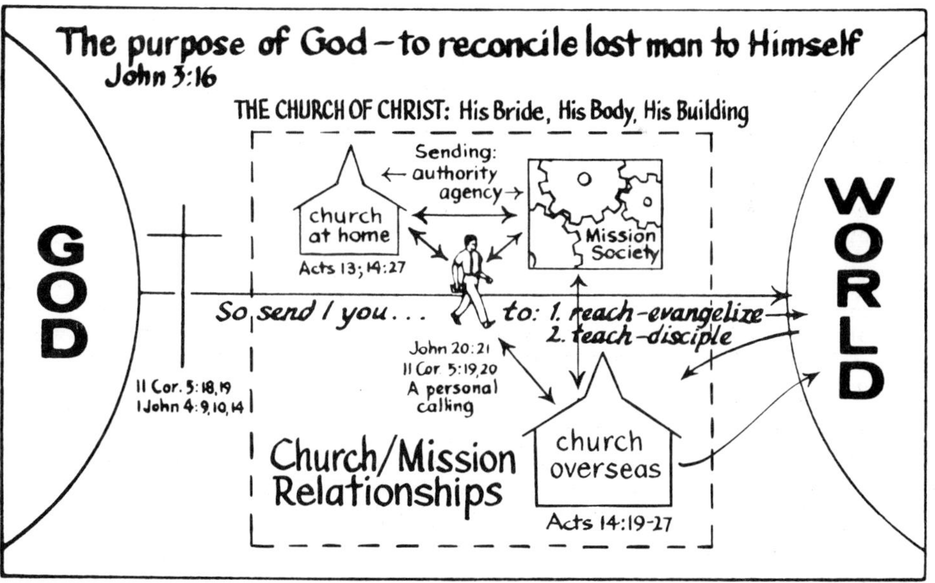

Fig. 8

When we differentiate within the Body for better understanding, we should not allow that differentiation to let us lose sight of the oneness that there is in His Body. At Urbana '70, one of the speakers said that when the church in the U.S. stubs its toe, the church in India should say "Ouch". For those who are within the Body of Christ, His Church, by faith in Jesus Christ and the resultant new birth, there is One Body and Jesus prayed:

> "That they all may be one as Thou Father art in me and I in Thee, that they also may be one in usñ that the world may believe that Thou hastsent me"[22]

And so God's Purpose is accomplished.

Ian M. Hay

FOOTNOTES

1 John 3:16
2 II Corinthians 5:18, 19
3 Galatians 4:4, 5
4 Philippians 2; John 1
5 I John 4:9, 10, 14
6 John 17:4
7 John 20:21
8 I John 1:1-3
9 II Corinthians 5:19, 20
10 Acts 1:8
11 Acts 13:1-3
12 Webster, Douglas, <u>What is a Missionary</u>? (London, Highway Press, 1958) P. 13
13 Schaeffer, Francis A., <u>The Church at the End of the 20th Century</u>, (Downers Grove, Ill., Inter Varsity Press, 1970) p. 54
14 Peters, George W., <u>Saturation Evangelism</u> (Grand Rapids, Zondervan, 1970) p. 22, 23
15 Acts 13:1-3
16 Acts 14:26, 27
17 Lovering, "Who Sends Him? the Church? or the Mission Board?", <u>Africa Now</u>, #53, November-December 1970
18 <u>Ibid</u>.
19 Peters, <u>Op</u>. <u>cit</u>.
20 Troutman, Charles, "Where is God Pushing Us?" From an unpublished study paper prepared for Latin America Mission, 1971.
21 Acts 14:26
22 John 17:21

This overview is a preliminary study paper in preparation for GL'71, a joint IFMA/EFMA conference on "Missions in Creative Tension" to be convened at Green Lake, Wisconsin, September 27 - October 1, 1971. The author is North American Director of the Sudan Interior Mission and president of the EMIS board of directors which is sponsoring the conference.

FEEDBACK QUESTIONNAIRE #1
for participants

Please read instructions carefully

1. Your answers are important to us and to you. In preparation for the sessions, they will be classified, tabulated and a summary of the results sent to discussion group leaders without identification of the source.

2. After you have read the study paper, answer questions on the basis of your first-hand knowledge and experience. If not applicable to your situation or if you do not feel qualified to comment, simply leave it blank.

3. Be sure to sign your name, address and organizational relationship. This is our identification for the next mailing.

4. Use typewriter if possible.

5. Participants Study Paper #2 will be sent to you upon receipt of this questionnaire.

QUESTIONNAIRE #1

. *List 4 major areas of tension which you sense between missions and their churches at home.*

. *What type of mission/church relationships are you acquainted with or does your mission have overseas? Fusion ____, Partnership ____, Service ____, Other (specify) ________________*

What specific problems do these relationships create?

continue on other side -------->>

3. *What guidelines would you suggest for missions in terms of positive, creative relationships with churches overseas and at home?*

4. *What should the missionary's relationship be to the mission, the home church and the church overseas?*

5. *What phase of church/mission relations do you want to discuss at GL'71? (Suggest 3 in order of importance to you.)*

Return to: **evangelical missions** INFORMATION SERVICE • BOX 794 • WHEATON, ILLINOIS 60187 •

Sent in by:

NAME ______________________________

ADDRESS ______________________________

______________________________ ZIP __________

ORGANIZATION to which you are related:

____

Date received:

for delegates to

To help you
in your preparation
for GL'71....

William Carey Library has arranged to make five important but out-of-print volumes on church/mission relations available to GL'71 delegates at a fraction of their original cost. For only $5.00 postpaid (a savings of almost 80%) you will receive:

TITLE	AUTHOR	PAGES	VALUE
The Missionary Between the Times	R. P. Beaver	210	$5.95
The Responsible Church and the Foreign Mission	P. Beyerhaus H. Lefever	199	2.95
On the Growing Edge of the Church	T. W. Street	144	3.95
The Missionary Nature of the Church	J. Blauw	182	3.95
Missionary, Go Home!	J. Scherer	192	4.95
Total		927	$21.75

A "must" in your study on the subject, all five books are being printed in a special, single MULTIBOOK edition under the title: CROSSROADS IN MISSIONS. The book has gone to press and will be ready for mailing by the end of July.

DON'T WAIT! Return this coupon with your check to EMIS now! (No order will be accepted unless accompanied by a check.)

Please rush my copy of CROSSROADS IN MISSIONS to:

NAME ________________________________

ADDRESS ________________________________

________________________ ZIP ____________

check for $5.00 must accompany order

evangelical missions INFORMATION SERVICE • BOX 794 • WHEATON, ILLINOIS • (312) 665-1200

GL'71
Mailing No. 2
to delegates

INSTRUCTION SHEET #2

Enclosed...

1. This Instruction Sheet #2
2. An orientation for delegates
3. Further information from the GL'71 registrar
4. Your second set of study materials which includes:
   (a) Participant's Study Paper #2 by J. Allen Thompson
   (b) Feedback Questionnaires #2 and #3
   (c) Glen Eyrie Conference Findings

For background reading and study...

Under separate cover you will receive your copy of the MULTIBOOK, "Crossroads in Missions", IF you sent in your order with the $5.00. (Overseas personnel will receive their copy at Green Lake if they put a foreign mailing address on their questionnaire form.)

Please note that...

QUESTIONNAIRE #1 (received in the first mailing) was SUBJECTIVE in nature, designed to get a free expression from you as to the tensions which you see in church/mission relations.

QUESTIONNAIRE #2 & #3 (encl) is OBJECTIVE in nature for the purpose of statistical analysis and classification of data.

We are pleased to have the expertise and assistance of MARC (Missions Advanced Research and Communication Center) in the preparation and analysis of this information.

PLEASE COMPLETE BOTH FORMS of Questionnaires AND RUSH THEM BACK TO US BY RETURN MAIL. Help us effectively prepare discussion group leaders, recorders and feedback personnel, and make meaningful group assignments of delegates where you can make the greatest contribution and receive the greatest benefit.

Papers enclosed are hole punched for your convenience and a hard-cover WORKBOOK will be provided at Green Lake to keep them all together.

INSTRUCTIONS FOR QUESTIONNAIRES #2 and #3

 primary purpose of GL '71 is to bring together people who have had, or are xperiencing, common church/mission tensions. In order to place you in the iscussion groups in which you can give and receive the most benefit, your ommittee needs some more details. We have attached two questionnaires. The irst (questionnaire #2) applies to tensions between home church and missions... he second (questionnaire #3) deals with tensions between missions and national hurches.

uestionnaire #2: Tensions in Home Church/Mission Relationships.
Numbers in parentheses refer to column numbers at the top of the questionnaire.)

1) Your name and organization is again needed and Primary Area of Interest.
2) The tension areas listed have been compiled from Question #1 of Questionnaire #1. Each one of these tension areas was mentioned in one way or another by several of you. Spaces have been provided at the bottom of page 2 for additional tension areas you may feel have been overlooked.
3) Please check with an X those tensions you or your organization have now, or sense exist and for which you are seeking solutions.
4) Please check with an X those tensions you or your organization have now, or sense exist and with which you are making progress toward solution.
5) Please check with an X those tensions you or your organization have had in the past with which you coped successfully.
6) Please place an X in the column which represents, in your opinion, the magnitude of the tension in the view of the home church. (1 is the greatest magnitude.)
7) Please place an X in the column which represents, in your opinion, the magnitude of the tension from the view of a missionary involved. (1 is the greatest)
8) Please place an X in the column which represents, in your opinion, the magnitude of the tension from the view of the mission.
9) After you have completed columns 1-8, & 10, please review your answers and for each of the tension areas which you noted were of first magnitude in columns 6, 7 or 8, place an X opposite those which you consider highest for your area of primary interest (home church, mission or missionary).
.0) Please place an X in the proper column for each tension as indicating, in your opinion, the one primary source of this tension.

uestionnaire #3: Tensions in Mission/National Church Relationships
Similar to Questionnaire #2 with exceptions noted below.)

2) The tension areas listed have been compiled largely from Questions #2 and #5 of Questionnaire #1. Again, each one of these tension areas was mentioned in one way or another by several of you. As before, add others you think have been missed.
6) Applies to magnitude of the tension in the view of mission.
8) Applies to magnitude of the tension in the view of the national church.
.0) The same tension may have quite different causes and solutions depending on the stage of development of the church in the country of concern. Please indicate with an X in the appropriate column the mission/church relationship that exists in the place where you are having this tension. If the same tension is occuring in more than one situation check each appropriate column.

Participants STUDY PAPER NO. 2
by J. Allen Thompson

Church-Mission Relationships: The Principal Missiological Issue of the 1970s.

AGENDA FOR GL'71

"Missionary organizations are always in peril," writes Arthur F. Glasser. "They begin as vital movements of God calling His people to goals of the highest order. Inevitably, however, they involve themselves ever increasingly in organizational life. With the passage of time they become complicated expressions of Parkinson's laws. They tend to lose initial vision and verve, and unconsciously transform themselves into mere human institutions that are capable of jogging along with little evidence of the dynamic of God in their life and service." *1*

This is particularly true of mission organizations that view their structures rigidly and refuse to respond to the opportunities of a new day and its accompanying pressures. One of the exciting features of the 70s is the wholesome attitude that mission and church leaders are taking toward their organizational relationships. There is increasing evidence of a willingness to accept God's "painful, costly, gifts of openness, flexibility and mobility." New structures are being established in creative response to the present problems and opportunities.

Working relationships sometimes grow out of an intense drive to innovate, more often they represent a desperate response to deteriorating inter-organizational relationships. Seldom do they arise from a deliberate attempt by leaders to analyze goals and restructure a relationship that is Biblically defensible and evangelistically dynamic. Today the latter approach must be taken to excite a great surge in evangelism and church growth.

In anticipation of the Green Lake '71 conference on church-mission relationships, I have written my own agenda. I don't expect all my questions to be answered, but underscore the following as basic. What are the presuppositions in Scripture that relate to church-mission structures? Are they clearly delineated, and understood and applied? What structures or combinations of structures are currently in use? Can a formula be devised to assist mission and church leaders in setting a practical course toward solutions?

What follows is an attempt to "flesh out" these questions. Basically approach the problems of structures from the premise that they are flexible many types, forms and varieties) but not neutral. They must in every instance eflect the nature, purpose, and will of God. Otherwise they are invalid. No ingle form of church-mission relationship is absolute or binding. A variety f structures may be necessary to accomplish the will of God at a particular ime in the life of the mission and the church. Each form should be examined s to its legitimacy in fulfilling God's purpose. In the absence of theologi-al imperatives practical considerations may guide in the choice of alterna-ives.

UNDERLYING BIBLICAL PRESUPPOSITIONS

Meaningful structures flow out of sound presuppositions. When the elegates of the Wheaton Congress on the Church's Worldwide Mission (April, 966) drew up their recommendations on church-mission relationships they did o on the assumption that church and mission were equally valid entities. The mission society exists to evangelize, to multiply churches, and to trengthen the existing churches," they wrote. "Therefore, we recognize a ontinuing distinction between the church established on the field and the ission organization."[2] Today some missiologists would take issue. They ould claim that it is impossible to make a New Testament case for the con-inued existence of the missionary society, especially as a massive parallel tructure distinct from the church.

Little wonder that church-mission tension is today's great tension. bviously clarification of Biblical principles and their implications for the ormation of right relationships is urgent.

Those of us who serve under interdenominational boards feel the rgency of isolating Biblical principles that affect ecclesiology. We eel this perhaps more than denominational missionaries because we sense our istance from the sending churches. Also, not always pressed upon to follow uniform church polity, we quickly discover our theological illiteracy.

This creative tension among us is not new. J. Hudson Taylor, founder f the China Inland Mission, after serious soul searching regarding his organ-zation observed, "I look on the foreign mission as a scaffolding round a ising building; the sooner it can be dispensed with the better - or, the sooner, ather, that it can be transferred to serve the same temporary purpose else-here."

More recently the China Inland Mission pounded out a series of prin-iples to validate its continued existence as the *OVERSEAS MISSIONARY FELLOW-HIP* and provide a solution to the tangle of church versus mission relation-hips. These presuppositions merit in-depth study.

1) The Missionary

The validity of the role of the missionary arises from the continuing function of the New Testament apostle. He proclaims the Gospel to the unbelieving world (Romans 1:5; Galatians 2:7-9) and organizes converts into local congregations (Acts 14:21-23; Titus 1:5). This role is distinct from the prophetic and pastor-teacher roles (Ephesians 4:11). Furthermore, the missionary is as permanent an expression of the life and witness of the Church as the pastor-teacher. From this we conclude that missionaries are to be part of God's work until Christ returns. This fact demands that we give highest priority to discovering how this role is to be performed in the present context of the emerging Church in East Asia.

2) The Mission

The New Testament distinguishes between structured local congregations (churches) and the structured apostolic band called by God to evangelize the heathen and plant new churches. Whereas the apostles were of the Church, their corporate ministry of missionary outreach necessitated among themselves patterns of leadership and organization, recruitment and finance, training and discipline, distinct from comparable patterns within local congregations. This significant distinction gives Biblical sanction to today's structured missionary fellowship. Since we accept the thesis that missionaries have a continuing role in East Asia, we also conclude that missionary fellowships somehow also have their place in God's purpose in East Asia in the days ahead.

3) Church and Mission

Because of the absence of Biblical precedent, it seems questionable for any missionary society to allow itself to become fully assimilated into any local ecclesiastical structure. Its functions cannot be successfully duplicated by any one congregation, or by several congregations working together. If attempted, this eventually reduces the missionary task of God's people to mere Church-to-Church interchange, something that would soon eventuate in no one 'coveting earnestly' the apostolic gift (I Cor. 12:28-31). Hence, if God intends both Church and Mission to retain their separateness there must be some solution to the tension that currently exists between national Church and Western Mission throughout East Asia.

4) Cooperation in Mission

The Apostle Paul in his missionary activity never sought to commence a new work in any locale without first seeking to relate himself to that which God had begun in the area prior to his arriving on the scene (Acts 19:1-7; Romans 15:23,24). A parochial outlook was foreign to his spirit and practice. Today's missionary must likewise be concerned to strengthen the life and witness of each congregation he touches, while not losing his sense of priority for 'the regions beyond.'

5) Flexibility in Mission

Missionaries are not to regard themselves individually or corporately as either central or enduring, when compared with the local Christians and churches that have resulted from their ministry. In the final analysis, national Christians and local congregations, by their permanence of existence and possibilities for continuous outreach, are God's tools for preaching the Gospel to every creature (Acts 19:10). On the other hand the permanence of the apostolic calling implies the inevitability of its constant change and adaptation. We in the OMF are deeply persuaded that God will continue to deal with our Fellowship, so that it might creatively accomplish its unique task, in each successive generation, until the Church Age is consummated. [3]

In the West Indies Mission I have witnessed a renewed interest in Biblical theology as a basis for decision making and strategy planning. Two years ago, after reviewing thoroughly the doctrine of the church, the leaders of the Mission established guidelines to assist in establishing church-mission relationships.

1) God has ordained that world evangelism should be the responsibility of His church. Churches are therefore responsible and accountable to God to carry out His missionary purpose.

2) Historically, God has raised up organizations to assist and serve the church in fulfilling God's missionary purpose.

3) While retaining its identity the Mission should increasingly surrender its functions as the church is able to assume them. The church may mature to such a stage that the presence of the Mission will no longer be needed. In such a case the Mission will consider its objectives completed and shall be free to rechannel its resources to other fields.

4) Missionaries should identify with the church on their field, worship and serve through it, and shall be under its authority in this relationship.[4]

I hope that GL'71 will not let us down on a fresh view of Biblical theology that relates directly to church-mission tensions.

KINDS OF MISSION STRUCTURES

Armed with his set of Biblical directives, the mission-church leader now approaches the step of structural analysis. Most of us seldom explore the informal ties between missions and churches overseas. Much less do we analyze who the decision makers are, or where the spheres of influence lie. Consequently it is most difficult to evaluate relationships and correct those that are deteriorating or moving toward ineffective goals.

Ralph D. Winter, writing from an engineer's viewpoint, has classified Christian organizations as vertical and horizontal. For this definition he is not as interested in theological distinctions between "churchly" and "non-churchly" structures as he is in a descriptive definition that helps untangle the vast array of organizations involved in overseas ministries. His two terms, borrowed from the labor movement, make helpful distinctions. The horizontal are the interdenominational mission agencies that run horizontally across the whole country, and to other countries, expressing the concerns of a mission-minded minority within many different Christian denominations and independent churches. The vertical are the agencies that express the mission interest of whole denominations.[5]

Interdenominational missions are therefore horizontal in their home support structure since they reach across to a number of denominations for financial support and personnel. When overseas, however, they assume various patterns--vertical-horizontal (church planting primarily and some service ministries), horizontal-vertical (primarily service ministries and occasional church planting), or horizontal (service ministries). Few, if any, actually become purely vertical (solely church planting).[6]

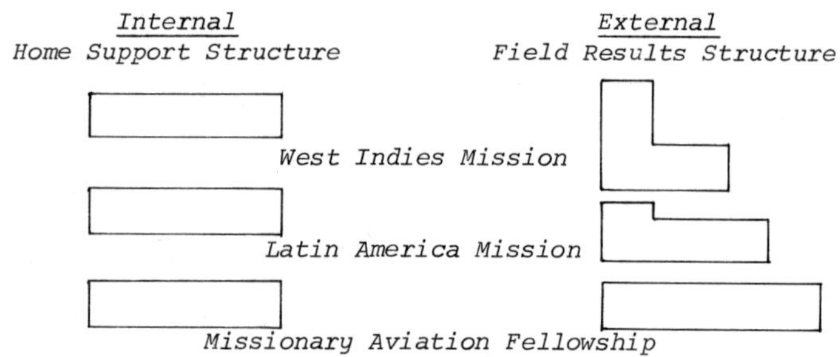

Though this description generally fits most interdenominational issions, each individual mission has variable structures from field to ield. The West Indies Mission, for example, actually has three differing tructures within a narrow geographical area.

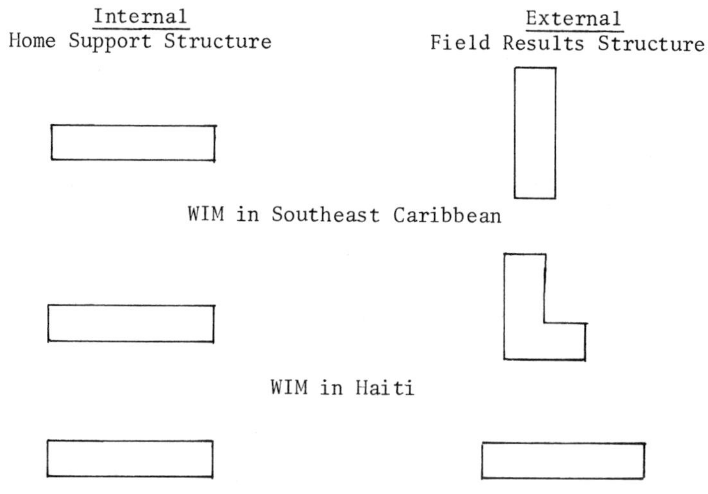

To make matters even more complex the exact nature of the verti- l or horizontal ministries of interdenominational missions overseas differs eatly. Vertical structures may embrace independent local congregations, a mily or association of inter-congregations, and/or fellowships of churches. me interdenominational missions have espoused all three types.

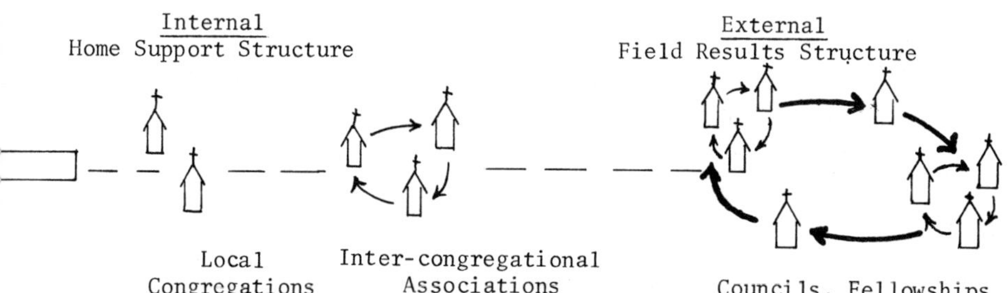

Horizontal ministries (including institutions, schools, hanages, hospitals) and functional ministries (communications, trans- tation, linguistics, and research), some directly related to churches church planting, others not.

Horizontal Structures Overseas

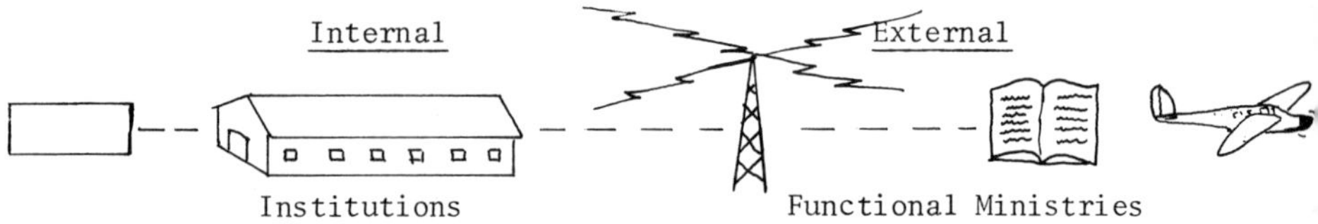

Without question the overseas character of a Mission and its doctrine of the church are the major factors in determining the approach to mission-church relationships. If the Mission espouses an independent local congregational system in its view of the "church," then obviously, a very limited relationship is possible. On the other hand, if the main objective of the mission is service ministries and church planting one of its many interests, then a totally different structure must be defined.

This great divergence in the nature of interdenominational missions abroad requires a flexible approach. New patterns for mission-church relationships will need to be designed. Those missions engaged in church planting (vertical structures) will move from spontaneous relationships to more formalized structures as churches mature. These structures may include amalgamation, amalgamated autonomy, and mutual autonomy, depending on the stage of church growth and the particular needs of the church. [7]

Those missions engaged in service ministries (i.e., Missionary Aviation Fellowship, Latin America Mission) may find it necessary to establish national autonomous organizations, with flexible relationships to the international body to be a dynamic force in evangelism as they serve the national churches. Current studies by Latin America Mission establishing autonomy-partnership-in-community entities is a step in this direction.

"COPING" STRATEGIES

Careful exploration of structures will assist missions in discovering their identity. As this is done and priorities are realigned some tensions will be eased, others heightened. Internal pressures to force a decision in favor of service ministries or church planting will emerge. The implementation of new structures to separate the vertical ministries from the horizontal will test the unity of organizations. Some missions will discover that they need two kinds of structures overseas, one to define the mission (church planting)--church relationships; the other to clarify mission (service ministries)--interdenominational relationships. The same missions will find that no two fields can be approached identically.

Is it too much to expect strategies out of GL'71 that will help us cope with these tensions and other problems? I hope not.

Creative approaches are needed to establish correct attitudes, formulas and models. A positive outlook toward church-mission relationships is basic. Defensiveness or fear will prove disastrous. A strong drive to establish formal structures too early may prove futile, since the functional interaction of mission and church is paramount. An attitude of identification, oneness, confidence, openness must be demonstrated before any defined structure will prove beneficial. This attitude is tested by our willingness to discuss and change lines of authority in finances, deployment and supervision of personnel and decision making. It is honored by a demonstration of confidence in the work of God, through weak and erring vessels, whether these instruments be expatriate missionaries or national leaders.

Formulas to help us identify critical areas are needed. Let me venture a possible equation.

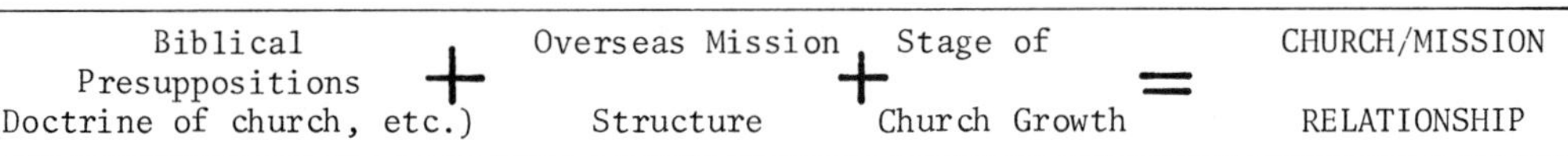

Apply this to the case of the West Indies Mission in the Southeast Caribbean and the following pattern emerges:

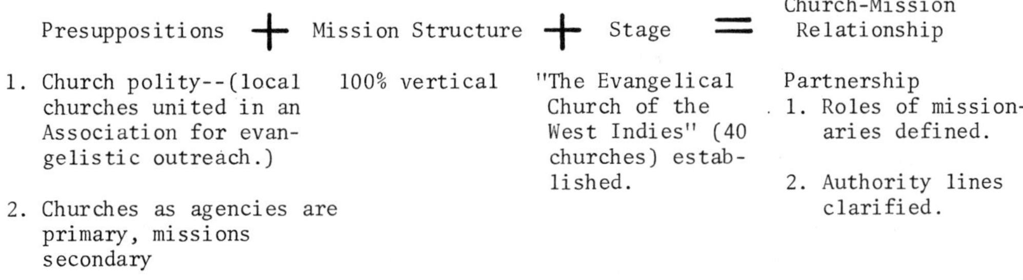

Presuppositions +	Mission Structure +	Stage =	Church-Mission Relationship
1. Church polity--(local churches united in an Association for evangelistic outreach.)	100% vertical	"The Evangelical Church of the West Indies" (40 churches) established.	Partnership 1. Roles of missionaries defined. 2. Authority lines clarified.
2. Churches as agencies are primary, missions secondary			

Of course a much more difficult example could have been chosen, but the point is made. We need pegs on which to hang our thoughts to wrestle meaningfully with solutions in a given country.

Then, finally, I would hope that some ingenious person would produce a series of <u>models</u> for different kinds of church-mission relationships. I have heard and used terms like partnership, fusion, amalgamated autonomy, autonomy-partnership-in-community. What do these tags mean? How are they similar and in what aspects do they differ? A clarification of vocabulary listing the variables and fixed elements would be most helpful. Models of structures to fit service missions, church planting missions and church planting-service missions would be useful.

GL'71 will come and go. Its role in clarifying terminology, encouraging interaction, and sharing of insights will be helpful. But only as we become theological activists will enduring changes occur. It is not enough to produce papers defining the problems and giving theoretical answers, though this is helpful. We need theological activists who not only conclude that the "river is polluted," but get in to "clean it up." We need leaders, missionaries and nationals, who are Biblically literate and willing to grapple with issues at the scene of activity with the church.

J. Allen Thompson

FOOTNOTES

1 Arthur F. Glasser, "The 'New" Overseas Missionary Fellowship," study paper prepared for the OMF, mimeographed, 1965, p. 1.

2 Harold Lindsell, ed., *The Church's Worldwide Mission,* (Waco, Texas: Word Books, 1966) p. 230.

3 *Op. Cit.,* pp. 1-2.

4 Minutes of The West Indies Mission Executive Board, May 1969, p. 86.

5 Ralph D. Winter, "The Anatomy of the Christian Mission," *Evangelical Missions Quarterly,* Winter 1969, pp. 74-89.

6 Fred Edwards, *The Role of the Faith Mission, A Brazilian Case Study,* (William Carey Library, 1971); Mr. Edwards presents a helpful analysis of interdenominational missions in Brazil, classifying them as horizontal or vertical.

7 Harmon A. Johnson, "Research is the Key to Church Development," *Evangelical Missions Quarterly,* Winter 1968, pp. 75-88.

This "agenda" is the second of the preliminary study papers being sent to delegates in preparation for their participation at GL'71, a joint IFMA/EFMA conference on "Missions in Creative Tension" to be convened at Green Lake, Wisconsin, September 27-October 1, 1971. The author is General Director of the West Indies Mission and serves as Discussion Group Coordinator for the conference.

evangelical missions INFORMATION SERVICE • BOX 794 • WHEATON, ILLINOIS 60187

(1)			(2)	(3)	(4)	(5)	(6)			(7)			(8)			(9)	(10)			
	(NAME)	(ORGANIZATION) Primary area of interest: ☐ Home Church ☐ Mission ☐ Missionary ☐ National Church	QUESTIONNAIRE #2 HOME CHURCH/MISSION RELATIONSHIPS DESCRIPTION OF TENSION AREAS	HAVE OR SENSE NOW (SEEKING SOLUTION)	HAVE OR SENSE NOW (MAKING PROGRESS)	HAD IN THE PAST (COPED WITH IT)	MAGNITUDE OF TENSION IN VIEW OF HOME CHURCH (check one)			MAGNITUDE OF TENSION IN VIEW OF MISSIONARY (check one)			MAGNITUDE OF TENSION IN VIEW OF MISSION (check one)			RANK ORDER OF FIRST MAGNITUDE TENSIONS YOU HAVE OR SENSE NOW	PRIMARY SOURCE OF TENSIONS (check one)			
							1	2	3	1	2	3	1	2	3		HOME CHURCH	MISSION ORGAN.	MISSIONAIRES	NATIONAL CHURCHES
1	Discrepancy between living standard of missionaries and national workers.																			
2	"Designated, personal gifts" versus "pooling" systems of fund handling.																			
3	Pressures for overseas funds at the expense of home projects.																			
4	Competition for financial resources among missions.																			
5	Personal fund raising increasingly objectionable to missionaries.																			
6	Home churches increasingly reluctant to fill missionary meeting requests.																			
7	Short-term commitments preferred to long-term ones.																			
8	Tendency of mission to "run its own show".																			
9	Disillusionment of laymen who have visited missionaries on the field.																			
10	Perception of missionary's loyalty to mission or to home church.																			
11	Trend favoring small cell mission-sending groups vs usual mission.																			
12	Continual struggle for personal involvement with missionaries.																			
13	Shift of emphasis from missionary leadership to national leadership.																			
14	Ambivalence as to home church or mission being final authority for missionary.																			
15	Detrimental separatist views held.																			
16	Increasing scrutiny of mission doctrine and practice.																			
17	Lack of emphasis on sound theology in missions.																			
18	Unrealistic attitudes toward the missionary and his tasks.																			
19	Difference of opinion regarding indigenous church principles.																			
20	Lack of participation in decision making of mission plans and policies.																			

(1)		(2)	(3)	(4)	(5)	(6)			(7)			(8)			(9)	(10)			
(NAME) (ORGANIZATION) Primary area of interest: ☐ Home Church ☐ Mission ☐ Missionary ☐ National Church		QUESTIONNAIRE #2 HOME CHURCH/MISSION RELATIONSHIPS DESCRIPTION OF TENSION AREAS	HAVE OR SENSE NOW (SEEKING SOLUTION)	HAVE OR SENSE NOW (MAKING PROGRESS)	HAD IN THE PAST (COPED WITH IT)	MAGNITUDE OF TENSION IN VIEW OF HOME CHURCH (check one)			MAGNITUDE OF TENSION IN VIEW OF MISSIONARY (check one)			MAGNITUDE OF TENSION IN VIEW OF MISSION (check one)			RANK ORDER OF FIRST MAGNITUDE TENSIONS YOU HAVE OR SENSE NOW	PRIMARY SOURCE OF TENSIONS (check one)			
						1	2	3	1	2	3	1	2	3		HOME CHURCH	MISSION ORGAN.	MISSIONAIRES	NATIONAL CHURCHES
21	Doctrinal differences between home church and national church.																		
22	Shorter furloughs reducing personal contact with home churches.																		
23	Reluctance to donate money to missions for distribution by national leaders.																		
24	Growing resentment of mission cost with shift to national leadership.																		
25	Tendency to report trivia rather than hard news on status of evangelism.																		
26	Inadequate representation of home churches on mission boards.																		
27	Polarization in real perspective - Ghetto (my country) vs Global.																		
28	Competition for personnel by home churches and missions.																		
29	Lack of involvement and commitment of church members.																		
30	Apathy and indifference toward mission.																		
31	Failure of home church to take responsibility for recruiting.																		
32	Churches feel useless to relate to missionary because of mission control.																		
33	Pressures of ecumenicity, modernism and social action.																		
34	Meagre understanding of cultural differences between home and field.																		
35	Failure to provide information essential to parties concerned.																		
36	Failure to adequately educate about new trends and movements in evangelism.																		
37																			
38																			
39																			
40																			

(1)			(2)	(3)	(4)	(5)	(6)			(7)			(8)			(9)	(10)			
	(NAME)	(ORGANIZATION) Primary area of interest: ☐ Home Church ☐ Mission ☐ Missionary ☐ National Church	QUESTIONNAIRE #3 MISSION/NATIONAL CHURCH RELATIONSHIPS DESCRIPTION OF TENSION AREAS	HAVE OR SENSE NOW (SEEKING SOLUTION)	HAVE OR SENSE NOW (MAKING PROGRESS)	HAD IN THE PAST (COPED WITH IT)	MAGNITUDE OF TENSION IN VIEW OF MISSION (check one)			MAGNITUDE OF TENSION IN VIEW OF MISSIONARY (check one)			MAGNITUDE OF TENSION IN VIEW OF NATIONAL CHURCH (check one)			RANK ORDER OF FIRST MAGNITUDE TENSIONS YOU HAVE OR SENSE NOW	STAGE OF MISSION/ CHURCH DEVELOPMENT FOR FIRST MAGNITUDE AREAS OF TENSION			
							1	2	3	1	2	3	1	2	3		PIONEER	MISSION DOMINANT	TRANSITION	CHURCH DOMINANT
1	Feelings of superiority on the part of missionaries.																			
2	Unwillingness of leadership to relinquish control and position.																			
3	Lack of trust toward nationals in distribution of finances.																			
4	Difficulties involved with difference in cultural background, thought patterns.																			
5	Missionary withdrawal from spiritual fellowship by new responsibilities.																			
6	Tensions in partnership when one or other not fully committed.																			
7	Problems of shifting from subsidy to indigenous responsibility.																			
8	Differences in financial emphasis on workers vs institutions.																			
9	Degree of trust in assignments by board predominantly national.																			
10	Mission as foreign agency in position of authority overseas.																			
11	Definition of missionary's role under authority of national church.																			
12	Insensitivity to new missionary's need for pastoral care.																			
13	Political maneuvering from attempts to fuse national churches.																			
14	Tendency of missionaries to act independently of mission home office.																			
15	Inadequate understanding of program and direction of the national church.																			
16	Differences in educational levels of missionaries and nationals.																			
17	Tendency to impose points of view and authority upon others.																			
18	Status of missionary as foreigner, elite representative of rich church.																			
19	Imposing of principles which go against the social/ethnic structures.																			
20	Lack of adequate attainment in language skills.																			

(1)

(NAME)

(ORGANIZATION)

Primary area of interest:

☐ Home Church ☐ Mission

☐ Missionary ☐ National Church

(2)

QUESTIONNAIRE #3

MISSION/NATIONAL CHURCH RELATIONSHIPS

DESCRIPTION OF TENSION AREAS

	DESCRIPTION OF TENSION AREAS	(3) HAVE OR SENSE NOW (SEEKING SOLUTION)	(4) HAVE OR SENSE NOW (MAKING PROGRESS)	(5) HAD IN THE PAST (COPED WITH IT)	(6) MAGNITUDE OF TENSION IN VIEW OF MISSION (check one)			(7) MAGNITUDE OF TENSION IN VIEW OF MISSIONARY (check one)			(8) MAGNITUDE OF TENSION IN VIEW OF NATIONAL CHURCH (check one)			(9) RANK ORDER OF FIRST MAGNITUDE TENSIONS YOU HAVE OR SENSE NOW	(10) STAGE OF MISSION/CHURCH DEVELOPMENT FOR FIRST MAGNITUDE AREAS OF TENSION			
					1	2	3	1	2	3	1	2	3		PIONEER	MISSION DOMINANT	TRANSITION	CHURCH DOMINANT
21	Disparity between the self-images and expectations.																	
22	Unbending, "dictatorial" attitudes vs "too humble," wishy-washy.																	
23	Theological positions which nullify search for middle ground.																	
24	Unbalanced emphasis leading to legalism.																	
25	Lack of appreciation of central emphasis in the New Testament.																	
26	Degree of emphasis on long-range plans for evangelism.																	
27	Negative attitudes acquired by experience.																	
28	Transition to partners and fellow servants of Christ.																	
29	Shifting emphasis from institutions to evangelism and training programs.																	
30	Relinquishing initiative to national church and assuming supporting role.																	
31	Paternalistic oversight of national church affecting partnership.																	
32	Tendency for mission services and institutions to "outrank" national ch.																	
33	Relations between mission national workers and pastors.																	
34	Degree of orientation training of missionaries for current problems.																	
35	Factor of vested interests, personal pride in withdrawal of mission.																	
36	Mutual lack of confidence.																	
37																		
38																		
39																		
40																		

ORIENTATION for GL'71 delegates

GL'71 is *different* from other conferences you have attended.

1 in PURPOSE

- we do not expect to find final solutions to the problems of church/mission tensions.
- we do not expect to find uniformity among ourselves in dealing with these problems.
- we do not expect any "pronouncement" or "declaration" to come out of GL'71.
- we do not expect to speak either to or for national churches and leaders overseas.

What we do hope to do is

a) Identify the points of tension which exist today between mission and church.

b) Share experience input and cross-fertilization of ideas that will help each of us to constructively cope with these tensions and to chart his own course of action in terms of changes which must take place.

c) Come up with a study guide similar to that which came out of the Glen Eyrie Conference a few years ago.

in PARTICIPATION

GL'71 is PARTICIPANT-oriented. To accomplish our objectives the conference actually begins with you....long before we convene at Green Lake September 27th.

GL'71 is a WORK conference. Already 70-some delegates have accepted responsibilities of one kind or another. Although paper writers and their consultants have put scores of hours into their preparations and presentations, the real work will be done by the delegates before and at the conference. Your thorough reading on the subject before the conference, your prompt response to the feedback questionnaires now, and your creative input to discussions at the conference are the active ingredients which will enable us to accomplish our goals.

Feedback from the questionnaires will help us not only to determine needs, but also where you as a delegate can make your greatest contribution and at the same time receive the greatest benefit.

Although EFMA/IFMA sponsored,limited invitations have been extended to include mission leaders and representatives from other evangelical societies and agencies, mission professors and missionary-oriented students from Christian

evangelical missions INFORMATION SERVICE • BOX 794 • WHEATON, ILLINOIS 60187 • (312) 665-1200

over

schools, missions-related pastors and a select group of overseas national leaders (as resource consultants). We are especially grateful to God for the top-notch national church leaders who will be there to help us evaluate objectively the tensions which exist.

in PROGRAM

Unlike most conferences the number of speakers and papers at GL'71 will be few. The program is geared to delegate participation rather than platform and positional presentations.

One single subject will occupy our attention: CHURCH/MISSION RELATIONS under the theme "Missions in Creative Tension".

The growth and success of churches overseas now firmly rooted in national soil in every part of the world have also created new relationships and new problems. Missions and missionaries, instrumental in part at least in bringing about this phenomenon of the '70s, now find themselves in the midst of positive tensions between North American churches and their overseas counterparts.

The subject of CHURCH/MISSION RELATIONS will be treated under two headings: a) At home and b) Overseas.

The conference program will begin on Monday night (Sept. 27th) with a paper by Rev. Jack Shepherd on the first phase of the subject: "Church/Mission Relations at Home." This in turn will provide the basis for discussion on the following day. On Tuesday and Wednesday nights Dr. Louis King and Dr. George Peters will both introduce the second phase of the subject, the first night dealing with principles and the second with practice on the field. These will then be discussed respectively on the following days.

Dr. Edmund Clowney will lay the Biblical/theological foundations each morning, Tuesday through Friday.

On Tuesday and Wednesday afternoons from 1:30 to 3:15 p.m. IFMA and EFMA will conduct their business sessions.

4 in PROCEDURE

ince GL'71 will be a work conference and participant-centered rather than plat-orm-oriented, the following procedure has been set up for the conference itself:

1- EXPOSURE of the sub-ect on Mon/Tues/Wed ights via carefully repared papers.

2- EXPANSION of the ubject on each of the ollowing mornings led y a panel with questions nd input from the floor.

- IDENTIFICATION of the oints of tension in maller groups allowing or individual expression y all.

4- COLLATION of feed ack from discussion roups by feed back team.

5- INTERACTION on the eed back with ample time or corroborative ex-erience input.

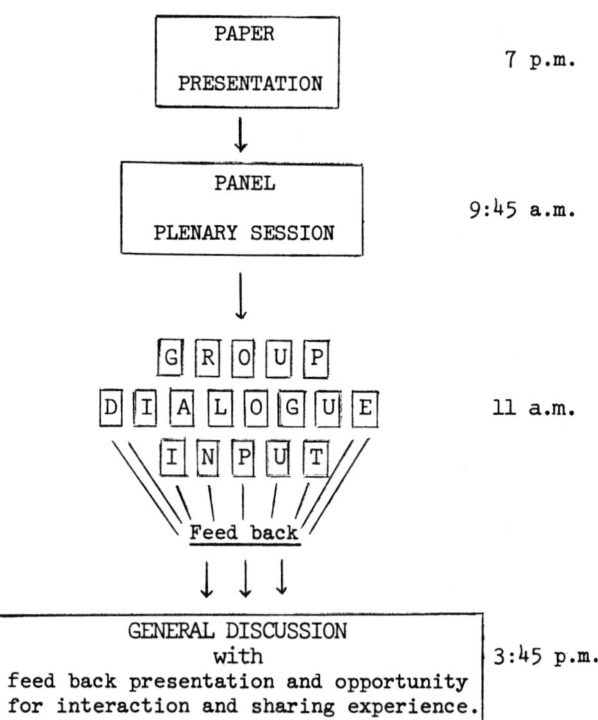

t the close of each day a special FINDINGS COMMITTEE will sift, classify and re-ine the results of the discussions and present them in a final Wrap-up Session n Friday morning.

FINAL WRAP-UP - FRIDAY A.M.

Presentation of summary findings. Open sharing of what has been gleaned from the week's experience together and how these principles and suggestions apply to our individual spheres of activity.

L'71 Study Conference • Sept 27-Oct 1 • Green Lake, Wisc • Dr. Vergil Gerber, Coordinator

Part 3

the conference handbook

welcome to

Your presence
and preparation are
warmly appreciated.

Some 400 other IFMA/EFMA related leaders join you this week in grappling with the crucial issue of *MISSIONS IN CREATIVE TENSION.*

Identifying the tensions, finding guidelines for coping with them are of course only for the purpose of reaching the more than 2 billion on 6 continents who as yet do not know Jesus Christ as Saviour and Lord.

God grant that in the midst of serious dialogue and debate this week, we may also be very sensitive to what the Holy Spirit wants to say to us and do through us to accomplish His missionary purposes through the Church.

Yours and His,

V Gerber

Vergil Gerber
GL'71 Coordinator

Sponsored by

evangelical missions
INFORMATION SERVICE • BOX 794 • WHEATON, ILLINOIS 60187

Quick Reference PROGRAM
Sept. 27-Oct. 1, 1971

EMIS Study Conference
Green Lake, Wisc.

"Missions in Creative Tension"

Discussion theme: "CHURCH/MISSION RELATIONS"
I- At Home (Areas shaded)
II- Overseas (Areas shaded)

	Monday Sept. 27	Tuesday Sept. 28	Wednesday Sept. 29	Thursday Sept. 30	Friday Oct. 1
AM 6:45 – 7:30		EARLY MORNING PRAYER GROUPS (locations posted in dormitories)			
7:30		*breakfast*			
8:45		"The Ministry of the Church" (CLOWNEY) *"Patterns of Service Together"*	*"Formed in God's Presence"*	*"Called in God's Service"*	*"Ordered in the Spirit"*
9:45		PANEL Questions/Input from floor	PANEL Questions/Input from floor	PANEL Questions/Input from floor	FINAL WRAPUP — Summary Findings — Discussion of their implications and application
10:30		*coffee*			
11:00		GROUP DIALOGUE	GROUP DIALOGUE	GROUP DIALOGUE	
PM 12:30		*lunch*			
1:30 – 3:15		IFMA Annual Mtg. EFMA Board Mtg.	IFMA Annual Mtg. EFMA Board Mtg.	Special Committees Free time	
3:15		*coffee*			
3:45		Plenary INTERACTION Session	Plenary INTERACTION Session	Plenary INTERACTION Session	
5:30	*dinner*				
7:00	I "Church/Mission Relations at Home" (SHEPHERD)	II "Mission/Church Relations Overseas" A-In Principle (KING-PETERS)	"Mission/Church Relations Overseas" B-In Practice (KING-PETERS)	PRAYER & PRAISE *"Building His Church"* (ARMSTRONG)	

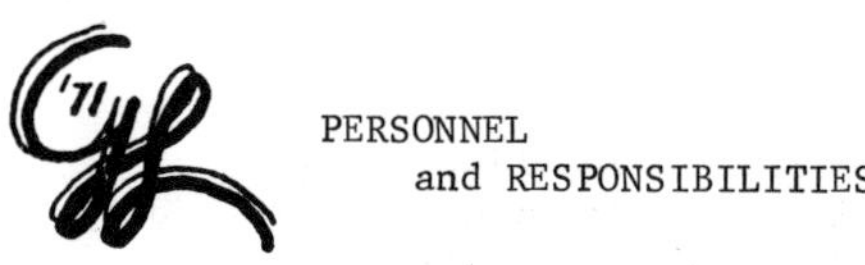

PERSONNEL and RESPONSIBILITIES

Coordinator: VERGIL GERBER - Evangelical Missions Information Service

Sponsoring Co-chairmen

PHILIP E. ARMSTRONG - President, Interdenominational Foreign Mission Ass'n
WESLEY L. DUEWEL - President, Evangelical Foreign Missions Ass'n

EMIS Executive Committee

IAN M. HAY - President (Sudan Interior Mission)
LESTER WESTLUND - Vice President (Evangelical Free Church of America)
CLYDE W. TAYLOR - Secretary (Evangelical Foreign Missions Association
E.L. FRIZEN, JR. - Treasurer (Interdenominational Foreign Mission Association)
WADE T. COGGINS - Alternate (Evangelical Foreign Missions Association)

Bible Exposition: EDMUND P. CLOWNEY - Westminster Theological Seminary, Phila, Pa.

Paper writers and Consultants

JACK F. SHEPHERD - Christian and Missionary Alliance
OLAN HENDRIX - American Sunday School Union
GEORGE LINHART - Grace Chapel, Havertown, Pa.
J. ROBERTSON MCQUILKIN - Columbia Bible College
J. MURRAY MARSHALL - First Presbyterian Church, Flushing, N.Y.

LOUIS L. KING - Christian and Missionary Alliance
JOHN GRATION -Africa Inland Mission
AKIRA HATORI - Pacific Broadcasting Association, Japan
GADIEL T. ISIDRO - FEBIAS College of Bible, Philippines
CHARLES D. KIRKPATRICK - Free Methodist Church of North America
J. ALLEN THOMPSON - West Indies Mission

GEORGE W. PETERS - Dallas Theological Seminary
BYANG KATO - Sudan Interior Mission, Nigeria
SAMUEL O. ODUNAIKE - Association of Evangelicals of Africa and Madagascar
WILLIAM H. TAYLOR - Central American Mission
I. BEN WATI - Evangelical Fellowship of India
RALPH WINTER - Fuller Theological Seminary

Panelists

EDMUND P. CLOWNEY - Westminster Theological Seminary
WILLIAM G. CROUCH - Sudan Interior Mission
J. PHILIP HOGAN - Assemblies of God
LOUIS L. KING - Christian and Missionary Alliance
J. MURRAY MARSHALL - First Presbyterian Church, Flushing, N.Y.
GEORGE W. PETERS - Dallas Theological Seminary
JACK F. SHEPHERD - Christian and Missionary Alliance

Overseas Resource Personnel

MOSES ARIYE - Christian Nationals' Evangelism, Nigeria
DAVID C. CHO - Korea Evangelistic Intermission Alliance, Korea
JOHN C. CHO - Seoul Theological Seminary, Korea
ARSENIO DOMINGUEZ - Christian Nationals' Evangelism, Philippines
HECTOR ESPINOZA - Mexican Evangelistic Institute, Mexico
BYANG KATO - Evangelical Churches of West Africa
SAMUEL I. KIM - Korea Evangelistic Intermission Alliance, Korea
JOHN E. LANGLOIS - World Evangelical Fellowship, United Kingdom
HENRY LOEWEN - Mennonite Brethren Conference, Brazil
AUGUSTUS MARWIEH - Christian Nationals' Evangelism, Liberia
JUAN CARLOS MIRANDA - Brethren Church, Argentina
CLAUDE NOEL - Evangelical Baptist Mission, Haiti
JOSE REINOSO - World Radio Missionary Fellowship, Ecuador
PETER SPENCER - Missionary Church, Jamaica
WALFORD THOMPSON - Men In Action, Caribbean
ERNEST VATTER - Conference of Evangelical Missions, Germany
PIUS WAKATAMA - Rhodesia Christian College, Rhodesia

Prayer and Praise: PHILIP E. ARMSTRONG - Far Eastern Gospel Crusade

Feedback Chairman: HORACE L. FENTON - Latin America Mission

Co-Chairman: FRANK A. INESON - Missions Advanced Research & Communications Center

Assistants: KERRY LOVERING - Sudan Interior Mission
JAMES REAPSOME - Evangelical Missions Quarterly
CHARLES A. TIPP - Ontario Bible College
WARREN WEBSTER - Conservative Baptist Foreign Mission Societ

Findings Committee

WADE T. COGGINS - Evangelical Foreign Missions Association
HORACE L. FENTON - Latin America Mission
E. L. FRIZEN, JR. - Interdenominational Foreign Mission Association
IAN M. HAY - Sudan Interior Mission
FRANK A. INESON - Missions Advanced Research & Communication Center
KERRY LOVERING - Sudan Interior Mission
GORDON MACDONALD - First Baptist Church, Collinsville, Illinois
JAMES REAPSOME - Evangelical Missions Quarterly
CLYDE W. TAYLOR - Evangelical Foreign Missions Association
J. ALLEN THOMPSON - West Indies Mission
C. PETER WAGNER - Fuller Evangelistic Association
WARREN WEBSTER - Conservative Baptist Foreign Mission Society
LESTER WESTLUND - Evangelical Free Church of America

Registration: MILTON BAKER - Conservative Baptist Foreign Mission Society

Bibliographer: DONALD G. PETERSON - Wheaton College Library

Exhibits: WALTER FRICKE - Conservative Baptist Foreign Mission Society

Morning Prayer Coordinator: JOSEPH S. MCCULLOUGH - Andes Evangelical Mission

Daily News Sheet: C. PETER WAGNER - Fuller Evangelistic Association

Music: DAVID L. SUNDEN - Harrington Press, Harrington Park, N.J.

Discussion Groups

Coordinator: J. ALLEN THOMPSON - West Indies Mission
Assistant: FRANK A. INESON - Missions Advanced Research and Communications Center

Leaders:

HOLLIS F. ABBOTT - World Gospel Mission
MILTON BAKER - Conservative Baptist Foreign Mission Society
WILLIAM G. CROUCH - Sudan Interior Mission
NORMAN L. CUMMINGS - Overseas Crusades
RAYMOND J. DAVIS - Sudan Interior Mission
WALTER FRANK - Greater Europe Mission
WALTER FRICKE - Conservative Baptist Foreign Mission Society
PHILIP HOGAN - Assemblies of God
CHARLES D. KIRKPATRICK - Free Methodist Church of North America
GEORGE E. LEDDEN, JR. Far Eastern Gospel Crusade
CHARLES J. MELLIS - Missionary Aviation Fellowship
VERNON MORTENSON - The Evangelical Alliance Mission
PETER STAM - Africa Inland Mission
ALFRED LARSON - Unevangelized Fields Mission
WILLIAM H. TAYLOR - Central American Mission
WARREN WEBSTER - Conservative Baptist Foreign Mission Society

Recorders:

ROBERT D. ANDERSON - South America Mission
WILLIAM D. BELL - North Africa Mission
CHARLES T. BENNETT - Missionary Aviation Fellowship
DALE W. BJORK - Baptist General Conference
ROBERT DILLON - Evangelical Free Church of America
ARNO W. ENNS - Conservative Baptist Foreign Mission Society
DELMER R. GUYNES - Assemblies of God
M. VIRGIL INGRAHAM - Brethren Church Missionary Board
EDWIN E. JACQUES - Conservative Baptist Foreign Mission Society
T. GRADY MANGHAM, JR. - Christian and Missionary Alliance
JOSEPH S. MCCULLOUGH - Andes Evangelical Mission
EDWARD G. SCHUIT - Africa Inland Mission
ARNI SHARESKI - Christian and Missionary Alliance
EDWIN TOMLINSON - Sudan Interior Mission
VERNON R. WIEBE - Mennonite Brethren Church
RICHARD WINCHELL - The Evangelical Alliance Mission

"CHURCH-MISSION RELATIONS 'AT HOME'"

by Jack F. Shepherd

for presentation at GL '71

INTRODUCTION - GL '71 PURPOSE AND THEME

The primary concern of this study conference is with organizational structures for world mission. We are not here to "rethink missions" from the standpoint of our commission, message or objectives. IFMA/EFMA commitment to these basic unchanging issues is clear and unqualified. It is as we affirmed it at the Wheaton Congress on the Church's Worldwide Mission.

Willingness to review and revise the shape of mission structures should not involve any modification of the message which we proclaim or the purpose of its proclamation. Evangelicals, in insisting that the Bible does set out things that are fundamental for the Christian mission, may appear to claim explicit Biblical authorization for missionary methods and organizations. We must avoid that kind of "morphological fundamentalism"(1) in which structures become sacrosanct and thus inflexible. The truth we seek to proclaim is fundamentally unchangeable, but the techniques and agencies for its transmission can be amazingly varied.

We must admit that the Bible does not give clear specific patterns, particularly for mission organizations. Probably most of us would agree with those scholars who maintain that there is not a single normative New Testament pattern for the organized life of the church. W. D. Davies, a representative of that point of view, says:

> ". . . New Testament studies in the last seventy-five years have revealed a curious dichotomy. On the one hand, there has emerged a marked unity as to the essential nature of the church as the eschatalogical people of God in Christ. On the other hand, there has emerged equally marked disagreement as to the way or ways in which that people was organized. . . To use Quick's metaphor, the relation of the church to its external order in the New Testament is analogous not to the relation of a man to his own body, which is joined indissolubly to him under all earthly circumstances, but to that of a man to his clothes, which he can change at will. The church in the New Testament can assume many forms, and is not limited to any one particular form which is peculiarly the expression of its very being."(2)

If such a claim can be made concerning church organization, it seems certain that structuring for mission is defined with even less specificity. This does not mean, in any sense, that it is unimportant, or that we can get on without any. In fact, just as the church must have some form, and the sort of form that will be expressive of its essential nature and a means to the fulfillment of its function; so, if mission is to be more than an impulse or an ideal, it will have organizational shape. Just as the theological principle of legitimate variation in the external form of the church has been effective and productive in "indigenous church" developments, so it can now be fruitful and corrective in thinking about organization for mission.

There is a special reason, with a positive and a negative side, which makes it urgent and appropriate to consider this issue at this time. There is the basically happy problem of the need to relate to the vital growing churches overseas so that we can share more effectively with them in ministry to their own nations and also have them become involved along with us in world missions. Over against this evidence of progress and achievement in Christian mission is the frankly acknowledged fact that there are tensions that threaten to limit outreach and diminish effectiveness in the task of world evangelization. We are just not doing well enough to insist that we are doing things the right way. If we are determined that the whole church should take the whole gospel to the whole world, then we must work at the problem of church-mission relationships.

The GL '71 theme with its Gerberian logo is intended to dramatize the tensions arising in the two-sided relationship of church to mission at the sending end and mission to church in the overseas situation. The accelerating rate of extension and growth is a complicating factor that can hardly be illustrated in the diagram. Tensions are on the increase because missions are on the move out into the complexities of the modern world. This kind of movement necessitates our updating and even retooling methodology, strategy and organization.

Stephen Neill, the great missionary scholar, must have been the first to suggest that the stress and strain within the mission-church dichotomy has already been and can still prove to be a "creative tension."(3) Without stretching the analogy or "getting uptight" about it (two common forms of tension, incidentally), it needs to be acknowledged that tensions must be reduced or relieved or they invariably have a deleterious effect. We are honest, not just nervous, in admitting that the tensions are there; now let us be imaginative and industrious in making the adjustments that will utilize and eliminate them. Dr. Zwemer, a wise and experienced missionary statesman, once urged me to remember that "anything that moves through space makes friction." However, it must also be remembered that just as you can have friction without purposeful movement so you can have tension without creativity. But if, as our stated objective here has it, we can "identify the points of tension" and then find ways "to cope with them constructively," they will prove to be creative tensions.

PURPOSE AND PLAN OF THIS PAPER

A. PURPOSE

This is to be a working paper not a **position** paper. The Peters/King presentations are more in the nature of a debate, a confrontation of two differing positions. The issue is to be joined so that two contrasting points of view concerning church-mission relations overseas are set out, the one against the other, in what is hoped will be "creative tension." My assignment is to be descriptive and analytical rather than evaluative, corrective or pontifical.

Accordingly, the purpose of this paper is threefold: first, to show how church-mission relations at home and overseas are inextricably bound together; second, to formulate some guidelines for use in evaluating, modifying or updating church-mission organizational relationships at home; then to suggest, for purposes of discussion at least, some possible directions toward change in the structuring of these church-mission relationships.

B. THE OUTLINE OF THE PAPER

I. An Enumeration of the Tensions
II. Probing for the Source of the Tensions
III. Biblical Sanction for Church-Mission Organization
IV. Present Structures as Products of History
V. Guidelines for Continuity and Change in Organizing for Mission
VI. Some Suggestions for Change in Church-Mission Relationships

I. AN ENUMERATION OF THE TENSIONS

Part of this assignment is to review the areas of tension in our home-base church-mission relationships. It is to be hoped that these can be discussed in a direct and open way in our various sessions so as to produce practical approaches to cope with them. You have identified points of tension in your own experience. It has been helpful to have had these shared in conference preparations. Having a certain homogeneity of tension classification will now determine our groupings. I will only list the categories I used for these points of tension and pass over the comments:

(See Appendix for comments , page 147)

1. Organizational Alignments
2. Administrative Participation
3. Personnel Problems (Note the important place of the school here.)
    a. Recruitment
    b. Training
    c. Evaluation
    d. Service and Assignment
    e. Furlough
    f. Retiral
4. Finances
5. Communication

II. PROBING FOR THE SOURCE OF THE TENSIONS

1. To What Do the Tensions Point?

If in this conference, and as a result of it, we can reduce the intensity of some of these acknowledged tensions, we will be more effective in mission. However, we cannot be satisfied with just that. We must ask about the causes of these tensions. Are they inevitable? Can they be removed? Perhaps the best possible use of these tensions will be stimulation to search out the basic problems and then to plan not only for a cure but for a permanent correction of the tension-producing situations.

We must not leave here having simply provided for quick relief if it is only of short duration. It is imperative to probe for the source of the tensions. Undoubtedly we can discover personal, social, cultural, and even demonic factors that figure in the kinds of sample tensions we have listed. But I believe we will all agree with the planners of this conference that the source of certain significant aspects of the tension is in the very structuring of church and mission relationships. If that is so, we can work for adjustments, shifts, and reshaping so that efficiency will be increased, tensions minimized, and the work of world mission will be accelerated, expanded and multiplied.

Now I will not agree that, because there are tensions, the structures are necessarily improper or outmoded. There may, and probably will be tensions in the most nearly perfect of structures or relationships. However, the presence of multiplying tensions certainly is an indication that we should examine and test our structures, and correct them as needed. Part of the problem may be the very uncertainty and ambiguity in our thinking about these matters. We may have become so equivocal about basic church-mission relationships and responsibilities that we may hastily undertake dangerous and even compromising revisions of mission nomenclature. Worse than that, we may jeopardize the basic principle and idea of mission by letting it evaporate in the kind of "shapelessness" against which the Frankfurt Declaration discerningly warned.(6)

2. Self-examination at the Sending End of Mission

As has already been noted, this paper has to do with our end of things here "at home." We begin our probing there. As a matter of fact, all of these tensions have been listed with this side of the church-mission dichotomy in mind.

Without attempting to formulate fixed definitions, it does seem worthwhile to seek to discern the shape of that frequently maligned relationship.

Stephen Neill, for example, speaks of the "disastrous dichotomy" of church and mission.(7) Without consenting altogether to that description, we must admit that the variety of categories used in defining both "church" and "mission" are disastrously diversified. One gets impatient with attempts to define and redefine, but careful definition and design of organizational structures, with close Biblical scrutiny and testing, might have prevented developments described by Newbigin and later Scherer in the self-contradictory terms "unmissionary churches" and "unchurchly missions".(8)

It is necessary to further divide up this dichotomy so as to see the distinction between church and mission at home and overseas, as we have it on the preliminary outline of the program. This does not mean that more should not be said on "What is the church?" and "What is its mission?" We will certainly have to keep on asking that. But now to make this initial distinction, it seems to me that the most helpful and least offensive way to rephrase the traditional "home base--foreign field" dichotomy is to speak of "sending" and "receiving" churches, both of which have their particular kind of "mission" relationship. It is well to have as a frame of reference and order of procedure in our discussion a consideration of the sending church in relation to its mission agency. Then we can turn to the receiving church as it relates to the mission agency of the sending church and perhaps also to its own agency for mission, if that is different. Without taking sides in the debate on the issues on the agenda for subsequent days (and perhaps we should follow the formula of the Keswick week--"no crisis before Thursday!") it is evident that whether we talk "integration" or "separation," we are generally talking about two churches, one sending and one receiving, but one mission. So the mission society or board itself is dichotomous in nature, at least it has to stretch to simultaneously assume two roles, one toward the sending and one toward the receiving church. If we can get that into perspective, we are looking at the primary structural source of tensions.

If this assumption as to the shape of mission is correct, then there is special logic in looking first at church-mission relations at the sending end. Alfred Larson is probably right in saying that "the relationship to the receiving church has become increasingly more complex through the years."(9) Probably for that reason we are properly concerned to get at the overseas issues. We do need to bear in mind, however, that what is there is the result of our aggressive exporting operations. It is also right that we should look for solutions knowing that we have created the problems, at least in part. As Professor Freytag of Hamburg put it some years ago, "Missions have always had problems, but now missions themselves have become a problem."(10) It is to be hoped that we can be part of the solution as we have been part of the problem. If we succeed in that, we must do some self-examination and be ready for changes in our traditional sending structures in order to lessen and absorb some of the tensions.

3. Two Perspectives on the Sending End

Ralph Winter, who ranks with the world's most avid students of missions, has stimulated many of us with his ingenious graphs and probing articles on "The Anatomy of Missions."(11) He has begun at the right end with his analysis. This is in contrast to great missionary strategists and thinkers like Venn, Anderson and Allen. They produced their classic theories of church and mission in connection with field situations. Winter, partly because he has the historians' instinct, has begun his "anatomical analyses" at the home base, the sending end. He has undoubtedly been informed and influenced by missionary thinkers who have been concerned with mission in relation to conciliar unity. We need to be aware of their work and try to understand their perspective over against the one Winter is getting into focus.

It may not be quite fair to set Winter in complete antithesis to ecumenical thinkers, but I will do that in order to introduce what I regard as a necessary element in this discussion. There is a polarization between two basically different viewpoints on organization for missions, particularly here in North America.

I identify Winter with "Conservative Evangelical Free Association" as opposed to "Ecumenical Inclusive Conciliarism." I am not seeking to elicit prejudice against the integration position by putting it in guilty association with ecumenicity. However, there is a historical connection there that cannot be overlooked. In ecumenical integration there is the danger that mission as we know it will get lost in ecclesiastical structures and programs. On our side, we should see the danger of missions operating without a proper vital churchly relationship. It soon becomes evident that there is need of balance between the two points of view, balance along with flexibility.

(a) "Ecumenical Inclusive Conciliarism":

Most recent studies which have seen church and mission separation as a scandal and an inconsistency have been concerned with the conciliar movement. These have begun by giving primary attention to Western-based structures. For example, Newbigin, Neill and others who have written helpful and exciting things about church and mission have sought to make a case and plead the cause for union of the World Council of Churches and the International Missionary Council. We know that consummation of that union and its consequent implementation has not increased missionary concern or activity. We do well, however, to study the literature produced in connection with these developments. We can learn much from what has been written and experienced within this movement. One thing does seem tragically clear: that is, that following the conciliar merger there has been a sharp diminution or perhaps even repudiation of the very missionary motivation and concern that brought the ecumenical movement into being.

The ambiguities resulting from integration of "mission" into "church"--or, even more, the corollary theory that has identified the one with the other--have left things in such an amorphous state that obligations, objectives and functions are obscured. There are exciting, up-to-the-minute high decibel declarations, but they issue a call with an uncertain sound to communicate a message of ill-defined content.

The ecumenical authors to whom we refer repeatedly as offering profound and helpful insights have raised their warning cries against this tragic departure from the missionary task of the church. However, they probably get a better hearing and understanding from us nonconciliar evangelicals than from their own company. A basic ambiguity in which they have been caught is the shape of the structures in which church and missions are to be organized. Is there not a connection between the absorption of mission organization into "the church" and the loss of clear, purposeful missionary identity and action?

Ecumenical thinkers and writers, it seems to me, have suffered from a confusion about structures partly because of lack of the very kind of intimate knowledge of and appreciation for evangelical missions that characterizes Ralph Winter's work.

He is a vocal champion of our kind of mission even when he is speaking in ecumenical precints. Winter has shown that the new or independent missions, and most of us are included there, are the best hope for filfilling the mission of the church.

This joint conference would provide a fascinating diagram of vertical-horizontal, modality-sodality, warp and woof configurations if Winter began to show us how we are put together and fit into the total pattern. He has done more than enlarge our vocabulary and provide us new tools for missions research and evaluation. He has introduced concepts that require our doing basic and even radical thinking about church-mission relationships and world-mission strategy. His stimulating page in the provocative GL '71 issue of CGB probes right down to show up errors that can be detected in the defective church-mission perspective promoted within the ecumenical movement.

> "The first error wars against the Western-based missionary society and says it isn't needed. The second error is the strange assumption that not even the younger churches need missionary societies .. that the formation of a truly indigenous church precludes the necessity of a truly indigenous mission!"(12)

There is an ecumenical doctrinal inclusiveness of which we must be critical, but what I am protesting is the kind of structural inclusiveness in which organizational unification can become an end in itself. It is not irrelevant to our concern to observe that there is danger in the drive for a uniform alignment of churches into denominations, denominations into more extensive mergers, with conciliar incorporation as a parallel development.

In this organizational evolution, vital functions and creative initiatives get locked into compromisingly inclusive bureaucratic structures. Is this not what we have seen happen to missions in the course of denominational and ecumenical developments? We should at least be alert to things as they are here, before we too quickly offer proposals for organizational unification of church and mission overseas.

(b) "<u>Conservative Evangelical Free Association</u>":

Our two associations have in common not only a critical reluctance toward the ecumenical movement, but on the positive side deep respect for a spirit of freedom and voluntarism in missionary activity and organization as long as it does not compromise evangelical doctrine. We may be called fissiparous, fragmented, and even divisive in our toleration of "fission for mission." But we are a part of the great tradition that has kept alive and given discernible shape to mission and world evangelization as a distinct part of the ministry of the church.(13)

R. Pierce Beaver, who has shown a remarkable understanding of both sides of the ecumenical tension, has recently given an instructive word on the crucial importance of "voluntarism" in missions. It is significant that he deals with this topic in a paper given to the Association of Professors of Missions in a kind of final prophetic word to them in this year of his retirement. He calls his paper "A Plea for New Voluntarism," but shows that the idea of free association in mission has a respectable and productive history. He reflects a wistfulness for recovery of this vitality and freedom when he says:

> "The encouragement of voluntarism is necessary to recovery and advance. Most British and European mission agencies and the American inter- or undenominational missions are still voluntary societies. Twenty years ago Max Warren and Hans-Werner Gensichen were suggesting that the voluntary principle is essential to mission. Here in America, however, we claimed that official commitment of denominational churches through official boards was a better way and better justified by Bible and theology. But our boards were put into the straightjacket of denominational structure and budget, became administratively rigid, were subjected to American business managerial principles and methods, and eventually deprived the local disciples and congregations of meaningful and conscious part in the sending operation. The whole thing became depersonalized. Now many members have been lost to the cause, alienated or discouraged.
>
> "Actually all through the nineteenth century and the first quarter of the twentieth the expanding American overseas mission was sustained by a tremendous volume of voluntary participation. . . Managerial, administrative centralization and uniformity gradually destroyed this spontaneous participation, and we now pay a very heavy cost for its elimination."(14)

Beaver is hopeful, a vain hope in my opinion, for a revival of voluntarism within ecumenical structures. Winter has been industrious in seeking to promote free horizontal forms of mission within his own denomination. So neither of these scholars would identify this principle of freedom within organizational separation of mission from churches.

Winter's appeal is for balance and close articulation of movement between the two. To follow his analogy, we need to weave and perhaps reweave the fabric of the Christian movement so as to have a balance of churchly warp and mission woof. Winter puts his finger on the problem and tension that is a real threat to both church and mission in the sending situation. He points out what he regards as "an almost inevitable tension" between ecclesiastical organizations and mission societies. He says that mission societies have had a "diversity producing spontaneity of Christian growth and vitality" which has disregarded and even been a threat to "requirements of a unity based on organic centrality."

This is his way of describing the rise of mission society type horizontal sodalities along side of denominational vertical modalities. The threat in this development is not that they are separate, but that they are so far apart. Winter calls attention to the dangerous situation in which the newer missions"have been so organizationally distant from the churches." He says "that the problem consists precisely of this unprecedented degree of alienation between mission and church."(15)

Apparently Winter's discontent over these developments arises from a concern to keep missions somewhat integrated into ecclesiastical structures. Actually, it seems to me, he ends up showing that separateness of this sort has a special kind of vigor and vitality. Of course, I think he is one of those who are generous but imprecise in calling so many levels and segments of ecclesiastical organizations "church." Missions may do well to keep "organizationally distant" and even be "alienated" from some of these structures. As a matter of fact, some of the missions which Winter usually describes as "independent," and Scherer and others by less complimentary terms, may well have a sounder ecclesial instinct than those who end up moving down through geographical, national and hierarchical levels to come down to the local congregation as perhaps the lowest form of ecclesiastical life!

If "faith mission" people have no better ecclesiology than is expressed in terms such as "inter- un- non- or anti-denominationalism," then we do well to ask, "What kind of churches can those kinds of 'mission' plant?" I suspect their emphasis is more likely based on a persuasion that the form of the church which seems to have special prominence in the New Testament is the local assembly. If that is so, they may be better churchmen than they are often considered to be. In fact, it is to the credit of missionary thinkers of this genre that they have steadfastly and accurately insisted that the mission is not the church.(16)

4. <u>The Source of the Tensions:</u>

Tensions are multiplied and become a threat to both churches and missions when the relationship between them is not clearly defined, mutually respectful, constantly kept in balance, and sensitively adapted to the environment of the changing world of mission.

It is not that the existence of distinct organizational forms is wrong. It is not that one must be assimilated into the other. It is not that there is one fixed and final structure, deviation from which will inevitably produce tension. It is not that situations become so complex that the church must seek some alternative to mission as we have known it. The need of the hour is to look at our structures, test and examine them in the light of the Bible and history, and then work continuously for change that will be creative and effectual but without compromise.

III. BIBLICAL SANCTION FOR CHURCH-MISSION ORGANIZATION

The principles that we must carefully avoid compromising are those set out in Scripture. We can learn much from history but only as we look at it in the light of the Bible. We have available to us a wealth of scholarship, both theological and historical, in the preparatory materials and study resources for this conference.

I must limit myself to a brief Biblical statement and then a historical footnote, acknowledging that there is still a vast amount of work to be done in both areas.

When it comes to trying to bring concepts of church and mission organization under judgment of the Word in order to formulate theological guidelines, we are confronted with two highly respectable schools of thought, both of which would claim Biblical authority. On the one hand, there is the view of Roland Allen, quoted approvingly by Boer and echoed by Neill and others, that in the New Testament, speaking particularly of organization or institution, there is only "church" not "mission":

> "The Church was first established and organized with a world-wide mission for a world-wide work. It was a living organism composed of living souls deriving their life from Christ, who was its Head. It was an organism which grew by its own spontaneous activity, the expression of that life which it had in union with Christ, the Saviour. Its organization was the organization fitted for such an organism; it was the organization of a missionary body. Consequently, there was no special organization for missions in the Early Church; the church organization sufficed. It was simple and complete. There was abundant room in it for the expression of the spontaneous individual activity of its members; for every member was potentially a missionary; and the Church, as an organized body, expected that activity and knew how to act when its members did their duty. . . . The new modern missionary organization is an addition. . . . If we compare our modern missionary work with the missionary work of the Early Church, this is what differentiates them; with us missions are the special work of a special organization; in the Early Church missions were not a special work, and there was no special organization."(17)

As we shall note, most readings of the history of the post-apostolic period seem to maintain the same position. Mission societies and agencies which were distinct from the church in their institutional form were abnormal and substandard in Biblical terms.

Recently such a point of view has come to be convincingly challenged. Arthur Glasser is the one I have been hearing speak most persuasively to this issue. His conviction won the consent and support of his colleagues in the 1965 restatement of principles when the China Inland Mission was reshaped into Overseas Missionary Fellowship. Allen Thompson quotes approvingly their statement on "The Mission" in a paper on our subject:

> "The New Testament distinguishes between structured local congregations (churches) and the structured apostolic band called by God to evangelize the heathen and plant new churches. Whereas the apostles were of the church, their corporate ministry of missionary outreach necessitated among themselves patterns of leadership and organization, recruitment and finance, training and discipline distinct from comparable patterns within local congregations. This significant distinction gives Biblical sanction to today's structured missionary fellowship."(18)

I think I hear echoes of that sound pronouncement in Glasser's mild rejoinder to Scherer in the helpful and generous introduction to the GL '71 multi-book.(19)

Undoubtedly there is an increasing number of scholars who could identify with such a position. It is to be hoped that they will devote themselves to the study and exposition of it. If Scripture does indeed suggest and sanction a separate missionary organization in the New Testament period, then this may well be a norm from which we should not deviate or we may produce tensions of a more serious nature than some of those now resultant from organizational dichotomy.

I want to try to make three points from Ephesians 4:11,12, which is surely the key text on this issue. These points are in support of the proposition that both church and mission should exist in organized form. They are essential the one to the other, and should function in accordance with New Testament principles.

1. <u>Mission Has a Permanent and Well-defined Place in the Total Ministry of the Church:</u>

Ephesians 4:11 and 12 may be understood to present, in a striking way, unity and diversity of the church's ministry. The risen Christ gives to His church men of various gifts, complementary the one to the other, so that the people of God will be fully equipped for all He purposes for them to do. Attention should be turned from the <u>official</u> idea usually associated with verse 11 to the <u>functional</u> emphasis; in that way the scope of the church's ministry is dramatized. It is to be: apostolic, prophetic, evangelistic, pastoral and didactic. Just as our Lord himself incarnated the Servant image of the ministry (vss. 9,10), so these specially gifted men incarnate and demonstrate certain aspects of the

the whole ministry.

There is good reason now to assume that "apostolic" here is to be understood as "missionary." We can agree with those who lament the tendency to place the entire emphasis on apostolicity in doctrine while neglecting the apostolate of worldwide witness. In spite of Scherer's equivocation, there is a good case for regarding missionary vocation as in proper succession from the "apostles."[20]

Could all of the several aspects of this total ministry be fulfilled directly through the organized life of a local congregation? Perhaps the prophetic function, which may relate in a special sense to social responsibility in the world, should be looked at carefully as possibly requiring a paraecclesiastical structure, though the prophetic aspect of ministry can and does go on in and through the congregation.[21] The didactic or pedagogical aspect of ministry has been carried on in schools which took on institutional form apart from the church.

The apostolate, however, which involves reaching out into the world to see new congregations brought into being through the preaching of the Word and work of the Spirit, was certainly carried out by an organized apostolic company, strategy and program. Is this not best conceived of as separate in structure as well as function? If that is correct, the local churches in the New Testament fulfilled the missionary part of their ministry in fellowship with the apostles and their work. New Testament examples of this come readily to mind.

2. There is a Proper Distinction Between the Evangelistic and Missionary Functions of the Church's Ministry.

I am encouraged to press this point as fundamental to this whole issue because of the fairly full discussion of it in Beaver's book, The Missionary Between the Times.[22] In a provocative and helpful way he seems to distinguish between "evangelism" and "missions." Evangelism may be regarded as that local witness which the church directly bears in its own world. It is the outreach of the local congregation in programmed and personal witness to share Christ. The structure of the congregation is adequate for that. To call men to Christ is to invite them into the fellowship of the Body, "the household of God," of which you are a part. In contrast to this direct witness in evangelism, missions is that sending of missionaries "to the regions beyond" (2 Cor. 10) in order that other churches might be planted. In them that total ministry which will include missions and evangelism will be reproduced. Missionary ministry then is indirect; that is to say, it is carried on through delegated representatives.

This concept seems to me to save us from that superficial notion that "the church is mission," that everything it does is "mission." It does mean that neither missions nor evangelism is the sole, complete and final function of the church. Of course, in terms of the text, missions would have a kind of priority, but the church has a total fivefold ministry to fulfil that incorporates all that God purposes for it in service and witness to Christ in the world.

3. The Missionary Vocation Is a Continuing and Necessary Type of Ministry.

Stephen Neill has argued in colorful words that we should get rid of the word "missionary," but he concedes that he, at least, cannot get on without it. He agrees that "if everything is missions, nothing is missions," but warns in a winsome way against just what I am presumptuous enough to try to do. He says:

> "By reaction against this too general formulation, we are in danger of thinking really in terms of a theology of missionary societies and of missionaries, of a theological justification of what we have done in the past and of what we are trying to do in the present. And this, in my judgment, is exactly what cannot be done. To put it in oldfashioned language, you can have a theology of substances, but not of accidents. Missionary societies, as we know them today, are in no sense a necessary part of the existence of the Church; they are simply temporary expedients for the performance of certain functions that could be performed in entirely different ways. 'Missionary' does not signify status; it has reference to an activity and a relationship. It is possible to have a theology of ministry, but not of mission board secretaries. ... A correct theology of the Church would include everything that we now regard as the special and separate problems of 'missions'; and a correct theology of ministry would include everything that now perplexes us as the special problem of the 'foreign' missionary. Yet in fact, 'foreign missions' have come to be largely divorced from the general life of the Church, and 'the missionary' tends to be regarded as a man who holds a special office in the Church, to which this special title has been assigned." (23)

Now I am in hearty agreement with much of what Bishop Neill says; however, I think there is theological substantiality for both the mission structure and the person with a sense of guidance to missionary vocation. This is not to argue the special call. It is not to say that the function or institution has for all times the same characteristics. In fact, we might do well in our day to consider a distinctly churchly missionary ministry as differing from supportive "functions." I simply think no church, here or overseas, is a proper church unless it has a missionary dimension to its ministry. Having missionaries to send is the most logical way to carry on. In that sense, the missionary is needed primarily by the sending church. What makes a person a missionary is that he is sent, not the foreign place to which he goes.

I am, in fact, favorably impressed with Neill's novel suggestion, which might even reduce some tensions. He says, "It seems clear to me that a missionary ceases to be a missionary on the day on which he sets foot on the shores of the land in which he has been called to work. From that moment on he is a servant of the church in that place and nothing else. ... Paradoxically, the missionary becomes a missionary again when he sets foot once more on the shores of his own country. In the overseas church he has no status as a missionary."(24) Now that may create problems for the other side of this whole debate, but it is a positive note for my side of the discussion. A mature church is a sending church and the mission agency and the missionary are the divinely patterned instruments to allow for the fulfilment of the high calling of involvement in God's mission, the primary part of the church's total ministry.

IV. PRESENT STRUCTURES AS PRODUCTS OF HISTORY

The historical background of the development of distinct church-mission structures deserves more time and attention than will be allowed for it here. It has already been emphasized in a helpful way in Ian Hay's preparatory paper which included Charles Troutman's capsule review of the formation of mission societies. This reference should whet our appetites to explore those periods of church history that have special significance for missions. Champions of the Anabaptists, like Littell, and defenders of the Reformers, like Latourette,(25) can contribute much to our understanding of the present shape of things.

Again Ralph Winter must be referred to as one who revived and popularized the whole subject in missionary circles. His enthusiastic promotion of Latourette's seven-volume set with his own exciting addendum, The Twenty-five Unbelievable Years, has caused many to look at missions history with renewed interest.

It is to be hoped that a careful reassessment of the history of missions will correct Scherer's casual claims: "In the infancy of the church there were no 'missions' in the modern since. ... Historians cannot find a missionary strategy or a plan for Christian expansion in the records of the early church. ... Since the fourth century, mission has been thought of as something quite distinct from the mainstream of the church's life."(26)

Scherer certainly is a competent scholar and he has contributed much to keep missions in Biblical perspective, but he is in danger of relativizing New Testament teaching on missions so that it can be regarded as a temporary arrangement in the history of the church's expansion. Worse than that, the implication comes through that mission agencies, as distinct from churches, were the product of political and other factors when the church was in decline.

Harry Boer handles this period of history in a similar manner though his perspective on it is especially stimulating. He insists that the Holy Spirit has always been at work among Christians to keep alive the fires of missionary ardor even where, in his opinion, it has been out of order organizationally. I cannot resist including this extended but instructive quotation from Pentecost and Mission out of the chapter, "Quench Not the Spirit!"

> "The Protestant Churches have, since their inception, wandered far from the missionary ideal set forth in the New Testament. They have through default permitted to come into being that characteristic phenomenon known as the missionary society. The voice of the Spirit cannot be silenced. His work continues. When the church organization and organism, as a whole, proved deaf to his promptings, as a whole, the Spirit began to work through some part of the Church. So it happened that the refusal of the Church to acknowledge the Great Commission as still binding upon her led 'friends of missions,' 'mission enthusiasts,' people who were 'mission-minded,' to bring into being missionary societies. These societies have done the work that the Church in her totality should have performed. The missionary is, scripturally speaking, an abnormality. But it has been a blessed abnormality. As such, it has been at once evidence of the power of the Spirit and a judgement upon the Church. It has heen the salvation of hundreds of thousands, it has prevented the witnessing Spirit from being wholly quenched, and it has spread the faith and the Church to the ends of the earth. But it has meant that the Church allowed her proper task to fall into the hands of groups of her members. It has meant that the Church permitted the obedience that she should have rendered in her entirely to be rendered by the proxy of a few."(27)

It is hopeful to see that the "disastrous dichotomy" became a "blessed abnormality" when we look at the subject from Boer's historical standpoint. However, any historical interpretation of missions history that maintains that missions, because they are products of history, are merely accidents of history has a blind side. We can begin from the New Testament assumption that no fixed form is prescribed for either church or mission. But it seems consistent to maintain that missions, like the church, must have had some form. It was visible and identifiable and on the move. I want to believe that this dimension of participation in the apostolate was one of the most strikingly observable characteristics of the apostolic church as it was thrust out in obedience to the mandates of the risen Lord.

The very diversity of mission organizations throughout history is a reminder that, like the church, it can appear in different shapes in order to express its nature and fulfil its function. If we just see missions as products of history without realizing that they conform to a Biblical principle and ideally are the result of the Spirit's working, we might be tempted to say they have outlived their usefulness in our time and we will scrap them and busy ourselves with other good things. On the other hand, we must be aware that, in a very real sense, they are products of history and share in its relativity. Therefore, they can be changed, dismantled and redesigned, but there must be some functional substitute that gives form to or, in a sense, incarnates the mission of the church. This is "the identity crisis" for mission and accordingly for the church.

V. GUIDELINES FOR CONTINUITY AND CHANGE IN ORGANIZING FOR MISSION

The stated objective of this conference is to discover guidelines that will help us to cope in a constructive way with the tensions which we are discussing.

My list is offered as part of the process of discovering more comprehensive guidelines. Mine are based upon my own general understanding of church and mission in the light of things specifically considered in this paper. I have tried to divide them up into four sides of the missionary sending relationship. These are not instructions for those in any one side of the relationship, but rather as pointers toward the kind of perspective needed by all of us not only in coping with, but thinking constructively about, the total shape of these relationships.

1. Guidelines on the Place of the Mission in the Sending Relationship

a. Though we cannot claim that there is a specific Biblican delineation of the organizational form of mission, the apostolic mission can best be understood as standing in some such relation to New Testament churches.

b. The New Testament certainly indicates in detail what is to be comprehended in the total ministry of the church. That mission was an aspect of the total ministry is certain. It seems logical to take the basic elements of this New Testament pattern as a general norm for church-mission relationships throughout history.

c. The fact that there was an institutional form, though it varied even within the New Testament, but was adapted to the cultural, social, and economic situation of that day, is another patterning factor that has scriptural sanction.

d. The mission must operate in the knowledge that it is dependent upon and subordinate to the church which is the sending authority under Christ's Lordship.

e. Mission societies must look for ways to relate to churches at every organizational level so as to accept the responsibility delegated to them in terms of resources--spiritual, personal and material--which churches invest through them in mission.

f. The program and strategy of every kind of mission agency should look to the planting, strengthening and serving of churches which the Lord will bring into being in the situation which is the object of missionary outreach.

g. It is a part of the sending mission's service to stimulate and be available to help the new churches in their own missionary sending.

h. In issues of organizational alignment, the mission should see itself as standing between the sending churches and the receiving churches, being responsible to the one and respecting the integrity of the other.

i. Missions, even in a denominational structure, should recognize that churches are not a means to a missionary end, but that they are only a part of the total comprehensive ministry of the church. The one is essential to the other.

j. The mission must see the value of a vital disciplined church experience as an essential qualification for missionary personnel. Practical structured plans for involving churches in recruiting, evaluating and training are essential.

2. Guidelines on the Place of the Church in the Sending Relationship

a. Every church should have a missionary dimension to its total ministry. This should be something in which every believer has a share. Efforts in evangelism are not to be seen as fulfilling missionary obligation.

b. A church is responsible to delegate management of its missionary outreach to soundly evangelical and methodologically efficient mission agencies. Churches should not attempt to control in areas where they have delegated authority.

c. The church should assume responsibilities for a continuing supply of people to serve in mission and work at providing support for them in adequate and regular ways.

d. The sending church should be aware of the special relationship that is established for it through the sending agency. This new church, as the objective of mission, should be the object of prayerful, loving concern and support.

e. Leadership within the church is most effective in promoting missions and developing a balanced program adapted to local conditions. Missions have resources for this available, but coordination and selection must be made at the congregational level.

f. Supporting churches should have the sort of education in mission that will enable them to see that church growth is the end and objective of mission.

g. Since the receiving situation and overseas relationships are so crucial in mission work, churches must place their confidence in mission leadership and let them make decisions relating to these matters.

3. Guidelines on the Place of the School in the Sending Relationship

a. A school with special concern for missionary training should cultivate in students an understanding of and a respect for the church.

b. Church experience, in terms of orderly participating both in membership and in service opportunities, can be provided for in relation to school programs.

c. The school stands in the sort of special relationship to both church and mission to serve in creating understanding and better communication between them.

d. In many ways the school has a greater opportunity for a more profound influence at a crucial life period than the church. The school should look to both church and mission for assistance and cooperation in this strategic ministry and it should be provided.

e. Missionary courses have too often only been provided for those already committed to missionary vocation. All programs of training for Christian vocation should include an emphasis on mission in the total ministry of the church.

f. Ideally home and overseas workers should be trained together, especially in the basic phases of theological education. This makes for wholeness in ministry.

g. Along with theology the social sciences can be brought to the service of church and mission, especially in those matters of organizational form where cultural factors are crucial.

4. <u>Guidelines on the Place of the Missionary in the Sending Relationship</u>

a. The missionary is very much the "man in the middle" in all of this. He must be a sensitive person and well grounded in doctrines relating to both church and mission.

b. As a Christian believer, he should have a primary relationship to a congregation with which he maintains fellowship wherever he is located. He should establish just this kind of relationship with a congregation where he lives overseas. He should be in the church, first as a believer in relation to others who are with him in Christ, then as a missionary colleague seeking to serve the receiving church.

c. Since in most cases missionaries will probably continue to maintain those relationships and connections that make him a "foreign" missionary, he is most directly amenable to the mission and through it to the church authority in the overseas situation.

d. The missionary is the key person whose love and spirit will hold churches and missions together when organization and administrative structures may tend to keep them at a distance one from the other.

VI. SOME SUGGESTIONS FOR CHANGE IN CHURCH-MISSION RELATIONSHIPS

I conclude with some suggestions for change in church-mission relationships. Since preparation of the first draft of this paper, Dr. McGavran's thunderous and searching challenge has been issued to us. As he warns, we can become so absorbed with change and restructuring that we neglect our urgent, primary task.

Additional cause for alert caution comes from the fact that, in the ecumenical enterprise, industrious and ingenious champions of changes similar to those I suggest have certainly not seen the work of the saving world mission expanded or accelerated.

Nonetheless, there are some areas in which, in my judgment, even the willingness to attempt to work for change and renewal in mission will have a salutary effect. Here then are some directions for possible change. I will limit myself to the mission side, though implications for church and school should come through as well.

I want to second the Winter motion for extending and broadening mission structures horizontally. I do not mean multiplication of them. As a matter of fact, the present concern with merger, consolidation and elimination of competition and duplication is all to the good.

What I want to encourage is an increase of interdenominational and intercongregational cooperative participation in mission. It appears that there is inevitably limitation on continuous and healthy growth of mission within denominational structures. The need is for more inclusive voluntary involvement even though, from the denominational standpoint, it is limited to selective utilization of the mission section of an organization rather than a joining of the denomination itself.

A corollary to the breaking over the boundaries of the vertical structure of denominational missions should be the flexible accommodation of nondenominational societies so that they can cut across and maintain orderly and approved relationships with churches even when they have denominational affiliation.

Productive change, in my view, should involve a shift toward centralized support arrangements and away from personalized faith-mission type support. Denominational patterns of financing mission seem more effective than some others which become so free and individualistic as to be irresponsible. If the element of voluntarism can be cultivated and retained within the more uniform structures, vital horizontalization will be created. A crucial factor in this will continue to be the provision of the closest kind of relationship between local churches and missionaries.

Not only do we need to move even farther in the direction of inter-, intra-, and transdenominational relationships, but this must be broadened to include the internationalization for which many are now calling. This will not be primarily an overseas accommodation. It must involve an acceptance of change and venturesome readjustment here at the sending end. In fact, international mission must be truly reciprocal, not just an acceptance of overseas nationals into our structures.

One effect of internationalization for which we will have to be prepared is the necessary anonymity of sending agencies and the sharing of denominational distinctives within the broader, larger structures for mission. This will also involve a loss of distinct national identity with its attached loyalties. At this point the traditional "foreign" element in missions can be quietly discarded.

Some mission societies have nurtured the development of national missionary agencies for the receiving churches. This may be the hope for the future rather than what I have in mind. However, it is to be hoped that we will not see in the Third World a duplication of our own wasteful and inefficient diversification. We may argue that we can afford the luxury of this pluralization. The new world and next stage of mission cannot. It might have been ideal if, through our combined efforts, we could have seen the establishment of one church fellowship with one mission agency in receiving situations. We are now well past such a possibility. However, since mission in overseas churches seems only to be at its beginning (I say this to our shame!), let us do all we can to encourage true unity in mission. We may see the geographical center of the sending relocated. We may revise and vitalize our self-support theories; but we can see, if we work at it with humility and unselfishness, a genuine oneness in world mission. This is a New Testament ecumenism.

Another change that can go along with internationalization, but which is needed with or without it, is a rethinking of the missionary vocation. Much more is involved than a hasty and thus superficial revision or deletion in the nomenclature.

A basic argument in this paper is that "mission" and "missionary" have come to be applied too broadly and undiscerningly. This has resulted not only in a loss of primary usefulness, but has caused confusion.

I believe we need to keep all of the classic vocabulary, except "foreign." We must use it with precision, faithful to the source but relevant to the contemporary task.

I think we need to distinguish "the missionary" as one called and committed directly to evangelization with church multiplication and growth as its defined objective. This role and function should be distinguished from that of those who serve the mission in vital supportive ways or those who serve the established receiving church more directly in evangelistic, prophetic, pastoral or didactic aspects of its ministry. Let us revive the idea of "the apostle" through whom the church fulfills its call to involvement in the apostolate. Is this not consistent with Romans I where a general "apostleship" is fulfilled through identification with a designated "apostle"?

Could there not be a "specific task ordination" for this very purpose? This is a church-mission issue, but it needs to be grappled with on the mission side. This may mean that service agency people, or those in certain mission "communities," as we now call them, would not be classified as "missionaries." This is not so bad. "Servant" and its cognates have a longer and nobler history than "apostle" and "apostolic."

This sort of reconception of the missionary role can prepare for the kind of bifurcation of the sending missionary force that would make provision for some to serve in appropriate aspects of ministry in and under the receiving church. The "missionary" division could, along with other missionaries called out of the national churches, reach on out toward the billions in the "regions beyond." This could follow a formula used for higher theological purposes. Church and mission could each have its own farm "without change, mixture or confusion."

* * * * *

APPENDIX

I. AN ENUMERATION OF THE TENSIONS (see pages 126 and 127)

1. Organizational Alignments

How do churches and missions get connected in supportive and cooperative relationships? In the case of the vertical denominational-type structures, there is theoretically a built-in coordinating function to tie the mission board and its activities into the program of the local churches. It becomes apparent immediately that mission agencies of the horizontal type have no such structurally provided arrangements to align them with congregations and individuals from whom support is obtained. This is one of the really remarkable things about those missions with no organizationally defined constituency. They do seem to have an unfailing supply of revenue "by faith alone!"

It becomes apparent then that the relationships established in these more decidedly voluntaristic associations are personal rather than institutional. It is generally the individual missionary who initially establishes and continues to maintain support relationships with individuals and churches. He, or she, is the crucial link in horizontal mission relationships. It has frequently been recognized that even within denominational structures "personalized" giving has a strong appeal. The missionary interests and loyalties of pastors is another very important factor in introducing missions to churches and building bridges of fraternal relationships. Mission board promotion will for the most part follow upon contacts made on the more personal basis.

So the very variety of forms of organizational relationship that can be established between different type mission boards and the various levels of church organization is a potential for tension. This is made the more complex by the fact that in both vertical and horizontal structures connections are very much dependent upon individuals. Here, again, is a point for tension, not the least of which is the person who may come to be sensitive to being used like this, or one who takes advantage in improper ways of the influence he comes to have. So we must ask, "Are there ways to improve the kinds of necessary organizational alignments that exist between churches and missions?"

2. Administrative Participation

There is tacit acknowledgement of the priority of church over mission in the fact that we are not usually asking how can missionaries get involved in the government of the church. However, it does seem legitimate to ask how churches can participate inthe administration of mission agencies for which they provide support. It will be interesting to share in group discussion, ways in which those who invest in our mission boards earn the right to vote in certain elections and send delegates to conferences in which mission business is transacted. However, when the multiplicity of gifts from so many different sources is taken into consideration, it becomes clear that no simple pattern of enfranchisement on the basis of finances is feasible. This kind of representation is provided in a denominational structure, but it is evident that actual participation in governing affairs is limited to the few and there is little direct participation on the part of individual members and congregations which provide missionary support. Ways must be found to satisfy those supporters who are asking about the relationship of support to administration in the missionary enterprise. Another possible source of tension of this sort is the desire on the part of individual missionaries in both vertical and horizontal structures to participate in decision making. We have a reflex of this problem overseas, but we have not really solved it here at home.

3. Personnel Problems (Note the important place of the school here)

We may very well ask in the light of the issues being discussed if there is any vocation that has the built-in potential for stress that the missionary calling has. The missionary stands between the sending and receiving church with responsibility to both, but without a direct one-sided relationship to either. Overseas under any system, there is almost invariably a kind of duality of control under which a missionary serves. Here at the sending end he is between supporting churches (how many?!) and the mission board. On both sides are those to whom the missionary feels himself to be under authority. Where one congregation provides full or majority support the situation is somewhat clearer, but does that church exercise its authority through the mission or in other ways?

In looking at the several areas, all with a potential for tension, in which there are personnel problems between churches and missions, it soon becomes apparent that schools also enter in here to complicate things even more. Again, within the denominational structure, schools are expected to fulfil their function for and along with the mission board. While there is somewhat more potential for control and limitation, the basic problems and tensions are not so different from those of independent churches, interdenominational missions and self-governing schools. Of the six basic personnel concerns, the school is very directly involved in the first three.

a. Recruitment: Who has primary responsibility in enlisting people for the missionary enterprise? We must certainly say that the Holy Spirit is the one to do this. But then we must ask which is going to be his primary instrument for doing this--church, mission, or school? Again, our discussions here will yield some valuable information. It does seem certain that while all three are needed, the local church, in its formative influence on family and children, has the first word to speak. Mission board recruiting is essentially dependent on access through both church and school. Probably final decisions for commitment to missionary vocation is going to be made in the course of college experience. This makes the missionary influence of campus ministries so very important. How can these kinds of relationships be created, strengthened and coordinated in order that there may be a continuing supply of people available for service in the world mission?

b. Training: As George Linhart made clear to the members of the IFMA Board Retreat this spring, the local congregation is the best training ground to develop skills so crucial to the ministry of the missionary.[4] There is a very real danger that on a campus where he is engaging in theological study, a candidate may suffer a cooling off of evangelistic fervor or develop the kind of sophistication over doctrine that makes truth seem theoretical and conceptual rather than personal. One urgent aspect of training for world mission responsibility concerns the preparation of pastors so that they will see the equality of missionary responsibility and obligation on all ministers, churches, and Christians regardless of the particular kind of calling within which they fulfil it. Education in mission must not be reserved entirely for those that are to be involved in mission professionally. This is too often true both in Bible College and Seminary. Training must be designed to involve the whole church in world mission. Obviously, there are many points of tension in relation to missionary training. Such a question as the responsibility for support in the training period becomes an increasingly urgent one with the financial pressures of our day. Cooperative training programs for overseas service could be economically, intellectually and spiritually beneficial, but openness and even venturesomeness is needed for this, and that kind of need can cause tension.

3. Personnel Problems (continued)

c. Evaluation: This is an area, again, where sensitivity, seriousness and mutual concern on the part of churches and schools toward mission boards is very much needed. How can we get more adequate and honest measures of the character and abilities of those who apply for missionary service? This is another area in which missions people are doing much to share information and services. This is surely something to investigate and increase. Perhaps the potential of experience in the local church has not been fully appreciated or utilized by mission boards. If missionaries have been careless about essential aspects of the life and affairs of a church congregation, it may be because of insufficient or defective experience at home. No campus experience is a substitute for living and service in close fellowship to a committed community of God's people.

d. Service and Assignment: At this point there is inevitably an almost complete transfer of authority to the mission board which must then relate, on the other side, to the receiving church. However, the sending church may get involved in these matters in such a way as to induce tension. A North American church may seek to influence decisions about cooperation or in relation to standards of behaviour. While it is proper for a church supporting its missionaries with money and prayers to have a concern in these matters, there is great danger of an improper attempt to bring influence to bear in matters that are not easily understood at such great distance. The missionary family and education of missionary children is another issue that can be a cause of tension. We may discover in our conversation about these matters special instances of tension and ways to deal with them.

e. Furlough: This is surely a point of three-sided tension. The missionary has his plans and personal obligations. The supporting church wants to see him and have him around. The mission board sees the "live missionary" as the most valuable public relations instrument. Again this same tension is present in the denominational structures. Of course the school figures in here also. In some cases they are anxious for the right kind of missionary to come at specified times for special appearances. That can complicate schedules. Another academic aspect of things is the increasing need for furlough study which drastically affects deputation. What can we say to these kinds of tension? How about Dennis Clark's proposal of annual vacation rather than regular furlough?(5)

f. Retiral: Who is tense over retiral? It may be the missionary himself who has most apprehension about it, but undoubtedly both churches and missions share a concern that those who have given a life of service to missions, and thereby forfeited ordinary opportunities to provide for personal security, may be properly cared for when they need to retire.

4. Finances:

In some ways this seems to be the primary point of tension in missions. This is often so at home, and gets exported to the field in a somewhat different form. Communication is suggested as another area of tension between church and mission, but it can also be mentioned under finances, because free flow of information about use of money is very important to harmonious and stable relationships. Is it possible that in our concern as missions to trust God and have faith that we have seemed to be piously unrealistic and at the same time have not shared facts that responsible and intelligent donors want? Churches, both independent and denominational, are wanting to know about expenditures for administrative costs and overhead, especially promotion. Is there tension because we are not open enough in these matters? Another sore point with laymen in our churches who pay the bills, concerns the alarming proliferation of organizations, expensive duplication of services, costly surveys and conferences, like this one, competitive programs that introduce confusion and denigrate worthy and respected organizations. There are multiplying tensions that could be avoided by honesty, economy, investigation and sensitivity. We are learning much in missions these days about management principles; perhaps the financial area is one that will directly reflect the benefits of this kind of efficiency.

5. Communication:

In many ways this is the best tool for reducing tension between churches and missions. So much of the tension is due to misunderstanding or lack of information. However, the communication process itself has to have real integrity. How much of the sad side of missions when it is critically observed is the result of an eagerness over promotional communication. The missionary knows that his success in selling himself to his supporters depends on his deputation presentation. He is sure that he knows what they want to hear and what will really "grab" them in terms of generating missionary interest. So he proceeds to use the communication techniques to get his message across. One danger is that there will be a complete caricature of the missionary role which may make him a hero to the friends in the home church but at the same time may result in his rejection by sensitive well informed young people. This same kind of missionary promotion when it is tied up to support appeals and still leaves missionary standards here at home at the subsistence level, is creating a bad image and having a reverse effect. What can be done with the missionary communications gap? How can churches be informed as to real missionary objectives and the strategy for attaining them? How can we magnify the missionary function in fully honest and realistic ways?

NOTES

1. Wieser, Thomas, Ed.; Planning for Mission, W. C. C., New York, 1966, p. 134.

2. Davies, W. D.: Christian Origins and Judaism, Westminster, Philadelphia, 1962; pp. 208 and 217.

3. Neill, Stephen; Creative Tensions, Edinburgh House Press, London, 1959.

4. Linhart, George; "Missions and Sending Churches--A Pastor's Viewpoint"; IFMA Board Retreat Paper, 1971.

5. Clark, Dennis; The Third World and Mission; Ward, Waco, Texas; 1971, p. 62.

6. One World, One Task; Evangelical Alliance, London; 1971; p.162. (Appendix II, "The Frankfurt Declaration.")

7. Neill, Stephen; The Unfinished Task; Lutterworth; London; 1957; p. 158.

8. Newbigin, J. L.; The Household of God; Friendship, N.Y.; 1954; p. 148.
   Scherer, James; Missionary, Go Home; Prentice Hall, Englewood Cliffs, New Jersey; 1964, p. 41.

9. Larson, Alfred; "Church-Mission Relationship - A Fused Partnership"; IFMA Board Retreat Paper; 1971.

10. Viz. Beyerhaus, P. and Lefever, H.; The Responsible Church and the Foreign Mission; Eerdmans; Grand Rapids; 1964; p. 9.

11. Winter, Ralph D.; "The Anatomy of the Christian Mission"; EMQ; Vol. 5, No. 2, 1964.

12. Winter; "Churches Instead of Missions"; CGB; Vol. III, No. 6, July 1971.

13. Warren, Max; "Why Missionary Societies and Not Missionary Churches?" from History's Lessons for Tomorrow's Missions; W.S.C.F.; Geneva, 1960.

14. Winter, Ralph D.; Beaver, R. Pierce; The Warp and the Woof, William Carey Library; South Pasadena, California; 1971, p. 47, 48. (Reprint of original paper).

15. Op. cit. p. 36 (Reprint of "The New Missions and the Mission of the Church")

16. Lindsell, H.; Ed.; The Churches' World-wide Mission; Word; 1965; pp. 220, 230.

17. Allen, Roland; The Spontaneous Expansion of the Church; World Dominion; London; 1960; p. 96.

18. Thompson, Allen J.; "Mission-Church Structures: A Key to Evangelism," IFMA Board Retreat Paper; 1971.

19. Crossroads in Mission; William Carey Library; South Pasadena, California; 1971. p. xv.

20. Op. cit. Weiser et al. p. 38.
Haekendijk, J. C. The Church Inside Out, Westminster; Philadelphia, 1964. pp. 13-85.

21. Taylor, John V. "Preparing the Ordinand for Mission" I R M, Vol. LVI; No. 222; pp. 145 ff.

22. Beaver, R. Pierce; The Missionary Between the Times; Doubleday; N. Y.; 1969, pp. 1-23.

23. Neill, op. cit.; Pg. 82.

24. Ibid. pg. 92.

25. Anderson, Gerald; Ed.; The Theology of the Christian Mission; Abingdon; Nashville; 1961; pp. 99, 112.

26. Scherer; op. cit. pp 41, 46.

27. Boer, Harry; Pentecost and Mission; Eerdmans; Grand Rapids; 1961; p. 212.

MISSION/CHURCH RELATIONS OVERSEAS

PART I: IN PRINCIPLE

by Louis L. King

for presentation at GL 71

I. INTRODUCTION

The current and most crucial debate among evangelicals concerns mission-church relationship. Both evangelical missions and the overseas churches with which they are associated exhibit the deepest interest in this widely considered subject. Almost everyone rates the relationship pattern of the past as obsolete and unsatisfactory. The young churches very definitely want a new working relationship and, with us, are making earnest efforts to discover what form it should take.

When we turn to the New Testament for examples or precedents to guide us, however, we are somewhat at a loss. For although the New Testament talks of missionaries, there is no information about a missionary society or a board of missions, and certainly there is no indication that missionaries continued as helpers to the new churches for uncounted years. Also, there were no mission-established institutions to be taken over by the young churches or maintained by foreign personnel or funds. The New Testament, then, offers no direct example or precept analogous to today's situation in mission-church relationship.

Foreign mission societies and boards have developed historically as a functional and pragmatic way of carrying out the Great Commission. They are neither biblical nor unbiblical. Only indirectly are they rooted in the New Testament. We can hope, therefore, for only indirect guidance from the New Testament concerning them.

II. THE CHURCH[1]

The New Testament is concerned wholly with the Church -- not with the organizational structure of the Church but with its nature and function. Once we ascertain what the nature and the function are, then the relationship between the foreign missionary society and the younger church can be so arranged that the church truly exists according to the New Testament presentation. And this, I hold, is where to begin our search for a proper mission-church relationship.

What, then, does the New Testament disclose concerning the Church -- The Church Universal or the local church which is but a microcosm of the whole? Most noticeable by its absence is any concept of the Church as a kind of tinker-toy to be put together and held together by missionaries. Also missing is the Church's acquiring and possessing the blessings of education, industry, civil liberty, and social order as essential to her being. Neither do we find the Church commissioned to carry out every good thing that needs doing in education, medicine, economics, and the social and political structures. As worthwhile as these are -- and even though missions may have specialized in them -- they are not of the nature and function of the Church.

A. THE CHURCH -- THE BODY OF CHRIST.

The New Testament presents the Church as the "body" of Christ (Eph. 1:22,23). The Church is composed of all regenerate believers in Christ. It is a living organism and is infused with life from its head (Eph. 1:22,23; Col. 1:18). All of the Church's life and nourishment and direction flows from the Head to the members. The Church (His body) is as full of resources for its needs, and ability for its activities, and guidance for its decisions, as is its very Head. He Himself provides for the Church's total needs from His limitless, exhaustless riches (Phil. 4:19).

B. THE GOVERNING HEAD OF THE CHURCH -- CHRIST.

In the New Testament, the voice of the Head is supreme in the decisions of the Church. The Church conforms to His directing and correcting voice in matters of faith, worship, prayer, stewardship, holiness, witness, and mission. As seen in the New Testament, it has no super body over it. Christ alone is its Head. His Word is final. Submitting to His sovereignty, it seeks to do those things which He has commissioned it to do. These are not optional, but essential; not peripheral, but central. For just as no person can repent and believe for another, so no church can successfully assume another church's obligations to biblical life, faith, and mission. Further, these obligations -- towards itself and towards the non-Christian world -- are given to newly started churches. No portion of Scripture suggests an initial period when a new church need not comply or when peculiar economic circumstances automatically cancel out obedience or when its members can delay until their educational and living standards are cared for.

C. THE MISSION OF THE CHURCH -- WORLDWIDE WITNESS.

The New Testament sets the Church in this world for the purpose of carrying the gospel to the ends of the earth (Mark 16:15, Acts 1:8). Altogether apart from financial aid from others, all believers are commissioned to participate actively in carrying the gospel into all the world. To this end the most telling New Testament Scriptures dealing with the obligations of liberal giving (I Cor. 16:1-3 and II Cor. 8 and 9) and pastoral support (Gal. 6:6-10) are written to newly started mission-land churches. Churches are obligated to support the spread of the gospel with men and money. The New Testament presents a church that has the ability to be missionary from its inception. It has been given the full resources of God's gifts and graces for all of its assigned activity. Therefore, the church's attention should be focused on Christ and the non-Christian world outside its doors, or there will be disobedience to Christ, grieving the Holy Spirit, and an atrophy of spiritual faculties.

The New Testament is especially clear about the witnessing role of the Church:

> "The biblical material out of which the church's missionary consciousness, comprehension, and compliance have commonly been drawn is neatly distilled in the words of the Great Commission, found at the end of Matthew's Gospel (28:19,20), with variations in the other Synoptic Gospels (Mark 16:15,16; Luke 24:47,48) and in Acts (1:8). This simple scriptural command -- to go and make disciples of all nations -- has much to commend it as a continuing source of fuel for the Christian mission. It is linked to Jesus himself. It is a clear and concise set of orders."[2]

In Matthew 24:14 the missionary task of the Church is set forth with particular clarity and forcefulness: "And this gospel . . . shall be preached in all the world . . . and then shall the end come." Here the mandate for world evangelization is viewed as the necessary fulfillment of prophetic predictions in the Old Testament as well as God's eschatological purpose for mankind.

The validity of the role of the missionary arises from the gift of apostolate (missionary) (Eph. 4:11). This gift and role is distinct from that of prophet, evangelist, and pastor-teacher (Eph. 4:11); and being one of the gifts of the Holy Spirit to the Church (I Cor. 12:28), it is as permanent an expression of the life and witness of the Church as that of the pastor-teacher. The missionary proclaims the gospel to the unbelieving world (Romans 1:5) and organizes converts into local congregations (Acts 14:23, Titus 1:5). The missionary band is presented as distinct from the local congregation -- being sent forth by them and reporting back to them. They strengthen and exhort the new churches (Acts 14:22 and 15:41) and guide them in correct doctrine and morals (I Cor.). Since the Church is to witness "to every creature" "to the uttermost part of the earth," the missionary is necessary to the end of the age.

Missionary outreach then is presented as valid, normative, and essential for the New Testament kind of church. On this account, every church should play its rightful part in the evangelization of its own country and participate in worldwide missionary outreach. And this activity of the Church is such that it calls forth a concentration of attention. That is what the Book of Acts is all about. Indeed, a loss of that attention on "the regions beyond" or a reduction of the task of God's people to mere church-to-church interchange must be rated as something less than the scriptural goal for the Church. So long as the work remains uncompleted, the Lord's command to publish the gospel to every creature (Mark 16:15) unto all nations (Matt. 24:14) to the uttermost part of the earth (Acts 1:8) should have priority attention (Mark 13:10) by every church -- older and younger alike. Indeed it is a perennial task. We should, therefore, seek that mission-and-church relationship pattern that will most certainly create an atmosphere for church growth, initiative, and self-reliance in the specific tasks of evangelism and missions by both.

III. FORMS OF MISSION-CHURCH RELATIONSHIP

Since the start of the modern missionary era, varied forms of mission-church relationship have been practiced, ostensibly to make it possible for both the sending church and the receiving church to be all that the New Testament intended each of them to be. Generally eight forms are indicated, as follows:

Mission dominance, or paternalism
No mission, only the church
Modified mission dominance
Dichotomy, cooperation of autonomous equals
Modified dichotomy
Partial or functional integration
Full integration or fusion
Partnership of equality and mutuality

Except for mission service agencies, all mission-church relations are comprehended in this list. For most 20th century evangelicals, however, partial or full integration and regular or modified dichotomy have dominated men's attention. It is for this reason I shall limit this discussion to these considerations.

A. FUSION.

Presently the organizational structure gaining favor for accomplishing the New Testament ideal for the church is one in which the mission is required to lose its identity by merging itself into the church's organization. We want, therefore, to examine some of the reasons argued in favor of amalgamating mission with church. Of necessity the list will be suggestive, not exhaustive. Each point, we know, has many ramifications that would need to be more thoroughly explored; but direction rather than a detailed road map is intended. Along the way we shall briefly examine those reasons either in relation to their scriptural undergirding or practical outworking in experience to learn whether or not fusion helps or hinders achieving a New Testament kind of church.

Here are some of the reasons offered in favor of fusion:

1. Oneness of the Church.

The merging of the mission into the church is considered essential in order to achieve the "oneness" of the Church. This emphasis came alive at the 1928 Jerusalem Conference. Tambaram 1938 was the conference where for the first time the younger churches were unconditionally recognized as equal with the older churches. Whitby 1947 went further and disregarded the difference between older and younger churches and called all churches everywhere to "expectant and worldwide evangelism in the spirit of partnership in obedience."[3] Since then the swing toward unification of mission and church has been strongly marked. At this point almost all ecumenically oriented missions and churches have been unified.

The strongest impetus in all this has been the enormous attention given to being "one" as set forth in John 17:21 and Ephesians 4:1-6. Arguing from these two passages, it is asserted that organizational relatedness is essential to the nature of the Church; therefore, the mission must not maintain a separate or distinct identity from the structured church. Since the Church is indivisible, the church and the mission must be joined. The mission must be so integrated that the mission's property, money, and personnel become the responsibility of the church. Anything less than this misses the biblical requirement. The younger churches have adopted the "oneness" concept with alacrity and lay it before mission leaders with forcefulness.

Another argument closely allied with the "oneness" doctrine maintains "that the principle of dichotomy [separate administration of mission and church] is not sound biblically . . . Biblically, it cannot be sustained. Dichotomy is not known in the Bible. It does not fit into the body structure of the church."[4] "Equality in partnership seems the only logical deduction from the Bible."[5]

The discerning student of the Word knows that these arguments are not based entirely on what the Bible itself teaches but upon what it is thought to teach. The proponents for the integration of church and mission have "eisegeted" (read into) rather than "exegeted" (read out of) the Scriptures. There is indeed teaching on the Church as "one" and as the "body," but not in the sense of organizational relatedness. They have taken these grand concepts of the Church and gone outside Scriptures to make some logical deductions. The validity of the position taken must be understood in this light. It is an assumed concept of the church.

The only certain position to take is that no specific structure or pattern of church organization or of mission-church relationship is prescribed in the New Testament. The Bible gives only ideals of relationships. Particularly the New Testament concerns itself with the life of the "body," the Church, and the relationship of its members to their Head and to one another as persons. If we are to "deduce" anything from the New Testament, it is that the "body" structure should be such that the life-giving channels from the Head are unrestricted and that nothing is permitted to paralyze the obedient response of members to their Head. When full response is inhibited, the "body" is not healthy. The nature of mission-church relations then should be such that best allows the church as Church to express and exercise maturely its life in Christ. The type of structure for relationship should be based on a functional relatedness to this principle rather than on a noncontextual interpretation that "oneness" and "body" necessitates organizational relatedness.

2. The Church IS Mission.

The "Church IS Mission" idea is also used to support the assertion that church and mission must be united. In this context, ecumenists and many evangelicals are saying: the church should be central in all missionary endeavor; missionaries must be a part of the church and amenable to the official leadership or else the nature of the Church is damaged; missionary work should be done with and through the existing church; the central administration of the national organization ought to decide and control when and where and how missionaries work. The contemporary view is that a church in a given country, or even in a region of a country, has "homestead rights" and no one may enter except to work under the direction of that church.[6]

But some of us have questions. Does the official leadership by itself constitute the church? Is the central administration of a denomination the church? Are missions legitimate only if carried forward through the structured church? If the answer is affirmative, then what should we say concerning CMS, and OMF, and TEAM, and a host of other missions which are not under any official church administration? Should we disallow them? or put "theology of the church" aside and admit that they are the Church -- the "Church in action" or an "expression of the Church"? In any event, on what scriptural basis has the Church defined as denomination become an adequate definition?

Again, has denominational administration been the best vehicle for achieving a worldwide witness of the gospel? Has the structured church leadership demonstrated necessary sympathy for missions, and do they have a record of achieving mobility?

The answer of western church history is not favorable. It shows that official leadership of the church can be out of sympathy with the missionary enterprise. Look at the disapproval and downright opposition that Justinian Welz[7] and William Carey and others since them received from church officers. Examine the various Reformation Churches in Europe and the Church of England also. Many of them do not conduct foreign missionary work from within the framework of the church organization. It is structurally and officially absent. They have not knit missionary work with the rest of the church's program. It is only the independent association of people within these churches that sustains missions through mission societies. Their money is not raised centrally. These voluntary agencies are not in any way controlled by the official administrative machinery of the church.[8]

It is primarily in North America that denominations have foreign missions within their organizational structure. But these came into being only after many mission societies had been established. With the passage of time, though, denominations have accumulated so many institutional and self-serving interests that missionary work does not receive the good will and concentration it deserves. Viewed historically and currently, missions has not received adequate, sympathetic, and financial consideration within the structure of the church: church governments greet this matter with great reluctance.[9]

With this knowledge, does it not seem strange to suppose that the younger churches will give more favorable attention to missions than European and North American denominations? Are the mission-land churches less concerned with their ecclesiastical and social self than the western churches? Is their specific missionary intent such that they are more willing or ready or eager for world evangelization? Are they so proclamation-centered that they do not neglect the non-Christian frontier? Or are they institution-minded, given to improving their resources, trying to get their membership to rise in the social structure, devoting themselves to the maintenance of church for nourishing their members spiritually? May not the national church's central organ of control be in the same danger of debunking missions as the Reformation Church -- although it may be for other reasons, such as finances? And have they not required that missionaries and an increasingly larger proportion of our resources be devoted to work among Christian people, for Christian people, and in Christian institutions? Does not a large proportion of our finances to the church simply become inter-church aid to support its organizational and institutional life without any missionary purpose? Do not the younger churches taking the aid, more often than not sink into the unexciting business of routine without growth or without evangelistic or missionary outreach? In fusion of church and mission, can our determination to be missionary be preserved and nutured and structured? In the fusion structure, are missionaries so organized that they can resist the inveterate tendency of the church to self-centeredness? If they do resist the younger church, what will happen?

Already, where churches and missions have been joined, the younger churches' pathological over-anxiety about their prerogatives in controlling the missions indicates what we can expect.

Here is Dr. Herbert C. Jackson's indictment of the younger churches. It was given in his inaugural address as Adjunct Professor on the Senior Faculty of Union Theological Seminary in New York City:

> "Quite unintentionally a tyranny has arisen which stifles apostolate and militates very greatly against any real fulfillment of the Great Commission and against the freedom of the Holy Spirit to move where He will . . . This has produced a retraction in the missionary witness that is worse than tragic, and at a time when there are still vast areas that have not heard the gospel and when the 'population explosion,' the resurgence of non-Christian religions and numerous

sociological factors are causing a steady decline in the ratio of Christians to non-Christians in the world . . . This has also provided us with the situation that has given rise to the appalling frustration that exists today among missionaries."[10]

By way of contrast, church history reveals it was the mission societies, standing independent of the churches and branded as "nontheological factors" by opposing church administrators, that pioneered with consumate courage and aggressiveness the worldwide advance of the gospel. The point is that mission administration separate from the church's control is valid and very often necessary for missionary endeavor.

3. A "Proper" Church.

Some younger church leaders have stated that the mission must lose its identity by integrating with them in order for them to be a "proper" church. Being "proper" also includes recognition and contact with established denominations, highly trained leadership, more respectable church buildings, wearing the clerical collar (since this is "proper" among the historic denominations), operating educational and medical institutions as appurtenances of respectability and influence, and belonging to a worldwide organization.

The mission joined to the church is viewed not only the "proper" structure but the logical agency through which these benefits can be achieved. The major issue here is not their desire to be "proper" but the possible exploitation of the mission. This occurs when the mission's resources are expended in supporting the church's ministry, establishing central offices, providing pension funds, and raising the salaries of officials -- when the mission is not permitted to focus on the world but on the church. The United Presbyterian Church has spoken thus on this issue:

> "It needs to be reasserted continually, without pomposity or irritation, that the Commission is more than a servicing agency for indigenous churches. It is an instrumental expression of the United Presbyterian Church's fulfillment of its mission to the world, and to assume that the ecumenical era demands a total subordination in program and the use of personnel to the individual determination of indigenous churches would be a restrictive error."[11]

To the exploitation of the mission we add the calamity wrought by the economic and political power that the fusion of church and mission affords. Concerning this, a recent correspondent wrote:

> "Where fusion of church and mission has taken the form of an effort to fuse the mission structures with the structures of an autonomous church, the experience has been disastrous . . . In the case of the Disciples' Church in Madhya Pradesh, India, the structural fusion of the church and mission saddled a small and poverty stricken church with a whole series of institutional structures for education and medical ministry which represents a tremendous reservoir of economic and political power. Struggle over these sources of security and power has very nearly wrecked the church."[12]

Examples abound of spiritual apathy, wrong relationships, quarrelsomeness over finances, litigations over property, distrust of church leaders, electioneering for office, and keeping missionaries home on account of the power and benefits accruing to the church bureaucracy through fusion. Making the mission's structure and strategy fit what is prescribed in the minds of Africans and Asians to make them "proper" certainly has helped neither the church nor the mission to accomplish their God-appointed roles more successfully.

The idea is scripturally inadequate. The "proper" church sends missionaries. Converts are won, new churches formed, which in turn evangelize and send until the whole world has heard. Churches were never meant to be ends in themselves but means for enlarging and extending the spread of the gospel. Nor do young churches exhaust their responsibility in local evangelism. They, too, are to send. This activity is natural to their essential nature and is required for their maturity.

4. Financial Assistance a "Right."

Since the fusion of mission with church gives the younger church equality with the older church, it is alleged that financial assistance is a "right." This concept comes to the fore because of "the new patterns observed in neighboring ecumenical churches, the service rendered by Inter-Church Aid and Refugee Service, the example of the World Health Organization and the operations of the United Nations. In all these relationships the poorer groups may pay a small contribution or none at all, but receive great benefits.

They find that this does not impair the sense of equality, involve sacrifice of proper pride or the sense of dignity and independence. They believe the international team of helpers or the financial assistance is received as a present from themselves to themselves since they also are members of that international body through which the gift came.[13] As applied to the church, it is stated: "Financial resources in one part of the church can be used in another part . . . the issue is never whether a church has a right to spend that money."[14] "Any gift that a church has belongs to the whole body of Christ."[15]

Our response to such specious reasoning is that such a "right" is not right. Indeed, much of the failure in maintaining successful fellowship between missionaries and national Christians comes from financial relations. Far down below almost every other problem of mission-church relationship the fundamental thing is money. It is this dependence upon foreign money that creates an abnormal and truly dangerous situation for the church. Therefore, if and when aid is given, it should be recognized by both parties as exceptional and not unattended with danger to (1) the faith and (2) the activity of Christians and (3) their relations with the missionaries.

Full maturity in finances and propagation and government is a necessary Christian virtue, and has proved to be essential to church growth. In Korea, Burma, the South Pacific, and Uganda where there has been dramatic church growth, less foreign money has been spent in proportion to membership than in other mission fields of the world. There are sufficient church growth studies to show that when a church can take care of itself financially it is more relevant to its world, more evangelistic and missionary. The practice of biblical stewardship helps make this possible and therefore should be given priority and be everywhere applicable. Indeed, the Scriptures point out that liberal giving or the lack of it is an indication of one's spirituality (II Cor. 8 and 9).

By promoting a structure of relationship which assumes that a Christian community, by "right," can continually receive and yet not give or give so little as to not really matter, we are cutting a main artery which leads to the very "heart" of the church.

Dr. John R. Crawford, Professor at the School of Theology of Congo's Free University, recently concluded a research on the most important causes of money problems in the struggling Congo churches. He lists these three[16] at the top of some 29 given causes:

1. Christians don't take giving seriously enough.
2. Bad or doubtful handling of church funds.
3. Christians expect help from the outside.

What an open but tragic witness that their heart is not in the Lord's work! (Matt. 6:21). And doubly tragic if the continual infusion of finances keeps it that way. J. Merle Davis, in commenting about the national church's economic life, said: "It is self-evident that if a tree is to live it must draw its nourishment through its own roots and leaves."

In addition to creating a spiritual problem, foreign financial aid cripples initiative. Take India as an example. In 1967 India received 10 billion dollars in foreign assistance. The bulk of this was provided as gifts or as loans on concessional terms. It was estimated that one of every five U. S. farms worked to feed India. But the foreign aid did not relieve India of hunger and starvation; in fact, it compounded them, for the availability of American food grains induced the Indian government into extravagant industrial undertakings to the neglect of agriculture. Also, the government sold the foreign aid grain at a subsidized price considerably below the open market price. The result of all this was that Indian farmers withheld grain from delivery or produced only for their own need. The eminent economic consultant, Walter Groseclose, summed it up as follows in his article, "Foreign Aid Fizzle":

> "The fact recognized by many in India, is that as long as U. S. agricultural aid is available, neither the government nor the people have incentive to improve domestic food sources."[17]

Illustrations abound to show that, even as for India, the continuous flow of foreign finances dulls the younger churches' incentive to give to sustain the Lord's work committed to them. It does not train them in giving. Necessity is not laid upon them. They become disobedient to the plain requirements of the Bible. Seldom do they catch the vision of <u>their</u> service to others. They will be strengthened <u>only</u> as they become instruments of Christ in sustaining His great mission through their own money gifts.

Also, the flow of the mission's more abundant financial resources into the young church divorces it from local financial and social realities. The structures the money supports are not related to the actualities of the church's own financial setting. There is little attempt to assess the programs in terms of the church's own obedience in stewardship. Furthermore, being beneficiaries of the system, they do not want to drop the comfortable status quo. They become myopic and think primarily of self-interests. The system enables them to live unrelated to financial actualities. It goes contrary to scriptural instruction regarding stewardship and actually trains them to be dependent.

5. Independence.

Some leaders of evangelical younger churches believe that an amalgamation of mission with church will give them independence. They are saying:

> Western missions continue to reflect, more or less, the colonial administrative pattern;
>
> The church is held in some subsidiary and subordinate relation to an organization outside its country; and
>
> This undermines their integrity and selfhood.

They therefore want an end to their uncertain and ambiguous status. They desire to rid themselves of every vestige of ingrained characteristics of the colonial era as epitomized in the missionary's attitude and in present mission-church structures. They seek the goal of possessing authoritative final control in every department of their church's life and ministry. This, they insist, calls for a new structure of relationship. They believe the union of mission with church is that which will accomplish independence.

But, will it? What do we learn from the many missions and younger churches associated with the ecumenical movement who in the 1950s revamped their relationship structure in the manner evangelical younger churches are requesting today? Has the specter of colonialism been obliterated and the exhilarating spirit of independence truly prevailed? The answer is NO.

a. Neo-colonialism.

We learn that after two decades the new relationship is being branded as neo-colonialism.[18] Younger church leaders are saying the new structure was designed to maintain a special relationship with them, to retain influence and power in just those areas which had been under the mission's subjugation, and to insure a continued projection of the mission's interests. Furthermore, they testify, western Christians (fraternal workers, servants, technicians) have not functioned in a manner to promote the goal of self-reliance, of modernization, and of economic progress. Missionaries have not been sufficiently aware of the nationals' aspirations or accepted their goals of development and conscientiously subscribed to them. Rather, missionaries are playing the old colonial game in a new form. The new partnership rejects colonialism in principle but continues it in practice. After several years of a fused relationship, traces of patronage, paternalism, and condescension remain. There is still no true equality, no real partnership.

b. International cooperation.

In ecumenical circles the complaint is voiced that the younger church often judges a missionary "by the funds . . . which he brings with him, together with the funds his presence attracts for projects he designs, and which are usually not available for the church if he withdraws or resigns."[19] Financial considerations all too often force church leaders to fulfill the wishes of the missionaries against their own judgment. "This makes it difficult for a church to use its freedom of decision . . . ."[20] And some ecumenists believe " . . . the present ways in which they try to manifest the universality of the Church by sharing personnel are distorted forms."[21] For this reason, the Uppsala Assembly of the WCC officially requested that "new forms and relationships" be structured. They are asking for "new relationships of genuine equality, new respect for one another's identity and calling and new ways of supporting one another in the task which God has given to each one, within the fellowship of the universal Church."[22] In particular they want a new structure that provides for "international cooperation" in which missionary activity will be internationally supported, controlled, and directed.

Furthermore, much of the data from evangelical and ecumenical sources discloses that the integration of mission with church has proved to be thorny for both sides. And although some see the fusion of the two bodies as not only desirable but also inevitable,[23] others do not consider it an altogether sufficient or final solution. Some consider it a temporary arrangement pending a better way. Through it the kind and extent of independence and equality the younger churches seek has not yet been achieved; it still evades them. Responsible men continue to question whether the pattern and the conception behind it is the right expression of the obedience God wants.[24] Since foreign personnel and money are still there, fusion has not produced -- and cannot produce or guarantee -- the "freedom" the younger churches seem to want. This is so because interpersonal and interorganizational relationships are still there -- because people are involved. Being evangelical or ecumenical makes no appreciable difference in this context.

6. Conclusion About Fusion

The relationship structure that fuses the church and the mission overclouds certain basic scriptural requirements. As popularized and practiced, it perpetuates weakness in the younger church in the very areas where maturity is needed. Fusion causes the younger churches to delay or ignore the implementation of biblical faith and mission. And in the sending churches it has produced a discouraging situation: they have degenerated into giving inter-church aid, of being "supply depots." Although it is not the sole reason, it has helped to produce a profound loss of initiative and money and personnel for world evangelization. Admittedly these drawbacks could be corrected, but the effort required would be enormous.

Fusion in its unmodified form, then, does not foster either in the sending church or in the receiving church the kind of church the New Testament portrays. Daniel T. Niles correctly said, "When a missionary church is reduced to the bare function of a recruiting agent of personnel and finances to support another church, then the heart of the missionary conviction has been betrayed."[25]

B. MODIFIED FUSION.

A modified fusion pattern has been proposed by Climenhaga and Jacques[26] and more recently improved upon by Dr. George Peters[27] who calls it "Partnership of Equality and Mutuality." Peters takes into account the three major problem areas of (1) administration of the missionary and the mission expansion program, (2) integration of the missionary into the full life of the church, and (3) finances from overseas. He then lists seven advantages of a total partnership of church and mission with all matters of the mission's activity including policy, finances, administrations, and personnel being church based.

Proponents of modified fusion rightly and scripturally, with Peters, insist that "Christian missions must be focused on the world, not on the church with its organization and program. Missionaries as such are not sent for police action or church programming, but in order that the attack forces of the churches may be bolstered and that churches might be multiplied. The energies of the sending church must not be spent in perfecting church structures, drafting constitutions, exercising church discipline and superintending institutions. The goal of missions is not the structural and institutional life of the church community, but the proclamation of the gospel to those who do not confess Jesus Christ as Lord and Savior."[28]

"Missions must also be the mission of the new church, not only for the church." "The missionary's ministry must be rendered through the church, but not mainly to the church. Principally, he works neither in the church nor for the church but with the church. His service is mainly to the unevangelized world."[29] "This assignment is his by divine calling and mutual agreement, between him, his mission, and the national church . . . he has become a part of a conference to serve as a missionary with the church to unevangelized areas that must be reached with the gospel."[30]

Modified fusion is purposely designed to keep the evangelistic and missionary function of both the sending church and the younger church truly inviolate in accordance with the New Testament requirements for the Church. In this, it is commendable. Nothing, however, is spelled out about the extent of the church's independence and its obligations in stewardship. It is possible that the old and irksome paternalistic control will be reimposed once again through the injection of foreign personnel and finances into the younger church. It could thus be tied to western power centers more securely than ever before, and that as a permanently weaker partner.

Unfortunately the plan is so relatively recent we do not have enough details of its application or an illustration of its success. We await these with deepest and sympathetic interest.

C. DICHOTOMY.

We turn now to the consideration of dichotomy. This is the cooperation of autonomous equals. It allows the mission and the church to maintain their own organizations. But does it help or hinder attaining the New Testament ideal for the Church? Let us examine it as we did the fusion pattern. And since it has been so fairly represented by Dr. George W. Peters,[31] an opponent of the plan, we present his analysis:

"This pattern is based on the principle of organizational dichotomy in the field. The ideal is functional co-operation rather than separation or integration. According to this pattern, the mission and the church form two autonomous bodies with separate legislative and administrative authorities though they operate in fraternal relationships and functional unity.

"The mission and the church are distinct, separate, and independent organizational bodies, parallel movements with distinct assignments. The missionary labors independently of the jurisdiction of the national church and under the direction of his board of missions. The degree of functional and spiritual interrelation of the two bodies, because of a goal-relationship of the two bodies, is either taken for granted or carefully delineated. Usually it is understood that the mission does not set up its own churches, but rather relates such to the national body and then becomes a functional serving agency to the ecclesiastical structure.

"This is basically the pattern of numerous faith missions whose supreme goal is the evangelization of the world and the establishing of local congregations as lighthouses in many communities, and who are less concerned for larger structural units in the various lands. However, it is also well exemplified by the Presbyterian 'Brazil Plan' of 1916, hailed as a unique success as recently as 1968 by the Reverend C. Darby Fulton.[32]

"This program functions best according to the following principles: (a) The mission practices intensive work rather than extensive evangelization. It practices geographical concentration rather than general dissemination of the gospel. To a certain degree, it follows the example of Paul who abode in one place for a considerable time, at least sufficient time for a church to be born. (b) Evangelism of a locality is undertaken for the purpose of establishing a functioning assembly or church. (c) After a church has come into being, it is led into fellowship with churches of similar persuasion and organization and thus linked to a larger national body. (d) The missionary officially dissociates himself from here on from the church and technically has neither right nor authority over this body of believers. He returns only upon invitation to assist and to minister as requested.

"The arguments for this pattern of operation must not be minimized. Based both on logic and sentiment, and in part on experience, they seem sound, convincing, and beneficial. In general they are somewhat as follows: (1) It best protects the autonomy and selfhood of the emerging national church. No missionary sits in the church courts to exert undue influence and to project his image into the image-forming and legislative body. Spiritual self-reliance and self-help become primary exercises from the beginning. It is hoped that thereby not only tensions will be eliminated and the western image of the church minimized, but also the selfhood of the church will evolve more fully, its national character will become apparent, and, above all, the church will from the very beginning learn to depend upon its own resources and particularly upon the superintendent of the church, the indwelling Holy Spirit. All of this is basic and crucial for a church if it is to function properly and to fulfill the design of God for it in the community and the world. Also, should an emergency demand the withdrawal of all missionaries, the church would continue its function without serious vibrations and interruptions.

"(2) It best protects the missionary in his primary calling and in his freedom and initiative as a 'sent one' for a particular task. It permits him to labor as a pioneer in the 'regions beyond' without becoming absorbed in a church-centered program and wrapped up in the organizational and institutional structure and life of the national church.

"This aspect must not be minimized. While mission and church belong organizationally together, the mission of the church is larger than missions, the total function of the church is larger than the sending forth of evangelists into the world of unbelief and gospel destitution, beyond its own area of operation and influence. At the same time, it remains a New Testament fact that a church ceases to be New Testament in spirit and design if it ceases to be missions as well as mission. No church sent into the world (mission) can afford not to send forth some of its members beyond its own region (missions). Most of these 'sent-forth-ones' are evangelists, not to other churches, but to the world in unbelief and without the gospel. To envelop them in another church program, no matter where this may be geographically, is doing injustice to their very calling and assignment. They are missionaries, sent-ones, beyond the borders of the church. This high calling must be clearly grasped, emphatically taught, and zealously guarded.

"It should be noted, however, that this evangelist-missionary concept may not exhaust the interchurch ministries between the older and younger churches and that there may be a place for fraternal workers.

"(3) It best protects the image of a board of missions as being an agent of a unique task and particular assignment. It is not a church board or a board that has legislative authority over churches. It does not represent the church in its total function. Neither is it merely a recruiting agency. It is a board of a particular design and mission, a board to send forth men and women of a particular calling into a particular situation -- the world of unbelief, destitute of the gospel -- for a singular purpose, the purpose of gospel proclamation by every legitimate means and effective method, and the establishing of functioning churches who will assume their New Testament responsibility and calling and develop their own selfhood and national character. This board is not a mere service agency or 'supply depot.' It has not received its authority and assignment from a national body, nor is its sending forth subject to invitations and requests. Its task is not completed with the rise of a national church. It stands before its risen Lord, is subject to His unique command, conscientiously observes the needs of the world, and boldly expresses the promptings of the spirit of missions. Only then can the true image of a board of missions be presented. This, too, must be zealously guarded and energetically pursued."

Although Dr. Peters has so ably and fairly delineated the dichotomy pattern, he does not think it proves "functionally most effective, filially most satisfactory, scientifically most helpful" or expresses "the highest Biblical idealism."[33] And except for a brief paragraph in which he states he cannot fit it "into the body structure of the Church,"[34] he does not elaborate further on his opposing views.

Conclusion About Dichotomy

As for me, I hold that the pattern of mission-church relationship ought not to have as its final criterion simply a compatible relationship. Rather, I look at the dichotomy pattern as I do that of fusion. I look to see if it allows both the older church and the younger church to be New Testament kind of churches. Does it meet the scriptural requirements regarding a church's function? Most essentially, does it foster or stifle a passion for evangelism and missions in both? That, it seems to me, is the test of all tests. And dichotomy passes it quite well. The record of evangelism and missionary activity in both the older and younger churches that have operated under this system is well known to us and speaks for itself.

Problems there have been and are, but these have become acute only when an exaggerated emphasis on developing the new church has supplanted evangelism; when service jobs have displaced persuasion evangelism (the kind that wins the lost and establishes them in visible churches); when both church and mission have concentrated their attention on the church rather than the unredeemed multitudes.

D. MODIFIED DICHOTOMY.

Those who practice modified dichotomy believe the existence of the new churches has without doubt added a new dimension to missionary work -- that younger churches do need assistance in certain specialized areas. They therefore propose the mission's resources in personnel and finances be divided. One segment would be (1) for maintaining liaison and vital support with the national church, the other (2) for pioneering and planting by the mission.

1. Maintaining Liaison and Vital Support.

In this the mission turns over to the church the development portion of its resources, usually without strings attached. The authority and maturity of the younger church is recognized, allowing it to use some funds and some missionaries as it sees fit. These missionaries are such as are willing and able to participate fully in the life of the church. The amount of money, the number of missionaries, and the length of time involved are determined by a negotiated agreement. At the end of the stipulated period, the agreement is mutually examined with a view to renewing or modifying it. The aim is for the church to work toward assuming full responsibility just as soon as possible. In this way the founding mission maintains a good relationship with the church, and gives help if it is needed.

2. Pioneering and Planting.

Since God is still calling, equipping, and sending pioneering, church-planting missionaries, the framework is provided for them to work unhampered by fragile considerations of church jurisdiction. Their full energies are directed to planting new churches, not merely servicing the existing ones. Their work, however, is not merely in terms of geography. This gives an unparalleled opportunity as well as responsibility for the missionary to advance the gospel. The new ground for missionary fresh starts is agreed upon, however -- if at all possible -- between the church and the mission. Generally, all populations not being effectively evangelized by existing churches are open to the mission to evangelize. The church is asked to participate by sending personnel. There are clear plans to incorporate the missionary-planted churches into the existing ecclesiastical structure.

This pattern of relationship is in its beginning stages and still too new to assess from experience. Like modified fusion, it seeks to recognize fairly some responsibility to the national church and at the same time to maintain its obligation to continually spread the gospel in an everwidening area. It is a pragmatic and functional approach to mission-church relationship.

E. NO MISSION-CHURCH RELATIONSHIP PATTERN FULLY IDEAL.

Although it is necessary and profitable to learn all that we can about mission-church relationship, it should not so absorb our attention that the evangelistic and missionary obligation of the Church is obscured. Further, the complexities of the subject strongly suggest that our presenting a consensus opinion about which pattern is the best is ill-advised. There are simply too many variables to deal with. Whether the church is newly started; large or small; burdened with institutional responsibilities or unencumbered; evangelistic and missionary or static -- all these factors have to be considered. Also the form of ecclesiastical government and whether the mission is a faith society or a denominational board will make a difference. And some things discovered to be helpful or hurtful in one country or area may not be so in another. Differences in cultures, national feelings, and the selfhood of the church must be taken under advisement.

F. GUIDELINES FOR MISSION-CHURCH RELATIONS OVERSEAS.

The following, though, should remain constant in any structure of mission-church relationship:

- The national church rejects the status of dependdence and recognizes its own responsibilities. It maintains its independence from outside direction or interference. An atmosphere in the mission-church relationship is created wherein evangelism and church planting are mutually desired and undertaken. The church assumes its full stature in Christ, having its own missionary outreach.

- The sending church is permitted to remain missionary in obedience to the essential obligation of a true New Testament church. The missionary can fulfill his personal, unique, and divine calling as a missionary.

- There is frank recognition that the great job which remains to be done cannot be accomplished by either the mission or the national church working alone but only by the combined operations of both working together to fulfill the Great Commission.

- The mission's relationship with the church is primarily at that point in which the church is engaged in witness and mission to the non-Christian world outside its door.

* * *

Notes

1. The word <u>ekklesia</u> (church) is found 115 times in the New Testament. The primary and literal significance of the word is the visible, local congregation -- a company of believers meeting in a given place for a given purpose. In this sense, it is used 90 times.

   The secondary and figurative sense is used to designate the invisible, universal company including all God's redeemed on earth and in heaven. In this sense it appears 11 times.

   In some passages the secondary sense grows directly out of the primary so that the primary meaning has been said to extend to 96 passages.

   The Church, the body of Christ, is composed of all the regenerate believers in the Lord Jesus Christ, alive and dead, without reference to geography, race, or ecclesiastical affiliation.

   The Church on earth manifests itself in visible communities which, according to the Scriptures, includes both those who by regeneration through the Spirit are truly His and some who in spite of their profession have not yet partaken of the life in Christ.

   The local church is the means, the agent, wherein God encounters human society. It is the witnessing community of God in the world.

2. Theodore Eastman, <u>Chosen and Sent: Calling the Church to Mission</u> (Grand Rapids: Eerdmans, 1971), p. 14.

3. <u>History's Lessons for Tomorrow's Mission</u> (Geneva: World's Student Christian Federation, 1960), p. 246.

4. G. W. Peters, "Mission-Church Relationship - I," <u>Bibliotheca Sacra</u>, July, 1968, p. 212.

5. G. W. Peters, "Mission-Church Relationship - II," <u>Bibliotheca Sacra</u>, October, 1968, p. 312.

6. H. C. Jackson, "Some Old Patterns for New in Missions," <u>Occasional Bulletin</u>, XII, No. 10, December, 1961, p. 5.

7. J. A. Scherer, <u>Justinian Welz -- Essays by an Early Prophet of Mission</u> (Grand Rapids: Eerdmans, 1969).

8. *The Encyclopedia of Modern Christian Missions*, ed. B. L. Goddard (Camden, New Jersey: Thomas Nelson & Sons, 1967); see various missions but especially pp. 161 and 215.

9. R. D. Winter and R. P. Beaver, *The Warp and the Woof* (South Pasadena: William Carey Library, 1970), pp. 33, 47.

10. Jackson, *op. cit.*, pp. 5, 6.

11. D. P. Smith, "Personnel Development Interviews," *Occasional Bulletin*, September, 1970, p. 7.

12. J. M. Smith, Executive Secretary, Department of East Asia, Division of Overseas Ministries, Christian Church (Disciples of Christ), in a letter dated May 12, 1971, to Boyd B. Lowry, Southern Asia Department, DOM-NCCC/USA. (*Note*: Appreciation is expressed to the Rev. Boyd B. Lowry, Acting Executive Director, Southern Asia Department of the National Council of the Churches of Christ (U.S.A.) for assistance rendered in preparing for my use an up-to-date bibliographical survey of pertinent doctoral dissertations on the fusion of church and mission and in supplying some documents and pertinent correspondence. Mr. Lowry's openness and friendliness in rendering full help was outstanding.)

13. L. L. King, "Who Controls the Missionary?" *His*, May, 1968, p. 14.

14. D. T. Niles, *The Message and Its Messengers* (Nashville, Tennessee: Abingdon Press, 1966), p. 44.

15. Bishop M. Arias, "Mutual Responsibility," *The International Review of Missions*, LX, No. 238, April, 1971.

16. *Africa Pulse*, December, 1970, p. 8.

17. Walter Groseclose, "Foreign Aid Fizzle," *Wall Street Journal*, Monday, November 27, 1967.

18. "The Ecumenical Sharing of Personnel," *The International Review of Missions*, LIX, No. 236, October, 1970, p. 443.

19. *Ibid.*, p. 445.

20. *Loc cit.*

21. *Ibid*, p. 443.

22. *Loc. cit.*

23. Rev. Robbins Strong, Deputy Director, DWME/WCC, in a letter dated June 7, 1971, to Rev. Boyd B. Lowry, Southern Asia Department, DOM-NCCC/USA.

24. *The Ghana Assembly of the International Missionary Council*, ed. R. K. Orchard (London: Edinburgh House Press, 1958), p. 139.

25. Quoted by T. K. Jones, Jr., "Mission, Unity, World Methodism and a Board of Missions," *The International Review of Missions*, LV, No. 218, April, 1966, p. 180.

26. A. M. Climenhaga and E. M. Jacques, "A Consideration of Principles in Mission-Church Relations," *A Symposium: Facing Facts in Modern Missions* (Chicago: Moody Press, 1963), pp. 213-220.

27. G. W. Peters, "Mission-Church Relationship - II," *Bibliotheca Sacra*, October, 1968, pp. 300-312.

28. *Ibid.*, p. 301.

29. *Ibid.*, p. 302.

30. *Ibid.*, p. 303.

31. G. W. Peters, "Mission-Church Relationship - I," *Bibliotheca Sacra*, July, 1968, pp. 208-211.

32. Cf. *Evangelical Missions Quarterly*, IV;2 (Winter, 1968), pp. 65-74.

33. G. W. Peters, "Mission-Church Relationship - I," *Bibliotheca Sacra*, July, 1968, pp. 208-211.

34. *Ibid.*, p. 212.

* * *

LLK:jrh 8/26/71

MISSION/CHURCH RELATIONS

PART II: IN PRACTICE

by Louis L. King

for presentation at GL 71

In presenting mission/church relations in practice, I shall draw upon that which I know best: personal experience. As a new missionary I entered into a mission-church relationship that must be rated a failure and had the joy of seeing it improve. Then as an administrator I've had to search for ways to win through in this always delicate area of relationships. And this has been done while keeping mission and church organizationally separate. Here is the story of how I came to practice four basic principles in relating to the church.

I. "MIND YOUR OWN BUSINESS"

I came upon mission-church relationship problems in an abrupt and direct way. After nine years of pastoral ministry, I was sent as a missionary of The Christian and Missionary Alliance to Gujarat, India. I had not had anthropological or sociological studies and was untutored in mission theory and practice. I went with the fixed persuasion that God intended me to serve Him on foreign soil -- that I was called of Him.

Gujarat was entered by our mission in 1893. At the turn of the century, a devastating famine broke out. Our missionaries living in the midst of it did something about it. They established two orphanages and soon were completely responsible for about seventeen hundred orphans. Also, many adult famine victims were employed in a works program, and paid with food and a small wage. They erected brick churches, mission houses, and school buildings. Following the great famine, four large tracts of land were purchased, subdivided, and developed into excellent farms for relocating new converts from Hinduism and also setling newly married orphans. An industrial training program was instituted. The young men were taught carpentering, tailoring, shoemaking, weaving, and cooking. Two boarding schools and forty village schools were established and operated through the years at mission expense. Annually a quota of students was sent to a teacher training college. Each missionary directed mission-paid evangelists and Bible women in the work of evangelism. The mission seemingly left nothing undone in terms of witness coupled with social concern. The result was a church almost entirely literate. All Christians were educated through the primary school level, and some had gone beyond. Many had risen to a middle-class status, a few were professional people, and some were well-to-do.

Despite the mission's lavish attention on the church and its members, the mission-church relationship was not harmonious. In 1932 signs were painted on the walls of mission compounds:

"Missionary go home!" Antimission leaflets prepared by Christians were copiously distributed to Christians and non-Christians alike. In these the churches' demands of the mission were explicitly spelled out.

In that same year the church was officially organized with a Presbyterian form of government. All missionaries were required to be members of the church. They were made coequal with Indian pastors, and eligible for any office in a local church, presbytery, synod, or the General Assembly.

When I reached the field in 1947, church membership approximated what it had been in 1920. No new congregations had been formed since the start of World War II. The number of ordained pastors had decreased, and some pastors had the oversight of two churches. They were not having converts from the non-Christian faiths. Additions to the church were from the Christian community, with new members equalling the loss by death or transfer. There was no church growth.

It was so difficult to get Christians to witness that a strenuous effort was made to have at least one "week of witness" a year. In spite of the church's being ardently evangelical, youths from Christian families were admitted to church membership by a neat formula: so much instruction plus so much water equals a Christian. The result was that some had had no saving experience at all.

The mission still occupied the same locations it had in 1893. Missionaries did the same things; namely, superintended the work and the staff of Indian evangelists and Bible women, itinerated three months each year, sat on many committees, and handled finances. The relationship between church and mission was tense. The presence of missionaries was not appreciated and frequently not wanted.

During language study I carefully observed the unsatisfactory mission-church relationship, and concluded that:

1. Although a member of the church, I should decline any church office at any level in order to make way for the splendid Indian Christians.

2. With church members well educated, holding secular positions of importance, and well taught in the Word, I should refrain from entering into the church's problems. I ought to depend upon the Holy Spirit to work in them as I believed He did in missionaries.

3. The church must look to its Head for all its answers and not to the mission or to me, a missionary.

4. My authority should be spiritual and emanate solely from preaching and teaching the Word of God in the power of

the Holy Spirit. I should studiously avoid preaching from Scripture passages that applied to the church's problems unless they came in natural sequence in an expositional presentation of a New Testament book.

5. I must set a diligent example in witnessing to the lost and in establishing churches.

6. Although acting differently from my missionary colleagues, I must not permit my new way to cause contention in the missionary ranks. My views would need to be successfully implemented to be convincing.

During my brief six years of missionary service, the mission allowed me to practice faithfully these guiding principles. I found they worked. They appreciably helped to better the mission-church relationship, and worked mightily to achieve a breakthrough in evangelism.

> I learned, therefore, as A FIRST PRINCIPLE that good relations with the church are achieved and maintained when missionaries refrain from accepting administrative functions in, and forego imposing their plans upon, the church. I learned, too, that rapport is heightened through a missionary's diligence and success in the spiritual work of Bible teaching, evangelism, and church planting.

II. OPEN FORUMS

Coming on my first and only furlough in 1953, I was given administrative responsibilities for The C&MA's activities in the Pacific Islands and Southeast Asia -- then ten countries with a missionary staff of 502.

Except for the Philippines and Viet Nam, the work throughout the area was heavily subsidized. Most pastors received the bulk of their support from the mission. Giving to the church according to scriptural standards languished, with Christians' giving exceedingly little. Witnessing for Christ as a result and expression of their spiritual life was not done generally. The idea prevailed that speaking to others about Jesus should be done by the mission-paid agents.

Pastors and congregations annually made demands for more and more money from abroad. Instead of an attitude of love, care, and self-sacrifice on the part of a pastor, his feeling toward his congregation was, "I get my salary paid whether I serve you or not and whether you like me or not." The congregation thought, "What is the use of worrying about it. The pastor gets paid whether or not we provide for him and whether or not we like him." This certainly was not a healthy state of affairs, and from a human point of view offered some serious temptations.

For instance, pastors were afforded a degree of power and security quite independent of the demands and requirements of the laity. And the laymen were relieved of the need and responsibility of paying for pastoral care.* Pastors did not and would not preach with conviction what the Bible teaches about giving money. Although they pled the economic inability of the people, in reality they did not have the heart to cease being the beneficiaries of the mission's subsidy system. And missionaries felt that so long as subsidy was provided, they were entitled to control. They clearly saw that when they no longer paid, their control would be in jeopardy. In most of the countries the mission-church relationship problem was acute. In one instance, the church had given the missionaries six months to leave.

The most important responsibility given me upon my assuming office was to bring to full implementation the indigenous church policy which The Christian and Missionary Alliance had officially adopted in 1927. The policy had not been faithfully or uniformly enforced. Clearly this assignment could bring me into unhealthy relationships with both the national church brethren and the missionaries. Indeed, in every country a relationship crisis of major proportions could be precipitated. Who likes change -- and especially when it results in the accustomed income and source of power being taken away?

The Foreign Department decided upon a nonlegislative approach as the way to achieve our desired end: the indigenous church goal. We believed cold legislation could so irritate people that a severe reversal in our work might ensue. We decided the better way would be a consultative, educational, persuasive, and biblical approach to both the missionaries and the national church brethren. We could well afford to spend the time and effort and money in doing it this way.

Each year, therefore, we met in conference with all furloughing missionaries to inculcate in their minds the scriptural necessity of obeying the Word of God, following Jesus Christ, and expecting in believers -- even though newly won from non-Christian faiths -- the fruits of the Spirit.

We also decided to educate national church leaders along the same lines by holding continent-wide conferences. To date eight area conferences and one world conference have been held. They have been of incalculable value, both in achieving the indigenous church goals and in forging wholesome mission-church relationships.

At the first mission-church conference in 1955 as well as in all subsequent ones, success came through following the same well-defined principles.

---

*Adapted from a privately circulated document entitled, "A New Financial Policy for the New Century," as prepared by the American Methodist Mission, North India.

1. The basic principle has been that the church should be first in our thinking and in our work. Secondary things should not be exalted in our enterprise at the expense of that which is vital; that is, our attention should not be diverted to the perpetuity of the mission or the mission's medical and educational institutions. Furthermore, the new fellowship -- the church -- should function in the midst of its own cultures, traditions, and economic conditions and not in a vacuum or in a splendid but ineffectual isolation from its own people. And evangelism should be thought of as the fruit and evidence of the faith and zeal of the new converts. The quality of their spiritual life and experience should be seen in their own evangelizing power. Hence the so-important thing is not the process whereby the mission operates and evangelizes, but rather the character of the spiritual life and experience of the church, which if healthy will lead it into evangelism itself. The objective is the creation of a witnessing church in which the Holy Spirit will achieve Christ's purpose in winning lost peoples.

2. We have sought to follow the New Testament in giving a minimum of attention to church constitutions and the mechanics of church administration. The New Testament is concerned with life -- the life of the Lord Jesus manifested and reproduced in the fellowship of the believers. We therefore have spent little time discussing that about which the New Testament is relatively silent.

3. Christ has been given His exalted place as Head of the Church -- the One who controls. We believe Christ has a threefold way of controlling the Church which is His body. First, when a man is born again by the Spirit of God, the new law of love comes as part and parcel of that new birth. It is the first fruit of the Spirit's work in the believer's life (Gal. 5:22). No one is born of God without it (I John 3:14). And Christ exercises His authority over us by this new law of love He has put within us. It causes us to act properly toward God and toward our fellowman.

The second method by which Jesus Christ the Head exercises authority and rulership in the body is through the Bible. All that needs to be known about the Church is in the Book. The answers to the Church's problems are found there, and not from the mission. The Bible alone is the Church's guidebook and ultimate constitution.

And the third method by which Christ controls and rules the Church is by establishing Himself as the standard of behaviour and action. Henceforth, "looking unto Jesus" is the Christian's aim. Instead of looking in the decalogue to see if any law has been infringed upon, the Christian is to look to Christ. In every department of life he is to endeavor through the indwelling of the Spirit to attain to the full measure of the stature of Christ.

4. Another principle has been to develop self-initiative in the national delegates to the conferences. As much as possible the conferences have been dominated by them. Church leaders from areas where noteworthy progress and attainments have been made explain their methods and experiences, while delegates of less progressive fields take note and discuss their peculiar problems with expressed desire for improvement. By sharing their successful experiences as well as their areas of difficulty, they convince themselves concerning the basic, essential requirements for building, strengthening, and expanding the Church. These sharing sessions have taken up self-support through tithes and offerings; self-government unhampered by missionary intervention; self-propagation by being an evangelistic and missionary church; mission-church relationships; the new stance of Roman Catholicism; non-biblical ecumenism as represented by the WCC; improving the Sunday school; and saturation evangelism.

5. A salient aspect of the conferences has been the healthy incentive created by comparison with others in the areas of self-support, aggressive evangelism, and missionary work. As a result the advance in these has been phenomenal.

6. We have also practiced complete integration. There has been no difference in the treatment of any delegate, missionary or national, as to travel arrangements, eating, sleeping, or use of bathroom facilities. Missionaries have been interspersed in the room accommodations. Consequently, fellowship -- daily, personal, spiritual, and social -- has been a most noticeable feature. This aspect of the conferences shall probably never be forgotten. And through the years numerous delegates have given praise to God for the fellowship in the Lord with kindred Christians of many lands.

These nonlegislative conferences have helped immensely The C&MA's relationship with the overseas churches in our fellowship. They have served as open forums in which questions are freely asked and answers openly and honestly given. Explanations are possible without misunderstanding or doubtful disputation. The mission's purpose and program throughout the world are exposed. Opportunity is afforded to explain why we do not always operate as other missions do. The churches' aspirations and desires are also made known. Indeed, there has been no limit to the probing of mission-church relations. And neither has there been any trace of irritation or residue of resentment due to the freedom of expression in this area. We have discovered that holding conferences of this nature affords a directness of learning that far surpasses the reading of theoretical books and papers on the subjects considered.

> The conferences have taught me A SECOND PRINCIPLE for achieving healthy mission-church relationship: this is to establish some kind of periodic open forum that permits a free exchange of ideas and opinions on a variety of important subjects between national church leaders of various countries and mission field administrators.

III. ADMINISTRATIVE BRIDGES

At the field level where certain ministries of the church and the mission coincide, we have discovered that administrative bridges are helpful. Although both church and mission maintain a legitimate independence of each other, it should not mean they thereby lose contact. Within the scope of administrative dichotomy, there is room and plentiful reason for mutual counseling and talking of ways to expedite the work jointly. This we do through regularly scheduled joint meetings of the executive committees of the mission and the national church. These meetings are essentially for sharing views and formulating plans.

In matters that involve the mission alone or the church alone, no minutes are recorded. Since the mission conference is the sovereign body of the mission and the church's general assembly is the supreme body of the church, it is recognized that a joint committee cannot legitimately originate action for the mission nor yet for the national church. Neither can it sit as a tribunal deciding the legality of the church's acts.

When the two committees meet in joint session, the heads of the two groups alternately preside; or, in some instances, the church's president always chairs the meetings. The mission does not act like an agency retiring from the scene, nor does the national church assert its prerogatives. It is a meeting of brothers in Christ who manifest their unity in the practical areas of service. This ordinarily takes the form of joint arrangements for evangelistic efforts in local churches, developing missionary interest, helping to translate the ideal of tithing into reality, Bible teaching in the churches, ministerial education, adult literacy campaigns, preparing for and fulfilling the literature needs of the Christian and non-Christian communities, and learning to understand each other when difficult relationships have hindered fellowship.

> Thus THE THIRD PRINCIPLE for achieving harmonious working relations between mission and church is to establish local administrative bridges that provide for free, open discussion about, and planning of, the work.

IV. DOCUMENTED AGREEMENTS

In our mission's efforts to achieve and maintain wholesome relationships with various national churches, documents concerning relationship have been mutually worked out. Although the specific agreements may vary from country to country, the purpose and the pattern are the same.

First, we work directly with the church. The scheme is not something imposed by the mission or extracted by the church. Normally we try to begin with the open acknowledgment that the interests of both church and mission involve certain areas in which we ought to cooperate and that there are many difficulties in learning how to do so. We admit, too, that in the Society of God we can live with each other, that we are equal, and that both will benefit from mutual response. The purpose is to provide ways to respond to each other which are not based on charity or sympathy or simple relief but rather on the dignity of individuals of equal value doing the will of God together.

Next, the mission and the younger church seek to come to a clear understanding as to what constitutes a mature church -- the New Testament kind of church. If both are not certain on this so very essential matter, we envision that tragic consequences for the church, the mission, and world evangelization will ensue.

After this, the actual relationship document is hammered out. The specific agreements normally cover the following:

1. Ultimate authority. The question is, who has ultimate authority for the mission's work and personnel within the country? This needs to fit into a given country's political and cultural situation. In central Africa the demand for "one head" has reached the point of crisis. Elsewhere this is not an acute problem. It is evident, therefore, that the answer as to authority will vary with the country, the character of the people, the character of the mission, and the maturity of the church.

2. Assignment of personnel. This is one of the most difficult areas to settle with the church. It seems clear, though, that whatever organizational structure is adopted will determine the issue. Even so, the terms under which a missionary is to labor -- and to be released from service if necessary -- should be spelled out. That missionaries exist primarily for work across the frontier of the non-Christian community should be made quite clear. If they haven't been engaged in church-multiplying evangelism, they must be freed to do so.

3. Exercise of initiative. Who exercises initiative in beginning or expanding various ministries should be part of the agreement. If at all possible, the mission should seek an agreement that safeguards its freedom to initiate work not directly related to the local church.

4. Proprietorship of institutions. If hospitals, schools, presses, and bookstores have not already been given to the church, it would seem best that these be set up as independent or semi-independent corporations. The philosophy behind this is that these institutions do not have their roots in redemption or the church. Schools especially are a normal mode of community existence, and Christians ought to "take their place in the community alongside their fellows.

There is little justification for Christians to run schools, where it is possible for these schools to be run by all members of a community together"[1] or under state auspices. This "does not mean closing the school. It means only that the school should cease to be an integral part of the church structure."[2] The task of the church is to preach the gospel to the lost and to shepherd the people of God. Institutional burdens, therefore, might well be shifted to commercial, profit-making organizations or to a trusteeship of local Christians. If this is not done, the institution becomes a source of secular power for the church, and the church will have little time or energy left for the giant task assigned to it by Christ.

5. Finances. For both sending and receiving bodies, agreements regarding finances need to be spelled out for (1) preserving the giver's intention, (2) preserving the receiver's self-respect, (3) requiring accountability of how money was spent, (4) honoring the right of donors to discontinue giving or drastically reduce giving, and (5) stipulating whether money will be given "without strings" or to specific projects. A real issue that has to be faced is whether or not the church has the spiritual character to spend money for the glory of God and without inhibiting their ability to take care of themselves.

6. Transfer and maintenance of property. Properties that will be given to the church, together with all that is involved in the cost of transferring deeds, should be fully discussed. A clearly understood agreement should be reached as to who pays such costs. The arrangement will vary from country to country depending on the capability of the church to pay the fees or the mission's plan to give these properties as unencumbered gifts. When all the mission's holdings are given to the church, the agreement should contain a stipulation that the missionary homes are reserved for missionary use as long as they are needed for that purpose. Furthermore, the question of who maintains the properties should be answered.

7. Missionary allowances. Some churches ask that their treasurer receive the missionary's monthly allowance and pay him. This can be avoided by the home office's depositing the missionary's funds -- including operating expenses as well as personal allowance -- in his personal bank account in the homeland. He is then notified and can draw on that account by check. In this event, no mission or national church office is involved. An explanation of the method is generally accepted without a problem.

---

1. D. T. Niles, *The Message and Its Messengers* (Nashville, Tennessee: Abingdon Press, 1966), p. 43.

2. *Ibid.*, p. 44.

8. Changes in policy. Both parties should respect and allow changes in policy in either body. In addition, if new methods are developed to deal with new or different situations, they will be described and agreed to by written memorandum.

9. Inauguration. Even though autonomy, property, and grants are presently and fully possessed by the national church, the church may still say this is not true. This obtains when the tension points have been dealt with piecemeal and over a period of time. This problem is often the result of not holding a study and negotiating conference; not reaching documented agreement of relationship; and not having a public, official, formal ceremony to celebrate its inauguration. The inaugural ceremony is important to the national Christians and therefore needs to be a part of the agreement.

10. Review, renewal, modification, termination. Our agreements concerning certain matters have had a five-year term, after which they are reviewed by both church and mission, and renegotiated.

> *Reaching negotiated, documented agreements in those areas that normally have caused tension is the FOURTH PRINCIPLE for achieving and maintaining a wholesome mission-church relationship.*

V. CONCLUSION

These, then, are the four basic and essential principles practiced in structuring a wholesome and workable association of the mission and the church; *viz.*, (1) "minding your own business," (2) holding open forums, (3) establishing administrative bridges, and (4) negotiating documented agreements. The aim in all of this is to consciously and consistently keep in view for both the mission and the church "the big end" of their existence: carrying out Christ's worldwide mission, "As my Father hath sent me, even so send I you."

MISSION/CHURCH RELATIONS OVERSEAS

PART I

by George W. Peters

for presentation at GL'71

AN ANALYSIS AND OBSERVATIONS ON MISSION/CHURCH RELATIONSHIP

Unless I am living in a grandiose historical illusion and glorious missionary mirage, the Church of Jesus Christ is entering upon the greatest time of world evangelization. I am confident that the remaining three decades (or almost so) of our century will see absolutely unprecedented miracles and movements in the world, make the Gospel of Jesus Christ available to vast multitudes and will see more people enter the kingdom of God than the last three centuries combined have witnessed. The most phenomenal triumphs of Christ are before us and are awaiting to be claimed by the Church of Jesus Christ. Let no one think of GL'71 as the last rites of the missionary movement, the demise of the missionary in the biblical sense or the betrayal of the 2 billions without the Gospel of Jesus Christ.

However, neither are we here to raise up a glorious monument of organizational structures by which we must stand in guard and for which we are prepared to battle. Neither are we here for a great debate, one seeking to win over the other. We are not sportsmen. We are men of God, earnestly seeking His way to greater usefulness in His kingdom. We are here to find direction on how to <u>relate</u>, enlist, mobilize, train and coordinate the total Church of Jesus Christ for the greatest coordinated evangelism thrust, to actualize the evangelism command of the Master unto the greatest ingathering of people that this world has ever witnessed. This is the will of God and this is the abiding purpose of the Church of Jesus Christ in its missionary outreach. May it please the Lord to purge our motives, to enlarge and clarify our vision, to tune our ears to His voice, to empty us of all selfish ambitions, desire for self-aggrandizement and set our minds upon His glory and unchanging purpose.

Carefully I selected the words relate, enlist, mobilize, train and coordinate and placed "relate" first. This is the major concern of GL'71. We cannot concern ourselves with the other aspects as vital as they may be to the cause of Jesus Christ and the life of the younger churches. Because of this I have declined to enter in upon the interesting subject artfully presented in such wordings as Missions as "Orders," and Modalities need Sodalities (Winter). A conference on those subjects belongs to other continents than ours. Our only concern here must remain

CHURCH -- MISSION -- CHURCH Relationships.

The latter concepts form the basis of my presentation.

General Observations.

Before we launch into the study of our subject I present a few general observations. My studies and surveys of mission -- church relationships have led me to the conclusions:

1. That the issues are not the same in denominational and interdenomimational missions. Both experience tensions but the tensions are not the same in intensity or quality. To consider them together complicates the matter considerably;

2. That the issues are not the same in countries which have not been under colonial domination and countries which have gone through this experience;

3. That the issues are not the same in the various missions and that the intensity and quality of tensions is determined to a considerable degree by the inner structure and functions of the mission;

4. That the time seems to have come for creative innovations in many areas of the world. A new approach becomes necessary. We are faced by many small groupings of churches which cannot hope to become self-sustaining and selfmaintaining entities in the full sense of the word. They will remain dependent upon other agencies for

many "helps" such as literature, education etc. It does not seem advisable to encourage them to develop such materials. Neither are they ready to merge with other movements and lose their own identity. However, the denominational emphasis even of the interdenominational missions makes it difficult for the groups to accept the graces of these agencies.

It seems to me that we must think more concretely and practically in this realm. The invitations and courtesies of the churches do not meet the need. It would be well to think in terms of mission and church unrelated project agencies functioning like corporations and operating specific projects on a broad basis for the benefit of all who need and desire their services. As an illustration permit me to use the camp projects of Word of Life in Germany and Brazil. Here at home we may think of Wheaton College or Moody Bible Institute, or the Scripture Press or Zondervan Publishing House etc.

It seems to me that a great deal of help would come to the evangelical cause from such an approach, many tensions between missions and churches because of institutionalism would be easier resolved,and greater effectiveness in the ministry of the church would be achieved. At the same time smaller groups of churches and demoninations would feel neither dependent upon another denomination or mission nor would they be under the pressure to bear the heavy burdens of their own institutionalism. This could preserve their self-image and self-respect.

With rare exceptions, will regular missions and denominations be able to serve this purpose? It seems to me, however, that some TEAM projects approximate this type of ministry. The Christian community knows that the services are available, yet no one feels imposed upon or feels obligated to accept the services.

I draw the attention of the convention to these facts and ideas in order to save us in arguing for or against certain positions which seem rather irrelevant to some. They may be crucially relevant to another party. Much wisdom and great care will be demanded to find truly relevant and workable principles and patterns and relate them purposefully to the various situations. Generalizations can no longer guide us. We have coasted too long. We will need to relate fearlessly and creatively specifics to specific situations.

With these <u>general observations</u> as background I turn to our main study. We shall think along the following outline. We shall briefly discuss three main eras of missions, raise questions about some underlying issues, present some guiding principles and relate several theories of relationships. It will be evident that no satisfactory solution has thus far captured the mind of the mission societies and national churches alike. Much work is awaiting us.

A. HISTORICAL AND CULTURAL CONTEXT

Since history is the record of cultural processes including organizational practices, let us first turn to history.

I. <u>Three main eras in the history of modern missions</u>.

The history of modern missions and the younger churches may be divided for study purposes into three eras. These eras are conditioned by world history and by mission and church development.

(1) The era of colonial predominance sets the stage for mission expansion in the nineteenth century. This produced the age of paternalism when the Western based, oriented, staffed and financed missions expanded their efforts over most of the globe. Their organization and legislation were unilateral and were patterned according to prevailing colonial structures. For this we must not condemn missions, however. It merely behooves us frankly to acknowledge it.

(2) The era of national awakening began to shift the platform of missions. The years from 1905 to 1945 may be spoken of as the age of devolution. The transfer of authority, administration, and property to the national churches became inevitable -- either because of a breakthrough of indigenous principles, or because of rising nationalism, or because of the maturing of the churches, or because of the prevailing of biblical principles and practices.

(3) World War II ushered in many drastic changes in the Third World which left their imprint upon the churches. The era of independent nations and autonomous churches brought about a revamping of the stage of missions. There was first a period of partnership following 1945. In 1959 the age of servanthood became dominant. In this period serious confusion set in and experimentation took place which is still continuing.

II. Underlying issues.

The era of autonomous, national churches has gained considerable strength in the last several decades. The Jerusalem Conference of the International Missionary Council in 1928 brought about such diligent study, numerous conferences, and much thinking along several lines seeking to find the answers to such questions as the following: (a) When is a church truly autonomous? In order to be autonomous, must it be absolutely self-sufficient in finances and personnel? Or, may it be considered autonomous when it is independent in legislation and administration even while still receiving assistance in finances and personnel? (b) With the establishing of autonomous national churches, have the sending churches completed their mission assignment to such countries? It is often deduced that Paul seemingly implied such in the self-evaluation of his work in Asia Minor and Greece (Rom. 16:18-23). (c) With the establishing of autonomous churches, is it still the responsibility of the formerly sending churches to reach the unreached masses of the cities and communities and geographical areas of the countries where autonomous churches of considerable number or strength exist, as in India, Japan, Indonesia, and some sections of Africa and Latin America? (d) If the assignment is not completed, how can it best be done? How can the mission program be related to the autonomous national churches? Should the entire mission work and missionaries be integrated into the ecclesiastical structure and thus be administered unilaterally by the national churches? Should the mission relate itself only functionally to the churches and carry on mission expansion while the national church cares for the churches? Thus the mission would serve as an arm of the churches, but would retain administrative and legislative independence. In such case, co-operation rather than integration would govern the relationship. Should the mission become more or less a service agency and carry on certain projects for the churches, such as training institutions, hospitals, literature and publication, or assist in certain programs, such as evangelism, Bible teaching, etc., supplementing the ministry of the church and making it more effective with the hope that gradually these projects and programs will also be turned over to the churches and the mission will have completed the assignment and withdraw? (e) Is the problem basically spiritual, theological, anthropological, sociological, or organizational in nature? Is the answer organizational dichotomy into mission and church, unilateral organization and administration on the part of the national church, or a clearly defined church mission partnership in which unilateral action or decision is not practiced in specified areas and yet which will involve both parties equally and in which both parties will share in responsibility and liability?

While we do not wish to exaggerate the complexity of the issue, it behooves us to be realistic and open in confronting the problem. No doubt, God has an answer for every one of the questions. However, only as we become aware of the scope of the issue will we apply all diligence to find the proper solution.

III. Guiding Principles.

Principles which could assist us in regulating the relationship between an autonomous church of a given country and an autonomous mission elsewhere.

We must keep in mind that:

. . . The local church and not a mission society is central in the New Testament. The independent mission societies as we know them are in the main accidents of history rather than biblical ideals. No doubt, they have become necessities and as such have served a noble purpose. God has richly blessed them. However, had the churches lived up to the ideals of the New Testament, most probably no autonomous mission societies would have come into existence. Whatever the situation, our Lord is building the Church.

. . . The autonomy of the church in any area is not actual until it has complete jurisdiction over and/or freedom in its total life and ministry. This includes the sponsoring of all institutions, literature, radio, <u>or</u> access to independent institutions and services that relate to the life, well-being, and out-reach of the church.

> . . . The principal charge of missions is to the world and not to the church. We are commanded to evangelize the world and disciple all nations. As missionary societies and missionaries we are "sent" into the world (John 17:18 -- to the people of unbelief and non-belief). Here lies our principal sphere of responsibility and operation. This mission has been given to us by the Lord and must be discharged in the name of the Lord and in His authority.
>
> . . . In keeping with the principles of divine authority, biblical brother-hood, corporateness, equality, and mutuality, and according to the practice of Paul, the churches ought not frustrate and dominate missionary endeavors in communities not under the immediate influence of the church and in geographical areas which the church has not evangelized and in ministries which the church is not rendering. As long as there are communities and groupings of people or tribes outside of the immediate influence and reach of the church, and ministries not rendered by it, there should be room for the mission and the missionary.
>
> . . . Christianity is basically a religion of life and relationships. Relationships are of deeper significance than organizational structure and identity. The struggle for the preservation of organizational identity must not be permitted to disrupt spiritual relationships whatever our rights may be.
>
> . . . No organizational pattern will suffice for all circumstances, cultures, and peoples. Patterns are not divinely inspired but historically, culturally and psychologically conditioned. Flexibility, creativity, must characterize every dynamic and growing movement, especially a movement of international, cross-cultural, multi-cultural, cross-racial dimensions. Sometimes I fear the "old age arthritic" inflexibility of many missionary societies more than I do fear the lack of maturity (?) of many of the younger churches.
>
> . . . That organization is most ideal which genders the deepest level of fellowship among the brethren, facilitates the freest flow of spiritual dynamics, enhances the speediest and most effec-

tive course of evangelism, advances the church in her attainment of maturity, selfhood, and identification in the purpose and program of God, expresses most fully the unity and equality of all believers under the same Lord, in the same church, and in the same family of God.

. . . In faith we must lay hold of the principle that our Lord stands ready to do a "New Thing" in our midst and in our days. As we venture out in faith, believing that God will do a new thing also in mission-church relationship, we will experience that He will "make a way in the wilderness, and rivers in the desert." Both mission societies and the church are His. In grace and sovereignty He may see fit to create a New Thing in our days.

B. EMERGING THEORIES AND PATTERNS.

At no time have missions remained unconcerned about tensions at home or abroad. So also in the issue of mission-church relationship. If today we find ourselves in a crucial situation it is not because we have willfully neglected the Lord's business. Preoccupation with numerous other concerns and pressures have kept us from creative innovations, hardly realizing that former ways of doing things are outmoded and that old patterns are worn out.

The critical questions raised before as "underlying issues" have only in recent years become evident in much evangelical work and only in the last decade have they become crucial. Neither dismay nor despair must be permitted to overwhelm us or to put us off balance. Christ does not forsake the vessel which He has launched when same is threatened by storm and raging waves. His "peace be still" will be heard again by all in tune with heaven. Thus we must listen as we seek solutions and search for projections. At the same time let us test theories which have developed and patterns of mission-church relationship which are being advocated.

Let us not fall into the snare of negligence dindifference or take a simplistic attitude in is matter. Relationships are not becoming more mple. Our world is moving into complexity and nsions are mounting because relationships in uralistic societies are compounding. Mission-urch relationships are also becoming more complex d patterns of relationships are multiplying as ople beset by frustrations and pressures are oping about seeking some kind of solution. To assify them accurately is difficult.

Students of these matters have suggested that l patterns can be divided into two major posi-ons with several modifications --

The union of church and mission which is also known as fusion, merger, integration etc.;
A dichotomy or parallelism in which both mission and church maintain separate organizational identity and structures and function in some kind of relationship, defined or undefined.

Such classification may be helpful, but it is oversimplification of complex structures and lationships. It presupposes that a thesis results ly in an antithesis. No synthesis is envisaged a possible third option.

For our purpose, I present three patterns of lationships, -- thesis, antithesis and synthesis.

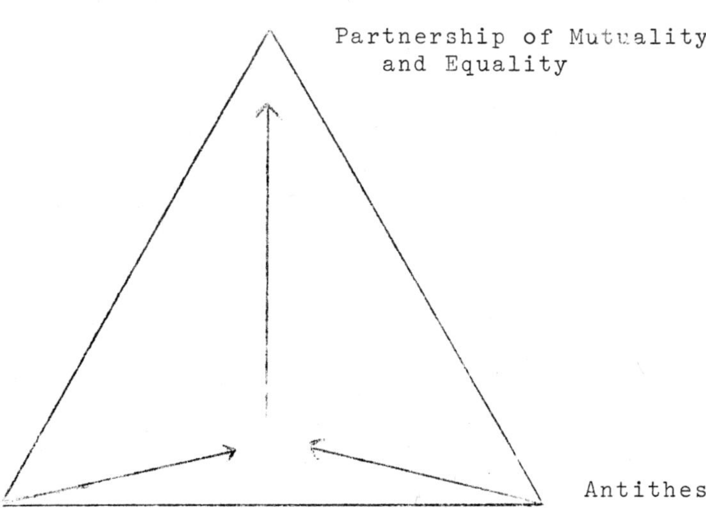

I. Organizational Unilaterality and Functional Servanthood- see pattern I, Appendix p. 226.

This pattern is also known as fusion, merger, integration and union of church and mission. In this program, all jurisdiction and administration on the field is transferred to the national church. The complete missionary program and missionaries are integrated into the national structure and conducted by that body with complete ownership of all property.

Usually the program calls for two things from the sending organization:

(1) An appropriation of finances, usually a specified but undesignated sum of money, completely under the administration of the national church.
(2) Personnel to assist in various ministries with no status and special position as missionaries assigned to them from home.

The missionary simply comes as a brother or fraternal worker, placing himself at the disposal of the national church. He receives his assignment from that church and becomes responsible to the church. Usually he receives his financial support from home either directly or through the church. Therefore, while the mission considers itself a partner of the national church, the missionary becomes a servant of the national church. The missionary partnership has been converted into "servantship." This relationship has been praised as true ecumenicity in practice and is to express real equality. At this occasion I shall not enter upon the long history and disputed theology of this pattern. It is found today in most ecumenical churches. It cannot be stated dogmatically that this pattern can not be made to work. It does work in certain areas of the world and in certain ecclesiastical systems. On purely functional basis, it cannot be rejected outrightly.

Carefully I have weighed more than twenty arguments against unilaterality or fusion. Some carry persuasion in them. Most can easily be negated. Few of the opponents to unilaterality (fusion) betray a high view of the local church as an agency of God. They advance most of their arguments from a deduced biblical idealism rather than from biblical realism. The latter finds its expression not in the "ideal Church" but in the local church in real life situations.

A second weakness which pervades most arguments against fusion is the fact that a certain predetermined stereotyped concept of the "indigenous church" is idealized beyond scriptural warrant and much to the impoverishing of the basic biblical qualities of fellowship, brotherhood, partnership, mutual burden-bearing, fellow-yoke-bearing and christian sharing. This is a rather serious matter and gives me much concern. Certainly God is more concerned about a truly Christian church than about a humanly defined and designed indigenous church.

Our arguments therefore are not as persuasive as they may seem to us. They may be as much rationalization of our predetermined patterns and ideas and a system of defense of our way, or a reaction to certain manifestations elsewhere as they are a result of deeper probing into tensions, conflicts and national feelings and thinking. Some of this feeling, even in the hearts of evangelicals, is fairly well but most politely expressed in a paper read by F. L. Kamasi as reported in Report of the Fifth Asia Conference, Bangkok, Thailand, February 18-26, 1969, pages 197-200. (Foreign Department The C&MA, New York). The national churches may be as pleased and thrilled to speak of "our missionaries" as we were only some years ago to report to our churches of "our native helpers" and "our native churches." We need to be very cautious and sensitive.

Having pointed to these apparent weaknesses of our arguments and expressed this caution, I join the opponents of unilaterality or fusion. To the arguments already advanced by others there are further reasons for a disapproval of this pattern.

First, the pattern of unilaterality destroys the relationship of true partnership. It should be noted that "partnership" in this relationship is a misnomer. Partnership and unilateral legislation and administration are mutually exclusive. In true partnership, mutuality, not unilaterality, governs. There is neither dominance nor absorption in true partnership. Dr. Max Warren has well stated that in partnership ". . . involvement and acceptance of both responsibility and liability presuppose the continuity within the partnership of each partner." This principle is completely erased. Mutuality is nonexistent.

Second, it distorts the concepts of mutuality and equality -- two basic concepts in the *body structure* of the Church of Jesus Christ. It makes one church subservient to the other.

Third, it reduces the sending church to a non-missionary church by cutting it off from direct access to the world and makes it into a "supply depot and service agency."

Fourth, it violates the principle of individual priesthood and the true calling of many missionaries and makes them servants within the church rather than missionaries to the world.

In addition it must be said that recent history is our evidence of the impracticality of this pattern in numerous instances. Many frustrated missionaries are our witness of its practical non-workablity in most circumstances.

Thus it is neither true partnership, biblical realism, genuine ecumenicity nor practical workability.

Dichotomy in Mission-Church Relationship.

The seeming opposite from unilaterality is dichotomy -- two organizations in some kind of workable relationship.

Two somewhat different patterns of dichotomy have been advanced and may be found in operation. I present them separately but evaluate them together.

II. *Organizational Dichotomy and Functional Co-operation*.- See pattern II, Appendix p. 227

This is the pattern of complete organizational disassociation of mission and church. The ideal is functional co-operation rather than separation or integration. According to this pattern, the mission and the church form two autonomous bodies with separate legislative and administrative authorities though they operate in fraternal relationships and functional co-operation.

The mission and the church are distinct, separate, independent organizational bodies <u>parallel movements with distinct assignments.</u> The missionary labors independently of the jurisdiction of the national church and under the direction of his board of missions. The degree of functional and spiritual interrelation of the two bodies, because of a goal-relationship, is either taken for granted or carefully delineated. Usually it is understood that the mission does not set up its own churches, but rather relates such to the national body and voluntarily becomes a functional, serving agency to the ecclesiastical structure.

This is basically the pattern of numerous faith missions whose supreme goal is the evangelization of the world and the establishing of local congregations as lighthouses in many communities, and who are less concerned for larger structural units in various lands. However, it is also well exemplified by the Presbyterian "Brazil Plan" of 1916, hailed as a unique success as recently as 1968 by the Reverend C. Darby Fulton (EMQ - Vol. 4, No. 2).

This program functions best according to the following principles:
(a) The mission practices intensive work rather than extensive evangelization. It practices geographical concentration rather than general dissemination of the gospel. To a certain degree, it follows the example of Paul who abode in one place for a considerable time, at least sufficient time for a church to be born. (b) Evangelism of a locality is undertaken with the purpose of establishing a functioning assembly or church. (c) After a church has come into being, it is led into fellowship with churches of similar persuasion and organization and thus linked to a larger national body. (d) The missionary officially disassociates himself from here on from the church and technically has neither right nor authority over this body of believers. He returns only upon invitation to assist and to minister as requested.

The arguments for this pattern of operation must not be minimized. Based both on logic and sentiment, and in part on experience, they seem sound, convincing, and beneficial. In general they are somewhat as follows:

(1) It best protects the autonomy and selfhood of the emerging national church. No missionary sits in the church courts to exert undue influence and to project his image upon the legislative body. Spiritual

self-reliance and self-help become primary exercises from the beginning. It is hoped that thereby not only tensions will be eliminated and the Western image of the church minimized, but also the selfhood of the church will evolve more fully. Its national character hopefully will become apparent, and, above all, the church will from the very beginning learn to depend upon its own resources, and particularly upon the Superintendent of the church, the indwelling Holy Spirit. All of this is basic and crucial for a church if it is to function properly and to fulfill the dwsign of God for it in the community and the world. Also, should an emergency demand the withdrawal of all missionaries, the church would continue its function without serious vibrations and interruptions.

(2) It best protects the missionary in his primary calling and in his freedom and initiative as a "sent one" for a particular task. It permits him to labor as a pioneer in the "regions beyond" without becoming absorbed in a church-centered program and wrapped up in the organizational and institutional structure and life of the national church.

This aspect must not be minimized. While mission and church belong together, the inclusive mission of the church is larger than missions. The total function of the church is larger than the sending forth of evangelists into the world of unbelief and gospel destitution beyond its won area of operation and influence. At the same time, it remains a New Testament fact that a church ceases to be New Testament in spirit and design if it ceases its missions as well as its mission. No church sent into the world (mission) can afford not to send forth some of its members beyond its own region (missions). Most of these "sent-forth-ones" are evangelists, not to other churches, but to the world in unbelief and without the gospel. To envelope them in another church program, no matter where this may be geographically, is doing injustice to their very calling and assignment. They are missionaries, sent ones, beyond the borders of the church. This high calling must be clearly grasped, emphatically taught, and zealously guarded.

It should be noted, however, that this evangelist-missionary concept may not exhaust the interchurch ministries between the older and younger churches and that there may be a place for fraternal workers.

(3) It best protects the image of a board of missions as being an agent of a unique task and particular assignment. It is not a church board that has legislative authority over churches. It does not represent the church in its total function. Neither is it merely a recruiting agency. It is a board of a particular design and mission, a board to send forth men and women of a particular calling into a particular situation -- the world of unbelief, destitute of the gospel,--for a singular purpose -- the purpose of gospel proclamation by every legitimate means and effective method, -- and the establishing of functioning churches who will assume their New Testament responsibility and calling and develop their own selfhood and national character. This board is not a mere service agency or "supply depot." It has not received its authority and assignment from a national body, nor is its sending forth subject to invitations and requests. Its task is not completed with the rise of a national church. It stands before its risen Lord, is subject to His unique command, conscientiously observes the need of the world, and boldly expresses the promptings of the spirit of missions. Only then can the true image of the board of missions be presented. This, too, must be zealously guarded and energetically pursued.

III. Organizational Dichotomy and Functional Partnership.- See pattern III, Appendix p. 228

This is the pattern of fraternal partnership in obedience. Although this pattern has many factors in common with the preceding one, it has some distinctives. According to this pattern, (1) each body has its own organization, personnel, budget, and program and thus remains a distinctive and autonomous entity; (2) with the understanding of the church, the mission functions more or less as a service agency to the national church and serves mainly two purposes.

The first of these is to loan workers to the churches for specifically agreed upon assignments and projects. These may be in the areas of pioneer work, institutional ministries, technical services, or church administration. The missionary may be spoken of as a fraternal worker on an assignment to the national church or a loaned missionary serving with the national church.

The second purpose is to promote certain specific projects for the benefit of the church and community, such as evangelism, hospitals, schools -- usually schools of higher learning and theological training centers -- literature, publications, radio, etc. In this way the work is integrated into the national church structure, but the worker and the organization are autonomous organizationally. The principle of partnership is evident on a somewhat different level than we saw before.

The two bodies are linked together, functionally and in purpose and fellowship. It is a fraternal partnership -- relationship with the mission doing something for the churches, lessening the load of the churches, yet without infringing upon the rights and privileges of the autonomous churches. Usually such projects are administered jointly by the church and mission.

Evaluation of Dichotomy

The arguments for dichotomy seem reasonable and strong. The question remains, however, whether parallelism proves functionally most effective, filially most satisfactory, spiritually and religiously most helpful, and whether it expresses the highest biblical idealism within the reach of Christian realism. I am forced by history, applied anthropology, and the Bible to place an emphatic "no" behind each one of these factors. While logic may not be faulty, it may be resting upon faulty premises or upon an inadequate embracing of the total substratum and biblical realism. To me dichotomy in the above sense is less Christian achievement and more human accommodation.

That the arguments for dichotomy are not as conclusive as they seem is evident from the fact that other theories are competing for consideration and are pleading to be heard. Some national churches reject it as unacceptable.

The honesty and rational depth of some of the arguments favoring organizational, legislative, and administrative dichotomy need not be questioned. The principle of dichotomy may be read into the Wheaton Declaration under the section of "Missions -- and Foreign Missions," at least into the last sentence of the declaration. Significantly, however, the statement had declared previously: "In the New Testament no clearly defined structure for church-mission relationship can be adduced."

This bespeaks a hesitancy, uncertainty, and a sense of haziness. It leaves the door open to human wisdom and cultural adaptation. This may be proper. However, it seems to portray more an unwillingness or a reservedness than an outright openness. The Bible does not prescribe detailed organizational structures and patterns; however, it does concern itself with basic principles and guidelines. While the former are matters of time and culture, the latter are matters of revelation.

The principle of dichotomy is not sound biblically, theologically, sociologically, or pedagogically, at least not to my judgement and my observations.

Biblically, it cannot be sustained. Dichotomy is not known in the Bible. It does not fit into the body structure of the church neither into the fellowship of the saints, nor into the co-laborer and fellow-laborer practice of the apostles. It must be recognized that the sole Lordship of Christ in the church argues at least as strongly for the unity of mission and church as it does for the individual responsibility of each member. The individual priesthood of every believer and the membership in the body of Christ find their common ground and unity in the Lordship of Christ. Here mutuality and equality meet in unity and obedience. Outside of the official apostles and their immediate associates and subordinates other apostles seemingly were known as the messengers of the churches (Phil. 2:25; 2 Cor. 8:23). They seemed to have been church related in their ministries.

The example of Paul is also not sufficient to prove this principle. It cannot be maintained on the basis that Paul did not become a member of the mission churches he founded. While this is true, it is so only superficially. It will be admitted that Paul did not join the church of his own nationality. He was not a member of the church in Jerusalem or Judea. His Home church was in Antioch, a church in the mission field, a product of missionary evangelism and a mother church of other mission churches. He was not a part of Jewish Christianity, but of Hellenistic Christianity. Here was the field of his labor and here was his spiritual home. He was part and parcel of the Hellenistic Christian church. So were his co-workers -- Timothy, Titus, Luke, Silas, etc. Only as they were involved in the internal structure and life of the movement they founded could they exert wholesome and maximum influence in the developing churches.

Dichotomy is not sound <u>theologically, sociologically, and pedagogically</u>. It must be kept in mind that syncretism, messianism, nativism, and Christopaganism are formidable enemies of the Christian gospel and the church. They seek by a process of reductionism, additionism, or modification to destroy the purity, uniqueness, and independence of the gospel of God and the dynamic life of the Church of Jesus Christ. These enemies are not overcome by sound conversion and the organization of an indigenous church. Indoctrination, according to the soundest pedagogical principles, is an essential part of missions. Applied anthropology makes no hiding of the fact that in general it takes several generations until a genuine "regeneration of culture" in language, ideas, and ideals has taken permanent shape and root.

<u>Evangelistic fervor</u> in the younger churches should not be taken for granted. Religious propagation has not been a part of the previous culture and religion. Evangelism must be caught by association as it is taught in the class room and in the churches. Only evangelism begets evangelism. God wants evangelizing churches. It cannot be proven that the evangelistic impact of parallelism in general has been impressive. There are some noble achievements, but these are the exceptions. Only recently and under very unique circumstances is evangelism becoming dynamic in some younger evangelical churches. Parallelism or dichotomy did not beget it at least not in full measure.

It was a rude awakening that over 80% of more than 300 national pastors and leading laymen in about 15 countries on three continents felt that the presence of a "parallel mission" along side the churches had unconsciously conditioned them to become church centered. It had become a part of them to think of the mission as being responsible for the evangelism program and the outreach to the world outside of the church. Very little of evangelism carry-over had resulted.

It should be noted that all pastors studied were part of the churches that have arisen through the efforts of EFMA and IFMA missions. To our humiliation it must be admitted that we have given birth to relatively few dynamic evangelistic churches and movements. The real evangelism impact around the world today comes mainly from the Assemblies of God, the Southern Baptists and some special agencies. This is a fact that is endlessly depressing. Where and when has our breakdown in dynamic evangelism come?

It must be kept in mind that the two most dynamic evangelistic movements just mentioned would not fit into our pattern of dichotomy. They operate on a higher level of relationships.

Far be it to think in paternalistic terms to legislate or to dominate the younger churches for a period of generations. This would not be tolerated, nor could it ever be desired. But be it just as far from us to abandon these churches, separate ourselves from personal and intimate relationship to their life, organization, and purpose, or to dis-associate ourselves from direct and brotherly involvement in their struggle, mission and evangelism. Only as we are properly related to them socially and as we administratively and functionally constitute an integral part of the church and are accepted members of the in-group, can we truly fulfill our teaching mission to them and participate with them in dynamic evangelism. Dichotomy in its simple version must be rejected. A better and higher way must be found within practical and spiritual ecumenicity.

(These papers will be coming out as part of Dr. Peter's new book: <u>THE BIBLICAL THEOLOGY OF MISSIONS</u>, Moody Press. Anticipated release - Spring 1972).

MISSION/CHURCH RELATIONS OVERSEAS

PART II

by George W. Peters

IV. Partnership of Equality and Mutuality.
See pattern IV, Appendix p. 229

In the pattern of partnership of equality and mutuality, we have a synthesis of the two extreme positions of unilaterality and dichotomy. Here both the church and the mission can live out their divine calling, preserve their identity on a certain level while they merge on a different level. The program is neither mission-centered nor church-centered, but church-based and world-faced. Of course, the danger is ever present that a church based program may become a church bound program. This must be avoided at all cost.

Christian missions must be focused on the world, not on the church with its organization, institutions and program. Missionaries as such are not sent for police action or church programming, but in order that the attack forces of the churches may be bolstered and that churches might be multiplied. The energies of the sending church must not be spent in perfecting church structures, drafting constitutions, exercising church discipline, and superintending institutions. The goal of missions is not the structural and institutional life of the church community, but the proclamation of the gospel to those who do not confess Jesus Christ as Lord and Savior.

The above principle, however, must be applied in wisdom and with care. It must not lead to dichotomy. There is a prophetic and teaching ministry for some servants of God within the church to assist the church in maturing into the stature of Christ, to come to oneness of doctrine, and to encourage fulfillment of God's purpose in this world. We should not deprive the national church of this vital teaching ministry which belongs to the church universal and not to a local or national church exclusively. The Bible provides for a pastor-teacher-missionary as well as the evangelist-missionary. Barnabas and Apollos seem to have been such missionaries performing their ministry within the church universal.

The travelling teachers as well as the evangelists in the church universal are missionaries in the full sense of the word. Though no sharp line of demarcation can be drawn, yet there is a difference of function, responsibility, and sphere of operation. The teacher functions mainly within the churches and the evangelist functions mainly outside of the churches; the one deepens and enriches the life of the church, and the other advances the borders of the church.

The main thrust of missions and of the majority of missionaries must remain a ministry to the unevangelized world. Thus evangelism and church planting are the main thrust and burden of missions.

Yet such a thrust should be church-based or church-related and not separated from the churches. Dichotomy of organization, purpose, and assignment may seem an easy way out of serious complications. But it creates new and insurmountable ones and offends biblical ideals and relationships. We dare not bypass the church nor separate missions from it. It must be involved on an equal basis and in closest collaboration and fellowship. Missions must also be the mission _of_ the new church, and not only _for_ the church. Fraternal partnership must be created. The church, too, must become actively involved in the ministry to the world and not only to itself. This must take place from the very beginning. This was so in the book of Acts. Partnership, obedience must begin when the church begins. Such partnership, however, must be carefully agreed upon to make it possible for both parties to function fully according to the calling of God. We must realize that the church's ministry is broader than missions only.

Missions must be related to the churches, and must become an integral part of the churches, fully involving the national churches. The missionary's ministry must be rendered through the church, but not mainly to the church. Principally, he works neither _in_ the church _nor_ _for_ the church, _but with_ the church. His service is mainly to the unevangelized world. Wherever his official membership may be, he is a full-fledged laborer of the board of missions _and_ the national church with rights, privileges, and responsibilities, serving in the missionary expansion _of the church_. This assignment is his by divine calling and mutual agreement between him, his mission, and the national church, and cannot be altered by unilateral action either by the mission or the church. Only in this manner is true partnership possible with equality and mutuality evident. Therefore, one is not over the other nor integrated or submerged. Here is organizational co-ordination, and functional unity.

It is evident that in this pattern the missionary may work himself out of a geographical area but not out of his divine calling as missionary (one sent with the gospel to the unevangelized). Starting as a missionary to a people he has become part of a conference to serve as a missionary with the church to unevangelized areas that must be reached with the gospel. He is not a temporary worker in a field. He has a life assignment to a ministry. He may change his status and relationship, but he does not change his work, assignment, or calling.

It should be noted here that it seems wise that in such evangelistic expansion ministry a missionary works not only in full agreement with the national church, but also side by side with a national brother designated and <u>subsidized by the church</u> who may continue in the ministry when the missionary moves to a new area. Thereby, not only is continuity of the work assured, but the church is directly involved in the missionary expansion and the work is national from the very beginning.

From the analysis it is evident that the mission society and the church are two separate entities, that the mission society recognizes the church from the very beginning as a functioning and responsible body, that the mission of the society is principally to the world, that the church must become involved from the very beginning in the program of evangelism, that such involvement is most effectively achieved when church and mission merge as equals.

In the program of evangelism and church expansion, that such a program must become church-based from the very beginning, that the individual missionary in his missionary outreach becomes responsible to the church-mission body which directs and administers the outreach program, that the initiative lies with the joint body and that therefore living ideas may come from either source.

Thus the church is not submerged and the mission society is not subjugated. The program of evangelism and church expansion, however, is merged and involves both the church and the mission. (See appendix p.230)

Tension Areas in Partnership

It would be unrealistic to assume that partnership in equality and mutuality presents no tension areas. Such there are. No dynamic movement can be and ever will be without tensions and problems within human situations and historical processes.

It is impossible to forecast all the areas in which tensions will arise. No prophet-minister has ever been able to tell the young couple before him ready to exchange marriage vows all the areas in which tension will crop up in their joint life's journey. So it is in any dynamic partnership. Too many factors are involved. They must not discourage us. There actually is a thing as creative tension. No high ideal has ever been achieved nor has it been able to function without experiencing difficulties, frustrations, tension and modifications. In general we can foresee that tensions will arise in areas of policy making and legislation, programming, missionary assignment, budgeting and property acquisition, usage and disposal.

<u>Partnership and policy making and legislation</u>.

Partnership begins on the highest level. This is the level of policy making and legislation. As stated before, partnership is meaningless as soon as policy making and legislation is handed over to or is taken over by one body. Unilaterality destroys partnership. It has been well stated that "progress in partnership"depends in a measure on human insight and adjustment, but its origin is not found in these. Its source is a <u>common obedience</u> to the living Word of God, given once for all in Jesus Christ yet given anew through the Holy Spirit in every generation.

" . . . Above all earthly circumstances stands unchanged the command of Christ to preach the Gospel to every creature. This command has not yet been fulfilled by the Church. It cannot be fulfilled unless all the forces of all the churches, older and younger alike, are gathered in a <u>common loyalty</u>, inspired by a <u>common task</u> and mobilized in a <u>common service</u>. This situation is one of extreme urgency." (Renewal and Advance, pp. 173,174, C.W. Ranson, editor, Edinburgh House Press, London, 1948).

The expressed commonness is not real nor dynamic unless there is partnership on the highest level -- the level of policy making and legislation. Mission and church must meet and melt on this level. Only as mutuality and equality are recognized, cherished and respected will the real dynamic of the Holy Spirit be loosed in full measure. There is no room in partnership for dominance and unilaterality. Commonness of interest, of concern, of rights, of privileges, of responsibilities and of accountability make for strong partnership.

As evangelicals we have been strong in our emphasis of the relationship of the body member to the Head. This is essential. However, we have been pathetically weak in our emphasis on the member to member relationship. This is why so often individualism runs rampant, team work becomes difficult and submission is spurned. Yet, the Bible knows as much of interdependence as of independence. God seeks not only independent churches but interdependent as well.

Partnership in policy making and legislation has its definite limitations. It does not extend into the areas of the local church--the area, district or national organization of the church or the institutions which relate to the life of the church. The autonomy of the church in these matters must be respected and safeguarded.

Partnership in policy making and legislation concerns itself with matters which directly involve the mission (mainly evangelization beyond the borders of the church and the expansion of the church). Basically this will revolve around five areas;

First, Projection and approval of expansion programs; (perhaps a three or five year program)

Second, Assignment and placement of personnel; (all missionaries and such national workers as serve in the program of the joint body)

Third, Projection, approval and allocation of annual budget;

Fourth, Acquisition, usage and disposal of properties in the expansion plan;

Fifth, Special delegated projects which are serving the community as well as the church and which by the consent and/or authority of the church have been initiated and/or are being continued -- radio, general literature, higher education institutions, hospitals, etc.

Partnership and Administration.

With policy making and legislation in missions being shared by the mission and the national church we ask: how is the program to be administered? Is the administrative base to be retained geographically in the area of the sending churches? Or is it to be located in the area of operation? If it is to be in this area, is administration to be in the hands of the mission or the church? We have thus two basic questions in relation to administration. The first concerns more the denominational missions, the second affects more the interdenominational missions. Many of the latter have their administrative offices in the field of operation.

Three reasons compel me to believe that the administrative base must be shifted away from the sending churches and into the area of operation.

(1) The efficiency of the work. No student of the history of missions can escape the embarrassing fact that we are touching upon one of the most sensitive points of modern missions. Perhaps in few other ways has colonialism influenced modern missions more than through superimposed administration procedures Much has been said about paternalism in methods and the colonial patterning of missions in the lands abroad. This is sadly true. But it is as much a fact of history that mission boards at home also fully operated on colonial principles with an office thousands of miles away from the sphere of operation, yet fully administering the work and the worker in those areas. Only slowly is the extra-scriptural basis of this principle being recognized and the inefficiency of the practice conceded. Even more reluctantly are changes introduced into the structure of administration. The mission administrative office thousands of miles away is the last but also the strongest colonial remnant of modern missions.

It was wisdom on the part of Hudson Taylor when in 1865 he decreed for the China Inland Mission that the base of administration must be related to the work and the worker, rather than to the supporting constituency. Legislation which affects the work and the worker must be related to the people directly involved, not only to an office across the ocean which provides funds. Here common sense, sound business judgment, and Christian insight triumphed over the prevailing colonial pattern of the day. Other faith missions adopted similar patterns. Though this system is not without serious perils, its efficiency has been demonstrated by several larger missions.

(2) The nature of the church. It lies within the nature of the church to be self-administrative as well as to administer the affairs related to her. It would seem natural, therefore, that as soon as a church has come into being in a geographical area the administration of the mission expansion program should be integrally related to the church in whose geographical proximity and cultural milieu the work is being carried on and toward whose expansion the work is to contribute. Only so will the work be actually a part of the national church and be integrated into her structure. To separate the administration of missions is unnatural and violates sound idealism.

Dr. Raymond J. Davis, general director of the Sudan Interior Mission, recently answered a question on the major policy changes of their mission within the past ten years. Said he: "Our policy is continually being reviewed in the light of new circumstances. Three of the most far-reaching changes during the past decade have been: [1] The participation of national church leadership (representative of the Association of Evangelical Churches of West Africa) in the major policy-forming body of the Sudan Interior Mission in West Africa; [2] the transfer of more than a dozen SIM stations to ECWA (Evangelical Churches of West Africa). . ." This is but the natural result of healthy development and Christian relationships. Ideally there should be no need for turning a work over to the church. It should be related to the church as the church grows up with it. In fact, the need for turning over (known once by the infamous word devolution) indicates that we have not been indigenous from the very beginning as we had hoped we were.

(3) <u>The natural resentment of foreign administration.</u>

Much has been written about the foreign missionary, his place in missions, his need and desirability in the field, and the advisability or inadvisability of his presence in the indigenous, autonomous work. Too much the unpopular missionary has been made popular to the discouragement of many young volunteers and ready contributors.

What are the facts behind the scene? The author has had the privilege of studying this matter quite extensively and has discovered that there are causes and conditions which create a favorable and a disfavorable atmosphere for the missionary. One of the principal causes of disfavor is the fact that the missionary operates as an agent under the direction of an administration located in a foreign country. The question is not one of motivation on the part of the missionary. Neither is it the fact that he is a citizen of another country, or a person of another color or race. His cause and purpose are widely appreciated and his services are wanted. In the main the problem is not the missionary.

It remains a fact that neither church, community or government appreciate an intrusion of an administrative office located in a foreign land. There is no scriptural precedent for such practice. To the contrary, in my estimation it violates biblical idealism and propagates colonial practices. The location of the administrative center is important.

<u>Administration -- church or mission?</u>

Equally important as the location of administration is the second question. Who is to manage the office of administration, the mission or the church? The administration should go into the hands of the church at the earliest possible date. Here indigenization should begin. There is no scriptural, historical or practical reason for a dual administration in a field where a church of like persuasion and common loyalty exists, especially a church which is the result of the mission's efforts. A high view of the church necessitates the unification and transfer of administration of the mission expansion program to the church.

In my studies of this issue around the world I soon discovered that American missions and missionaries experience more serious tensions than certain English missions in similar circumstances. This aroused my interest. In personal conferences with canon Douglas Webster and secretary John V. Taylor I asked for their comments on this matter. It was of significance to me that both men referred to the low view of the local church of many American missionaries and some missions. They spoke with concern about the issue. Their comments were substantiated by several other mission administrators. They confirmed my conviction and findings.

It needs to be recognized that there is a psychology and sociology as well as a theology underlying mission operations. Basic concepts, consciously or unconsciously held, are important. Our view of the church becomes determinative in this matter. A high view of the local church in the true New Testament sense of the word will find it relatively easy to see the biblicity and urgency to unify and transfer the administration of the total program to the church. Only then will evangelism and church expansion become truly church based. Christ is building His church; He loved her and gave Himself for her. The mission, too loves the church and must give herself for her.

A principal cause of tension in many fields is the fact of the dual administration which persists long after a church has come into existence. The fact that the national church has no part or only an advisory part in the legislation and administration of a work and worker in her midst and in her land is unnatural and remains a strong point of friction. It is neither the work or the worker, but rather the policy which is being resented. While we are apt to attribute this to nationalism, unspirituality or immaturity (which it may not be, perhaps it is a symptom of maturity, selfhood and concern) the fact remains that foreign administration in the presence of a national church is a violation of human rights and Christian relationships. It creates tensions within the body of Christ and disrupts fellowship on the deepest level.

It may be argued that the principle of equality and mutuality is being violated by what seems to be unilateral administration. Ideally this may be so. With mission-church <u>synthesis</u> becoming a reality in legislation, administration must be unified if the unity of the program is to be safe-guarded. By placing it under the church rather than under the mission the program is more likely to become church-related and not mission-related.

Partnership and Missionary Integration.

The question of the integration of the missionary into the national church and program is not a simple matter to decide. Denominational missionaries should find it natural to integrate themselves into the sister churches of their own denomination, no matter in what country or culture they may be found. Common confessionalism and other similarities bind them together into one body. This commonness of faith and purpose should supersede all other relationships.

This is not as simple for the faith missions whose missionaries constitute no such homogeneous group in doctrine and church polity. Their varied denominational or independent church background complicates matters seriously. Therefore, should they constitute a free-moving body of men and women serving in evangelism and church planting, relating themselves functionally to the national church but remaining outside her organizational structures? Here sentiments, convictions, and practices differ.

We quote at some length from an article in the Evangelical Missions Quarterly: "A statement of the problem and a resulting stance are expressed in the following quotation from a speech delivered at a conference in Limuru, Kenya, in 1962. While the address was given in an African setting, the reference to related experience in India shows that the problem stated and the general philosophy expressed represent a broad attitude in most regions where the emerging church is found. The speaker stated:

"' In Africa we find the missions in varying stages of integration with the respective churches. It is still a real issue and must be worked out vigorously and realistically as quickly as possible. Our experience in India follows very closely the patterns that are developing here in Africa. They are some of the very same principles, fears, and problems expressed here in Africa the past two weeks. For many years there has been a struggle between the mission and the church. The mission wanted to bring the church into the mission in one way or another, or wanted the mission and missionaries to completely integrate into the church. By 1952, the church won out and the mission integrated into the church.

"' What is it that the young churches want? Not indigenization in the older sense that we missionaries used to use it. They do not want a self-supporting, self-governing, self-propagating type of church that separates mission and church, missionaries and nationals.

"' At an African luncheon meeting sponsored by the Africa Committee, Division of Foreign Missions, National Council of Churches, at San Francisco, California, December 7, 1960, Bishop Lesslie Newbigin clearly gave the African viewpoint. This was just after his study tour of Africa. Young missionaries were saying: "We are the temporary people. We are here to help the African to stand on his own feet, then we shall go . . . We are merely scaffolding. You are the building. We are temporary. You are permanent." But African leaders said, "If this is the understanding of your task, it is better that you go now rather than later. We are not interested in an African church. We are interested in a Christian church in Africa, and we regard you as part of the church . . . We want the missionary who will come here, live with us, work with us, die with us, and lay his bones here in Africa."

"' The whole question involves identification. An African spoke to Newbigin about identification. He said there are two kinds. "One is the anthropological conception of identification; the other is identification in Christ. It is the second in which we are interested."

"' Is the view of the younger churches valid? Yes! This principle of interaction and interrelationship must be used in all human relationships if there is to be peace and progress. Separation of people is wrong. Walls dividing people into black and white, rich and poor, East and West are unchristian. This is sin. It is pride and selfishness that make us want to keep aloof from people.'" (Arthur M. Climenhaga EMQ Vol. 1, No. 2, Winter 1965, p.5).

We must learn to understand the sentiments of the leadership of the national church. At the same time we must learn to discern whether such language is a cry of the heart for identification on a deeper level and a yearning for closer fellowship than we have offered to the church thus far, or whether it is a desire for absorption into a church-centered program. History warns us that not always is the assignment of missions clearly kept in mind and differentiated within the total program of the church. Thus the missionary program becomes blurred and integration is mistakenly taken for assimilation to the degree that the missionary loses his identity as a missionary of the church as well as the board of missions. We must remind ourselves that the missionary has not gone forth mainly to join another church. He has been called of God and he has been sent forth by the mission with the commission to preach the Gospel of Jesus Christ to people outside of the church. His task is evangelism. He must go beyond the borders of the church although not without the church. His calling and assignment cannot be endangered or altered by a decree and arrangement of a church. Integration is not absorption; it is not assimilation; it is not subjugation. It is not one winning over the other. The missionary must remain a missionary. His activity in the main is directed toward the world and not toward the church unless he is a fraternal worker in the church. His status and assignment cannot be changed by unilateral decision and action of the church. He is integrated in purpose and relationship, but in legislation and assignment he remains under partnership of equality and mutuality by church and the board. Any other platform destroys partnership and makes missions on the part of the mission and sending churches impossible.

It may be a part of wisdom to encourage missionaries who are serving in church-related institutions and assignments to become active members of the national local churches, while missionaries who are serving in the program of evangelism and church expansion and thus are not related directly to specific local churches to retain their membership in the sending churches.

All of us, however must face the question realistically and honestly whether we have offered to the churches and leadership that degree of identification in Christ which makes fellowship on the deepest level in the Spirit possible. Or, has our cross-cultural, cross-racial and cross-organizational complex separated us on the deepest level and in areas of ministries from our brethren? Christ came to break down the middle wall of partition (Eph. 2:14). This can under many circumstances also include cross-organizational structures.

Partnership and Finances.

The projection and approval of an operational budget requires much wisdom. Many factors enter in to do the will of God in the matter of finances.

Modern evangelical missions has been dominated by an extra-biblical concept, if not by an outrightly unchristian ideal of indigenity. This has caused perilous difficulties in the work, serious disruptions in relationships, critical attitudes and unchristian demands as well as unchristian withholdings. The disperity in income and the ability to initiate and sponsor projects and programs with foreign finances by missions and missionaries which the national church has no hopes to carry on without financial subsidy has assured either the permanency of the mission or the paralysis of the mission as soon as the mission or missionary leaves.

I am not prepared to condemn the mission or missionary. Many ambitious projects were undertaken to get the Gospel of Jesus Christ out to the people for whom we felt a special burden and responsibility. Thus every modern means was employed to expedite the work. The motive and intentions were good. The wisdom of such proceedings may be questioned. We have come to a time and place in the history of world evangelization when the whole issue of finances is due a thoroughgoing review. Not only preconceived ideals of indigenity -- self-support, self-propagation, self-government -- but also needs, possibilities and the biblical principle of bearing one another's burdens should guide in this critical issue. Only so can we fulfill the law of Christ and hope to accomplish world evangelism.

In general three principles have prevailed in relation to finances:

(1) No foreign funds have been made available to national churches. This is the extreme application of the self-support principle under the label of

indigenization. Due to this practice, there are today thousands of small, impotent, ill-cared-for, anemic groups of believers in the world struggling for survival. There is as much peril in undersupply as there is in over-supply of foreign funds. Balance and common sense are much needed in this matter.

(2) Foreign funds are made available to the churches conditionally. Usually such provisions are made upon the recommendations of the missionaries and for projects approved by the missionaries. The missionary thus becomes the mediator between the churches and the board and the administrator of the funds.

(3) Foreign funds are made available directly to the churches and without any conditions. Usually such allowances are made in a lump sum to be used in special projects or in programs as the church deems advisable. The national church renders a careful account of the appropriations of the funds, but administers them independently.

As in other matters so also here, there should be no unilateral decision in the area of foreign finances. Partnership in equality and mutuality must prevail. Dollar diplomacy has no more place in Christianity than nationalism has. It takes as much grace to give humbly as to receive proudly, to give without a sense of condescension as to receive without losing one's own self-hood and not to acquire a habit of expectation.

Perhaps nowhere do we need the mind of Christ as fully as in money matters in order not to offend Christian principles, not to retard the cause of Christ, remain indigenous (in the economic patterns of the land), build spiritual relationships as well as sound economic foundations and express real brotherhood concern and unity. Within genuine partnership there is no reason why churches which are economically strong should not contribute the larger share in the mission outreach and expansion of the church through aggressive evangelism. This certainly would not violate indigenity or harm a spiritually minded church in her maturation process or the development of her self-respect, identity and sense of responsibility. Sharing is as much a biblical principle as training in stewardship. Both aspects should be evident in partnership.

In general budgeting should proceed according to the following guidelines:

. . . All finances must be negotiated within the legislative body, duly considering needs and resources;

. . . All available finances must be prayerfully allocated in the light of the purpose of the church and according to biblical priorities;

. . . Only in exceptional and emergency cases should foreign funds be made available to continuing programs except evangelism and church expansion in which mission and church are unified. Foreign funds may be applied to special projects and to special missions;

. . . Funds must be responsibly administered under the authority of the legislative body and in keeping with the negotiated budget and purpose and according to the agreed upon projects;

. . . Responsible accounting must be rendered through the legislative body to the constituency which supplies the funds.

It may sound reasonable that money given to the Lord's work is the Lord's money and that the Holy Spirit has the right to disburse such money anywhere He leads and deems wise. Such emphasis is, however only one side of the coin. Biblical stewardship does not only obligate to give unto the Lord the portion that belongeth unto Him. It also obligates to responsible administration. Responsible investment is an important aspect of biblical stewardship. The giver has a right to know how his money is being invested and administered. In stewardship mutual confidence does not exclude personal responsibility and accountability.

Summary

In the light of the historical development of the various practices and policies followed, the following guidelines could be accepted:

1. It is a matter of deep concern and great wisdom to find the right place of missions and the missionary in relation to the existing churches in the nations.

The Bible neither defines nor establishes a pattern for such relationships. It merely upholds ideals of relationships and forbids the violation of such relationships.

2. The place of the mission and the missionary in relation to the national church depends a great deal on principles practiced in the establishing of the church. Changes should not be instituted by unilateral action of either the mission, missionary, or the church, but by negotiation and mutual agreement.

3. No overall pattern will meet the need of all areas of operation. There are differences as there are differences in cultures, national feelings (nationalism), and maturity of the church, which factors do play a role in this matter.

4. There must be a unified approach in any given area. There must be agreement among the missionaries; otherwise grave discord will arise and confusion will result.

5. There must be consistency in this serious matter. Too much experimentation will prove detrimental. Yet, there must be flexibility and room for changes by negotiation and a place for progress as the church matures.

6. There must be the definite purpose of heart to help at any cost. The greatest cost is the willingness of self-limitation and sacrifice.

7. The missionary must practice the mind of Christ, who did not come to promote a cause and build institutions or to do a job and promote or perpetuate Himself indefinitely. He came to preach the gospel, to teach the Word, to mold lives, to give His life, and to make an impact that reaches our own day.

8. There must be utmost care not to offend and distort the biblical concept of brotherhood and <u>koinonia</u> (fellowship). The latter can be practiced only where a deep sense of oneness (interpenetration), sameness (relatedness), and equality exists. If an organizational or administrative structure disturbs the fellowship or distorts the brotherhood concept, a time for deep spiritual searching and organizational reorientation may have come.

9. There must be utmost care taken to see that the missionary responsibility of the younger churches is not stifled and that the self-hood of the church is not minimized, keeping in mind that only as a church grows (in its own community by missions) is it truly a New Testament church. A self-containing entity is not a New Testament church whatever it may be called. A New Testament Church is an evangelizing church.

Conclusion

Partnership is not an easy way out of tensions. Tensions are not our foe unless we make them such. Partnership in the true sense of the word is a high ideal -- a New Testament ideal -- expressing mutuality and equality in the body of Christ. Thus the sending church is neither lording the situation nor is she being lorded over. Rather, the sending church and the national church jointly become the servant of the Lord to a world destitute of salvation and the gospel of God.

Such partnership presupposes that: "The spirit of the servant must be found in all participants, in all members of the people of God in that place. All of the people of God, including missionaries and church members and church officials, must rediscover the vocation of being the servant. The one mission of the people of God in that place is the servant mission to each other and to the world. There is no place for insistence on rights and privileges or for any assumption that because one group contributes more it can control more. There is no place for the independent operator, the organization man, the dictatorial missionary administrator or church official. All must lead the servant life and work in the spirit of the servant. Only in such a life and spirit will there be found a way to give first priority to the good of the one Christian mission in that place."

Partnership of equality and mutuality is as much an attitude, a relationship, a philosophy, a way of missions as it is a pattern of legislation and administration.

It seems to me that only in the pattern of partnership of equality and mutuality do we -

1. ... Really enter into full partnership of obedience to the command of Christ, which was not committed just to one body, but to the believing churches wherever such may exist;

2\. . . . Truly express the biblical concept of brotherhood within the church, which knows neither race, national or cultural distinctions;

3\. . . . Fully honor the church as a church with full missionary responsibility;

4\. . . . Create an atmosphere and relationship in which it becomes possible not only to evangelize and plant churches, but to raise them to full stature in Christ, assist them in discovering and formulating the Biblical doctrines and "make disciples" in the full sense of the word;

5\. . . . Create a possibility for the missionary to remain related to and involved in the inner structure of the church as an integral and motivating force of the church, yet fulfilling his personal, unique, and divine calling as missionary;

6\. . . . Make it possible for a sending church to remain a sending and missionary church, and to do justice to the essential missionary demand of a truly New Testament church;

7\. . . . Truly involve the autonomous national churches in the missionary assignment which is theirs as well as ours.

Pattern I

ORGANIZATIONAL UNILATERALITY AND FUNCTIONAL SERVANTHOOD

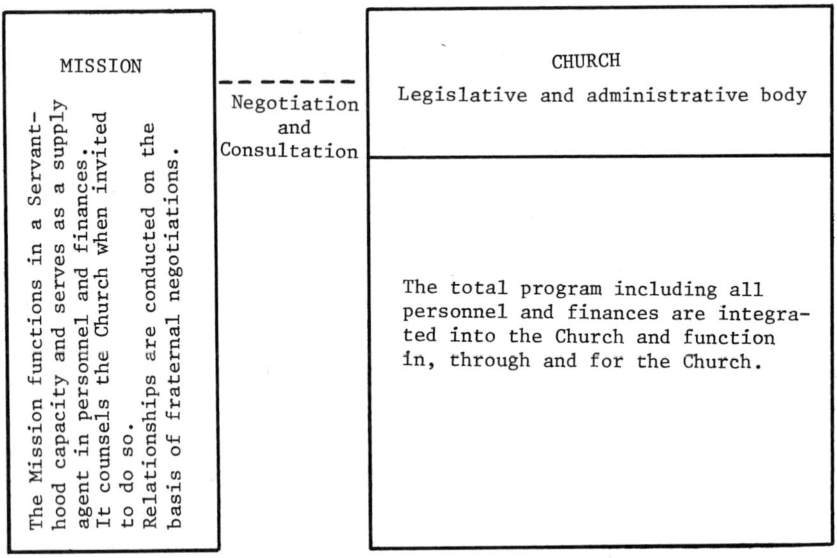

MISSION

The Mission functions in a Servanthood capacity and serves as a supply agent in personnel and finances. It counsels the Church when invited to do so. Relationships are conducted on the basis of fraternal negotiations.

Negotiation and Consultation

CHURCH

Legislative and administrative body

The total program including all personnel and finances are integrated into the Church and function in, through and for the Church.

Pattern II

ORGANIZATIONAL DICHOTOMY AND FUNCTIONAL COOPERATION

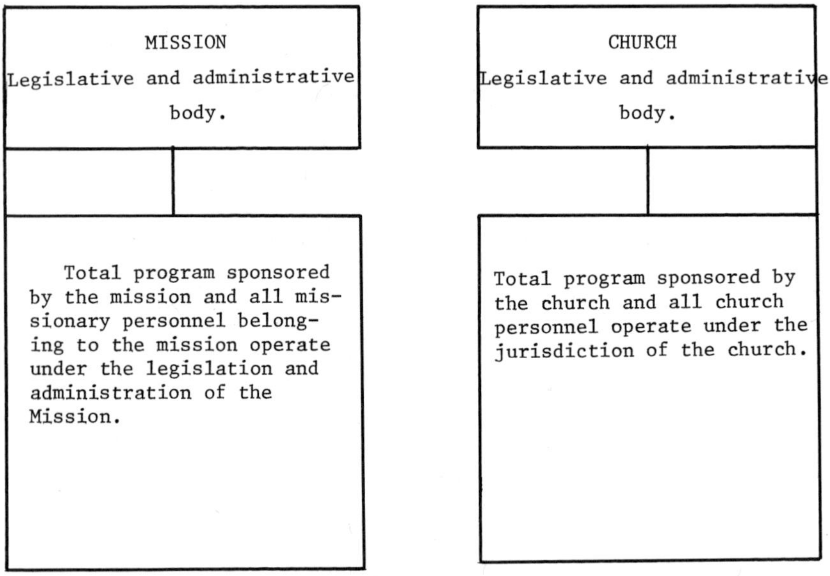

MISSION

Legislative and administrative body.

Total program sponsored by the mission and all missionary personnel belonging to the mission operate under the legislation and administration of the Mission.

CHURCH

Legislative and administrative body.

Total program sponsored by the church and all church personnel operate under the jurisdiction of the church.

Pattern III

ORGANIZATIONAL DICHOTOMY AND FUNCTIONAL PARTNERSHIP

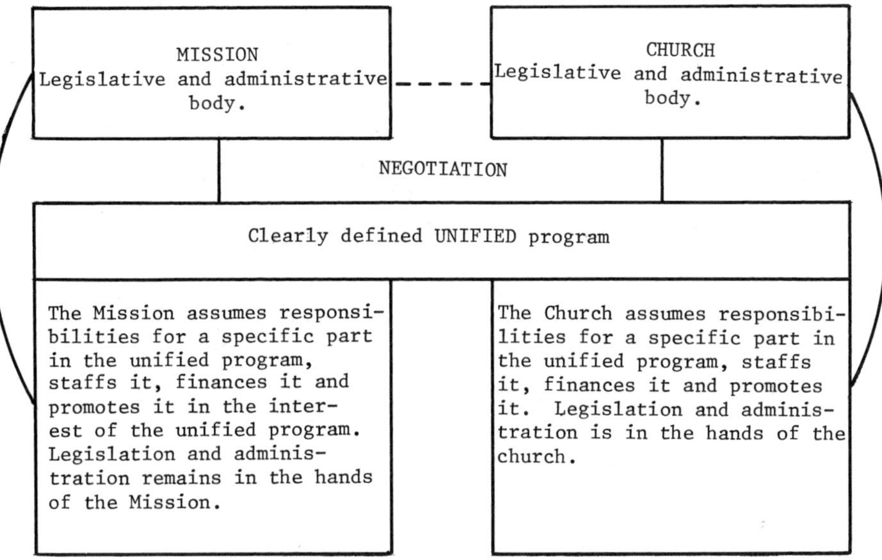

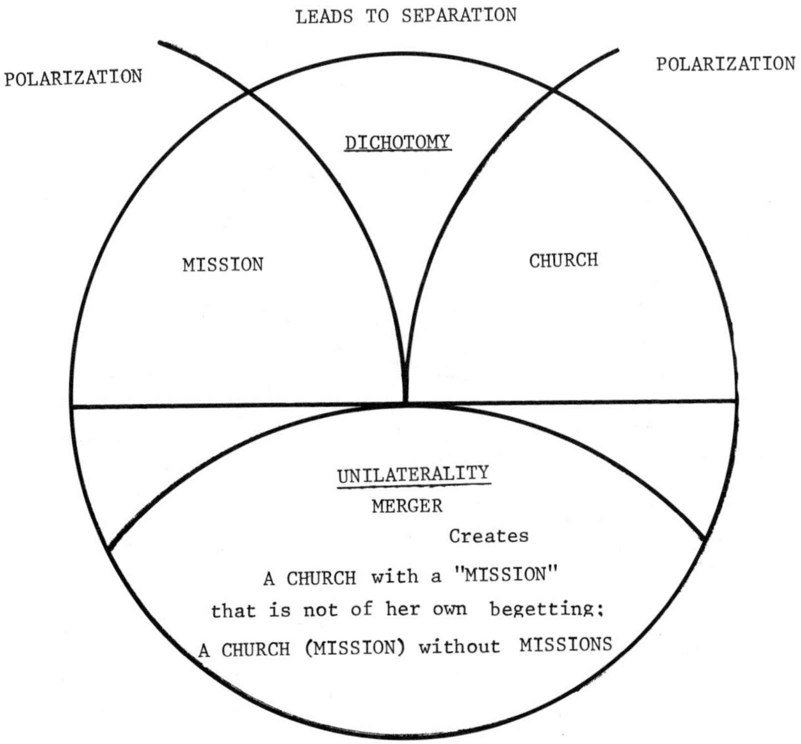

LEADS TO SEPARATION

POLARIZATION

POLARIZATION

DICHOTOMY

MISSION

CHURCH

UNILATERALITY

MERGER

Creates

A CHURCH with a "MISSION"

that is not of her own begetting;

A CHURCH (MISSION) without MISSIONS

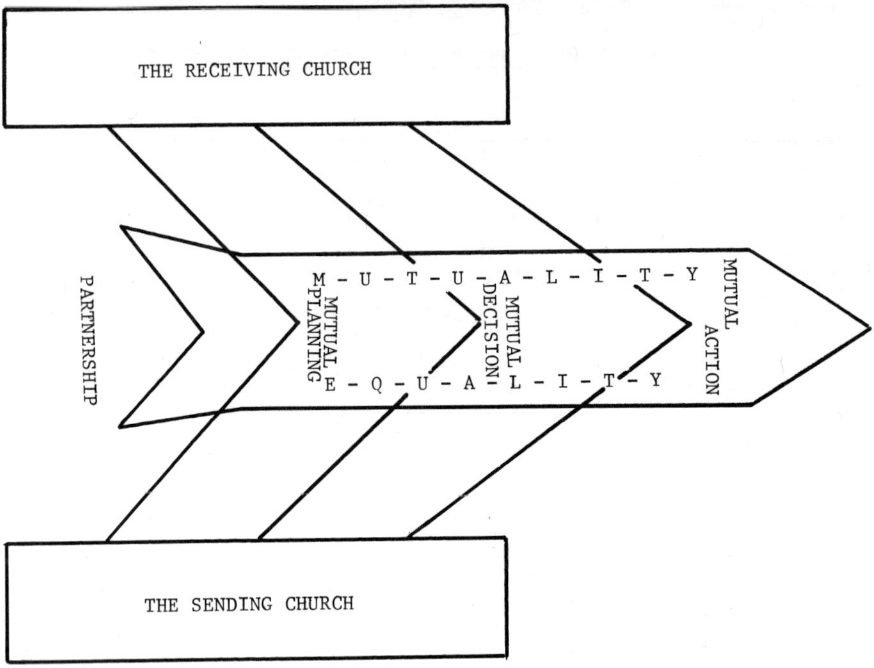

THE RECEIVING CHURCH
PARTNERSHIP
M - U - T - U - A - L - I - T - Y
MUTUAL PLANNING
MUTUAL DECISION
MUTUAL ACTION
E - Q - U - A - L - I - T - Y
THE SENDING CHURCH

Adapted from Japan Christian Quarterly
Winter 1971

THE RECEIVING CHURCH
PARTNERSHIP IN
STRATEGY PLANNING
CAPITAL INVESTMENTS
FINANCES
PERSONNEL
IN WORLD EVANGELISM
THE SENDING CHURCH
THE WORLD
THE WORLD
THE WORLD
THE WORLD
THE WORLD

Adapted from Japan Christian Quarterly
Winter 1971

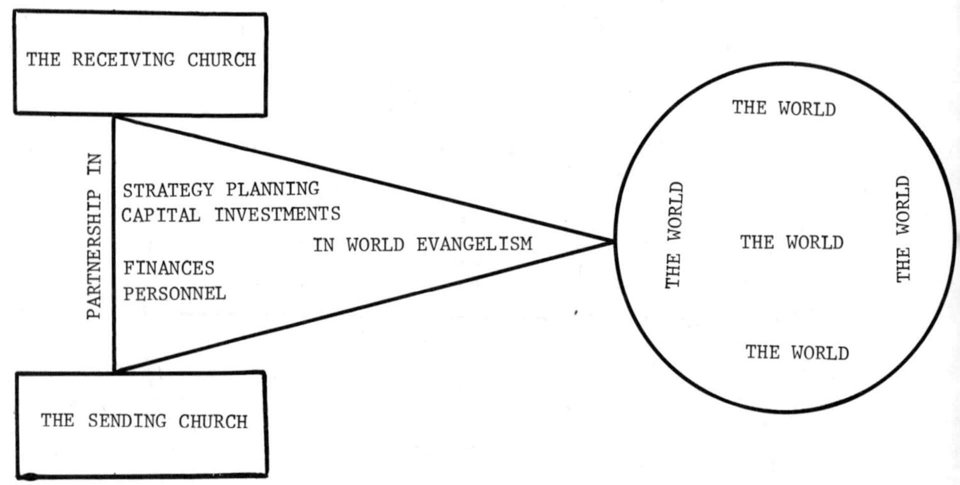

Appendix

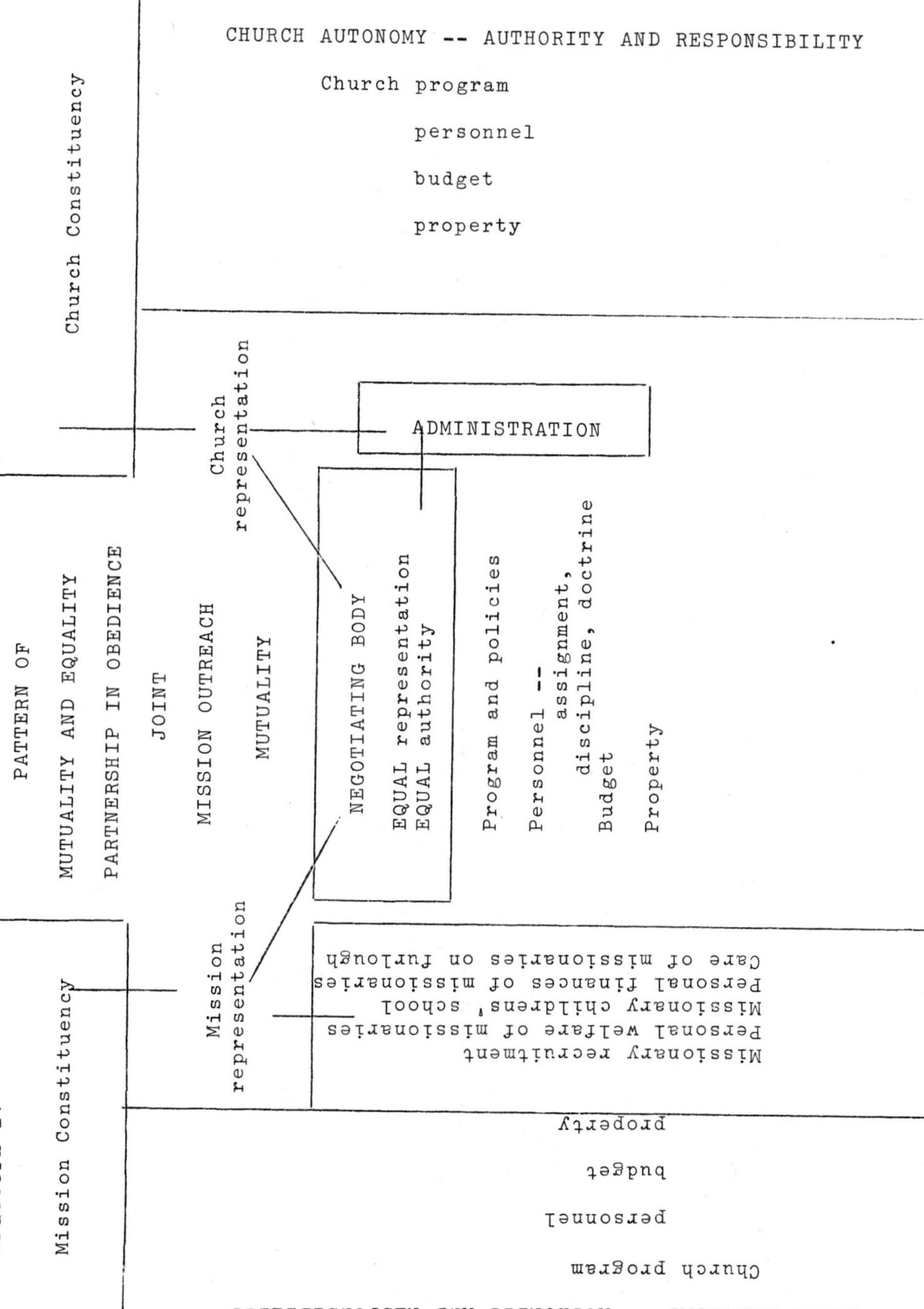

CHURCH AUTONOMY -- AUTHORITY AND RESPONSIBILITY
Church program
personnel
budget
property
Church Constituency
Church representation
ADMINISTRATION
PATTERN OF
MUTUALITY AND EQUALITY
PARTNERSHIP IN OBEDIENCE
JOINT
MISSION OUTREACH
MUTUALITY
NEGOTIATING BODY
EQUAL representation
EQUAL authority
Program and policies
Personnel -- assignment, discipline, doctrine
Budget
Property
Mission representation
Missionary recruitment
Personal welfare of missionaries
Missionary childrens' school
Personal finances of missionaries
Care of missionaries on furlough
Mission Constituency
Pattern IV
CHURCH AUTONOMY -- AUTHORITY AND RESPONSIBILITY
Church program
personnel
budget
property

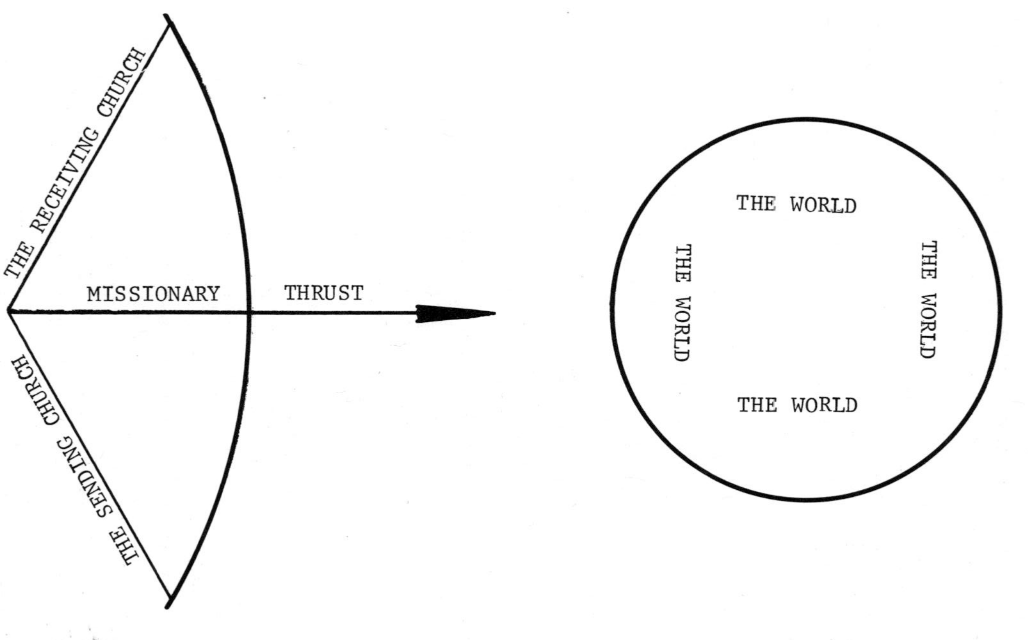

Adapted from Japan Christian Quarterly
Winter, 1971

The Biblical Doctrine of the Ministry of the Church

(Biblical Ecclesiology and the Crisis in Missions)

Edmund P. Clowney

Mission agencies and missionaries today feel the tensions of their position between the church back home and the church on the "field." Not only the structure of missions but the continuance of mission has been called in question. This study was prepared in summary form for an E. F. M. A. and I. F. M. A. conference at Green Lake, Wisconsin, September 27-October 1, 1971. It is neither a full ecclesiology nor a theology of missions, but an effort to set before mission leaders an outline of the Biblical doctrine of the ministry of the church in a form that is applicable to the problems they face.

I. The Bible and Patterns of Service Together

A. The normativity of Biblical theology

1. Sola Scriptura: redemption, revelation, and the church

The people of God are saved by his words and deeds. The word of God is always the expression of his divine wisdom and creative power (Ps. 33:6, 10, 11; Isa. 14:24-27). God who called creation into being by his fiat also calls and forms his people by his word. His word of saving promise is no less sure than his word of immediate creation (Isa. 55:10, 11; Jer. 1:11, 12). Man lives by every word that proceeds out of the mouth of God (Deut. 8:3; Matt. 4:4). God's word, spoken at Sinai, made Israel to be his covenant people. God not only spoke but gave his word in written form as his covenant, the treaty of the Great King (Ex. 24:12; 32:15, 16; Deut. 9:10).[1] The fact that it was written on tablets of stone made it an abiding witness to God's redemption--and an abiding claim on the life of his people (Deut. 6:20-25).

To the basic document of his covenant God added fuller revelation: the ordinances, the sanctions, the blessings of his dominion. His prophets kept his covenantal record, the sad history of an erring people. Even the songs of Moses and David were inspired of God to form part of God's "testimonies," memorials of his faithful dealings and witnesses against Israel's sin (Deut. 31:19; II Sam. 23:2).

God's use of human language and human spokesmen to communicate his word in no way reduces the divine authority of that word. Not only does the inspiration

---

[1] See Meredith G. Kline, *Treaty of the Great King* (Grand Rapids: Eerdmans, 1963).

of the Holy Spirit secure the result God intends; the structures of culture and history in which revelation takes place are themselves prepared of God for his appointed use (Ps. 33:6-15; Dan. 4:34, 35; II Pet. 1:19-21).

The principle of "Scriptura sola" was recognized in the Protestant reformation. The authority of God speaking in Scripture has no rival. The church does not produce Scripture but Scripture produces the church. The authority of Scripture is God's authority to which the people of God are obedient.

To be sure, the prophets and apostles through whom God's word is given are called to their task from among the people of God (Jer. 1:5; Isa. 6:5). In his grace God planned it that way, for so he prepares for the great prophet and apostle Jesus Christ. Christ who is the Son of God speaks God's Word in the midst of the church (Heb. 2:3, 12). But although the prophets are called from God's people, they do not speak in the name of the people but of God; Christ Himself speaks the words given him of the Father (Jn. 8:28, 47; 12:49, 50).

Reflection on the relation of the church to Scripture has fresh urgency today. From many sides the church is being tempted to abandon the objective authority of Scripture. For example, it is often held that the gospel message must be distinguished from the Biblical words in which it is conveyed. Similarly, Christ is set over against the Biblical witness to Christ.

Such distinctions are alien to Scripture and to the mind of our Lord. Jesus not only ascribed divine authority to the words of Scripture; he perfected his own obedience to God (including his death and resurrection) in full obedience to Scripture (Jn. 5:46, 47; 10:35; 19:28; Lk. 24:46, 47). Further, he promised to his apostles, as eye and ear-witnesses, the fullness of the Holy Spirit to bring his deeds and words to their memory (Jn. 14:26; Heb. 2:3, 4). Both the Old Testament (for the Spirit of Christ inspired the prophets--I Pet. 1:11) and the New Testament are more than man's witness to God; they are God's witness to man, the witness of the Father, of the Son, and of the Spirit (Heb. 1:1; I Pet. 1:11; Rom. 3:2).

For the great crisis that confronts evangelicals today our attitude to Scripture will prove to be determinative. Routine assent to the authority of Scripture is not enough. We are in grave danger of denying in practice the sufficiency, perspicuity, and unity of Scripture. We are far too ready to suppose that we know what the Bible says, and that in any case it is of little practical importance since the Bible somehow says too little and too much: too little, because its principles do not settle the real issues that divide us today; and too much, because we courteously assume unimpeachable Biblical support for almost every answer to any major question that has been enshrined in the historic position of some accepted ecclesiastical movement.

If the faith and obedience of the church is to be governed by the Word of God we must pray for the illumination of the Holy Spirit to give us a new and deeper understanding of Scripture. This means the willingness to be corrected by Scripture, not just enriched. If we are looking for practical working solutions in church-mission operations that will accommodate every misconception ancient and modern that has currency among us, we are certainly not looking for Biblical solutions. We should recognize that we have honest differences as to what the Bible teaches with respect to the church, its order and its mission. In these differences we may all be partly wrong but we cannot all be entirely right. Not every such difference is significant for the problems we face in church-mission relationships. But some of our differences have wide consequences for practice in ordering the life and mission of Christ's church. Until such differences can be resolved in genuine study of the Bible together we cannot avoid major conflicts in practice.

No doubt there is wisdom in taking account of our differences while they remain unresolved. But it would be disastrous for the application of Scriptural authority to make such working compromises final solutions.

2. Progressive revelation and the pattern of truth

God's word of revelation accompanies his work of redemption; both come to their climax in Jesus Christ. The progressive form of Biblical revelation does not lessen the normative force of Scriptural doctrine but enriches our understanding of it. Jesus did not come to destroy the law but to fulfill it. The most fruitful understanding comes as we perceive how God's work and word of preparation issue in his work and word of actualization. The Old Testament revelation prepares us to perceive the meaning of Christ's fulfillment, while Christ's fulfillment interprets and actualizes the meaning of the Old Testament preparation. The doctrine of the people of God, like every other doctrine of the Bible, is revealed, not in one systematic statement, but in the progress of the history of redemption. For example, the holiness of the Old Testament people of God had to be expressed in ritual cleanness as well as in moral rectitude. In Christ's fulfillment of "all righteousness" the ritual forms are transcended; the water of purification is made wine for the feast of the Bridegroom. Yet that separation to a jealous God which was symbolized by Israel's ritual cleanness is required of the New Testament church in spiritual realization (II Cor. 6:14-7:1).

The principle of progressive revelation applies within the New Testament period as well. Jesus could not give all the revelation he had received from the Father until after his death and resurrection (Jn. 16:12). Through his Spirit he inspired the apostles and prophets of the New Testament to communicate "all things" (Jn. 16:13, 14; Matt. 28:20) to the church.

Even these apostles did not at once present the church with a complete tradition of the teaching and deeds of Christ. Consider, for example, the prolonged process by which the church was taught that circumcision is not to be required for salvation because salvation is by faith, not works. We now recognize that the doctrine of justification by faith alone is clearly taught in the New Testament. But we sometimes forget the process by which the Spirit led the apostles and the brethren into this truth.

Liberal scholars, of course, deny the integrity and continuity of this process of Divine revelation. They assume that contradictory theological positions are taught by "inspired" apostles. Since real contradiction is alleged, the process cannot represent coherent development. At best there is a dialectic that issues either in the triumph of one viewpoint or in the forging of a synthesis. Often the moral drawn from it all is that since pluralism of theology existed in the New Testament church, it can thrive in a united church today. The attitude of theological permissiveness is commended in the name of the "catholicity" of the church.

Evangelicals, on the other hand, rightly insist that sensitivity to theological error marks the whole course of the apostolic proclamation and defense of the gospel. No ecumenical umbrella can shelter both the Apostle to the Gentiles and the false apostles of another gospel (whose theological error might seem so allowable in comparison to current heresies! Gal. 1:8).

With respect to a wide range of the fundamental teachings of the New Testament we do recognize that clear positions are presented in the process of the unfolding of revelation. Looking back on the full history of redemption we may seek to formulate succinctly what it is that the Bible teaches about this or that particular topic. Such formulations are always subject to correction from the Bible, and their very brevity involves some loss of Biblical richness. Yet we believe that the New Testament itself requires us to grasp the "pattern of sound words" given through the apostles, and to set this pattern over against error and misunderstanding (II Tim. 1:13; I Tim. 6:20).

Now we face an important question. Is there any reason for putting what the Bible teaches about the church in a different category from what it teaches about Christ? Do the principles by which we formulate Biblical doctrine apply to the apostolic teaching concerning the church, its order and ministry?

If we agree that Scripture is the Word of the Lord, we must confess that we cannot limit the subjects on which the Lord may choose to speak. We cannot therefore decide in advance that Scripture is authoritative in soteriology but not in ecclesiology. It may seem appealing to distinguish "matter" from "form," but we cannot restrict the authority of Christ to the <u>content</u> of the gospel by which his people are saved while claiming for ourselves the right to decide upon the form by which his people should live.

Further, if we recognize the progressiveness of God's revelation we will not make the mistake of supposing that an unfolding pattern is no pattern at all. The pattern of Christian worship, for example, is more fully revealed in the Epistle to the Hebrews than in the example of the early Christian church in Jerusalem as recorded in the Book of Acts. We must perceive not only the integrity of the history of redemption in the New Testament but also the fullness of the outcome.

There is in the New Testament no *Manual of Discipline* like that found in the scrolls of the Dead Sea community. The absence of such a formulation is in itself significant, for the spiritual discipline of the Christian community is too comprehensive and dynamic to be contained in such a summary of rules. But the lack of a *Manual of Discipline* does not mean that there is no New Testament ordering of the structure of the church. What that order is, how extensive and how universal--these are questions that cannot be answered in advance but only from the New Testament itself.

Let us not forget that the authority of God's Word with respect to the order and ministry of the church provides the divine Magna Charta of freedom from the tyranny of men. The easy yoke of Christ's commandments sets us free from bondage to the traditions of men; the light burden of his discipleship delivers us from the rule of other masters. We cannot assume that the structures of political and social organization can be baptized without prejudice into the form of Christ's kingdom. The will of our Master in heaven provides the perfect law of liberty where human exploitation is forever barred.

B. The importance of Biblical ecclesiology

1. Comprehensiveness of the Biblical doctrine of the church

God reveals himself to his people and declares his purposes of salvation for them: "I will be your God and ye shall be my people" (Lev. 26:12; Hos. 2:23). In the fulfillment of God's salvation in Jesus Christ the Lord promises to build his church (Matt. 16:18). The Spirit's ministry in building the new temple of God is central to the New Testament (Eph. 2:22). Scripture focuses on God and his saving work, but always in relation to those who are made joint-heirs of God's salvation.

The Biblical teaching about the church is therefore not an addendum, and consideration of it is not a sign of an introverted faith that has lost the Biblical perspective. Rather in discovering what Scripture teaches about the church we gain a concrete understanding of what God's saving purposes are. Indeed, the church is part of the content of faith ("I believe a holy catholic church") and the form of the church structures Christian service.

Further, we must begin with this broad Scriptural relation of God and his people. We dare not conceive of the church sociologically (or even architecturally!) and then seek for nominal Scriptural warrant for an institution that has already been defined.

2. Uniqueness of the Biblical doctrine of the church

Because the people of God are made the objects of his saving work in Jesus Christ, no account of them can be given apart from God's saving purpose. The church therefore cannot be set beside the family, the state, or other societal groupings. It cannot be understood as one social group among many but must be seen as the manifestation of the new society of the world to come. Other societal structures may be transformed by the new life of Christians, they may be penetrated or dissolved by the influences of the gospel; but the church is unique since it is established as the Lord's own structuring of his redeemed people. The church exists through the gospel and for the gospel; it represents another dimension, not another organization.

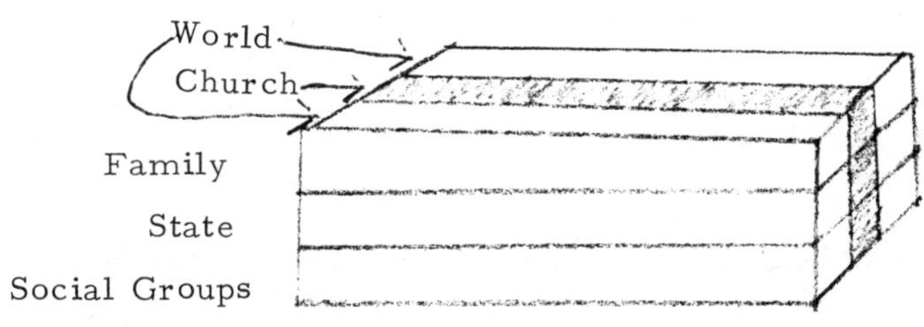

The church is not subservient to the state, neither is it sovereign over the state. Members of the church may be active citizens of the state insofar as the state does not claim that obedience and devotion which they owe to God alone. The state may be leavened by Christian influence, but no state may now be organized as the political form of the people of God in the world, for the Christian "polis" is heavenly and the church is already the appointed form on earth of that heavenly commonwealth (Matt. 16:18, 19; 21:43; Phil. 3:20; Col. 1:13; Heb. 11:16; 12:28; 13:14, 17). The church does not now bear the sword because Christ, in the program of his kingdom, forbids it (Jn. 18:11, 36; cf. I Cor. 4:8). Any political organization that seeks to take up the sword in the name of Christ denies the form of Christ's church and disobeys Christ's appointment.

Our appreciation of the uniqueness of the church must be drawn from the Biblical presentation of the church. To that we must turn.

II. The Church Is Formed in God's Presence

Scripture presents rich teaching concerning the church, but never at the expense of teaching concerning God and his saving grace. Rather, the calling and existence of the church is always in the immediate presence of God the Saviour. The doctrine of the church is directly God-centered, and in this sense "theological." This fact has most important consequences for our obedience.

The origin of the church as the people of God is theocentric. God constitutes the seed of Abraham as his people in his own presence. The fulfillment of the promise in the new people of God gathered by the Messiah is still more pointedly Christocentric. The Lord comes to gather his people to himself. With the coming of the Spirit to actualize the fellowship of Christ, the Divine presence possesses the church with heavenly fullness, power and reality.

We must learn from the amazing scope of this Scriptural pattern. The heirs of salvation are the people of God, the church of Christ, the fellowship of the Spirit. Through the history of redemption God works to call to himself a people for his own possession. All that God has done is written for our instruction upon whom the ends of the ages are come (I Cor. 10:11). It has been said with some justification that the Christian church has too often been modeled on a single pattern isolated from the rich history of redemption. Some have thought of the church in largely Old Testament terms as the new Israel, the people of God in covenant relation with him. Others have thought of the church in terms of Christian discipleship, or as the sacramental body of Christ. Still others have stressed the fellowship of the Holy Spirit. Lesslie Newbegin, for example, suggests that the first is the Reformed view of the church, the second the Catholic view, and the third the Pentecostal view.[2]

Any one of these views in isolation distorts the fullness of Biblical teaching. In the history of redemption we are not offered conflicting understandings of the people of God. The Spirit sent from heaven is the Spirit of Christ as well as the Spirit of the Father; the holy nation filled with the Spirit is the fullness of the people of God as well as the body of Christ. At Sinai, at Bethlehem, at Jerusalem God comes to be present with his people. There is a marvelous crescendo of fullness in the meaning of each "coming," but there is also a beautiful continuity of purpose.

A. Theocentric origin of the church: the people of God. (I Pet. 2:9, 10; Ex. 19:5, 6; Isa. 43:20, 21; Hos. 1:6, 9; 2:1)

The people of God are constituted in his presence by his redeeming power and royal call. God gathers the people to himself at Sinai by delivering them from bondage in Egypt. This physical deliverance symbolizes an even greater deliverance; the Exodus is used in the prophets as a picture of God's work of salvation in the latter days (e. g. Isa. 40; Ezek. 20; Hos. 2:14, 15). When Israel had been brought to Sinai, God said, "Ye have seen what I did unto the Egyptians, and how I bare you on eagles' wings, and brought you unto myself" (Ex. 19:4).

God's redemption is not simply out of Egypt, but unto himself. The purpose of the covenant given at Sinai is that Israel should be God's "own possession ... a

---

[2] The Household of God (London: SCM Press, 1953).

kingdom of priests, and a holy nation" (Ex. 19:5, 6). Here the emphasis falls on the intimacy of communion and service between God and his chosen people.

This relationship is dramatically presented as God appears in glory on the mount to the people who have been assembled to stand before him. The day of covenant-making at Sinai is called "the day of the assembly" (Deut. 4:10, LXX; 9:10; 10:4; 18:16). As an emperor might claim sovereignty over a people gathered in a great assembly before his throne, so God claims Israel as his people in solemn covenant. The sounding of the trumpet from Sinai marks this convocation in the presence of God (Ex. 19:16. Compare the sounding of two silver trumpets for later convocations in Num. 10:1-10 and the sounding of the trumpet at the great convocation of the _Parousia_ I Thess. 4:16; II Thess. 2:1).

Here is the Biblical source of the term "assembly" (_ecclesia_) as applied to the church. It is an active term, having in view the actual assembling of God's people, yet it has rich theological meaning. It is not because people find it convenient to gather together for worship that they are called the "assembly." Neither is it the local assembly of a house or city church that accounts for the New Testament name for the church. The assembly is the assembly of God, the holy ones who are gathered together before his face.

The later assemblies of Israel for worship, war, or covenant-making all reflect this same conception of gathering together to stand in the immediate presence of God. For this reason the festival assemblies for worship had to take place in Jerusalem, the place where God had set his name (Lev. 23; Deut. 16:11).

Further, the assembly of the earthly myriads at Sinai is linked with the assembly of the heavenly myriads. The Lord of the heavenly hosts is enthroned among them even as the earthly hosts are assembled at his feet (Deut. 33:2-5; Ps. 68:17; Heb. 2:2). The Dead Sea community reflected this understanding when they regarded membership in their assembly as joining one to the heavenly as well as the earthly "holy ones" (1QS 11:7-9; 1QH 3:21; _cf._ Deut. 33:3).

The assembly that defines the existence of the church is the present heavenly assembly convoked in the presence of God where Christ is, and where his blood is sprinkled on the throne of heaven. The author of Hebrews describes our access by faith to this assembly. He says that we have not come to Sinai but to the heavenly Jerusalem "and to myriads of angels, to the festival gathering and assembly (ecclesia) of the firstborn who are enrolled in heaven, and to God the Judge of all, and to the spirits of just men made perfect, and to Jesus the mediator of a new covenant, and to the blood of sprinkling ..." (Heb. 12:22-24).

The festival assembly at Pentecost binds the new people of God to the heavenly assembly from which the risen Christ sends the gift of the Spirit. The restoration of the people of God, promised by Joel in the figure of the assembly (Joel 2:15-17) takes place. Not only are Jews and Gentiles united in heaven's feast (Isa. 2:2-40; 56:6-8; Ps. 87), but the saints and angels join in praising the Lamb.

The fact that we worship in the company of mighty angels as well as the saints of all ages may well require a decorum touched with awe (I Cor. 11:10?). Yet the wonder of the church is that it is the assembly that gathers to God, or put the other way, has God in the midst (I Cor. 14:25; Isa. 45:14).

The author of Hebrews who describes the heavenly assembly to which we are come in worship also warns us not to forsake earthly assembling (Heb. 10:25). Those "who call upon the name of our Lord Jesus Christ" in any place of assembly (I Cor. 1:2) manifest in that place the existence of the heavenly assembly that defines the church. They await the final gathering of the assembly at Christ's parousia (II Thess. 2:1).

It would be a mistake, then, to think of the local house-church or the city-church on the one hand, or the church universal on the other as constituting the basic form of the church. Smaller or greater assemblies in Christ's name on earth all reflect the reality of the heavenly assembly that does constitute the church. The heavenly assembly is as real as Christ's risen body, as real as the power of his Spirt by which we live unto him.

Yet because our worship is in actuality on earth even as it is directed to heaven, we enjoy here in our fellowship with Jesus Christ and one another a foretaste of consummation blessing. The heavenly and earthly scenes of worship are not contradictory, for the way into heaven now stands open through our great High Priest. The stairway of Jacob's dream brings the Lord down to make the place of our pilgrimage Bethel, and the same stairway takes us up with Christ to his Father's throne. The Biblical doctrine of the church as assembly draws us together in Christ's name alone and demands that we do not deny by a secular institutionalization the heavenly reality of the assembly of God.

The people of God are described as his dwelling as well as his assembly. If the figure of assembly pictures the immediacy of God's presence, the figure of dwelling stresses the permanence of his presence.

At Sinai God's epiphany on the mount issued in his abiding presence symbolized by his glory in the tabernacle. The building of the tabernacle did not proceed smoothly after God gave his instructions to Moses on the mount. Rather there was the convulsion of a great crisis brought about by Israel's sin with the golden calf. After that sin had received stern judgment, God proposed that he go before the people in the angel of his presence and drive their enemies out of the promised land. But he would not go up in the midst of them, lest he consume them in judgment (Ex. 33:5). Rather than the tabernacle in the midst of the camp there would be a tent of meeting outside the camp where Moses would go to communicate with God on behalf of the people. This proposal was met with dismay on the part of Moses; the people mourned. In one of the most beautiful passages of the Old Testament, Moses intercedes with God and is given a revelation of his glory and grace. God will go up in the midst of the people yet forgive their sin. This is the incoming of the tabernacle (Ex. 32:30-34:9). In its gate stands the altar of sacrifice and the symbolism of atonement marks all of its ceremonies.

Again we see that it is God's presence that constitutes the people of God and that directs their service. God in choosing his people also chooses his place of dwelling in their midst (Ps. 68:16; Deut. 12:5, cf. 7:7). As a nation of priests, God's people know his presence among them, yet there is a focus of his presence in the sanctuary. The tabernacle and the temple cannot contain God, but they do represent the abiding presence of God in the midst. At the temple Israel worshipped the God who was there. The martyr Stephen, when he was accused of blasphemy toward the temple showed that through the whole history of redemption God's presence, not the temple, came first. The temple must remain a symbol; God cannot dwell in a temple made with hands (Acts 7:48, cf. I Kings 8:27).

What is symbolized by the temple becomes reality in the Incarnation. "The Word became flesh and tabernacled among us and we beheld his glory, glory as of the only begotten of the Father, full of grace and truth" (Jn. 1:14). The grace and truth proclaimed to Moses (Ex. 34:6) by the God who could not be seen by him (Ex. 33:23; Jn. 1:18) are revealed in the only begotten Son, who can say, "He that hath seen me hath seen the Father" (Jn. 1:18; 14:9).

The intensification of the "dwelling" of God in Jesus Christ has many implications for the New Testament church. Because Christ is the true temple and because in the risen body of Christ the true temple is "raised up" after destruction, the church can have no other sanctuary but Christ. Christ comes in the Spirit; Christ is the reality, the Truth. Worship in Spirit and Truth requires no holy place, so that Jerusalem is no longer the place where men must come to worship God (Jn. 4:21-26).

Instead, union with Christ defines the church as his temple, cleansed by his blood to be a house of prayer for the nations. The church as the sanctuary of living stones must show the holiness of the Lord's presence. So, too, the church is a new Jerusalem, a city set on a hill that cannot be hid, shining as a light in a dark world.

The close Biblical connection between the holiness of the church and its witness (cf. Phil. 2:14-16; I Pet. 2:9, 10) grows out of the reality of God's abiding presence in the midst of his people.

The people of God, then, are his assembly, gathered before him; and a nation of priests, even a temple, with God dwelling in the midst. They are also his possession, his chosen treasure. God's relation to his people is like that of a Father to his beloved son or of a Husband to his beloved wife (Hos. 1:10). Even these most intimate figures do not exhaust the language of God's love as he lays claim to the people of his own possession (I Pet. 2:9). The ground of God's choosing is not to be found in those chosen but in God who chooses in the good pleasure of his love (Deut. 7:7, 8; 4:37. Cf. Rom. 9:11-13). The purpose of God's election includes service, but service is not the final goal of God's love. God does not choose Israel just so that he may use Israel, nor does he select for service the serviceable. Rather the mystery of God's electing love is his desire that his people might be his and he their God forever. God delights in his chosen as his "portion," his inheritance (Deut. 32:6-10), he joys over his redeemed with singing and calls the true Israel Hephzibah--"my delight is in her" (Isa. 62:4). The glory of God's love is the glory of grace: a love that is not compelled by loveliness, but rather lavished on the unlovely and undeserving.

This wonder, too, is deepened and intensified in the course of the history of redemption. God's chosen people prove unfaithful. In wicked pride they even pervert God's election, thinking of themselves as a "choice" people. The vengeance of God's covenant is poured out (Lev. 26:25). The adulterous wife must be stoned (Ezek. 16:40), the rebellious son cast out (Hos. 11:1, 8; 12:1, 14), the precious vineyard wasted (Isa. 5:5, 6) and the vine uprooted (Ezek. 19:10f.; Ps. 80:12-16).

The people are driven into exile and the place where God set his name is destroyed with fire. But the electing purpose of God is not frustrated. First, there is a surviving remnant. Though it be as a few olive berries left in the top of a tree when it has been harvested, or a few ears of grain left in the corner of a field, it will nevertheless be spared. God will snatch some embers from the conflagration. Destruction will not sweep away every vestige of the people of God. But more--the surviving remnant will be made a renewing remnant. The dry bones in the valley are quickened by the Spirit of God and raised up to be given new hearts (Ezek. 37:14; 36:26, 27).

The theme of restoration and renewal fills the prophets. All will be restored: the temple (Isa. 2:2-4; Ezek. 40:2), the sacrifices (Isa. 56:7; Jer. 33:18; Ezek. 43);

the priests and Levites (Ezek. 44:9-31); the mediatorial position of Israel in the midst of the nations (Mic. 4:1-3; Isa. 66:23; 45:14; Zech. 14:16-19).

But the restoration becomes unimaginably great as it is described in terms of total renewal. For example, in the new Exodus the exiles of the nations are gathered in along with the outcasts of Israel (Isa. 56:6-8; Zech. 14:16-19). So total will be the restoration, indeed, that the Egyptians and Assyrians will share with Israel the privileges and titles of God's chosen people (Isa. 19:19-25)! The ark will not be missed (Jer. 3:16, 17), every pot in Jerusalem will be a holy vessel, the sacred engraving of the high priests tiara will be found on the bells of the horses: "Holiness to the Lord" (Zech. 14:20). Peace fills the animal world (Isa. 11:6-9; 35:9), the heavenly bodies have their light increased (Isa. 30:26), and there is no longer day and night (Isa. 60:20). The totality of renewal issues in a new heaven and new earth (Isa. 65:17; 66:22).

What can account for such unrestrained promises of blessing? Only God's own work in restoring, renewing, fulfilling the promises of his covenant. God's call to Abraham promised not only to bless him but to make him a blessing. The descendants of Abraham, beloved for the fathers' sakes, failed miserably in fulfilling God's covenant and brought upon themselves the curse of the covenant. But God, who is rich in mercy, is not content to vindicate his holiness. He must hallow his name in the miracle of grace by making those who are "no-people" to be the people of God. His promises are now so great that only he can fulfill them, and then only by his own presence. The prophets herald the appearing of the Lord who comes with the rejoicing of his creation to set up his kingdom on earth (Ps. 46:5-10; 98:7-9). His glory is revealed, marching through the desert as of old, dwelling in Mount Zion (Isa. 10:26; 35:1-10; 40:3, 10, 30; 52:12; 60:20; Ezek. 34:11-16; Zech. 14:16). He will spread his feast for the nations in his holy mountain (Isa. 25:6-8).

Yet even the coming of God in glory does not secure the redemption of his people. The consuming fire of his presence must bring destruction rather than deliverance unless provision is made for the sin of the people of God (Mal. 3:2). Before the year of jubilee is ushered in there must be judgment, not only to deliver and vindicate the oppressed, but to make atonement for their offenses. As in the pattern of the Exodus, the judgments that deliver the people of God fall not only upon the Egyptians, but upon the Passover lamb that receives the stroke of death instead of the son.

The mystery of suffering presented in the Old Testament prepares for the conception of the Suffering Servant of the Lord who is made to be a sacrifice for sin in the place of the people to whom the stroke was due (Isa. 53). It is God who provides the lamb for the sacrifice (Gen. 22).

The coming of God is joined to the coming of God's Anointed. God's covenant must be renewed from both sides: the covenant Lord must come, the covenant servant must come. God is the Shepherd-King who will deliver the scattered sheep (Ezek. 34:11; Isa. 40); but the Messiah, too, is the Shepherd (Ezek. 34:23; Isa. 42). The heightening of the glory promised reaches its climax in the figure of the Messiah. If every pot in Jerusalem will be holy (Zech. 14:21), and the feeblest man will be as David (Zech. 12:8), then who shall the King be like? He will be as God, as the angel of the Lord before them (Zech. 12:8). The name of the royal child who will rule forever is "Wonderful Counselor, Mighty God, Everlasting Father, Prince of Peace" (Isa. 9:6).

The Servant is the Son (Ps. 2; 110), identified with God as Lord, but also identified with the people (the "Servant Songs" of Isaiah, the "Son of Man" in Daniel). Again we must marvel at the way in which the redemption of the people of God is made the work of God himself. God redeems not only by coming himself (the true Shepherd as over against the false shepherds, Ezek. 34), but also by so uniting himself with his people in the coming of the Messiah that he makes perfect their obedience and bears their punishment.

B. Christocentric fulfillment of the church: the church of Christ

The New Testament proclaims the coming of the Lord. Jesus is born to his people as their Saviour-Lord (Lk. 2:11) who shall save his people from their sins (Mt. 1:21). He is the only begotten Son, the Divine Word incarnate, the true Light come into the world (Jn. 1:9, 14, 18), the Divine glory of God's people (Lk. 2:32). He is not only the Lord's Christ (Lk. 2:26), but Christ the Lord (Lk. 2:11).

His Lordship is revealed in the authority of his words and deeds. He announces the coming of the kingdom of God, as did John the Baptist his forerunner. But he does more. Not only does he show mighty signs of kingdom power in his miracles, he exercises that saving deliverance from the dominion of Satan which is the heart of the realization of the kingdom. The captives of Satan (the strong man) could not be delivered until the strong man was overcome (Lk. 11:14, 20-22). In his desert ordeal Christ initiated that triumph over the Prince of Darkness; in his death and resurrection he sealed his triumph (Col. 2:15; Jn. 12:31). The miracles of Christ were signs of the kingdom: the life and healing that Jesus brought gave a foretaste of the banishment of the curse from the new earth. But the miracles remained signs. The bread that fed the five thousand was not the true bread from heaven, nor was the wine at Cana the cup of the kingdom. Even Lazarus was not given the body of the last resurrection. Where the signs passed into reality was in the person of the Lord himself and in the saving work he accomplished. Jesus was not a sign of God's presence, he is Immanuel, God with us. His death is not a mere symbol of divine wrath, like the burning of the temple. Rather he bears the reality of wrath against sin and in his resurrection triumphs over death. Those, therefore, who come to Christ and trust in him find more than a sign of healing. They find the actuality of restoration to God, salvation, and life. Christ came to seek and to save that which was lost. He comes with God's power to forgive sins and thereby establishes the reality of the saving kingdom of God among men (Mk. 2:7-11).

John the Baptist is troubled and confused when Jesus performs the kingdom signs and pronounces the kingdom blessing without first establishing the kingdom in righteous judgment (Lk. 7:18-20). Jesus shows that his signs are fulfilling God's kingdom promise and requires John to trust in him without being offended--even though he does not intervene to deliver John from prison and death (Matt. 11:4-6; Isa. 35:5, 6). Jesus did not come to bring the final judgment of God's kingdom upon the world but rather to bear the judgment himself so that the world might have the gospel (Jn. 3:17). The day of judgment will come, but those who belong to Christ have already passed from death to life in him (Jn. 3:18). The reality and finality of Christ's saving work are not set aside by the span between his resurrection and the last judgment. Rather, the completeness of his victory and the exaltation of his triumph provide the basis for the epoch of God's longsuffering mercy when judgment is delayed while the sheep of Christ are gathered from the mountains of the world.

Christ the Lord, who fulfills Scripture by suffering and entering into his glory (Lk. 24:26), assembles the true people of God to himself. The sheep hear the Shepherd's voice and follow him (Jn. 10:4, 5). Christ begins his gathering in his earthly ministry among the lost sheep of the house of Israel (Matt. 10:6). In his heavenly glory as Prince of salvation, he continues to give repentance to Israel and remission of sins (Acts 5:31) but also to gather the other sheep that are not of this fold (Jn. 10:16) for he sends his apostles to make disciples of all nations (Matt. 28:19, 20).

The gathering **the** Father's "little flock" (Lk. 12:32) as the possessors of the kingdom is the purpose of Christ's work. Every stage of Christ's revelation of his Lordship makes its claim upon the people of God. His nativity is received by the worship of the poor who believe: Elizabeth, Mary, Zacharias, the shepherds, Simeon and Anna (Lk. 1). Gospel peace is declared to the men of God's good pleasure (Lk. 2:8-14). The rising of his glory will illumine the Gentiles (Lk. 1:79; 2:32); the coming of the wise men foreshadows the ingathering of the nations.

In his ministry Christ continues to gather a people. With his call the process of division that will be completed in the last judgment (Matt. 25:32f.; 13:41-43) begins (Matt. 10:34-36). He declares, "He that is not with me is against me, and he that gathereth not with me scattereth" (Matt. 12:30; Lk. 11:23). Christ's call to his disciples to follow him shows what is required of all who will bear his yoke (Matt. 11:28-30). He calls, not as a prophet (I Kings 19:19-21), nor even as an earthly king, but as the Lord (Cf. Isa. 40:9; 42:6; 46:11; 48:12, 15; 50:2; 51:2).

Christ calls as the Shepherd of the sheep (Jn. 10:3-16; Ps. 23). His gathering of the little flock that has been scattered is the work of God in which he is one with his Father (Ezek. 34; Isa. 40:11; Jn. 10:28-30). All things are ready and the Servant-Son summons men to the last feast (Lk. 14:17). To those who follow Jesus says, "I appoint unto you a kingdom, even as my Father appointed unto me, that ye may eat and drink at my table in my kingdom, and ye shall sit on thrones judging the twelve tribes of Israel" (Lk. 22:29, 30). In this appointment, Christ exercises covenantal Lordship; those who confess him in truth enter into the joy of their Lord (Lk. 13:25-30; Matt. 25:21, 23).

Further, Christ's disciples share with him in the gathering process (Matt. 10:5, 6). They are laborers in the harvest (Matt. 9:37, 38), "fishers of men" (Mk. 1:17; Matt. 4:19; Lk. 5:10). The number 12 is significant. In the apostles the new Israel is constituted (Matt. 19:28).

Over against the gathering process is the rejection of Christ by the unbelieving. In the parable of the wicked husbandmen Jesus uses the Old Testament symbol of the vineyard for the people of God (cf. Isa. 5). The husbandmen who kill the Son will be destroyed and "the kingdom of God shall be taken away from you, and shall be given to a nation bringing forth the fruits thereof" (Matt. 21:43). This "nation" (ethnos) is not a political state in the world of nations but the new people of God, who will replace the old Israel as the possessors of the gifts of the kingdom. The new Israel will bring forth the fruits of the kingdom, receiving the gospel of the kingdom in repentance and faith. Because the bidden refused God's kingdom feast, guests will be brought from near and far, for "none of those men that were bidden shall taste of my supper" (Lk. 14:24). Many shall come from east, west, north and south to recline with Abraham, Isaac, and Jacob at the kingdom feast, but those who have rejected the King will be cast out (Lk. 13:24-30). The stone which is rejected by the builders is made the cornerstone of the new temple (Ps. 118:22f.; Matt. 21:42; Lk. 9:22; Acts 4:11; I Pet. 2:6-8; cf. Isa. 28:16). The Messianic stone as the stone of God's kingdom is a stumbling-stone to those who reject Christ (Isa. 8:14; Lk. 2:34; I Pet. 2:6) and a crushing stone to those who oppose his purpose (Dan. 2:34, 44; Matt. 21:44), but it endures forever as the rock of foundation for the true people of God (I Pet. 2:6).

It is against this background of gathering and scattering, upbuilding and crushing, that Jesus reveals the constitution of the new people of God (Matt. 16:18, 19). Critics who have insisted that Jesus did not anticipate a period of time in which the church could exist have discounted other passages where such a period is in view. There is a time in which the harvest grows when judgment is deferred (Matt. 13:24-30); a time when the master has gone to a far country and his servants await his return (Matt. 25:14-30).

Christ's authorization of the new form of the people of God is not given until his disciples have some understanding of the distinctiveness of his Messianic claims. The time has come for his revelation of his death and resurrection. Peter's confession is solicited by Christ's questions when he has drawn his disciples aside at the crisis point of his ministry. The multitudes have shown themselves all too ready to follow Christ as a political Messiah, but they have found offensive the spiritual claims of his Divine Lordship as well as his refusal to execute retributive justice.

When Jesus asks, "Who do the multitudes say that I am?" the replies that he receives all express complimentary unbelief. The distinctive confession of the new people of God must recognize that he is more than a prophet, he is the Christ. Further, he is not the political Christ the crowds have been willing to accept, but Christ the Son of the living God, who demands religious devotion and is free to order his saving work in his own way to his own ends. The significance of Peter's confession lies not only in the clear assertion of Jesus' Messiahship but in the further heightening of the person and work of Christ in the kind of Messiahship that has been revealed--not only by Jesus, but by his Father in heaven.

Peter is declared blessed by Jesus because of his confession and more particularly because of its heavenly source. Divine revelation concerning Jesus provides the confession that is basic for the new community.[3] Peter's eyes

---

[3]The Dead Sea covenanters also confessed the need of divine enlightenment so that the community might be founded upon a grasp of the mysteries of God's counsel (e. g. 1QH 12:32ff. ; 1QS 5:5; 8:1-10; 9:3).

and ears have been opened by the Father (Matt. 13:16, 17; Lk. 10:23), who has hidden these things from the wise and understanding and revealed them unto babes (Matt. 11:25; Lk. 10:21). Just as only the Son can reveal who the Father is, so only the Father can reveal who the Son is (Matt. 11:27; Lk. 10:22). The deity of Christ implied in this necessity echoes also in the phrase "my Father" (Matt. 16:17).

The blessing pronounced upon Peter binds him to the Christ whose glory he has perceived by revelation of the Father. As he has pronounced Jesus the Christ so Jesus pronounces Simon the Rock ("and _I_ say to _thee_, Thou art _Petros_...").

To understand this passage we must hold together what we find joined here. Peter may not be isolated from the twelve. He is the spokesman in responding to a question Jesus has put to all. The power of the keys here granted to Peter is given to all the apostles (in the plural) in Matthew 18:18. One the other hand, Peter may not be separated from his confession. Protestant exegesis has gone too far in insisting that the confession rather than Peter is the referent for "upon this rock." Certainly Peter cannot be left out of account when the meaning of the name Christ gave him is so plainly in view.[4] But neither can the confession be dropped from sight. It is the confessing Peter who receives the blessing. Just below in the text of Matthew (16:22-23) Peter is called "Satan" and an "offense" when he would turn Christ from the cross. The term used here has in view a stone of another kind, a "stumbling-stone." Peter, speaking by revelation of the Father is a foundation stone; as the mouthpiece of the Devil, he is a stumbling-stone (_cf._ I Pet. 2:4-8; Isa. 8:14). Only as Christ prays for Peter that his faith fail not does Peter fulfill his apostolic calling. Apart from Christ and his word, Peter, too, sinks in the sea and builds on sand.

---

[4]Appeal cannot be taken to the change in gender between _Petros_ (the name masculine) and _petra_ (the rock, feminine) because the feminine noun for rock is most usual to describe foundational, bed-rock (in distinction from free-standing boulders).

But, filled with the Spirit, Peter speaks by revelation of the Father to open the door of the kingdom to thousands of Jews at Pentecost (Acts 2). Later, and again by revelation, he turned the key of the kingdom to admit Cornelius and his household as first-fruits from the Gentiles (Acts 10). Peter does not view his apostolic ministry as exclusively his own: he describes his apostolic authority and appointment as shared with others who also "ate and drank" with the risen Christ (Acts 10:41).

Yet there is an apostolic office and authority granted to Peter and the others (to whom the great Apostle to the Gentiles is added as one born out of due time, I Cor. 15:8). Christ's saying is a solemn assertion of the constitution of the New Testament church. The leaders of the old Israel are builders who have rejected Christ, the elect cornerstone, and who are building on sand. Their edifice will be swept away by the storm of divine wrath. The kingdom of God is taken from them and given to others; the remnant flock of Israel and the assembled strangers of the nations will inherit it. Peter is not the rock in contrast to the other apostles, for he is their spokesman. He is the rock in contrast to those teachers of Israel who claim to carry the key of knowledge (Lk. 11:52), to sit in Moses' seat (Matt. 23:1) and to be Abraham's seed (Jn. 8:33). Their authority is now to be removed and the people of God re-formed. God who can raise up of the stones children to Abraham reveals the mystery of his kingdom to Peter, the Galilean fisherman, one of the poor of the land, but a man of God's good pleasure, established as a remnant not to be moved.

Christ does not fail in his Messianic purpose. He will build the assembly, the people of God who are given the kingdom. He speaks in the future, for his death and resurrection form the center of his Messianic task. When the agony of the royal Sufferer issues in triumph he will praise God in the midst of the assembly while all nations worship and confess that the kingdom is the Lord's (Ps. 22:23-29; Heb. 2:12).

It is significant that Jesus uses the "building" figure to describe his work in raising up the new assembly of those who confess his name. In Scripture this verb, meaning build or rebuild, is used especially to speak of the temple (_cf._ Mk. 14:58). The restoration of the people of God is closely linked with the figure of the temple and the house of God. The building of the people of God in the latter days is God's own work: "In that day will I raise up the tabernacle of David that is fallen, and close up the breaches thereof; and I will raise up his ruins, and I will build it as in days of old: that they may possess the remnant of Edom, and of all the heathen, which are called by my name, saith the Lord that doeth this"(Amos 9:11).

This passage is quoted by James in the council at Jerusalem to justify the inclusion of the Gentiles in the people of God: "how first God visited the Gentiles to take out of them a people for his name" (Acts 15:14-17).

Christ's building of his people as a new temple is accomplished through the raising up of the new temple of his body (Jn. 2:19). By his death he redeems a people for his own possession, by his resurrection he emerges as the Living One, holding the keys of death (Rev. 1:18), by his ascension he leads captivity captive, giving gifts to men (Eph. 4:8), by his session at the Father's right hand he sends the throne-gift of the Spirit to perfect the temple of living stones for the day of his return.

All is of Christ: the church is the people of God as they are claimed by the Son of God. Peter, like Moses, is a steward in the house of God, but it is Christ the Son who builds the house and claims it as his own possession (_cf._ Heb. 3:1-6). The gates of death cannot prevail against the church because it shares the resurrection triumph of Christ. Jonah's prophetic cry from the depths of the abyss is fulfilled by a greater than Jonah: "Out of the belly of Sheol cried I ... The earth with its bars closed upon me for ever: Yet hast thou brought up my life from the pit ... " (Jonah 2:6; _cf._ the parallel in Psalm 18 between "the cords of Sheol" and "the floods of Belial," "the waves of death" vv. 5, 6. See also Ps. 9:13; 107:18; Isa. 38:10). The sign of Jonah seals the victory of the church (Matt. 12:39, 40). When the floods of death sweep forth in the final storm of destruction the city of God will remain (Isa. 28:15-18; Matt. 7:24-27; Ps. 46).

Since Christ himself brings in the new and abiding form of the people of God, it is he who gives the keys of the kingdom to Peter and the other disciples (Matt. 16:19; 18:15-20). Christ's coming, his life, death, and resurrection fulfill the covenant promises and change the form of the theocracy. The new form is not more secular or less theocratic. To the contrary, the theocracy comes into actuality through the immediate presence of the Lord. He has come, he has gathered his people to himself, and he will abide with them where even two or three are gathered together in his name (Matt. 18:20).

The assembly of the people of God that is built as the house and temple of God by the Messiah must be the place where the rule of God is fully evident; in it the kingdom of God must be manifested. Where God's Anointed is Lord, there the kingdom of God appears. The charter of authority for the new people of God is then granted in terms of the keys of God's kingdom.

Of course this charter does not identify the kingdom of God and the church as though Peter were being granted an imperial throne. The heavenly sanctions that validate the earthly exercise of authority are in themselves sufficient evidence that the rule is God's not Peter's ("bound in heaven ... loosed in heaven" Matt. 16:19).

The whole thrust of Jesus' ministry was to demand God's own royal authority against human pretension. The kingdom is not Israel's but God's, and the final offense of the wicked husbandmen is that they refuse to recognize the rightful claim of the householder (Matt. 21:33-44).

The church can be called a kingdom only as the plain assertion of God's total claim and Lordship: "he made us a kingdom, priests to God and his Father" (Rev. 1:6; I Pet. 2:9; Ex. 19:6). "Giving thanks unto the Father, who made us meet to be partakers of the inheritance of the saints in light; who delivered us out of the power of darkness, and translated us into the kingdom of the Son of his love ..." (Col. 1:12, 13).

Since the kingdom is totally God's, we can understand that it is spoken of more as a dominion than a domain. For Christ to come "in his kingdom" is to come in his sovereignty (e.g. Matt. 16:28). We can also understand that the rule of God and of Christ must be spoken of in the widest sense. God rules over all, his kingdom has no end (Ps. 47:7, 8; Dan. 4:34, 35). So also the rule of Christ is universal; he is given all power in heaven and earth as King of kings and Lord of lords until he has brought in the full consummation of the new heavens and earth (Matt. 28:18; I Cor. 15:24-28; Heb. 1:2, 3; Eph. 1:20-22).

But the universal rule of Christ, to which every knee must bow at last (Phil. 2:9-11; Isa. 45:23, 24) is distinct from the saving rule he exercises over those, who like Peter, confess his name in faith (II Thess. 1:5-10; Eph. 1:22).

Those who share in the blessings of Christ's saving rule are most naturally spoken of, not as composing Christ's kingdom, but as entering it, receiving it, even possessing it (e. g. Matt. 7:21; 21:31; 23:13; Mk. 9:47; 10:14f. ; Lk. 16:16). Their fellowship together as heirs of the kingdom is more often described by such terms as "people" and "nation" (I Pet. 2:9; Tit. 2:14), and "house" or "temple" (II Cor. 6:16) although the commonest term is, of course, "church." They are fellow citizens with the saints, of the household of God, the heavenly commonwealth of the new Israel (Eph. 1:11; 2:19, 21; *cf.* v. 12; Phil. 1:27; 3:20; Heb. 11:14-16; 13:14).

A further distinction between the concept of "church" and "kingdom" in the New Testament is the frequency with which the "kingdom" is used to describe the manifestation of God's power in the future when Christ comes again. The expectation of the future revelation of the kingdom presented in the Old Testament forms the immediate background for the preaching of the good news by John and by Jesus. The kingdom that was "at hand" was not, of course, simply God's universal sovereignty but that manifestation of his presence and power to judge and to save which would open the promised epoch. As we have seen, the epiphany of God is joined to the coming of the Messiah.

The kingdom was announced in the preaching of John and Jesus. Did the kingdom come? Or was it postponed to the second coming of Christ? Perhaps we can already perceive the direction in which the answer must be found. The kingdom centers on the King. We cannot deny the inauguration of the kingdom on earth from the very moment when Gabriel announces to Mary the fulfillment of the promise. Simeon in the temple was looking for the consolation of Israel;

his blessing expresses joy in its realization: "Mine eyes have seen thy salvation, which thou has prepared before the face of all peoples; a light for revelation to the Gentiles, and the glory of thy people Israel" (Lk. 2:30-32). The appearing of God's salvation, his glory before the nations, his Christ--this is the heart of the Old Testament promise concerning the coming of God's saving rule.

So when Jesus by the finger of God casts out demons "then is the kingdom of God come upon you" (Lk. 11:20). The forgiveness of sins he declares is more than kingdom preparation, it is the bestowal of kingdom blessing. In his life and death Christ conquers Satan; in his resurrection and enthronement at God's right hand he receives the full power of his kingdom. It is Christ's dominion that forms the authority of his commission to disciple the nations (Matt. 28:18).

We might readily conclude that all the kingdom promises are fully realized, that the New Testament teaches a "realized eschatology" as the last days have been ushered in.

But, of course, that would lead us back to the problem John the Baptist had. How can all the kingdom blessings be brought in without the judgment? The answer is that for the church Christ has borne the judgment, but for the world the judgment is yet in store. The new heaven and earth, the restoration of all things cannot be brought about until Christ comes again to judge.

Has the kingdom come? Yes, because Christ has come, not with just a promise of salvation but with its reality. Will the kingdom come? Yes, because Christ will come again with the glory of the Father and the holy angels (II Thess. 1:7). It is no more difficult to understand that the kingdom has come, is here, and is to come than it is to understand that Christ has come, is here, and is to come.

What we must not lose sight of is the fact that Christ is King in his sufferings as well as in his glory. By refusing to summon legions of angels as well as by coming on the clouds with the holy angels, Christ reveals the power of his kingdom. God's kingdom as the sphere of salvation cannot be revealed through force alone, for then it would be known only in wrath and judgment. Christ's death is the triumph of God's kingdom righteousness.

The church where the keys of the kingdom are used is not yet the kingdom of glory. Its members are called to fellowship with Christ's sufferings now, not to fellowship in his universal rule. When the Son of Man is revealed in the glory of his parousia, then the apostles will sit on twelve thrones (Matt. 9:28) and the least of the saints will judge angels (I Cor. 6:3).

But now the church receives not the sword of retributive justice, but the keys of the kingdom. On the surface it might appear that Peter was given much less authority than Moses, who was charged with the destruction of the idolaters (Who is on the Lord's side?). Since Peter is given the keys and told to put up his sword, surely his authority is greatly reduced from that of David who received Goliath's sword from behind the ephod in the sanctuary (I Sam. 22:9).

Yet such a conclusion would miss the significance of the authority of the kingdom. The temporal judgments inflicted under the old form of the theocracy were signs of final judgment adapted to a political and geographical picture of God's rule. Those whom David bound, loosed, or even put to death were not by that token so judged in heaven. The scribes and elders who pronounced the ceremonial binding and loosing of the clean and unclean were dealing with pictures, symbols, not spiritual realities. The point of Jesus' declaration concerning the keys is twofold: to show that the people of God are given new leaders, his confessing apostles; and to show that these leaders have new authority. Their declarations, made on earth, do not concern earthly or temporal matters alone, but heavenly matters, for their judgments, issued on earth are vindicated in heaven.

Binding and loosing were applied under the rabbis to both people and practices. A man who was "bound" was put under the ban, excluded from the congregation. A practice that was "bound" was declared unlawful, exposing one who did it to the ban.

It is clear from the Matthew 18 passage that the binding and loosing that Jesus speaks of has application to people. An offender may reject the overtures of a brother seeking reconciliation; he may further refuse to heed the judgment of the church in the matter. He is then to be "bound," that is, regarded as a Gentile or a publican.

The Matthew 16 passage is not limited to the discipline of persons, however. Especially since Jesus has emphasized the revelation received by Peter from the Father, it seems clear that the binding and loosing includes authoritative teaching as well as effective discipline. That this is the case is supported by what Jesus says about the abuse of the authority of the keys in Matthew 23. The scribes and Pharisees "sit on Moses' seat: all things therefore whatsoever they bid you, these do and observe: but do ye not after their works; for they say, and do not. Yea, they bind heavy burdens and grievous to be borne, and lay them on men's shoulders ..." (Matt. 23:2-4). These are the false "sons of the kingdom" (Matt. 8:12), who use their authority only to shut the kingdom against men; they do not enter themselves, nor do they permit others to enter (Matt. 23:13; Lk. 11:52).

The contrasts between the ordering of the kingdom under the rabbis and under the apostles are vast. They reflect the coming of the Lord of love. Yet there is a basic analogy by which we may understand the new form of the kingdom. Authoritative teaching, for example, not only remains but is strengthened in fulfillment. The rabbis must be heard as expositors of the law of Moses. Since Christ does not abrogate that law but fulfills it, it is he who succeeds to Moses' seat. The new people of God does not have many masters or rabbis, but only one, Christ himself (Matt. 23:8-12). Forgiveness is extended to the penitent an indefinite number of times (Matt. 18:21-35). The offended brother as well as the offender has the responsibility to seek reconciliation (Matt. 18:15). The "little one" must be protected from being caused to stumble (Matt. 18:6). The community is indeed transformed.

Yet it remains a community, indeed, <u>the</u> community of the people of God. Offences occur, witnesses are used to bear testimony, and through disciplinary and judicial procedures already quite familiar a verdict is to be rendered. The familiarity of procedure that Jesus assumes in Matthew 18 is so striking that some have argued that he is not speaking of the New Testament church at all but of the synagogue. In the context of Matthew this interpretation is not possible. Jesus cannot be telling his disciples that disciples rejected by the synagogue are to be regarded as heathen. Yet the plausibility of such an interpretation stresses the continuity of familiar procedures in the new form of the church. (For this reason, incidentally, it is not possible to assume that "tell it to the church," Matt. 18:17, marks an innovation in disciplinary procedure that would do away with the instrumentality of elders or judges in dealing with cases that came before the assembly.)

Jesus does not dissolve the community of the people of God into individualism. He respects such procedures as the use of witnesses and their participation in the decision of cases ("two or three" Matt. 18:16, 20). But what transforms the discipline of the people of God is his own presence as Lord. Judgment must be rendered in his name, and with the awareness that where the two or three witnesses or judges are met in his name, there he is in the midst (Matt. 18:20).

The same point applies to the teaching authority of the apostles. Because Christ is the only Master, their teaching, too, must be in his name. They open or close the gates of the kingdom according to his word. They are not legislators but witnesses, binding upon men's consciences the commandments of the Lord. The heavenly finality of their stewardship demands that they be ministers, not magistrates, declaring the Lord's word in his Name, not their words in their own name (I Cor. 4:1).

In the structuring of the new form of the kingdom, then, Christ applies the reality of his own Lordship. Through the authority given to the apostles his own immediate rule in the midst of his people is established. The kingdom is shut against any who oppose the apostolic declaration of the gospel. As the disciples shook off the dust of their feet against the town that would not receive their message (Matt. 10:13, 14; Acts 13:51), so to the end of the ages those who receive Christ must do so according to the apostolic word (Jn. 17:20; I Thess. 2:13).

The "Great Commission" expresses again the power of the keys in another form. The blessing of peace pronounced according to Matthew 10 upon those who received the gospel was a benediction in God's name. Baptism in the triune name in a yet fuller way seals the blessings of the kingdom shalom. Its administration is a use of the keys of the kingdom, a declaration of loosing from sin in the blood of Christ (Rev. 1:5). The Lord's Supper, is the symbolical feast of the new covenant, also seals the blessing of the remission of sins; its administration, too, as a use of the keys. The visible, temporal character of these signs, used where Christ's little ones are gathered in his name, marks the definiteness of the use of the keys. Christ's presence--"Lo, I am with you always"--gives eternal validity to the faithful and proper declaration of his will.

Christ, then, orders the new people of God as his people. He is the Lord of the covenant; he assembles his people in saving power and orders the form of their community by his own authority. Only through his presence in the Spirit can the new kingdom form be realized.

But Christ who is Lord is also Servant. In his presence by the Spirit he not only rules his people but is identified with them. He is the Source not only of their order but of their life. The church is not only the kingdom of Christ, it is also the body of Christ. Other figures, for example, that of the vine and the branches also express the unity of Christ with his people, but none is used so fully and expressively in the New Testament as the figure of the body. It is the Apostle Paul who presents this rich conception.

The figure is drawn especially from the meaning of the cross of Christ. There Christ died in the place of his people. He is their representative, the second Adam, the head of a new humanity (Rom. 5:12-21; I Cor. 15:22). The suffering Servant bears the curse of the covenant and fulfills the vow of the covenant (Isa. 42:6, 7; 49:3, 6; cf. 61:10; 53:4-9; Ps. 22:1, 22).

According to Ephesians 2:11ff., the gentiles were "separate from Christ, alienated from the commonwealth of Israel, and strangers from the covenants of promise." The Messiah, the commonwealth, the covenants go together. The blood of Christ is the blood of the new covenant that brings the gentiles into the commonwealth of the true people of God (v. 13). Gentile believers are no longer strangers and sojourners but "fellow-citizens with the saints, and of the household of God" (v. 19). Jews and Gentiles are reconciled "in one body unto God through the cross" (v. 16). The expression "in one body" is parallel to the phrases "in his flesh" and "in the blood of Christ." The body in which our reconciliation is accomplished is the crucified body of Christ. The enmity is slain in him, and we both have our access to the Father through him.

Our position "in Christ" is not at root mystical in opposition to the representative. It is fundamentally covenantal. "In Christ" we secure the blessings that are "through Christ" (cf. Eph. 1:3, 4, 5). Christ is the promised Seed who receives the inheritance of the Firstborn (Eph. 1:10, 11; Col. 1:18). Enthroned at the right hand of the Father, he awaits the day of consummation victory (Acts 2:34-36; I Cor. 15:25; Eph. 1:20). What is given to him is given to those who are his. They died with him, they rose with him and are exalted to heaven with him (= "in him," Eph. 1:3; cf. 2:6, 7; Col. 3;1, 2).

To be "in Christ" is like being "in Adam" (Rom. 5:12-21; I Cor. 5:22); the basic category is representational appointment in God's covenant, not subjective mystical experience. To be sure, the most intense fellowship is grounded in this relation. The Christian presses on to know Christ, but his hope lies in being known by Christ, in being "found in him" (Phil. 3:9, 10).

The background for calling the church the "body" of Christ is the fact that the church was redeemed in the body of Christ. We were "reconciled in the body of his flesh through death" (Col. 1:22). Through God's appointment, Christ the suffering Servant, "bare our sins in his own body on the tree" (I Pet. 2:24). Since the one physical body of Christ died and rose on behalf of the saints, they are united representatively in that one body, a fact that is symbolized in the bread and cup of the communion feast (I Cor. 11:24, 25). From this conception it is a small step to speak of the unity of the church in the figure of the body. Christians are one in Christ's body (Eph. 2:15, 16); they are one body in Christ (Rom. 12:5); they are a body of Christ (without the article: I Cor. 12:27); they are the body of Christ (Eph. 4:12).

If we understand the setting of the "body"

figure as applied to the church, we will not make the mistake of thinking of the church as an extension of the Incarnation. The reality of the risen body of Christ, in union with which the church can be spoken of as a body, keeps us from the gross misunderstanding of thinking of Christ as being risen in the church.[5] Further, we will be able to appreciate that the body of Christ is not thought of as a torso, with Christ as the head. Rather the figure of headship is distinct in Biblical use (Eph. 1:10; Col. 1:18; 2:10). Christ the head is related to the church his body as the husband is related to his wife (I Cor. 11:3). There is intimacy of vital and legal union but no question of absorption or loss of identity.

The relation of the church to Christ is personal, and the "body" figure assumes this personal relation. The community that is established is therefore not at the expense of the personality of its members. Paul expresses this in the organic figure of the body by speaking of the "members" of the body and their specific functions. He also shows the individual relation to Christ by speaking of the body of the individual believer as belonging to Christ so that the members of our body are Christ's (I Cor. 6:15). The same flexibility is shown in the temple figure, so closely connected with that of the body. Because Christ's body is the temple of the Holy Spirit, Christians are temples, and the church is a temple (Jn. 1:14; 2:21; I Cor. 6:19; II Cor. 6:16).

The figure of the body of Christ and the phrase "in Christ" express vital as well as representative union with Christ. Representative union is in view when Paul writes, "There is therefore now no condemnation to them that are in Christ Jesus" (Rom. 8:1). But when he salutes "the church of the Thessalonians in God the Father and the Lord Jesus Christ" (I Thess. 1:1; *cf.* II Thess. 1:1) he has broadened the phrase to describe communion, fellowship, living unity. "I can do all things in him that strengtheneth me" (Phil. 4:13).

---

[5] *Cf.* J. A. T. Robinson, *The Body* (London: SCM, 1952), p. 51: "It is almost impossible to exaggerate the materialism and crudity of Paul's doctrine of the church as literally now the resurrection *body* of Christ."

Not only does Christ dwell in us by the presence of his Spirit; we also dwell in him. Paul preaches the mystery of "Christ in you the hope of glory" in order that he may "present every man perfect in Christ" (Col. 1:27, 28). Just as Romans 6:1-11 emphasizes the representative side of our union with Christ, so does Romans 8 emphasize the vital side. Paul like John, reflects deeply on the personal union with Christ and with each other that is our experience "in him" (cf. Jn. 14:20; 17:21).

Those who have been representatively raised with Christ (Col. 3:1) have also been united to Christ as their life (Col. 3:4). Those who are in Christ must grow up into Christ (Eph. 4:15). The temple is not only united to Christ as the cornerstone, but it grows as a temple of living stones (Eph. 2:20-22; Col. 2:7; I Pet. 2:4, 5). The new Adam is united to the church as his wife, formed from his side (Eph. 5:31f.; II Cor. 2:2; Rom. 7:4).

Representative covenant union with Christ determines the position of the church; vital union with Christ is the source of the life of the church. Union with Christ therefore specifically determines the whole doctrine of the church.

Let us note some of the consequences for ecclesiology of this doctrine of union with Christ.

First, neither the individual nor the community can be made primary in the church for the reason that Christ alone has the pre-eminence. The individual is united to Christ, not first to the church. No intervening institution can mediate the Mediator. Each man has his own calling in Christ (I Cor. 7:7) to run with patience the race set before him (Phil. 3:13). In I Corinthians 10 Paul refutes any sacramentalist view of salvation. Those who have been baptized into Christ outwardly and come confidently to the Lord's table should remember the rejection of Israel in the wilderness. "The head of every man is Christ" (I Cor. 11:3). Every Christian is a temple of the Holy Spirit (I Cor. 6:13-20).

Yet, just as there is no salvation apart from Christ, so there is no salvation apart from union in the body of Christ. The sanctified in Christ Jesus at Corinth make up the church of God in that place (I Cor. 1:2). Divisions among those who call upon the name of Christ would imply that Christ could be divided (I Cor. 1:13). There is one Christ to whom the church is united; there is therefore one church, united to Christ. Apostles and prophets are sent and endued of Christ; the variety of their ministry serves the unity of the body.

The organic unity of the church as the body of Christ demands that Christian life, to be in Christ, be in the church as the body of Christ. To deny to others the ministry of one's gifts is to deny Christ (inasmuch as ye have done it unto the least of these, my brethren ... Matt. 25:40; I Pet. 4:10). To refuse to receive from others the ministry of their gifts is to refuse Christ, and to quench the Spirit (I Thess. 5:17-22).

The growth of the body is corporate. Edification is rarely used of the individual in the New Testament (I Cor. 4:14); it is regularly attributed to the church (I Cor. 14:4, 5, 12). The body grows in the image of Christ the Head through the proper functioning of each part: "till we all attain ... unto a fullgrown man" (Eph. 4:11-16).

The fellowship of mutual concern unites the members of Christ's body as they suffer and endure (Phil. 3:10; Col. 1:24; I Pet. 4:13; I Cor. 12:26). It also has a negative side. Bearing one another's burdens in the Spirit includes the gentle restoration of those overtaken in sin (Gal. 6:1-2); concern for Christ's body also demands the exclusion of those who defile the fellowship (Matt. 18:8, 17-20; Rom. 16:17; I Cor. 5:12, 13). The bride of Christ must be presented pure and spotless (II Cor. 11:2; *cf.* 6:15).

C. Spiritual actualization of the church: the fellowship of the Spirit

Christ came to claim God's people as his people through his finished work of redemption. Christ's work is not preparatory but final. He baptizes with the Holy Ghost and fire. We have seen that it is Christ's very presence that forms the church. He comes as Lord, and the church is the realm of his saving Lordship; he comes as Servant, and the church is united to him as his body. As Lord, Christ claims his people for God; as Servant, Christ claims God for his people. What Christ is and does for the church is realized through the Holy Spirit sent from the throne of his glory. The Spirit is Lord, as Lord he possesses the people of God. But as the indwelling Spirit he is also possessed by the people of God. The New Covenant is in this way made to be a reality and sealed by the Spirit of the Living God (Eph. 1:11-13).

Pentecost is a divine epiphany. God comes as Lord to possess his people. As at Sinai there are the signs of divine power: the mighty wind, the tongues of flame (Acts 2:1-3; cf. 4:31; Ex. 19:18; 20:18; I Kings 19:11, 12). The Spirit of God throughout Scripture manifests the presence and power of God. Whether in the thunder of God's wrath or in the still small voice of his counsel, the Spirit of God is supreme: "Not by might nor by power but by my Spirit saith the Lord of hosts" (Zech. 4:6). The great restoration that the prophets promise is wrought by the Spirit who will quicken the people of God (Ezek. 37). The prayer of Moses that the Lord would put his Spirit upon all his people (Num. 11:29) is fulfilled in the last days (Joel 2:28f.).

The Spirit comes not only as the Spirit of God but as the Spirit of Christ. Jesus' own ministry was carried out in the fullness of the Spirit (Luke especially records the anointing of the Spirit in Jesus' work and prayer). At Pentecost Christ sends the Spirit from the throne (Acts 2:33; 1:4, 5; 10:44, 45). The Spirit does not supplant the Son, but is sent in Christ's name (Jn. 14:26) to reveal the things of Christ (Jn. 16:13-15). In the Spirit Christ is present (Jn. 14:18, 22; Rom. 8:9, 10). Christ taught the disciples to desire his going away so that the Spirit might come (Jn. 16:7).

In the Spirit's possession of the church God's presence indwells the new temple. The presence of God that constitutes the church through the whole history of redemption is now actual in the full reality of the Holy Ghost. We often think of the spiritual as the insubstantial; we conceive of the Spirit Himself in ethereal terms. In the Bible, to the contrary, the Holy Spiritual is the real--the heavenly and abiding reality. To worship in Spirit and in truth is to worship in actuality, in realization.

The overwhelming reality of the Spirit's presence is spoken of in terms of "filling" and "fullness."

God speaks of his omnipresent power as his filling of heaven and earth (Jer. 23:23, 24). So in his saving presence the Holy Spirit fills the church, individually and corporately (Acts 2:4; 4:31). The filling of the Spirit is at the same time the filling of Christ and of God. In Ephesians 3:19 Paul's prayer for the church is "that ye may be filled unto all the fullness of God." To this end he prays "that ye may be strengthened with power through his Spirit in the inward man; that Christ may dwell in your hearts through faith" (vv. 16, 17). Through the Spirit, Christ is present in his fullness and the saints are given to know the breadth, length, height and depth of the fullness of the triune God. Christ fills all things in his ascended rule (Eph. 4:10) but gives his Spirit to the church that we may grow "unto the measure of the stature of the fullness of Christ" (Eph. 4:13). The church as the body of Christ is "the fullness of him that filleth all in all" (Eph. 1:23). The filling of the Spirit, of Christ, of God that the church both receives and continually seeks (Eph. 5:18) is the actualization of the personal presence of God with his people. Abundant life, power, and joy all spring from the reality of the indwelling presence of the Almighty. God's presence cannot be contained or restricted; with the coming of the Holy Ghost the church receives not merely a token of his favor nor a blessing from his hand, but all that the Lord himself is, in present and personal communion.

Again we must observe that the New Testament does not set the individual over against the community in presenting the indwelling of the Spirit. At Pentecost the disciples are assembled together in worship; the Spirit comes to the assembly with tongues of flame dividing to rest upon each one. Paul not only addresses Christians in the plural with his admonition to be filled with the Spirit; he also speaks of our growing together into the fullness of Christ. The "fullgrown man" (Eph. 4:13) he describes is not the individual Christian (although Paul labors to present every man perfect in Christ Col. 1:28), but the Christian church. The experience of the "breadth and length and height and depth" of God's fullness must be corporate experience "with all the saints." This "fullness" in Christ of the fullgrown church is approached through the ministry of each member of the body. Each member, in turn, is endued with gifts of the Spirit for ministry. The Spirit who is present as Lord actualizes his fullness therefore not only by immediate communion but also by a mediating process in which the members of the church are made channels of blessing.

The church is not pictured as an association of individuals whose growth in sanctification, whose "filling" of the Spirit is individual, and who may exercise the option of joint activities when they are so inclined. To the contrary, the church, not only the individual, is the temple of the Holy Spirit. The church is filled and edified and grows into a holy temple in the Lord. Life in Christ is life in the body; life in the Spirit is life in fellowship.

The Lordship of the Spirit in possessing the church is further evident in the direction of the Spirit who leads the church in accord with his own purpose. Again there is no division between the purpose of the Spirit and the purpose of Christ. The groaning of the Spirit in our hearts yearns for the complete "adoption" that will redeem our bodies and usher God's creation, delivered from corruption, into "the liberty of the glory of the children of God" (Rom. 8:20-26).

To this consummation goal the Spirit leads the church along the path of the calling of God in Christ Jesus. Since God calls his people to himself, and since the presence of the Spirit claims the people as God's possession, the goal of salvation is already realized in the fellowship of the Holy Spirit. But because the consummation fullness of salvation requires the gathering in and perfecting of all the saints, the leading of the Spirit directs the church in service, in ministry.

We must soon consider the form of this ministry, but since we are now reflecting on the Lordship rather than the ministry of the Spirit, it is enough for the present to recognize that God's Spirit powerfully directs the church to the accomplishment of his purposes. In the book of Acts major emphasis falls on the initiative of the Holy Spirit in bringing about the growth of the church, both in numbers and in holiness. Luke says, for example, that the "Word of God multiplied" (Acts 6:7; 12:24; 19:20), and by this expression describes the growth of the church in terms of the effective power of the gospel. Ministries are effective in the church because the ministers are filled with the Holy Ghost (Acts 4:8; 6:3, 5; 7:55; 11:24). Decisions are reached in wisdom given by the Spirit (Acts 15:28). Every major turning-point, every breakthrough, is prepared for and initiated by the leading of the Spirit: the baptism of uncircumcised

Gentiles (Acts 11:15-17), the launching of the Gentile mission (Acts 13:2), the turning of the apostles to Europe (Acts 16:6-10). We see in the Book of Romans how Paul perceives the pattern of the leading of the Spirit in directing him as the apostle to the Gentiles to carry his ministry to Rome (Rom. 15:19, 28, 29; 1:10).

No doubt the guidance of the apostles and the apostolic church is accomplished in a special way, appropriate to the calling of the apostles in the history of redemption. Through the apostles, Christ reveals his will for the future program of his church. Yet the Spirit abides as Lord in the church; his work in laying the apostolic foundation issues in his work of building the whole edifice. The Creator Spirit continues to lead and guide the true church of Christ. The Word of God increases; men filled with the Spirit are raised up to lead the church with wisdom and zeal. Doors of opportunity are opened. And the initiative continues to be with God: he moves the church toward his purposes, not toward the fulfillment of men's escapist fantasies or their imperial dreams.

Only the Spirit, present as Lord, can provide the realization of God's promise even as he leads toward its fulfillment. Human hope may create a speculative Utopia or it may project a planned metropolis. Yet its greatest dreams or blueprints are farthest from realization. God's Spirit, however, is a divine "earnest" or "down-payment" (arrabon) of completed redemption (II Cor. 1:22; 5:5; Eph. 1:14). The powers of the age to come, the glory of eternal life are present in the Spirit. The sons of God receive the first-fruits of the Spirit, the beginning of that restoration from corruption that is the liberty of the glory of the children of God (Rom. 8:21, 23). Down-payments are more than promissory notes. They are first installments of the final payment. The church is made a heavenly community on earth, bound together in the fellowship of eternal life. Not only does the Spirit seal to them their promised possession; he grants entrance into the possession. In him the church has the beginning of glory and more: the God of glory.

The New Testament describes the Spirit as the Spirit of Life and the Spirit of Truth. Here we are reminded of the original association of the Spirit with the breath of life and the breath of speech. As the Spirit of Life

(Rom. 8:2) he creates the church; as the Spirit of Truth (Jn. 14:17; 15:26; I Jn. 4:6; 5:7) he guides the church. The Spirit applies to the church both the redemption and the revelation of Christ.

The new life of the church is the work of the Creator Spirit. It is a new birth from above (Jn. 3:3-8). The radical circumcision of the heart, the giving of a new heart and a new spirit was the central promise of God's restoration of his people (Deut. 30:6; Ezek. 36:25, 26). Only by such radical cleansing and renovation could there be fulfillment of the covenant blessings rather than the covenant curse. All covenant renewal required cleansing (cf. Ex. 19:10, 14); the final renewal required total cleansing (Isa. 4:4; Mic. 7:19; Zech. 13:1). John's baptism was to purify the people in anticipation of the coming of the Lord; Jesus' baptism of the Spirit must cleanse as with fire and create new life by the outpouring of the Spirit of God (Matt. 3:11; cf. Isa. 4:4; Tit. 3:5, 6).

In his teaching about the new birth Jesus stresses the sovereignty of the Spirit (Jn. 3:6; cf. I Cor. 2:14). Not the will of man but the will of the Spirit quickened life in the womb of the virgin. As the King came by one great act of the Spirit's power, so those who enter the kingdom are "born, not of bloods nor of the will of the flesh, nor of the will of man, but of God" (Jn. 1:13). Faith in Christ, knowing and loving God, and righteous deeds are all declared to be fruits of the new birth in the First Epistle of John (2:29; 4:7; 5:1, 4, 18). The new life of the believer is life in Christ. The Spirit seals the individual's representative union with Christ (II Cor. 1:21, 22; Eph. 1:13; Rom. 8:9) and communicates the life of Christ (Gal. 4:6; Rom. 8:12-30).

The heavenly character of the life of the Spirit appears not only in the sanctification of the individual, but in the way in which believers are joined together "in one spirit, with one soul" (Phil. 1:27). Words that were used in judgment on Israel become a blessing for the New Testament church, "blameless and harmless, children of God without blemish in the midst of a crooked and perverse generation" (Phil. 2:15; cf. Deut. 32:5 LXX).

The work of the Spirit of life is individual but never isolating. The Spirit unites those who know the liberty of the children of God in the bond of peace (Eph. 4:3). The Spirit's "dividing" (diairesis) of gifts to each, according to measure (I Cor. 12:4, 11) is the opposite of fleshly "divisions" ('airesis, I Cor. 11:19). The Spirit's gifts rather unite the church in the interdependence of the bodily organism.

The unity of the church lies in the unity of the Spirit. There is one Spirit, one Lord (Eph. 4:4, 5). The "fellowship of the Spirit" in the Apostolic Benediction (II Cor. 13:14) means sharing either in the Spirit or in the blessings that he communicates (cf. Rom. 5:5). If we take it in the latter sense, the fellowship of the Spirit means the gift of fellowship with God through Christ mediated by the Spirit. "Through him we both have our access in one Spirit unto the Father" (Eph. 2:18).

The fellowship (koinonia) of the Spirit is far stronger than "comradeship" or "fellowship" in the modern sense. The participation of the church in the presence and blessings of the Spirit is a sharing of a common life, not in the sense of shared experiences, primarily, but of a shared nature: the new nature of new creatures in Christ. Those who share this Spirit are bound in the same mind, of one accord, united in the love of Christ (Phil. 2:1-2). Such fellowship readily includes the sharing of material blessings: those who share a common life will share daily bread or clothing (Rom. 15:26; II Cor. 8:4; Heb. 13:16). This is probably the meaning of koinonia in Acts 2:42. The fellowship is more than "espirit de corps"; it is also more than a mystical "spirituality" without observable results. The unity of the Spirit can be as tangible as a handclasp or a cup of water.

The Spirit of life is also the Spirit of truth. As we have noted, life and truth are not set over against each other in the Bible. A man speaks with the exhaled breath of his life; the Spirit of God creates as God breathes into Adam the breath of life; he also creates as God speaks the creative fiat, "Let there be light." The risen Christ breathes the Spirit of life into his disciples and the words that he speaks to them are spirit and life (Jn. 6:63). The commandment of the Father is life eternal (Jn. 12:50).

We have already reflected on the importance of the authority of Scripture for the life of Christ's church. God gave the written Word as his witness to Israel; an objective record sealed his covenant and memorialized his faithfulness. Christ did not come to destroy Scripture, but to fulfill it. Since the full meaning of the Old Testament promise was disclosed in Christ (Acts 3:20-26; II Cor. 1:20; I Pet. 1:10-12) his fulfillment both honored the Word of his Father and validated it. The "grace and truth" proclaimed to Moses was manifested in God's Son (Jn. 1:17, 18; Ex. 34:6). With the coming of the Spirit, the Word of God was brought to its fullness and completion. In the clear light of Christ's finished work the Spirit inspired the apostolic witness to his words and deeds (Jn. 16:12-15, 25). There is a crescendo of glory in Scripture itself as the obscure oracles by which God pointed the way across the ages are both fulfilled and surpassed in the grandeur of Christ's realization (Heb. 1:1-4). It was the Spirit of Christ who moved the prophets of old, and they testified to the sufferings of Christ and the glory that should follow (I Pet. 1:10, 11). But what they diligently sought to perceive has been openly revealed by the Holy Spirit sent forth from heaven (v. 12). Heavenly mysteries that intrigue the angels are publicly announced by the apostles. As the spirit of a man knows the things of his heart, so the Spirit of God searches the deep things of God's heart and teaches them through the apostles, giving them the words in which to express the mysteries (I Cor. 2:10-16). With the gift of his Son, God pours out his heart to his people. The secrets of the Divine counsels, hidden from generations like the treasure of a fortified city (Jer. 33:3; I Cor. 2:7-9; Isa. 64:4; 65:17) are now made known through Paul and Peter and John.

But again the fullness of the Spirit realizes but does not negate God's ancient work and Word. The Old Testament Scriptures were written by men who "spake from God, being moved (borne along) by the Holy Spirit" (II Pet. 1:19-21). Quotations from the Old Testament are therefore attributed to the authorship of the Holy Spirit (Acts 1:16; Heb. 3:9; 10:15). The sacred Scriptures are able to make one wise unto salvation; they furnish the man of God completely for every good work because they are "God-breathed" (II Tim. 3:16). Precisely because the Scriptures are known to be given by the Spirit, the New Testament authors concern themselves little with the <u>manner</u> of inspiration. As men who know the power of the Spirit sent from heaven, they naturally understand that the Spirit of God works as God, teaching, guiding, controlling, overruling to bring his word where, when, and how he pleases. The New Testament writers do not simply inherit a doctrine of inspiration from the Old Testament. Far less do they extend into the age of the Spirit a "mechanical" conception of inspiration inappropriate to the gospel. To the contrary, they grasp in the joy of the Holy Ghost the real meaning of his inspiring work. They know in fullness the presence of the Spirit and thereby perceive with fresh appreciation how that same Spirit moved the prophets to foresee what they are given to proclaim. God's Word as his witness to his own saving faithfulness is expressed in the apostolic testimony. They are ever aware, not only that they are called and chosen to bear witness to what they have seen and heard (Acts 10:41) but also that it is the Spirit who is the primary Witness, speaking through their word (Acts 5:32).

The church that is gathered to the Risen Christ by the power of the Spirit abides in the fellowship of the apostles, receiving the Word of Christ brought through them (Acts 2:42; I Cor. 14:37, 38; 15:2; Gal. 1:8; Heb. 2:3; cf. 12:25). Such fellowship is a joyful reality through the illuminating work of the same Holy Spirit who first led the apostles into the truth.

We now turn to consider how the church possesses the Spirit in the same fellowship in which it is possessed by the Spirit. Since fellowship with the Spirit is a personal relation these are complementary concepts. In our examination of the Lordship of the Spirit we could not escape speaking of the gifts of the Spirit; as we consider the Spirit's gifts we must understand his sovereign presence in bestowing them. Only by joining the gifts of the Spirit to the Spirit as giver can we avoid isolating certain Biblical figures for the Spirit so as to conceive of the Spirit in mechanical rather than personal terms. For example, the filling or fullness of the Spirit may be thought of impersonally, as though a quantum of spiritual power was transmitted. Whether one is "charged" with such power or not then has little to do with his personal fellowship with Christ. The insight of Paul's prayer in Ephesians 3 is lost, for the filling of the Spirit is cut off from growth in the love of Christ "that ye may be filled unto all the fullness of God" (Eph. 3:19).

Perhaps we may guard against an impersonal view of the Spirit's gifts by recalling that the Spirit is the Spirit of Sonship as well as the Spirit of Stewardship. Our possession of the Spirit is not first the possession of gifts that endue us for ministry in the world. Rather, our possession of the Spirit enables us to cry, "Abba, Father" (Rom. 8:15; Gal. 4:5, 6). When Jesus was endued with the Spirit for his ministry at his baptism, his Father's voice from heaven declared, "Thou art my beloved Son, in thee I am well pleased" (Mk. 1:11). This witness is not only public; it is also personal, the Father's testimony to his Son. So, too, the Spirit bears witness with our spirit that we are children of God (Rom. 8:16). Indeed, the Spirit in our hearts is the Spirit of sonship (Rom. 8:15) because he is the Spirit of the Son (Rom. 8:9, 14). Jesus rejoiced in the Spirit (Lk. 10:21), praising the wisdom of his Father, and we share the joy of God's Son as we use the very syllables that were upon his lips, "Abba, Father!" By the Spirit of the Son the love of God is shed abroad in our hearts (Rom. 5:5).

But the gifts of the Spirit of Sonship do more than grant to those who are in Christ the assurance of their adoption. These gifts also conform us to the image of God's Son. The Spirit leads the sons of God into the likeness of the Son of God (Eph. 4:15; II Cor. 3:18). The richly indwelling Word of Christ produces, by the Spirit's work, growth in wisdom. Such wisdom discerns the opportunities of obedience. It brings to the test the issues of life and approves the things that are excellent, in this way proving out in experience what is the acceptable will of God (Rom. 12:2; Phil. 1:9-11; Eph. 1:17; Col. 3:16; cf. Eph. 5:18).

We may distinguish between the gifts of sonship and of stewardship. The first have been called the "fruits" of the Spirit, the second the "gifts" of the Spirit. The gifts of sonship are the same for all Christians, for all those led by the Spirit of God are sons of God. These enduements make us like Christ, and therefore also like one another in Christ (Gal. 5:22). The gifts of stewardship, on the other hand, are gifts for ministry, and since there must be a variety of ministry in the organism of the body of Christ, these gifts differ (I Cor. 4:7; 12:4-11). Such diversity unifies the body of Christ in the mutual ministry of interdependence. Paul is at pains to show that the church, like the body, must function in sympathetic harmony (I Cor. 12:12-31). Our greatest need is for the gifts that are most unlike our own; we must therefore cherish and neither despise nor envy those whose gifts differ from our own.

Gifts for ministry constitute the calling of the individual; these gifts must not be wrapped in a napkin, but used in stewardship. The structure of this stewardship, the ministry of the church, must now be considered.

III. The Church Is Called in God's Service

In our study of the church as the people of God, the church of Christ, and the fellowship of the Spirit we have seen that the saving presence of God continually establishes and defines the church. In the unfolding of the history of redemption the divine presence is intensified until the church is filled with all the fullness of God. We cannot really appreciate this and then set it aside as mere "theology" while we proceed to organize the "institutional church" on the pattern of a social club or a sales organization. If the church exists in God's presence, then all the service of the church is service rendered before God. The Bible expresses this in another God-centered concept: the concept of calling. God calls his people to himself that he might possess them and they, him. He also calls them to serve. We may sum up both by saying that God calls us by a first and last name. The last name that we bear is the name of our Father, for he has called us by his name, and we are his (Isa. 43:6, 7). The triune Name of God is pronounced upon us as we are baptized into the Name of the Father, Son, and Holy Ghost (Matt. 28:19). Christians are united in that Name.

But we are also called in our own name, not only in the name of the people of God ("Israel" Isa. 43:1), but in our individual names, for he "calleth his own sheep by name" (Jn. 10:3). To him that overcomes, Christ will give a white stone, "and upon the stone a new name written, which no one knoweth but he that receiveth it" (Rev. 2:17).

In the pattern of God's call our gifts are joined to his purposes in personal fellowship with him and with each other.

A. Calling and the goals of service

What goals of service are set before us by the high calling of God in Christ Jesus? The goals of stewardship are directed first of all to God himself, then to the people of God, and finally to the world.

Our service of God directly is the service of worship in the widest sense. God called his people to himself at Sinai that they might serve him, and that service was given in worship. Redemption leads to praise. "Ye are an elect race, a royal priesthood, a holy nation, a people for God's own possession, that ye may show forth the excellencies of him who called you out of darkness into his marvelous light"... (I Pet. 2:9).

The first gifts of the Spirit manifested at Pentecost were gifts of praise; the disciples used the languages of earth to glorify God for his mighty works (Acts 2:11). Worship remains the first ministry of the church. Prayer does not simply prepare us for service; it is service. To pray in the Spirit, "Hallowed be thy Name" is to serve God. Paul saw his apostolic ministry as issuing in the "offering up of the Gentiles" (Rom. 15:16). Whether this refers to the Gentiles as presenting an offering, or being themselves presented as an offering, it puts Paul's service and theirs in the setting of worship. Paul rejoiced in the "tribute" brought to God by Gentile benevolence for the Jerusalem saints (Rom. 15:16, 25, 26; Isa. 60:5-7), in the self-offering of Gentile consecration (Rom. 12:1), and in the fruit of praise from the lips of the Gentiles (Rom. 15:9-11).

Not only does the worship of God come first in the ministry of the church. It also permeates all other aspects of service. Singing praise to God is blended with teaching and admonishing one another in psalms, hymns, and spiritual songs (Col. 3:16; Eph. 5:18-20). Giving thanks to God in the hearing and understanding of the church edifies believers (I Cor. 14:16, 17).

So also witness to the world must begin in praise. The New Testament presents doxological evangelism. In the passage from I Peter 2 quoted above, the church shows forth the excellencies of God who called them from darkness to light. The words "show forth" translate a word (exangello) that is used in the Septuagint Greek translation of the Psalms. This word and a synonym are used for a Hebrew word meaning to "recount" or "enumerate." The people of God praise him as they remember his saving deeds. "It is good for me to draw near unto God: I have made the Lord Jehovah my refuge, that I may tell of all thy works" (Ps. 73:28, cf. 9:4; 71:15; 79:13; 107:21, 22). Peter is also reflecting on similar language in Isaiah 43:21 "The people which I formed for myself, that they might set forth my praise."

Setting forth God's praise, declaring his excellency, is supremely an act of worship, but worship that witnesses before the nations to the true and living God. In the Psalms, as God's glory is celebrated, the nations are invited to join in the praise (Ps. 107:21, 22). The ideal of God's name being praised in his holy hill remains throughout the Old Testament. Since God is the God of the whole earth, and since Abraham was made a blessing to the nations, the full praise of God should rise from the nations too, as they join in the hallelujahs of his people. With the great manifestation of God in the latter days, the nations are brought in to God's feast in Mount Zion (Isa. 2:2-4; 56:6-8; Zech. 8:22, 23; 14:16).

How then does the movement change from the Old Testament to the New? In the Old Testament the nations are drawn in to worship at God's holy hill. In the New Testament the disciples are sent to the ends of the earth (Matt. 28:19; Acts 1:8). Actually, as I Peter 2:9-11 shows, the concept of the nations being drawn to the praise of God has not been lost but reinforced. The mount of God is indeed exalted--exalted to the heavenly Zion where Christ is, seated at the right hand of God. The Risen Christ is the Lord who calls the nations. The mission to the ends of the earth summons men to the heavenly mount of assembly, to the city with foundations, whose Builder and Maker is God.

It is not a passing fancy of the Apostle Paul, therefore, to think of his ministry as the assembling of a chorus of praise from the lips of the Gentiles (Rom. 15:6, 9-11). Nor is it strange that his explanation of God's counsels of mercy should culminate in doxology (Rom. 11:36). Praise is the hallmark of witness borne in the power of the Holy Ghost.

The two other goals of stewardship flow from the ministry of worship and they are closely tied together. We are called to minister the gifts of the Spirit in service to the church and to the world. Both of these goals of ministry toward men are emphasized in Scripture. For all the closeness of their interrelation we cannot dissolve one into the other. The statement that the church exists in mission alone rests ultimately on an unbiblical universalism. If the whole world, in the sense of every man, is saved, the church is distinguished from the world not by being saved, but by being sent. The church is then seen as that part of the world that is aware of the world's salvation and has the task of telling men that they are redeemed in Christ.

This view, far from exalting the mission of the church, removes its seriousness. The concern of the "servant church" of the universalist is with men's present consciousness, not with their eternal condition. But Paul's gospel ministry was a savor of life unto life and death unto death (II Cor. 2:15). The whole New Testament pronounces doom upon the unbelieving (e.g. Jn. 3:36; II Thess. 1:7-10). Men are called by the gospel to flee from the wrath to come (I Thess. 1:10).

God's great work of redemption delivers men in Christ from death to life, and therefore also divides between saved men and lost men. The terrible reality of this eternal issue causes Paul to cry, "Who is sufficient for these things?" (II Cor. 2:16). Were it not for our Lord's assurance that all whom the Father has given him shall come to him (Jn. 6:37-39), no preacher could bear the burden of his charge. But our sufficiency is of God, and all things are not only to him but from him, who gives life from the dead.

Since God has the people of his own possession, chosen in Christ before the foundation of the world (Eph. 1:4), God's purpose rests on them. In one sense, therefore, the mission to the world has for its goal the gathering of the church. Christ has "other sheep" who must be brought in (Jn. 10:16); he appears in a vision to Paul at Corinth to assure him that he has "much people" in the city (Acts 18:10).

The people of Christ are not only to be gathered to him; they are to be "discipled"--taught the things that Christ commanded, and thereby built up together as a holy temple of living stones (Matt. 28:19, 20; Eph. 2:20-22). We have already noted that the process of edification is both individual and corporate. Paul labored both to present each man perfect in Christ (Col. 1:28) and to present the whole church to Christ as a pure virgin (II Cor. 11:2).

The "body" figure in the New Testament is never used to describe the ministry of the church to the world but always to picture the mutuality of the ministry of Christians to Christians in the church. Some of the fullest discussions of the gifts of the Spirit are found in these "ministry of the body" passages (I Cor. 12:4-31; Rom. 12:3-7; Eph. 4:11-16). There can be no doubt that the goal of ministering to the building up of the church has a central place in the New Testament doctrine of stewardship. Ecclesiology must include the theology of nurture as well as of witness, and must relate both to the theology of worship.

From what we have been considering it is clear that witness to the world cannot be isolated as the ministry of the church, nor even as the primary ministry of the church. On the other hand, it does not follow that witness to the world is subordinate, or optional, --a goal to be sought only after the church has been at great pains to take care of itself. The Biblical emphasis has often enough been caricatured by churches that have justified huge expenditures for architecture, stained glass, and pipe organs under the rubric of worship. To this outlay they have added even vaster investments in staff and facilities for those multiplying programs that plead edifying purposes. Witness runs a poor third. It is left to a few missionaries who receive nominal support (and, of course, the women's missionary society).

This calamitous pattern comes, of course, from an underevaluation of the place of mission in the goals of ministry. But it should also be recognized that this pattern does not seek the other goals in their Biblical perspective, either. Biblical worship celebrates God's name before the nations, not in isolation. It becomes the warp in which the daily confession of Christ's name is woven. The church that truly worships will always draw in those who will fall down to declare that "God is among you, indeed!" (I Cor. 14:25). The same is true of Christian nurture. Biblical nurture sets the church on a lampstand and trims the wick of holiness. It strengthens witness in both life and word that men might "see your good works" and hear the "reason for the hope that is in you" (Matt. 5:16; I Pet. 3:15).

When the ministry of the church to the world is neglected the other goals of ministry cannot escape distortion. Worship dries up; edification becomes formal indoctrination. But when the church in obedience to Christ seeks to make disciples of the nations, then worship rises up: men cry out in prayer for boldness and for doors of opportunity (Acts 4:29; Col. 4:3; Eph. 6:19), the praises of the newly converted join with the thanksgiving of the saints. The church is edified together in obedient service, each member ministering to make the others more fruitful contributors to the whole ministry of the church.

B. Calling and the gifts of service

Since the Lord sets the goals of ministry and bestows the gifts for ministry no gift is useless or undirected. Further, the gifts are personally given and the value of each gift is expressed in the individual calling of the one who receives it as well as in the corporate fellowship in which it is exercised. That is to say, there is a pattern in the calling of each person as well as in the body of Christ, and the individual patterns are blended in the corporate. Behavioral science has sought to relate theories of personality and society within the limits of humanistic assumptions. Such assumptions exclude the true liberty of man in Christ. The Christian can respond to the question of identity, "Who am I?" in terms of his calling by Christ. He is a new man in a new society. He is not socially defined, for he is more than the sum of his social roles. Neither is he self-defined. Yet his identity and his function are united in the creative purpose of Christ's call.

The new name given to Simon is in a sense a title. We have seen how Jesus uses it in response to the title "Christ" as Peter applies it to him (Matt. 16:16, 18). Peter as an apostle is called to be a foundation rock of the church. Yet Petros, Cephas, is also a name, the key to Peter's distinctive identity: the man for whom Jesus prays that his faith fail not, and who is restored and filled with the Spirit to minister the Word. So every Christian is called with a title in the peerage of the saints. He has a role to fulfill in which he finds his own fulfillment as a servant of Christ.

Individual gifts are limited and specific: "but unto each one of us was the grace given according to the measure of the gift of Christ" (Eph. 4:7; cf. Rom. 12:3ff.). Yet a glad stewardship discloses the pattern of the Lord's giving: "But by the grace of God I am what I am, and his grace which was bestowed upon me was not found vain, but I labored more abundantly..." (Rom. 15:10). Since the gifts set the scope of one's service, a man must not glory beyond his measure (II Cor. 10:13) or think of himself more highly than he ought to think (Rom. 12:3). Yet he must think soberly, not despising the gifts he has received but regarding himself as a debtor to use them in service (Rom. 1:14). Further, in the course of service he may desire greater gifts (I Cor. 12:31; 14:1, 19; cf. Lk. 11:6, 9-13), and every steward must "stir up" his gifts in the flame of devotion (II Tim. 1:6; 4:5). Contrast Samson and Samuel: they differ not only in the service each rendered, but in the pattern of life each wrought in the stewardship of the gifts of the Spirit.

Christian experience is not an addition to life in the sphere of religious attitudes. It is the whole life of the new man. So, too, membership in the church is not a religious affiliation added to an intricate pattern of social relationships. The man in his identity and life calling is a new creature in Christ; the church is the form of the new humanity, the fellowship in which the stewardship of the Spirit's gifts is exercised. Unless this fellowship (described in Ephesians 4:12-16) does exist, the pattern of the church cannot develop as the one new man in Christ, and the individual cannot "find" himself in the service of Christ's calling. We are not pressing the body metaphor too far if we consider that ears, or hands, or feet cannot find their meaning apart from the body where they have been placed (I Cor. 12:15-20).

From the pattern of gifts granted by Christ for the goals of ministry we may trace a structure of ministry among the new people of God. We find that the gifts are grouped in three areas of ministry. First, there are gifts associated with the ministry of the Word of God. The importance of this gift is seen, for example, in Acts 6:2, 4, where the apostles say that it is not fit to "forsake the word of God and serve tables... But we will continue steadfastly in prayer and in the ministry of the word."

The administrative task of supervising the distribution of daily food to needy widows is necessary and important. The men chosen to discharge it are to be "of good report, full of the Spirit and of wisdom" (Acts 6:3). Yet in the church the ministry of the Word has priority even over the sharing of daily food. Those with the gifts and responsibility for ministering the Word have a necessity laid upon them to set aside other tasks as distractions. We are reminded of Jesus' teaching about the bread by which man lives and of the telling incident of Mary and Martha, recorded by Luke with obvious application to real situations in the early church where the demands of elaborate hospitality might keep the women of a house-church from the ministry of the Word (Lk. 10:41, 42).

In lists of gifts, too, the ministries of the Word occupy first place (I Cor. 12:8, 28; Rom. 12:6, 7). Indeed, in one passage, only ministries of the Word are listed. The function of these gifts is described: "for the perfecting of the saints, unto the work of ministering, unto the building up of the body of Christ" (Eph. 4:11-16).

Since Christ rules his church by his Word and Spirit there is a sense in which all ministry in the church is a ministry of the Word. Yet we have seen that the apostles were compelled to distinguish between their ministry of the Word and administrative tasks to be taken over by the Seven. The Word must be taught, but the life of the community must be ordered in obedience to the Word. It would appear that in Corinth, as at Jerusalem, the prominence of spiritual ministries of the Word overshadowed the development of administrators in the church who might adjudicate disputes (I Cor. 6:4, 5). Paul recognizes governing functions as distinct gifts (I Cor. 12:28; Rom. 12:8; I Tim. 5:17). The recognition of community elders in the Old Testament (Ex. 24:1, 9-11; Num. 11:6; Lk. 20:1) offered a ready pattern for the New Testament church, one that was particularly important for life in a fellowship governed by the law of love. Of course the commissioning of men with special responsibilities for administrative and judicial order in the community did not remove the responsibility borne by every member of the community for the soundness of the whole. A brother seeking the correction of an offense need not take an elder of the community with him as a witness (Matt. 18:16). Every member must be alert to admonish an erring brother (Phil.

2:4; Col. 3:16; Rom. 15:14; 16:17; II Cor. 2:6, 7; James 5:19, 20). The man to whom more has been committed by Christ bears the greater responsibility.

In addition to the ministry of the Word and of order in the church a third area is also singled out: the ministry of mercy. This, too, like the ministry of order is demanded by the gospel. Where the love of God rules and every man cares for the things of others a ministry of compassion must flourish. In the ministry of Jesus, the signs of kingdom power were deeds of mercy: Christ healed the sick and fed the hungry. In the teaching of Jesus the parable of the Good Samaritan grounded the full ministry of mercy in <u>compassion</u>, the attitude that must rise in the hearts of those who have themselves received the undeserved mercy of God (Lk. 10:25-37). The obligation of those who have received mercy to show mercy could not be more strongly put than when Jesus identifies himself with the least of his brethren who is hungry, thirsty, homeless, naked, sick, or in prison (Matt. 25:31-46). Christian love must be shown not in word only but in deed (James 2:15, 16). Jesus teaches prayer for the Holy Spirit against the background of a father feeding his son, or a friend urgently seeking bread to set before one who comes at midnight on his journey (Lk. 11:5-13).

The New Testament is full of teaching regarding the ministry of mercy. Not only did the apostles continue the ministry of healing Jesus had begun, the humblest disciple found a part in the church's ministry of caring. The joining of stewardship to fellowship in the early days of the Jerusalem church provided for all the needy. Every Christian recognized that he was a steward, together with the community, of what was possessed, and therefore each freely exercised his stewardship by selling possessions to meet the need (Acts 4:32-37; <u>cf.</u> 5:4). We have many other examples: Dorcas and the clothing she made (Acts 9:36, 39), Phoebe and her ministry (Rom. 16:1, 2), the Gentile churches in Greece and Asia Minor that contributed to the poor in Jerusalem. We have already seen that the Apostle Paul saw the fulfillment of prophecy in this giving of the Gentiles to the needs of Jerusalem (Rom. 15:16, 18, 25-28; II Cor. 8:19; 9:12-14). Hospitality, gifts and deeds of benevolence are spiritual sacrifices, thankofferings of praise to God (Heb. 13:16).

The ministry of mercy is not confined to the church; to them without also the compassionate concern of the gospel must be shown (Gal. 6:10). This is the thrust of the parable of the Good Samaritan in answer to the question, "Who is my neighbor?"

When we review the New Testament in general, or when we examine Paul's lists of spiritual gifts in particular (I Cor. 12:28; Rom. 12:6-8), we find gifts of ministering the Word, of governing, and of showing mercy. The Word is primary and central: the order of the community is the application of the law of love; mercy in the community is the manifestation of that same love on the part of those who have found mercy in the gospel.

The whole community is active in this total ministry, but since gifts differ, so do ministries: some are called to labor in the Word of truth, some in the establishment of righteousness, some in the showing of mercy. Further, gifts differ not only in kind but in degree. Some possess gifts in such extraordinary degree that they are called to be leaders of the community in the areas of their ministry. In such functions a measure of authority is necessarily entailed, and therefore certain outstanding gifts must have public recognition for their proper exercise. Office in the church does not begin with an institutional structure arbitrarily set up, but with the perfect harmony of Christ's appointment and calling. Christ grants gifts from the triumph of his enthronement. These enduements constitute men as apostles, prophets, evangelists, pastors and teachers (Eph. 4:7, 8, 11). Paul appeals to his apostolic authority when he says "by the grace given me" (Rom. 1:5; 12:3; 15:15; I Cor. 3:10; 15:10; Eph. 3:2, 7). The authority of officers in the church does not derive from the consent of the governed but from the enduement and calling of the Lord. "Take heed unto yourselves, and to all the flock, in which the Holy Spirit hath made you bishops, to feed the church of the Lord which he purchased with his own blood" (Acts 20:28). The submission the Christians render to those who govern in the church is motivated by the understanding that these rulers are accountable to Christ: "Obey them that have the rule over you and submit to them: for they watch in behalf of your souls, as they that shall give account..." (Heb. 13:17; _cf._ I Tim. 5:17; I Thess. 5:12; 2:13). The bishop is God's steward, accountable to his Master (Tit. 1:7; I Cor. 4:1-4; I Pet. 4:10, 11).

Of course the spiritual reality of such enduement and calling makes its possessor a minister and not a magistrate (I Pet. 5:3). The steward is a servant (doulos, Rom. 1:1; diakonos, Col. 1:7; oikonomos, I Cor. 4:1).

Further, the community is active in recognizing the gifts given to men. A man cannot normally exercise authority in the church until that authority has been recognized by the church. The apostles appealed to the Lord to choose a successor to Judas through the casting of lots, but the two candidates, Justus and Matthias were put forward by the company of 120 brethren. Similarly, the Seven were chosen by the brethren as men full of the Spirit and of wisdom (Acts 6:3). The community also has fellowship with those that exercise authority as they discharge their office. The decisions taken by the apostles and elders meeting in council at Jerusalem were publicly discussed. (Although the letter, according to the best text, was addressed by "The apostles and the elders, brethren" (Acts 15:23). The representatives who carried the letter to Antioch were chosen by "the apostles and the elders, with the whole church..." (Acts 15:22). Paul's pronouncement of discipline upon one guilty of a moral offense takes account of the fact that he can be present only spiritually. Yet he describes the community setting in which even an apostolic judgment could be rendered: "I...have already...judged him...in the name of our Lord Jesus, ye being gathered together, and my spirit, with the power of our Lord Jesus, to deliver such a one unto Satan for the destruction of the flesh, that the spirit may be saved in the day of the Lord Jesus" (I Cor. 5:5).

We have, then, what has been called the "general office" of all believers. Every Christian is called to participate in the ministry of Christ's church and therefore to have fellowship in the ministry of the Word, of order, and of mercy. Yet the diversity of Christ's gifts is such that we dare not argue that any Christian can perform any ministry. Not only are men warned not to estimate their gifts too highly (Rom. 12:3); they are also specifically warned against assuming that they are qualified to teach in the church (James 3:1, 13). Rather, they are exhorted to be more ready to hear than to speak, to learn than to give instruction (James 1:19). The New Testament presents an evangelistic church, but not a church in which every member is an evangelist. It is the whole fellowship of the church that accomplishes the evangelistic task, each member using to the full the gifts he has received and desiring greater gifts. Every Christian shows mercy in Christ's name, orders his life in holiness, and confesses Christ's name before men, giving reason for the hope that is in him. Some Christians can accomplish all this only very weakly and imperfectly. Yet each joins in the full fellowship of the church, praying for those with greater gifts as well as seeking by Christ's grace an increase of his own.

How do we relate the goals of ministry to the patterns of ministry? Evidently the patterns are directed to the goals and are not goals in themselves. Further, the patterns are formed both by kinds of gifts and degrees of giftedness. We have, then, three dimensions for the structure of ministry in the church. These are represented in the attached diagram of a truncated pyramid. Since the Mediatorial ministry of Christ is total, his office has been set as the capstone of the pyramid. No doubt it is a weakness in the diagram that it can indicate only Christ's transcendent authority and not his intimate presence in all ministry through the gift of his Spirit.

Yet the diagram serves to stimulate our thought as to the Biblical model of ministry. We see, for example, that mission, like edification and worship, is a goal of all ministry in the church. The function of the special office in mission is not limited to the ministry of the Word. Those with gifts for showing mercy to the sick, the poor, the homeless, the imprisoned--these deacons and deaconesses have a calling to share in the missionary outreach of the church. So, too, the ministry of order must be exercised by those called and gifted for administrative leadership. Again--these church governors do not labor alone but in fellowship with other church officers and with the brethren who are members of the church.

The goals of mission are best met by the whole fellowship of the church ministering the gifts of the Spirit. Certainly we have now perceived that mission is not the task of the preacher of the gospel alone. There is even some danger of an error in the opposite direction. We hear it said that every member of the church is a "missionary" and that the ministers of the church have no other responsibility than the training of members for mission. This new "laicism" can be as misleading as the "clericalism" it would replace. Mission is the work of the whole church, but each member contributes to it by serving with the gifts of the Spirit that are his. When God endues men with great gifts for evangelism and "discipling" those gifts must be used at the cutting edge of the church's ministry. "Do the work of an evangelist, fulfil thy ministry" (II Tim. 4:5).

The Biblical emphasis on structured fellowship in the ministry of the gifts of the Spirit does not mean that individual ministry is impossible. Paul labored alone at Athens for a period (Acts 17:14-16). There is no doubt that the apostles possessed unusual gifts of the Spirit for the ministry of the Word, order, and mercy. (We have seen how the apostles appointed the Seven to carry part of the responsibility they had borne. All other offices in the church are an "unpacking" of apostolic gifts.) But Paul was greatly distressed in his lonely labors, and his ministry was intensified when Silas and Timothy joined him (Acts 18:5, *cf.* II Cor. 7:6, 7). New Testament evangelistic ministry is more than "team" ministry; it is fellowship ministry carried forward not only by a minimum of two ministers of the Word, but also by what we can only describe as everyone else available by whatever means possible. Consider the hospitality of Lydia (Acts 16:14, 15); the fellowship and support of Aquila and Priscilla (Acts 18:2, 3, 18, 26); the help of Phoebe at Cenchrea (Rom. 16:1, 2); the gifts of the Philippians (Phil. 4:15, *cf.* 1:5). Paul sends salutations not only from his fellow-workers (Col. 1:1; Rom. 16:21; I Cor. 1:1) but from all the brethren with him (Gal. 1:2; Phil. 4:21, 22; Rom. 16:21-23; II Cor. 13:13). Indeed, the fellow-workers are themselves drawn from the churches of Paul's missionary endeavors (Timothy, Acts 16:1-4; Epaphroditus, Phil. 2:25; Sosthenes, I Cor. 1:1, *cf.* Acts 18:17; Titus, Gal. 2:1, 3; II Cor. 8:16, 23). The list of travelling companions in Acts 20:4 can be compared with Paul's description (II Cor. 8:16-24) of those who labor on his behalf and on behalf of the churches in collecting and transmitting the offering for the poor at Jerusalem. We learn of at least one leader who was appointed by the churches to travel with Paul in particular reference to this offering (II Cor. 8:18, 19), and of brethren who are "messengers (*apostoloi*) of the churches" (II Cor. 8:23).

The flexibility and fullness of fellowship revealed here is overwhelming. Men whose gifts have earned them recognition throughout the churches are appointed to minister with Paul; they serve on their initiative (II Cor. 8:17) and at his request (vv. 17, 18) to bring to realization a tremendous ministry of mercy, eloquent with the message of compassion, but significant also as fulfillment of the promises of the glorifying of God in the gospel.

Important questions remain with regard to the order of the Spirit by which the church lives and serves, but the structure we have observed helps us to survey the many areas of ministry directed to the goals of worship, edification and mission. Each of the volumes contained by the intersecting grids of the diagram has a content in terms of the exercise of the gifts of the Spirit. What the diagram does not show is the living flame of the Spirit that kindles this service and the flexible life of the community in which this structure comes to expression.

C. Calling and the program of service

We have been examining the structure of ministry as defined by its goals and gifts, with the help of spatial analogies. But what we are considering is God's calling in the Spirit. We must also reflect on another pattern in God's calling: the pattern of his program for the service of the church. The question is not just what the goals of ministry are, and what gifts are furnished to these ends, but what plan God has appointed for the service of his church.

Here we must take account of both the cross and the crown, sufferings and glory. We have already observed that the Holy Spirit seals our sonship in a twofold way. As the Spirit of sonship he teaches us to cry "Abba, Father" now (Rom. 8:14-16). But to this first-fruit of the Spirit's presence must be added the "adoption, the redemption of our body" (Rom. 8:23) for which we hope. This expresses, in terms of the work of the Spirit, the same tension between what is now realized and what is not yet realized that we also find in reference to the kingdom and the appearing of Christ. Further, Christ's sufferings are finished and his glory is complete. As the Spirit descended on him at baptism, so he has given the church the baptism of his Spirit at Pentecost. When we receive the redemption of our bodies we will be made in the likeness of his glorious, resurrection body. Yet the Spirit of Christ's resurrection is already given to us, and with him not only the guarantee but the foretaste, the "down-payment" of glory. What makes the picture complex is this wonderful intrusion of glory in the life and experience of the church, an intrusion which is found in the personal presence of the Lord, the Spirit.

Yet the presence of the Lord of glory with us does not mean that we are spared from suffering. Rather the Spirit of glory sustains us in the fellowship of suffering for Christ's sake. We are heirs together of God and of Christ, united not only to one another in sufferings now and glory to come, but also having fellowship with Christ as we take up our cross to follow him (I Pet. 4:13; Phil. 3:10; Rom. 8:17), knowing that if we suffer, we shall also rule with him.

The fact that our calling now is a calling to the cross means that self-fulfillment cannot be the ruling consideration in our use of the Spirit's gifts. We must take account, not only of the urgency of the situation, but of our own expendability for the name of Christ. God was totally glorified in the cross of Christ where the one Man who possessed the Spirit without measure was cut off. How much less are our gifts of the Spirit "wasted" when, through persecution we are barred from a full exercise of our calling.

We find that the Apostle Paul cheerfully foregoes many of the privileges he might have claimed in order to fulfill his ministry. Here we see a careful priority in the value of gifts ("I am debtor... woe is me if I preach not the gospel"). Even beyond that, Paul hazards his life and ministry to fulfill his own calling to the Gentiles, confident that God will preserve him so long as his presence is needful for those to whom he ministers.

In the ministry of the Spirit's gifts the church recognizes the priorities of the Spirit's leading. Paul rebukes the Corinthians for failing to recognize the program of the Spirit and to evaluate the gifts of the Spirit accordingly. The Corinthians treasured their role as possessors of startling gifts of the Spirit, acting as though they were already ruling. Paul only wishes that the day of glory and of rule had arrived, for then he too would reign! (I Cor. 4:8).

The secular theologies of our time have not only removed the distinction between the church and the world; they have also abandoned the promise of Christ's second coming. Inevitably the promise of the new heavens and earth that will follow judgment is also lost, and men speak in religious terms of the secular city.

The whole structure of ministry in Christ's church rests upon the program of his calling. He does not give the sword to his people to be used in his name. He withholds the outpouring of justice in a day of longsuffering grace. His people are not called to slay the wicked to deliver the oppressed. But they are called to die when necessary for the sake of the gospel.

Yet the ministry of the Spirit is not a ministry of weakness, but of power. The spiritual weapons of the church are proof against all the assaults of the devil and are mighty to the casting down of every imagination exalted against God (II Cor. 10:3-6).

The ineffectiveness of much of the contemporary church comes from the fact that it is fighting the wrong battles with the wrong weapons. Where the Biblical goals of ministry are sought with the rich gifts of the Spirit according to Christ's program, the fruits have not been lacking.

IV. The Church Is Ordered in the Spirit

A. Foundation of the church in the Spirit

1. Christ inaugurates the New Testament church with the gift of the Spirit

The baptism of the Spirit is inaugural of the new epoch after Jesus is "received up." The Spirit is given in fulfillment of the promise of Jesus' own preaching (Acts 1:4) and of God's promise in the Old Testament (v. 4). The disciples' question about the kingdom is not answered in reference to the consummation of the kingdom, but in reference to the present power of the kingdom realized in the coming of the Spirit (Acts 1:6-8).

Jesus received the Spirit at his own baptism to inaugurate his ministry; he gives the Spirit now, as the fruit of his finished work, to inaugurate the ministry of the church in his name.

All that Jesus "began both to do and to teach" (Acts 1:1) is now to be completed through the Spirit in the establishment of God's kingdom. The book of Acts describes this foundational period, beginning at Jerusalem and continuing to Rome, the capital, where the great Apostle to the Gentiles bears his witness.

2. Christ forms the New Testament church with the ministry of the Spirit

The Spirit that fills the church forms it, using men gifted of the Spirit who minister among brethren. In the foundation of the church the apostles have a unique calling of Christ. Jesus was received up "after that he had given commandment through the Holy Spirit unto the apostles whom he had chosen: to whom he also showed himself alive after his passion by many proofs, appearing unto them by the space of forty days, and speaking the things concerning the kingdom of God" (Acts 1:2, 3).

The apostles are chosen of Christ for their unique and unrepeatable ministry. They are witnesses of all that Jesus said and did (Acts 10:38, 39), and especially of his resurrection, for he was "made manifest, not to all the people, but unto witnesses that were chosen before of God, even to us, who ate and drank with him after he rose from the dead" (v. 41).

They witness also to the teaching of Christ, not only before the crucifixion, but in his post-resurrection instruction. Yet they are not commissioned for this witness until the Holy Spirit is given: they must wait at Jerusalem. Although their witness is grounded in their intimate association with Jesus, its expression and authority stem from the inspiration of the Holy Spirit who brings to their remembrance things past and reveals fuller truth that could not be received before Christ's resurrection (Jn. 14:26; 16:12, 13).

The apostles are organs of revelation; they bring the Word of God not only as prophets, but as men chosen and prepared to bear witness of what they saw and heard. The church is founded upon the apostles and prophets (= original inspired witnesses and other inspired men, Eph. 2:20). The prophets spoken of here are New Testament prophets (see Eph. 3:5). The mystery of Christ has "now been revealed unto his holy apostles and prophets in the Spirit."

In this foundational function the apostles are called as the "twelve," and Judas' vacated place must be filled by a new appointment. The community can recognize those who have the experience required of a witness, but the final choice is sought from the Lord. The number twelve itself points to the founding of the new people of God.

Paul's extraordinary apostleship springs from Christ's appointment and enduement. His seeing of the risen Christ qualifies him as a witness, not merely as a prophet (Gal. 1:12; 2:8; I Cor. 15:8, 9).

The apostles, too, serve as authoritative heralds. They are not only qualified to bear witness to Christ, but are charged to carry his name before kings and nations. Peter uses the keys of the kingdom for Jews and Gentiles; Paul fulfills his appointment as a herald of the gospel (I Tim. 2:7; II Tim. 1:11). The apostles are prophets, wise men, scribes of the kingdom who bear witness publicly and therefore suffer for Christ's name (Matt. 23:34).

In their heralding, too, the apostles fill a foundational role. Paul's urgent desire not to build on another man's foundation is not simply the zeal of a pioneer missionary. Rather it is the apostolic consciousness of the Apostle to the Gentiles. He is a wise master-builder who must lay the foundations of the church among the nations (Rom. 15:15-21; I Cor. 3:10).

B. Ordering of the church as the Spiritual community

1. Realism of Spiritual existence of the church

Because the church is the new creation of the Holy Spirit its existence is heavenly and eschatological: "For our citizenship is in heaven; whence also we wait for a Saviour, the Lord Jesus Christ" (Phil. 3:20). This is not simply the ideal or the hope of the church, but its real existence. The Spirit is the seal and the foretaste of this sonship. The church now worships in heaven where Christ is (Heb. 12:22; Eph. 2:6). This center of worship is as real as Christ's resurrection body and our union to him. Because the Spirit indwells the church, we actively participate on earth in this heavenly assembly.

In the same way the truth in which the church grows is heavenly doctrine: the words of the Father, communicated by the Son, and transmitted to us by apostles and prophets who were inspired of the Holy Ghost.

So, too, the discipline of the church is heavenly. It ministers unbounded forgiveness and seeks the reclamation of the offender. By the declaration of God's will it opens the gates of the kingdom to the penitent believer. But it also pronounces eternal doom in God's name upon those who refuse to repent and who trample under foot the blood of Christ.

As the community of heaven on earth, the church is possessed with fullness of spiritual life. Power, joy, freedom, peace and love--every blessing of Christ's own presence is poured out. Yet the church is restrained from the pursuit of vindicative justice. The Old Testament theocracy was vindicative within the limits of an institutional model of God's rule. The sword of King David did not execute final judgment any more than the knife of Aaron offered final atonement. When Christ came to fulfill the symbolism, he took both the knife and the sword. First, as Priest and Sacrifice, he bore the thrust of the spear on the cross. Now, as King of kings, he restrains the nations with the sword of his lips. When he comes again bearing the sword of judgment every enemy will be destroyed and God's righteousness will be forever vindicated.

The church as the kingdom of the Son of God's love is under his absolute rule and subject to his judgments, both spiritual and temporal. But the church can only declare God's judgment, it is not called to execute it. Here the very fullness of the church's actualization of Christ's kingdom restrains it from the execution of temporal penalties.

2. Manifestation of the Spiritual existence of the church

The heavenly reality of the church's existence does not remove the church from earth or make its earthly manifestation somehow shadowy. The distinctions between the church as visible and as invisible or between the church as institution and as body of Christ have sometimes confused this issue. But the "invisible church" is simply the church as God sees it; the visible church is the church as we see it. It would be reckless to conclude that because we cannot see the church as God sees it, we cannot see it at all! Surely, by God's grace, it is the task of the church to be visible, not only to the saints, but even to the world. The body of Christ figure describes in organic symbolism the visible and concrete relations of Christians to one another. There is reason for warning against a kind of ecclesiological docetism that would deny the reality of the church's appearance in the world.

Neither does the heavenly character of the church diminish the positive exercise of authority in the church. This authority is spiritual in the sense that it does not execute temporal punishment but pronounces eternal judgment as its final sanction. It is also spiritual in the sense that it is exercised in the power of the Spirit on the basis of the Word of the Spirit. Further, it is spiritual in the sense that it operates in the communion of the Spirit. No authority in the church is exercised apart from the fellowship of brethren. Those with gifts for rule share their ministry with those ruled; those who are charged to submit to the rule of gifted men have a voice in recognizing those very gifts and as brethren must discern if the gifts are being properly exercised.

C. Transcendent eschatological structure

The heavenly and eschatological character of the church does establish a pattern of authority that transcends both the rigidity and the pragmatism of secular institutions. For example, the Roman Catholic conception of church authority used the model of Roman imperial rule. This was justified under the claim of a continuing apostolic office and of a devolution of authority by which the pope claimed to be Christ's vicar on earth. This effectively secularized the Biblical conception of the church. But if the Jerusalem above is our "mother," there is no ground for awarding authority to the church of one city over others.

But the heavenly reality of the church should also warn us against absolutizing any geographical manifestation of the church. In insisting that only the local assembly is the church, some have thought of the kind of gathering that is described in the New Testament as "the church in thy house." Others have transferred this to a rather different assembly, the parish church. Still others have thought of the primary church assembly as the city church. (This is the pattern of the "presbytery" of the Westminster Assembly Form of Government.)

In the New Testament both house-churches and city churches are spoken of. (Rom. 16:5; Col. 4:15; I Cor. 16:19; I Cor. 1:2; Rom. 16:1) So, too, ecclesia in the singular may be applied to the church in an area (Acts 9:31; 15:3), as well as to the whole church, including all the scattered saints (I Cor. 10:32; 12:28; 15:9; Eph. 1:22, 23; 3:10, 21).

When the Spirit thrust forth Paul and Barnabas to proclaim the gospel, he used the prophets and teachers of the church at Antioch (Acts 13:1-3). This gathering of the recognized teachers of the church in a metropolitan area provides an example of one "presbytery" that lays hands on those commissioned for service (cf. Acts 13:3 with I Tim. 4:14). Their blessing would doubtless be accompanied by the exercise of their prophetic gifts (I Tim. 4:14).

It is most unfortunate that this account has been used as Scriptural warrant for making a parish congregation (or an independent church in one locality) the only proper sending agency for mission. Surely one reason that Luke gives the names and cosmopolitan origins of the teachers at Antioch is to indicate how representative was the complexion of that gathering of teachers in a city that had already become a notable center of mission interest and activity among the Gentiles.

The point, however, is not the precise magnitude of the church or churches among whom these teachers at Antioch labored. We are not to think, for example, that missionaries could be consecrated only in a "house-church" or a "parish-church" or a "city-church" or a regional church. (We are pointed, however, to the importance of the ministry of the Word and prayer in the functions of church leadership.)

The point is that gatherings of the brethren, or of teachers and leaders of brethren, have the right and duty to deal with matters that are of common concern in a way appropriate to the measure of authority (and therefore scope of service II Cor. 10:13-16; Rom. 12:3; Eph. 4:7) given to them by Christ with the recognition of his people. Fellowship in the gifts of the Spirit is the key to the exercise of authority in the church.

Where the organization of the church has become institutionally rigid (whether in decentralized or centralized units) the wider or narrower scope of proper common concern and action has often been forced to find expression apart from this institutionalized order. These "para-ecclesiastical" movements often become institutionalized in their turn. The danger in this fragmentation of the life of the church is that the flexible fellowship of the church is further impeded, even by the remedies sought for inflexibility!

D. Liberty of Spiritual order

The Spiritual order of the church is one of liberty, for the Spirit is the Spirit of liberty. Undue rigidity of structure need not be the greatest curb on liberty in the ordering of the church. Spiritual order may also be undermined by the tyranny of tradition. Here again the heavenly reality of the Word of God sets men free from bondage to the commandments of men. The church may not legislate new commandments to bind men's consciences, but only to teach and rule by the Word of the Lord. The church that requires for membership what Christ does not require has also become to that degree "para-ecclesiastical."

E. Spiritual order for the mission of the church

1. Missionary calling of the church and office

Since mission to the world is one goal of the whole ministry of the church, all Christians (the "general office" of believers) and all specially called and gifted leaders ("special office") have a role in mission. The Old Testament promises of the ingathering of the nations color all the New Testament teachings: the Great Commission of our Lord, the praise of the apostles at Pentecost, the vision of the Apostle Paul. "Foreign" missions therefore have a prominent place, not in the sense that crossing cultural barriers has theological significance, but in the sense that

God's mercy is magnified, his name exalted, and Christ's rule vindicated when the most remote parts of the world have heard the gospel and when all the tongues of man are united to confess in faith the name of Christ. The Christian who is conformed to God's only begotten Son is not only prepared to welcome sinners, to sit down to eat with them. He knows something of the Father's heart of mercy, and of the joy of the Father in welcoming the lost to heaven's feast. He is therefore particularly concerned to seek the lost to the ends of the earth.

The mission of the church is undertaken, however, in fellowship. As we have seen, the ministries of the Word, of order and of mercy all participate in the full mission of the church. We are not surprised to find Stephen and Philip engaged in evangelistic preaching and teaching, even though they had been charged by the church in the ministry of mercy among the poor widows. Similarly, the officers who participated in Paul's great offering for the poor at Jerusalem fulfilled the ministry of mercy with evangelistic purpose.

Certain officers, however, have particular gifts for evangelism, and their ministries both represent and lead the church in mission. The apostles, as we have seen, bore a unique responsibility as "foundation-layers" in heralding the gospel as well as in transmitting the gospel. But just as there were New Testament prophets who shared with the apostles the receiving of revelation from God, so there were evangelists who shared with them the work of heralding the gospel to the nations. The evangelists are named after the apostles and prophets in the list of the teaching officers given by Christ (Eph. 4:11, 12). Philip, one of the Seven chosen to assist the apostles is also described as an evangelist (Acts 21:8), and Timothy chosen to accompany Paul, is charged to do the work of an evangelist (II Tim. 4:5).

Because of the close association of evangelists with apostles it has been held that the evangelists were apostolic assistants bearing apostolic authority, and sharing in the foundational task unique to the apostolic age. One consideration that made this appealing was the fact that the evangelists were plainly not settled in one pastoral charge, and appeared to exercise authority beyond one local church. Were they bishops, then, with control of local pastors? To remove a possible wedge for Roman hierarchy it seemed much better to be able to conclude that the office of the evangelist was temporary, limited to the apostolic age.

But we must distinguish between the foundational ministry of the apostle as a herald and the continuing necessity for the heralding of the gospel to the ends of the earth and the end of the age. Perhaps Timothy and Titus were given certain charges under direct apostolic authority. It by no means follows that the work of evangelism to which they were called was limited to their possible service as apostolic delegates. Far less does it follow that there can be no calling of an evangelist after the initial apostolic proclamation. William Carey pointed out that the promise of Christ's presence through the agesshows that the Great Commission is not limited to the apostles, however significant their initial discharge of it might be.

Since the noun "evangelist" occurs so seldom, we must also consider the use of the verb and reflect on the importance of evangelizing to appreciate the importance of this gift.

Others who travelled with Paul under commission from the church, or who were recognized by the churches, doubtless had the gifts of evangelists. They could be called "apostles" because they were messengers of the churches, sent out and commissioned to herald the gospel (Acts 14:14; _cf._ Phil. 2:25).

We must recognize that such terms as minister (_diakonos_), elder (_presbyteros_), and apostle are capable of being used, not only in technical and non-technical senses, but even in a number of different technical senses (_cf._ our "governor"). The apostleship that Paul claimed (Rom. 1:5; Gal. 2:8; I Cor. 9:2) was on a level with that of the twelve: unique, foundational, of abiding authority in the church. This must not be confused with the authority of an evangelist like Barnabas who may also be called an apostle as an emissary of the church for evangelistic work. (Acts 14:4, 14).

Those who are evangelists must carry the gospel beyond those regions where it has been presented and believed. Their work cannot be regarded as simply the functioning of one local church in another, perhaps remote, area. Rather they labor in fellowship with the church in a broad region. We see the apostles reporting to the churches the triumphs of the gospel among the Gentiles. This reflects, not journalism, but fellowship. The concerted exercise of missionary evangelism does not go beyond the fellowship of the church when it goes beyond the bounds of a "parish," a city or a province. Rather, a wider representation of the church is involved in its maintenance and direction.

The missionary task force is then a most regular part of New Testament, Holy Spiritual, church order, equipped by gifts of the Spirit to be recognized by the brethren and thrust forth with the laying on of the hands of blessing by those called to declare God's Name to his people.

Paul's example shows us how thoroughly this task force is integrated with the spiritual government of the new churches that are established. Gentile evangelists are on the "team"--whose composition keeps changing--and Paul, even in the most serious discipline cases where his foundational apostolic authority must be exhibited, still scrupulously respects the disciplinary authority and responsibility of the church.

2. Missionary structure of the church

Not surprisingly, the problems of church and mission drive us back again to consider the attributes of the church in Biblical teaching. Many of the problems originate in the disunity of the "sending" church--whether in denominational division or in independent fragmentation. Churches which have no regular means of acting together in concerns that they have in common cannot escape difficulties when the opportunities of carrying the gospel abroad confront them. To some extent independent agencies may provide means for working together; but the absence of concerted discipline with respect to both doctrine and conduct remains.

In this situation, consultative relations represent a distinct gain, lest competitive direction and discipline prove self-defeating. But surely we must renew our consideration of the New Testament teaching respecting the unity of the church. Do the denominational churches that are true to the gospel show a concern like that now seen among the mission agencies? Consider, too, how great a part of the problem is the captivity of so many conservative churches in denominational fellowships whose leadership labors to substitute a new secular gospel for the gospel of Christ.

The church that is apostolic is one that remains on the apostolic foundation of gospel teaching and heralding. When that is rejected for secular theology and revolutionary action the mission of the church is not merely weakened, it is subverted. Yet what we need to stand against contemporary apostasy is apostolic church structure: full, obedient fellowship under the Word of God in the fellowship of the Spirit.

Only so can the real catholicity of the church be achieved. Otherwise the secularism inherent in the colonialist attitude may be replaced by the secularism patent in the revolutionary attitude, but the saving rule of Christ will not be made known.

Our discussions here can only be a beginning. Even in this project we need the wisdom of our brethren in the churches, here and abroad. For we need not only to talk about the church, but in the church in the fullest manifestation of its fellowship.

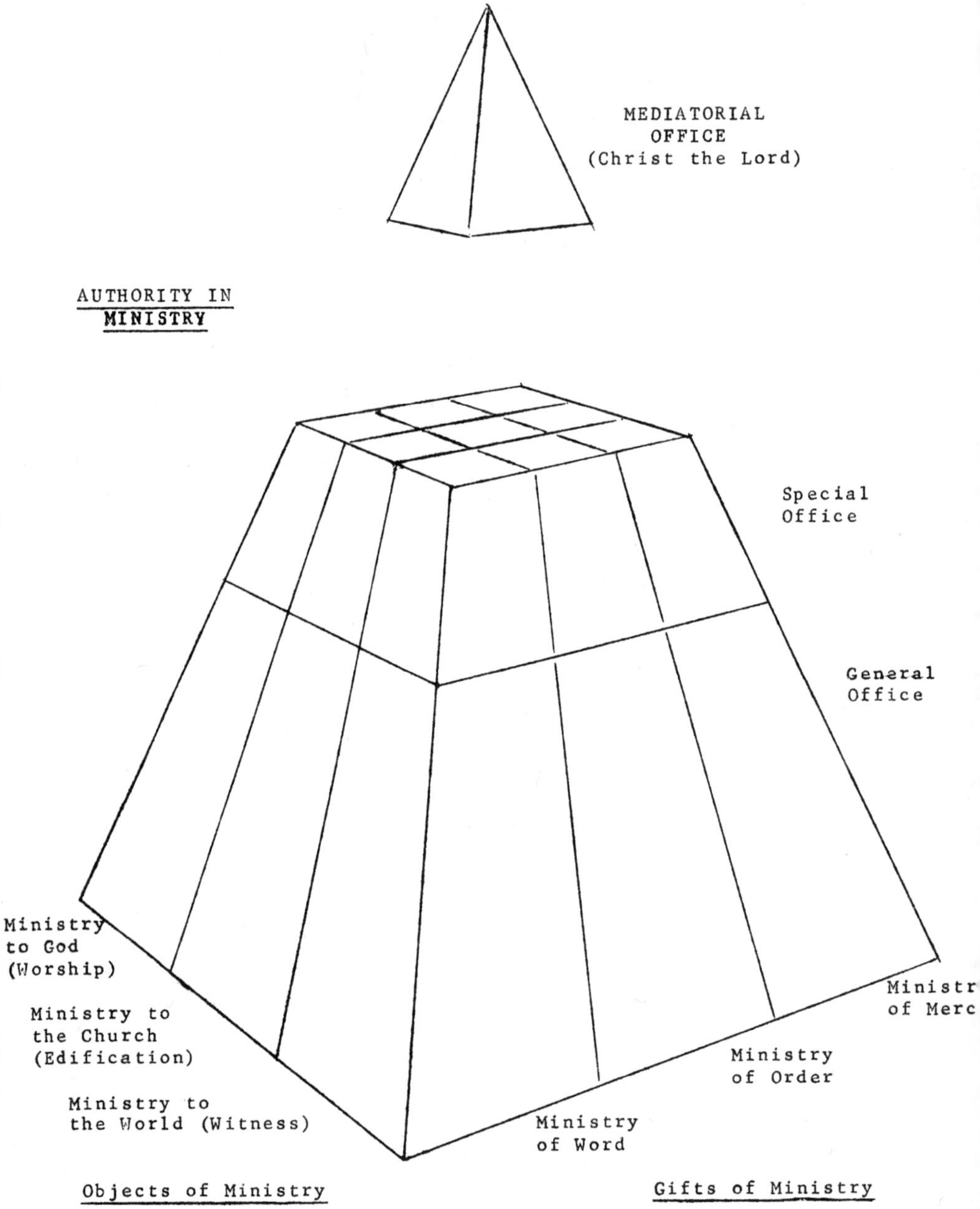

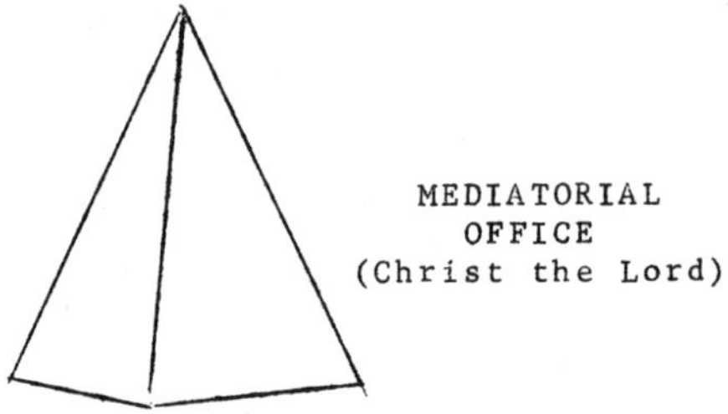

MEDIATORIAL
OFFICE
(Christ the Lord)
AUTHORITY IN
MINISTRY
Special
Office
General
Office
Ministry
to God
(Worship)
Ministry to
the Church
(Edification)
Ministry to
the World (Witness)
Ministr
of Merc
Ministry
of Order
Ministry
of Word
Objects of Ministry
Gifts of Ministry

STRUCTURE OF MINISTRY OF THE CHURCH

B I B L I O G R A P H Y

proposed for the

GREEN LAKE '71 Conference on CHURCH/MISSION TENSION
Donald G. Peterson, Bibliographer
Wheaton, Illinois

The preparation of the G. L. '71 Bibliography has been a formidable challenge to this neophite cataloger. It is submitted with the knowledge that it is far from complete, but with a prayer that its usefulness will have been worth the time and the effort of the writer and those who have contributed to it.

There are two preliminary comments with which this work should be prefaced. First, as to sources; many missionaries, professors, and mission executives have co-operated in responding to two questionnaires sent out to make up the list and I am indebted to each and all. The first of these asked for the "most crucial" book on this theme and five additional books. This largely formed the "Preliminary Reading List" which appeared in the summer issue of E.M.Q. The compiler also searched his library and other sources to complete the list. Since many of the contributions came without complete bibliographic details, when search failed to complete the information, they have been printed in their incomplete form.

The second comment has to do with arrangement. While the entire Bibliography bears directly upon the theme of Church/ Mission Tension, it was felt wise to divide the list into several subject classifications for easier reference. It is hoped that this arrangement will make it a continuing valuable tool.

ANTHROPOLOGY AND COMPARATIVE RELIGION

Buddhism and the Claims of Christ, Niles, D. T.
Richmond, Virginia, John Knox, 1967, p, 1.75
"Increasingly, the dialogue between Christianity and other faiths is calling for attention. The author has produced an important statement in Buddhism and the Claims of Christ. He respects Buddhism without compromising the uniqueness of Christianity."

The Church and Cultures: an applied Anthropology for the Religious Worker, Luzbetak, Louis
Techy, Illinois, Divine Word Publishers, 1963, 416 p.
A Roman Catholic text which gets to the heart of what paternalism and idigenization really are.

The Church between Temple and Mosque, Bavinck, J. H.
Grand Rapids, Michigan, William B. Eerdmans, 1966, 2.65 pb
The problems of Christianity's relation to other religions is the subject of this posthumous work by Prof. Bavinck. He believes, in spite of differences, dialogue is possible, men share a common religious consciousness and are equally the recipients of God's general revelation.

Cross and Crucifix in Mission: A Comparison of Protestant-Roman Catholic Missionary Strategy, Horner, Norman A.
New York, Abingdon Press, 1965, 223 p.

Customs and Cultures: Anthropology for Christian Mission, Nida, Eugene A.
New York, Harper & Row, 1954, 5.95 p.

Eyes on Europe, Harris, W. Stuart
Chicago, Illinois, Moody Press, 1971, 156 p., 1.95 p.b.
A nation-by-nation survey of a strategic continent reveals population, racial origins, prominent religions, size, topography and other details of 43 European countries, states and Islands. Europe is often a forgotten mission field, a continent divided by opposing religious and idealogies, the scene of a dangerous cold war between East and West. What is Christianity's role in Europe today?

The "Jesus Family" in Communist China, Rees, D. Vaughon
Fort Washington, Pa., Christian Liturature Crusade Inc., 1970 p. .89 pb

Major Religions of the World, Bach, Marcus
New York, Abingdon Press, 1970, p. 1.25 pb.
Brief sketches of the major religions of the world.

Message and Mission: The Communication of Christian Faith, Nida, Eugene A.
New York, Harper & Row, 1960, p. 5.95
Basic dynamics of communication between cultures.

People Movements in Southern Polynesia, Tippett, Alan R.
Chicago, Illinois, Moody Press, 1971, 400 p., 6.95
An engrossing, statistic-saturated treatment of 19th century mass conversion movements in Tahiti, Tonga, Maoriland and Samoa. A significant contribution to the church-growth movement.

Readings in Missionary Anthropology, Smalley, William A.
Tarrytown, New York, Practical Anthropology, 1967
The collection here of the best from Practical Anthropology is an excellent "Reader's Digest" from the best sources of common sense study about missions available today.

Religion Across Cultures: A Study in Communication of Christian Faith, Nida, Eugene A.
New York, Harper & Row, 1968, 111 p.
An introductory book to cross cultural communications.

Revival in Indonesia, Koch, Kurte
Grand Rapids, Michigan, Kregel, 1970, p. 2.95 pb.

Studies in Philippine Church History, Anderson, Gerald H.
Ithaca, New York, Cornell Univ. Press, 1969, 421 p.

What Would You Do? Ways of Sharing with other Faiths, Fleming, Daniel Johnson
New York, Friendship Press, 1949, 170 p.
New York, Association Press, 1929, 268 p.

Winning a Hearing: An Introduction to Anthropology and Linguistics for Missionaries, Law, Howard W.
Grand Rapids, Mich., Wm. B. Eerdmans, 1967, p. 3.95
Designed to help laymen and missionaries seeking special insights into the problems faced by churches which seek to serve various ethinic groups in this country and abroad.

World Cultures and World Religions, Kraemer, Hendrik
Philadelphia, Pa., Westminster Press, 1960
A historic background book for understanding concepts in a changing world.

World Mission and World Communism, Hoffman, Gerhard and Wille, Wilhelm, editors
Richmond, Va., John Knox Press, 1970, p. 2.45
Seven essays which look at the challenge of communism to missions in Asia, Africa, and Latin America.

The World's Religions, Braden, Charles S.
Ashville, Tenn., Abingdon, 1954 rev. ed., 3.00, 1.50 pb.
A concise account of the key facts concerning the origin, development and sacred literature of each of the great religions, ancient and modern.

CHURCH GROWTH--GENERAL

Christianity in Tropical Africa, Baeta, C. G., editor
London, Oxford Univ. Press, p. 8.80

The Christian Advance in Indonesia, Smith, Ebbie C.
South Pasedena, Cal., William Carey Library, 1970, 216 p., p. 3.45 pb.
The fascinating details of the penetration of Christianity into the Indonesian archipelago make for intensely interesting reading, as the anthropological context and the growth of the Christian movement are highlighted.

Church and Mission in Modern Africa, Hastings, Adrian
New York, Fordham Univ. Press, 1968, p. 5.50

Church Growth in Central and Southern Nigeria, Grimley, John B. and Robinson, Gordon E.
Grand Rapids, Mich., Wm. B. Eerdmans, 1966, 386 p., 3.25 pb
Detailed analytical studies of mission progress in two of the most productive mission outposts in the world, written by men who speak from within the missionary movement. Conclusions drawn are backed up by statistical figures, charts and graphs.

Church Growth in Sierra Leone, Olson, Gilbert W.
Grand Rapids, Mich., Wm. B. Eerdmans, 1969, p. 3.95
Basic approaches to mission activity as applied to Sierra Leone, assessed as well as various programs used to implement those approaches.

The Church of the United Brethren in Christ in Sierra Leone, Cox, Emmett D., Executive Secretary, United Brethren in Christ Board of Missions.
South Pasedena, Cal., Wm. Carey Library, 1970, 184 p., p. 2.95 pb.
A readable account of the relevant historical, demographic and anthropological data as they relate to the development of the United Brethren in Christ Church in the Mende and Creole communities. Includes a reformation of objectives.

Come Wind, Come Weather: The Present Experience of the Church in China, Lyall, Leslie T.
Chicago, Ill., Moody Press, 1960, 95 p., op
From personal experience and the gathering of news items, the author describes what has happened to the Church in China under the communist regime.

God's Impatience in Liberia, Wold, Joseph Conrad
Grand Rapids, Mich., Wm. B. Eerdmans, 1968, p. 2.95 pb
Readers of this book will come to have a new understanding of the lines along which Christ's followers may co-operate intelligently with Him in accomplishing His urgent purposes in every land. (McGavran)

istoric Patterns of Church Growth, Cook, Harold
Chicago, Ill., Moody Press, 1971, 128 p., p. 1.95 pb.
This volume (originally presented as a lecture series) delves into the ethnic, religious, cultural, and social backgrounds of five churches analyzed. It focuses on the Armenian church, the Celtic church of Ireland, the Karen church of Burma, the Hawaiian church and the Batak church of Sumatra.

History of Christianity in Japan, Drummond, Richard
Grand Rapids, Mich., Wm. B. Eerdmans, p. 4.95 pb
Confrontation with the Japanese culture was from the beginning one of the greatest challenges faced by the Christian Church, and is here analyzed in depth.

ow Churches Grow, McGavran, Donald A.
New York, Friendship Press, 1966
Originally published by World Dominion Press, London, 1959 (available in U.S. through Friendship Press), p. 2.50 pb.
Description of ways churches grow - or fail to grow. Including the influence of mission decisions (at home) on the growth of the churches on the field.

he Indigenous Church: A Report from many Fields, Reynolds, Arthur T.
Chicago, Ill., Moody Colportage Library, 1960, op
Covers many themes. "To give or not to give" - pros and cons of finances.

et Europe Hear: The Spiritual Plight of Europe
Chicago, Ill., Moody Press, 1963, 528 p., p. 5.95 o.p.
A survey of 16 countries of free, western Europe, stressing the conditions which have made them mission fields in our generation.

ation-building in Africa; Problems and Prospects, Rivkin, Arnold
New Brunswick, N.J., Rutgers Univ. Press, 1969, 312 p., p. 10.00
His book reveals that polycentrism and a desire for individual national sovereignty have become the guiding force in African interstate relations rather than Nkrumah's dream of an African super state. It challenges those who would apply to Africa conclusions predicated upon Asian and L-A models. His is a different approach to nation-building. He begins with the view that nation-building is the central process in life of all new states of Africa.

ew Branches on the Vine: From Mission Field to Church in New uinea, Kaschade, Alfred
Minneapolis, Minn., Augsburg, 1967, 175 p.
Theme developed "not missions but churches," some of the chapter titles are indicative of its themes: indigenization, Papuan thought, towards an indigenous theology. The author is a Lutheran missionary in Papua.

New Buildings on Old Foundations, Davis, J. Merle
New York, International Missionary Council, 1945, 320 p.
An old book, but excellent discussion on indigenizing of fields - especially self support.

The Nevus Plan of Missionary Work Illustrated in Korea, Allen, Charles
Seoul, Korea, Christian Literature Society, 1937
From South Minneapolis, E. G. Heinz, 3624 - 5th South.
Grand Rapids, Mich., Wm. B. Eerdmans, 1966

Notes on Christian Outreach in a Philippine Community, Mayers, Marvin Keene
South Pasadena, Calif., Wm. Carey Library, 1970

Peoples of Southwest Ethiopia, Tippett, Alan R.
South Pasadena, Calif., Wm. Carey Library, 1970, 304 p., p. 3.95 pb
A recent, penetrating evaluation by a professional anthropologist of the cultural complexities faced by Peace Corps workers and missionaries in a rapidly changing intersection of African states.

Planting and Development of Missionary Churches, Nevius, John L.
Philadelphia, Pa., Reformed and Presbyterian Publishing Co. 1958, 92 p.

The Planting of the Churches in South Africa, Sales, James M.
Grand Rapids, Mich., Wm. B. Eerdmans, p. 3.45
The liberal tradition in S. Africa is due in part to early missionaries. The great gulf between the white and non-white populations is the story of the failure of the Christian Churches to express the Gospel in the social orde

The Primal Vision (Christian Presence Amid African Religion), Taylor, John V.
Philadelphia, Pa., Fortress Press, 1964, p. 3.25

Profile for Victory in Zambia, Randall, Max Ward
South Pasadena, Calif., Wm. Carey Library, 1970, 224 p., p. 3.95
"In a remarkably objective manner the author has analyzed contemporary political, social, educational and religious trends which demand a re-examination of traditional missionary methods and the creation of daring new strategies... his conclusions constitute a challenge for the future of Christian missions, not only in Zambia, but around the world." - James DeForest Murch

Reform in Leopold's Congo, Shaloff, Stanley
Richmond, Va., John Knox Press, 1970, p. 5.95
Tells the story of the fight for racial equality and social justice in the Kasai region of the Congo during the critica years, 1890-1921.

Soka Gakkai: Japan's Militant Buddhists, Brannen, Noah S.
Richmond, Va., John Knox Press, 1968, p. 5.50
First study in depth of the beliefs and practices of the third largest political force in Japan. A broad survey of the historical background religious and philosophical beliefs, organizational techniques, and political activities of this important movement.

The Story of the Christian Church in India and Pakistan
Neill, Stephen
Grand Rapids, Mich., Wm. B. Eerdmans, p. 3.95
The history of the church in these countries is told in relationship to the history of the countries themselves.

Taiwan: Mainline Versus Independent Church Growth, A Study in Contrasts, Swanson, Allen J.
South Pasadena, Calif., Wm. Carey Library, 1970, 216 p., p. 2.95 pb.
A provocative comparison between the older, historical Protestant churches in Taiwan and the new indigenous Chinese churches; suggests staggering implications for missions every where that intend to promote the development of truly indigenous expressions of Christianity.

Toward an Indigenous Church, Idowu, E. B.
London, Oxford Univ. Press, 1965

Understanding Church Growth, McGavran, Donald
Grand Rapids, Mich., Wm. B. Eerdmans, 1969, 382 p., p. 7.95
Understanding church growth declares that the processes, by which God multiplies His churches throughout the world are extremely complex and must be understood with care. It examines the social and anthroplogical milieus in the midst of which churches multiply and shows how knowledge of social structures aids obedient servants of God to be faithful.

The Weathercock's Reward, Bentley-Taylor, David
London, Overseas Missionary Fellowship, 1967 (formerly China Inland Mission)
A historical examination of mission-church interplay in East Java, Indonesia. Significant because Indonesia has perhaps seen more ex-Moslems baptized than all the rest of the Moslem world combined.

Wildfire: Church Growth in Korea, Shearer, Roy E.
Grand Rapids, Mich., Wm. B. Eerdmans, 1965, p. 2.95 pb
An analytical, statistical case study outlines in detail how the Presbyterian Church and other major denominations in Korea grew in the past and what roles were played by missionaries and nationals in this growth. The author prescribes, his own recommendations for a more efficient and purposeful missionary program.

The following books will be released in 1972 in the Moody Press Church Growth Series:

Frontiers in Mission Strategy, Wagner, Peter
Chicago, Ill., Moody Press, June 1972
Church growth series.

Give Up Your Small Ambitions, Griffiths, Michael C.
Chicago, Ill., Moody Press, 1972, 160 p., p. 1.95 pb.
A helpful guide, spelling out what it's like to become a missionary. A reprint from I.V.C.F.

The Unresponsive: Resistant or Neglected, Liao, David
Chicago, Ill., Moody Press, 1972, 160 p., p. 2.95 pb.
A church growth study using the Haaka Chinese to illustrate a common mission problem.

CHURCH GROWTH -- LATIN AMERICA

The Church and Social Change in Latin America, Landsberger, Henry T., (ed.)
South Bend, Ind., Univ. of Notre Dame Press

Church Growth in Mexico, McGavran, Donald
Grand Rapids, Mich., Wm. B. Eerdmans, 1969

Church Growth in the High Andes, Hamilton, Keith E.
Lucknow, India, Lucknow Press, 1962, 146 p.

The Development of Christianity in the Latin Caribbean, Gonzalez, Justo L.
Grand Rapids, Mich., Wm. B. Eerdmans, 1969, 136 p., p. 2.65 pb.
This book is concerned not only with the history of the establishment of the church in these various countries, but with the development of the resulting churches.

El Seminario de Extension: Un Manual, Emery, James H., Kinsler, F. Ross, Winter, Ralph D., Walker, Louise J.
South Pasadena, Calif., Wm. Carey Library, 1969, 256 p., p. 3.45
Gives the reasons for the extension approach to the training of ministers, as well as the concrete, practical details of establishing and operating such a program. A Spanish translation of the third section of "Theological Education by Extension".

The Emergence of a Mexican Church: The Associate Reformed Presbyterian Church of Mexico, Mitchell, James Erskine
South Pasadena, Calif., Wm. Carey Library, 1970, 192 p., p. 2.95
Tells the ninety-year story of the Associate Reformed Presbyterian mission in Mexico, the trials and hardships as well as the bright side of the work. Eminently practical and helpful regarding the changing relationship of mission and church in the next decade.

The Growing Church in Haiti, Johnson, Harmand
West Indies Mission, Coral Gables, Florida, 1970

Growing Young Churches, Hodges, Melvin
Chicago, Ill., Moody Press, 1971, 126 p., p. 1.25 pb
Originally published as "The Indigenous Church", this paperback is based particularly on the author's experiences in very successful missionary work in Central America.

Hammered as Gold, Howard, David M.
New York, Harper and Row, 1969, 187 p., p. 4.95
Story of the growth of the church in northern Colombia through bloody persecution, defeats, tragedy, and ultimate triumph. Reveals many of the problems faced in contemporary missionary work.

Justinian Welz: Essays by an Early Prophet of Missions
Scherer, James A.
Grand Rapids, Mich., Wm. B. Eerdmans, 1969, p. 2.45 pb
Welz died almost three hundred years ago in South America. His treatises occupy a deserved place in the annals of mission history, and are available here, almost entirely, in the English language.

Latin American Church Growth, Read, William R.
Monteroso, Victor and Johnson, Harmon jt. eds.
Grand Rapids, Mich., Wm. B. Eerdmans, 1969, p. 6.95
The most complete analysis to date of the church on any continent. A must for every missionary executive, since it deals with the growth of churches in an area where they are growing phenomenally.

The Protestant Movement in Bolivia, Wagner, C. Peter
South Pasadena, Calif., Wm. Carey Library, 1970, 264 p. p. 3.95 pb
An excitingly-told account of the gradual build-up and present vitality of Protestantism. A cogent analysis of the various sub-cultures and the organizations working most effectively, including a striking evaluation of Bolivia's momentous Evangelism-in-Depth year and the possibilities of Evangelism-in-Depth for other parts of the world.

Social Justice and the Latin Churches
Richmond, Va., John Knox Press, 1969, p. 2.95
These essays by key Protestant thinkers in Latin America wrestle with the question of the role of the church (particularly protestant denominations) in the face of rapid social change.

A Study of the Older Protestant Missions and Churches in Peru and Chile, Kessler, J. B. A., Jr.
Oosterbaan and Le Cointre

Tinder in Tabasco, Bennett, Charles
Grand Rapids, Mich., Wm. B. Eerdmans, 1969
Tinder box in Tabasco: Church growth in tropical South East Mexico. Story of the church in this small Mexican state is a significant chapter in the annals of church history with insight which might be applied to the church around the world.

LEADERSHIP EDUCATION - PERSONNEL - BIOGRAPHY etc.

All Loves Excelling, Beaver, R. Pierce
Grand Rapids, Mich., Wm. B. Eerdmans, 1968, p. 2.95
First book in a series on women in mission. The author traces the development of that movement from their involvement with benevolent activities at home to active participation abroad.

Christian Collegians and Foreign Missions, Barkman, Paul F., Dayton, Edward R., and Gruman, Edward L.
Monrovia, Calif., Missions Advanced Research and Communications Center, 1969, 424 p.

Facing the Field, Soltau, Stanley T.
Grand Rapids, Mich., Baker Book House, 1959, 135 p., p 1.75

Fire on the Mountain, Davis, Raymond J.
Grand Rapids, Mich., Zondervan, 1966, p. 3.95
A missionary biography dealing with the hardships encountered in the New Testament pattern, just as Peter suggested it be treated, and glorifies Christ and tells of the spread of the Kingdom.

For Missionaries Only, Cannon, Joseph L.
Grand Rapids, Mich., Baker Book House, 1969, p. 2.95

Missionary Life and Work, Cook, Harold R.
Chicago, Ill., Moody Press, 1962, p. 5.95

Pioneers of the Younger Churches, Seamands, John T.
Nashville, Tenn., Abingdon Press
Biographical sketches of fourteen missionaries who make great sacrifices in their fields.

The Quality of Mercy, Steensma, Juliana
Richmond, Va., John Knox Press, 1969, p. 3.95
A human interest account of how the author's husband helped Korean War amputees overcome despair and regain normal lives. Provides insights for anyone who faces the question "how do I really go about helping people?"

Theological Education by Extension, Winter, Ralph D., Ph.D.
South Pasadena, Calif., Wm. Carey Library, 1969, 648 p., p. 7.95
A husky handbook on a new approach to the education of pastoral leadership for the church. Gives both theory and practice and the exciting historical development of the "largest non-governmental voluntary educational development project in the world today." - Ted Ward, Professor of Education, Michigan State University.

The Uyo Story, Weaver, Edwin and Irene
Elkhart, Ind., Mennonite Board of Missions, 1970

Who Shall Ascend?: The Life of R. Kenneth Strachan of Costa Rica, Elliot, Elizabeth
New York, Harper and Row, 1968, 171 p., p. 5.95
Reveals the agonies and struggles of soul of a very human man who nverthele ss was an outstanding missionary statesman and architect of Evangelism in Depth. Profoundly honest biography.

The Young Life Campaign and the Church, Simandle, Warren
South Pasadena, Calif., Wm. Carey Library, 1970, 216 p.
If 70 per cent of young people drop out of the church between the ages of 12 and 20, is there room for a nationwide Christian organization working on high school campuses? After a quarter of a century, what is the record of Young Life and how has its work with teens affected the church? "A careful analysis based on a statistical survey; full of insight and challenging proposals for both Young Life and the church."

PRINCIPLES, PHILOSOPHY, AND THEORY OF MISSIONS

To Advance the Gospel, the Collected Writings of Rufus Anderson, Beaver, Pierce
Grand Rapids, Mich., Wm. B. Eerdmans, p. 5.95, 2.95 pb
Anderson refused to accept civilization and evangelization as the two inseparable halves of mission activity, and to this day practically every North American mission board adheres to the principles first articulated by him: that missions should become self-governing, self-supporting, and a self-propagating church.

The Call to Mission, Neill, Stephen
Philadelphia, Pa., Fortress Press, 1971
This little book, though over priced, is one of the most recent by Bishop Neill, and contains many of his mature observations.

Concise Dictionary of the Christian World Mission, Neill, Stephen, ed., Anderson, Gerald H. and Goodwin, John jt. eds.
Nashville, Tenn., Abingdon, 1971, p. 10.50

For All the World, Taylor, John V.
London, Hodder and Stoughton
Even when it is not totally persuasive, it is healthily provocative.

For All the World: The Christian Mission in the Modern Age
Philadelphia, Pa., Westminster Press, p. 1.45 pb.

Living As Comrades: A Study of Factors Making for Community
New York, Agricultural Missions, 1950, 180 p.m.
Studies in principles and methods of world missions.

Missionary Administrations, Matthews, George W.
Des Plaines, Ill., Regular Baptist Press, 1970, p. 3.95

Missionary Methods, St. Paul's or Ours?, Allen, Roland
Grand Rapids, Mich., Wm. B. Eerdmans, 1962, p. 1.95
One of the most stimulating and provocative treatments of missionary methods which has come out in this century. The principles deserve the most careful study.
-- Eugene Nida

Missionary Principles, Allen, Roland
Grand Rapids, Mich., Wm. B. Eerdmans, p. 1.45 pb
A clear, compelling presentation of this extraordinary missionary's thoughts and faith.

Missionary Principles and Practice, Lindsell, Harold
West Wood, New Jersey, F.H. Revell, 1955, 384 p.

Modern Mission Dialogue, Theory and Practice, Pt. III
Kerkhofs, Jan

Paternalism and the Church, Hollis, Michael
London, Oxford Univ. Press
An Anglican bishop who also served for some years as bishop in the Church of South India, has some keen observations on the matter of paternalism as it has related to church work in India.

Revolution in Missions: From Foreign Missions to World Mission of the Church, Lamott, Willis Church
New York, MacMillan Co., 1954, 228 p.

The Spontaneous Expansion of the Church and the Causes Which Hinder It, Allen, Roland
Grand Rapids, Mich., Wm. B. Eerdmans, 1962, p. 1.95 pb
In chapter 7, on Missionary Organization; our organization immobilizes our missionaries; the term "mission station" is a contradiction in terms. "A challenge to all our complacencies."

Upon the Earth, the Mission of God and the Missionary Enterprise of the Churches, Niles, D. T.
New York, McGraw-Hill, 1962, 269 p.
Miss theory or theology.

Verdict Theology in Missionary Theory, Tippet, A. Richard
Lincoln, Ill., Lincoln Christian College Press, 1969, 161 p.

The World of Mission, Sundkler, Bengt
Grand Rapids, Mich., Wm. B. Eerdmans, p. 6.95
This survey contrasts with most surveys of Christian missions, by adopting an approach that is not primarily historical, but rather ecological. It is concerned with the environment in which the church exists and with which it interacts.

STRATEGY FOR MISSIONS AND EVANGELISM

Bridges of God, McGavran, Donald A.
New York, Friendship Press, 1955, p. 2.50
A study of how entire peoples become Christians and the significance of this for missionary strategy.

Christ the Liberator, Stott, John R. W. and others
Downers Grove, Ill., Inter-Varsity Press, 1971, p. 2.95
Chapter by Samuel Kamaleson, "The Local Church and World Evangelism", good on strategy.

The Christian World Mission In Our Day, Latourette, K.S.
New York, Harper and Row, 1954
A brief study in expectation of what to expect and the need for methodological change.

Church Growth and Christian Mission, McGavran, Donald
New York, Harper and Row, 1965, 252 p., p 5.95
A re-appraisal of the role of Christian missions and the evaulation of their success in bringing about church planting and growth.

Church Growth Through Evangelism-In-Depth, Bradshaw, Malcolm R
South Pasadena, Calif., Wm. Carey Library, 1969, 152 p., p. 2.45 pb
"Examines the history of Evangelism-in-Depth and other total mobilization approaches to evangelism. Also presents concisely the 'Church Growth' approach to mission and proposes a wedding between the two... a great blessing to the church at work in the world." - World Vision

For All the World; The Christian Mission in the Modern Age
Taylor, John V.
London, Hodder and Stoughton, 1966, 92 p.
Christian Foundations no 12
Even when it is not totally persuasive, it is healthily provocative.

Jerusalem Missionary Conference, 1928
Meeting of the International Missionary Council, March 24 - April 6, 1928
New York City, IMC., 8 vols.
Vol. III, Younger and Older Churches.

The Master Plan of Evangelism, Coleman, Robert E.
Old Tappan, N.J., F. H. Revell, p. 3.50, p. 1.25 pb

Missions at the Crossroads: The Indigenous Church, A Solution for the Unfinished Task, Soltau, T. Stanley
Wheaton, Ill., Van Kampen Press, 183 p., 1.95 pb

Missions in Crisis, Re-thinking Missionary Strategy, Fife, Eric S., and Glasser, Arthur F.
Downers Grove, Ill., Inter-Varsity Press, 1961, 270 p., p. 1.95
A re-thinking of missionary strategy. It combines factual examination of current forces at work with evaluation of the church's past, present and potential effectiveness.

ew Face for the Church, Richards, Larry
Grand Rapids, Mich., Zondervan Publ., 1970, 288 p., p 5.95
Excellent appraisal and restatement of the method and manner of operation for the N. T. Church. Structures new patterns for our time.

ew Life for All, Lager, Eileen
Chicago, Ill., Moody Press, 1971, 144 p., p. 1.25 pb

n the Growing Edge of the Church, Street, T. Watson
Richmond, Va., Knox Press, 1965
A fresh study of the program of missions.

ut Your Arms Around the City, Angel, James W.
Old Tappan, New Jersey, F. H. Revell
Winner of the $10,000 award Centennial contest.

esponse: The Church in Mission to a World in Crisis, Cogswell, James A.
Richmond, Va., John Knox Press, 1970, p. 2.50 pb

evolution in Evangelism, Roberts, W. Dayton
Chicago, Ill., Moody Press, 1967, 127 p., p. 1.25
The story of Evangelism in Depth, and its contribution to missionary strategy, especially in Latin America.

aturation Evangelism, Peters, George W.
Grand Rapids, Mich., Zondervan Pub. House, 1970, 237 p., 3.45 pb
Contemporary evangelical perspectives.

econd Thoughts on Missions, Lees, William C.
Fort Washington, Pa., Christian Lit. Crusade, p. .50
Develops the theme that God has indeed given gifts to the national Christians and that in many instances the missionary needs to learn to keep hands off.

trategy of Missions in the Orient, Christian Impact on the agan World, Lit-sen Chang
Nutley, N. J., Presbyterian and Reformed Publishing Co., 1968
This book deserves a careful reading by every executive of missions. In it we hear the church in Asia proclaiming its program for spreading abroad the sweet savor of Christ. - McGavran.

tudent Power in World Evangelism, Howard, David
Downers Grove, Ill., Inter-Varsity Press, 1970, p. 1.25 pb.
Chapter 4: The Church - the Agent of World Mission.

TENSIONS

TENSIONS - CHURCH AND MISSION TENSIONS. - NATIONAL AND MISSIONARY

The Christian Message in a Non-Christian World, Kraemer, Hendrik
Grand Rapids, Mich., Kregel, 1961, 455 p.
Published for the International Missionary Council
A classical study prepared for the Tambaram meetings of the I.M.C. in 1938 by an outstanding Dutch scholar - a watershed in missionary thinking. This work has long been overlooked. We may disagree with Kraemer, but we dare not disregard him.

Church and Mission in Modern Africa, Hastings
Roman Catholic author gives a realistic and true insights to church-mission relationships.

The Church at the End of the 20th Century, Schaeffer, Francis A.
Downers Grove, IVCF Press, 1970, p. 3.95
Chapter on form and freedom in the church as well as many other parts of the book applicable to the theme church/mission relations.

The Church Inside Out, Hoekendijk, J.C., translated by Isaad C. Rottenberg
Philadelphia, Pa., Westminster Press, 1971(?), p. 1.95 pb
Representative writings by this outspoken Dutch church man, selected for their relevance to the current American Church situation.

Creative Tension, Neill, Stephen
Edinburgh, Edinburgh House Press, 1959, 115 p. p. 2.00
Especially chapter IV.
Insights with some prejudice of a high churchman in his evaluation of Church and mission.

Don't Sleep Through the Revolution, Rees, Paul S.
Waco, Texas, Word Books, 1969, 130 p., p. 2.95
Comes to grips with most of the great problems the church is facing today... he confronts the racial problem with honesty, candor and imagination. Human suffering, eschatology, death and even Viet Nam, come into new focus under his vivid scrutiny. (Billy Graham)

Honest Religion for Secular Man, Newbigin, Lesslie
Philadelphia, Pa., Westminster Press
Especially chapter IV
Present world, West and East, are both caught in the p rocess of seculariation and the Church, West and East, can be the church in its full nature or succumb to secularism.

Mission and Unity in Lutheranism: A study in Confession and Ecumenicity, Shere, James A.
Philadelphia, Pa., Fortress Press, 1969, 272 p., p. 8.00
The author presents a lively account of the ambivelance of the Lutheran traditional position on ecumenicity, and the kinds of tension to which it leads, particularly in the younger churches. The detailed descriptions of inter-church discussions in Africa and of union negotiations in India reveal both the peril and the promise for churches everywhere.

Missionary Go Home: A Reappraisal of the Christian World Mission, Scherer, James A.
\# Englewood Cliffs, N.J., Prentice-Hall, 1964, 192 p., p. 3.95 op
A comprehensive and critical survey of current issues in world missions with penetrating analysis in relating problems of today to biblical directives. Excellent development.

Missions in a Time of Testing: Thought and Practice in Contemporary Missions, Orchard, R. K.
London, Lutterworth Press, 1964
An ecumenical and pessimistic look at the future shape of missions, which is never the less valuable for completing the total picture for the provocative new shapes of mission suggested and as a basis for reaction for evangelicals.

The Other Side of the Coin, Isais, Juan
Grand Rapids, Wm. B. Eerdmans, 1966, 104 p., p. 1.45
Realistic novel by a Mexican who is himself a missionary in Latin America. Shows the tensions between missionaries and nationals and offers solutions to this age-old problem.

People and Cities, Verney, Stephen
Old Tappan, N.J., F.H. Revell
This book concerns the urgent problems now confronting the human race - what is happening to people.

Protestant Crosscurrents in Mission: the Ecumenical-Conservative Encounter, Horner, Norman, ed.
Nashville, Tenn., Abingdon Press, 1968, p. 4.50
A discussion of the motivations, objectives, and strategy of world mission by competent representatives of both conservative evangelical and ecumenical view points.

The Responsible Church and Foreign Mission, Beyerhause, Peter
\# and Lefever, Henry
Grand Rapids, Mich., Wm. B. Eerdmans, 1964, p. 1.95 pb op
Challenge presented to the foreign mission by the church overseas, which church wishes to be treated as responsible body. Unique on church-mission relations.

Schism and Renewal in Africa: An Analysis of Six Thousand Contemporary Movements, Barrett, David
London, Oxford Univ. Press, 1968, p. 7.25

Sermons to Men of Other Faiths and Traditions, Anderson, G.H.
Nashville, Tenn., Abingdon Press, p. 3.25
Explorations of the conflicts within modern day Christianity.

Solomon Islands Christianity, A Study in Growth and Obstructio
Tippett, Alan R.
New York, Friendship Press, 1967
An excellent study of the historical interplay of church and mission decisions in the Solomon Islands. Growth is on the part of the churches. Obstruction is often provided by the mission.

The Supreme Task of the Church, Seamands, John T.
Grand Rapids, Mich., Wm. B. Eerdmans, p. 2.45 pb
From his rich experience in missionary work, the author gives a realistic picture of the tremendous opposition the Church faces.

The Third World and Mission, Clark, Dennis E.
Foreword by Paul S. Rees
Waco, Tex., Word Books, 1971, 129 p., p. 3.95
A healthy blend of evangelical candor and sensitiveness.

The Ugly American, Lederer, William J., and Burdick, Eugene
New York, W. W. Norton, 1958, 258 p., p. 1.85 pb

THEOLOGY, BIBLE BASIS, AND HISTORY OF MISSIONS

Asia-South Pacific Congress on Evangelism, Singapore, 1968 - "Christ Seeks Asia", Mooneyham, Stanley Walter
Minneapolis, Minn., W. W. Publishers, 1969, 267 p.
Originally, Hongkon, the Rock House.

Bible Basis of Missions, Glover, R. H.
Chicago, Moody Press, 1964, p. 3.95

Christian Mission in Theological Perspective: An Inquiry by Methodists, Anderson, Gerald H., ed.
Nashville, Tenn., Abingdon Press, 1967, 286 p., p. 2.50 p

he Church Growth Bulletin, Volume I-V, McGavran, Donald A., Ph.D.
South Pasadena, Calif., Wm. Carey Library, 1969, 408 p., p. 6.95
The first five years of issues of a now famous bulletin which probes past foibles and present opportunities facing the 100,000 Protestant and Catholic missionaries in the world today. No periodical edited for this audience has larger readership.

he Church, An Organic Picture of its Life and Mission, Brow, Robert
Grand Rapids, Wm. B. Eerdmans, 1968, p. 1.95 pb
A succinct analysis of the Church fulfilling its nature in practical function.

he Church Crossing Frontiers. Essays on the Nature of Mission
Beyerhaus, Peter and Hallencreutz, Carl F., Ed., in honor of Bengt Sundkler.
Lund, Gleerup, 1969, 282 p.
Includes bibliographical references.
Contents - Jesus and the Gentiles, by D.T. Bosch - Translating the Gospel in New Testament time, by H. Riesenfeld - Crossing the frontiers in the second century, by P. Beskow - The ministry of crossing frontiers, by P. Beyerhaus - Religion and Politics by T. Furberg - Indian Christians in political affairs, by S. Neill - The changing society, by M. Wilson - Writing African church history, by J. F. Ade, A. and E. A. Ayandele - The spirit and the religions, by E. J. Sharpe - Dialogue with Chinese religion, by J. Beckmann - Christian presence across the frontier, by G. Rosenkranz - Mission as dialogue, by C. F. Hallencreutz - Servant of the frontier church, by A. I. Berglund - Selfhood: Presence or persona? by J. V. Taylor - The new praise in ancient tunes, by H. Weman - The church in Buhaya, by J. Kibira - Redemption for the wrongs of history, by L. Thunberg - Negotiating for church union, by D. T. Niles - Can Lutherans cross frontiers? by H.W. Gensichen - Towards renewal in mission, by P. Potter - Call to mission, a call to unity? by L. Newbigin - Bibliography of Bengt Sundkler, by S. Axelson

hurch Growth and the Word of God, Tippett, Alan R.
Grand Rapids, Mich., Wm. B. Eerdmans, p. 1.95 pb
Spells out the Biblical basis for the concept of church growth held by Dr. McGavran and his colleagues at the School of World Mission and the Institute of Church Growth at Fuller Seminary.

he Church's World Wide Mission: An Analysis of the Current tate of Evangelical Missions, and a Strategy for Future Activity,
Congress held at Wheaton, Illinois, 1966
Lindsell, Harold, ed.
Waco, Texas, Word Books, 1966, 289 p., p. 3.95

Colonialism and Christian Missions, Neill, Stephen
New York, McGraw-Hill, p. 7.95

The Discipling of West Cameroon: A Study of Baptist Growth
Kwas, Lloyd Emerson
Grand Rapids, Mich., Wm. B. Eerdmans, p. 3.45
Approximately 500 Baptist congregations have been established in West Cameroon, but the author dramatically illustrates the fact that the growth potential of the church is far from reached.

Ecumenical Beginnings in Protestant World Mission, Beaver, R. Pierce
New York, Thomas Nelson and Sons
Beaver writes with a bias towards the W.W.C.

An Evangelical Theology of Missions, Lindsell, Harold
Grand Rapids, Zondervan, 1970, 234 p., p. 2.45 pb

Evangelism in the Early Church, Green, Michael
Grand Rapids, Wm. B. Eerdmans, p. 6.95
Traces the evangelistic activity of the church from N.T. period through the middle of the third century. Strengths and weakness of the earily church examined.

Facing the Unfinished Task: Messages Delivered at the Congress on World Missions at Chicago, 1960
Sponsored by Interdenominational Foreign Missions Assn. of North America. Compiled by Percy, J.O.
Bennett, Mary, ed.
Grand Rapids, Mich., Zondervan Pub. House, 1961, 281 p.

A Faith for this One World, Newbigin, Lesslie
London, SCM Press, 1961, 128 p.
Centrality and universality of Christ discriminatingly set forth.

The Finality of Christ, Newbigin, James Edward Lesslie
Richmond, Va., John Knox Press, 1969, 120 p.,
Bishop Newbigin examines the various Christian interpretations of finalty. He advances the debate by showing that the way to move beyond Kraemer's position is to look for the place of the gospel in secular history. The gospel is the announcement that all men make a decision for or against.

God's Mission, Roels, Edwin
Grand Rapids, Mich., Wm. B. Eerdmans, 1962, 303 p.
The Epistle to the Ephesians in mission perspective. A valuable study.

God's Mission and Ours, Smith, Eugene L.
Nashville, Tenn., Abingdon Press, 1961, p. 3.25

History of Christian Missions, Neill, Stephen
Baltimore, Md., Penguin Books, 1964, 622 p., p. 2.25
A massive and heroic chronicle, in one volume, of the history of world wide expansion of all Christian denominations from the time of Christ up to the year 1962.

The Household of God: Lectures on the Nature of the Church
Newbigin, James Edward Lesslie
New York, Friendship Press, 1954, 177 p.
Admittedly written to encourage the merger of the WCC and the IMC, it reflects the missionary urgency inherent in God's purpose for the Church. Newbigin is one of the most instructive of ecumenical mission leaders.

The Inescapable Calling, Strachan, R. Kenneth
Grand Rapids, Wm. B. Eerdmans, 1968, 227 p., p. 1.65
This book develops in clear and concise fashion the contemporary challenge to mission, the biblical basis of missions, and how mission is fulfilled today.

An Introduction to Christian Missions, Cook, Harold
Chicago, Ill., Moody Press, 1971, p. 4.95
A helpful introductory study of missions.

An Introduction to the Science of Missions, Bavinck, J.H.
Philadelphia, Pa., Presbyterian and Reformed Press, 1970, p. 4.95, Grand Rapids, Mich., Baker Book House, 1960, 323 p., 4.95
Chapter 10 deals with the role of the mother church and the relation of old and new churches. A scholarly introduction for the more advanced reader to the theory of missions, the foundations, aim and history of missions.

The Kingdom of God, Bright, John
Nashville, Tenn., Abingdon Press, 1953, 288 p., p. 3.75
London, Lutterworth Press, 1955, 292 p.
Beginning with the formative years of the Hebrew nation, Dr. Bright presents a comprehensive survey of Hebrew history and religion, tracing the concepts of the Kingdom of God, from beginning to consummation.
The missionary nature of the church is disclosed in God's design for His people whether in the O.T. or N.T.

Latin American Theology: Radical or Evangelical?, Wagner, Per
Grand Rapids, Mich., Wm. B. Eerdmans, p. 2.45 pb
A broad description of the theological scene in the Latin American Protestant Church, the first analysis of this significant movement. The critique is from the point of view of the "church growth" position of McGavran.

The Missionary Manifesto, Morgan, G. Campbell
New York, F. H. Revell, 1906, 157 p.

The Missionary Nature of the Church, Blauw, Johannes
New York, McGraw-Hill Book Inc., 1962, 182 p., p.3.95 op
A survey of the Biblical theology of mission showing the relationship between the O.T. and the N.T. concepts of world outreach of the church.

The N.T. Order for Church and Missionary, Hay, Alexander R.
Audobon, N.J., New Testament Missionary Union, 1947, 540 p., p. 4.65
Presents historical and scriptural evidence to develop the principles and methods of church planting.

The Normal Christian Church Life, Nee, Watchman
Los Angeles, Calif., The Stream Publishers, 1962
Helpful discussion on the gifts of the spirit, ministries, and finance. Makes the point that the "work" of apostles is separate from the management of the churches.

One Body, One Gospel, One World: The Christian Mission Today
Newbigin, James Edward Lesslie

Pentecost and Missions, Boer, Harry R.
Grand Rapids, Mich., Wm. B. Eerdmans, 1961, 270 p., p. 1.95
An excellent exegetical and historical study, showing that the real motive behind the missionary outreach of the apostolic church was the experience of Pentecost which gave the power for outreach.

The Philippine Church: Growth in a Changing Society
Tuggy, Arthur Leonard
Grand Rapids, Mich., Wm. B. Eerdmans, p. 3.45 pb
Develops the principle that the Church grows in a specific context. To achieve maximum growth the church must understand the society in which it is growing.

Planning for Mission: Working Papers on the Quest for Missionary Communities, Weiser, Thomas, ed.
New York, U.S. Conference of the WCC, 1966, 230 p.

The Scripture Doctrine of the Church: Historically and Exegetically Considered, Bannerman, David Douglas
Grand Rapids, Mich., Wm. B. Eerdmans, 1955, 589 p.
Reprint of 1887 edition, Edinburgh, Scotland

The Church, Kung, Hans
New York, Sheed and Ward
This Catholic scholar presents some aspects of the church which may assist us in understanding our present problems.

<u>A Survey of World Missions</u>, Thiessen, John C.
Chicago, Ill., Moody Press, 1961, 350 p., p. 5.95
A one volume survey of world missions today, with brief sketches of other religions, biographies of outstanding individuals, charts giving principle facts on each country, and other details.

<u>Symposium: Facing Facts in Modern Missions</u>
Foreword by Taylor, Clyde
Chicago, Ill., Moody Press, 1963, op
Discusses missionary relationships, international cooperation and mission/church relations.

<u>The Theology of the Christian Mission</u>, Anderson, Gerald H., ed.
New York, McGraw-Hill, 1961, 341 p.
Nashville, Tenn., Abingdon, Press, 1969, p. 2.45
Essays developing the theological foundations of Christian Missions.

<u>Time for Action</u>, Broomhall, A.J.
London, Inter-Varsity Fellowship, 1965, 152 p., p. 1.25
A powerful call to action to bring the gospel to the fast changing world of today. Presents the world and its need, the church and her responsibility, the Christian and his personal response.

<u>The Twenty-Five Unbelievable Years</u>: 1945-1969, Winter, Ralph D., Ph. D.
South Pasadena, Calif., Wm. Carey Library, 1970, 116 p., p. 1.95 pb
A terse, exciting analysis of the most significant transition in human history in this millenium and its impact upon the Christian movement. "Packed with insight and otherwise unobtainable statistical data... a brilliant piece of work."- C. Peter Wagner

<u>To Apply the Gospel, Selections from the Writings of Henry Venn</u>
Warren, Max, ed.
Grand Rapids, Mich., Wm. B. Eerdmans, 1970, p. 7.95
Selections from the voluminous writings of Henry Venn, arranged and clarified by introductory sections.

<u>The Unfinished Task</u>, Neill, Stephen
London, Lutterworth, 1957, p. 2.10 pb

<u>Unitive Protestantism: The Ecumenical Spirit and Its Persistent Expression</u>, McNeill, John T.
Richmond, Va., John Knox Press, 1964, p. 1.00
A basic resource for understanding the background of the ecumenical movement, especially in the Reformation period. Valuable for getting historical perspective on what is happening today.

World Congress on Evangelism: One Race, One Gospel, One Task; official ref. Volumes: papers and reports
Berlin, 1966
Henry, Carl F., and Mooneyham, W. Stanley, ed.
Minneapolis, Minn., World Wide Publishers, 1967

MISCELLANEOUS - UNCLASSIFIED, INCOMPLETE INFORMATION ETC.

Emphasizing Missions in the Local Church, Pierce, Robert
Grand Rapids, Mich., Zondervan

Missionary Education Helps for the Local Church, Pearson, Dick
Overseas Crusades

Missions Idea Notebook
Suggested by Gould, R. Howard of Dallas Bible College

Mobilizing for Saturation Evangelism, Taylor

The Missionary Between the Times, Beaver, R. Pierce
New York, Doubleday, 1968, p. 5.95

The following were submitted for inclusion in the lists. Either their bearing on the subject is unknown to me, or full verification has been impossible.

Missionary, Come Back, Almquist, Arden
New York, World Publishing Co., p. 5.95

The Other Revolution, Isais, Juan
Waco, Texas, Word Books

A Place to Feel at Home, Welbourn, F.B., and Ogot, B.A.
Publisher unknown

Reform of the Ministry, Allen, Roland
London, Lutterworth Press, 1968

Sons of Fire, Rubingh
Grand Rapids, Mich., Baker Book House

Triumphant Missionary Ministry in the Local Church
Lewis, Norman
Lincoln, Neb., Back to the Bible Publishers

Yes to Missions (or Say Yes, to Missions), Webster
Naperville, Ill., SCM Press

The following were received too late to classify in other subject headings.

Approaching the Nuer of Africa through the Old Testament
McFall, Ernest A.
South Pasadena, Calif., Wm. Carey Library, 1970, 104 p., p. 1.95
The author examines in detail the similarities between the Nuer and the Hebrews of the O.T., and suggests a novel Christian approach that does not make the initial use of the N.T.

The Challenge for Evangelical Missions to Europe: A Scandinavian Case Study, Malaska, Hilkka
South Pasadena, Calif., Wm. Carey Library, 1970, 192 p, p. 2.95
Graphically presents the state of Christianity in Scandinavia with an evaluation of the pros and cons and possible contributions that existing or additional Evangelical missions can make in Europe today.

The Emergence of a Mexican Church: The Associate Reformed Presbyterian Church of Mexico, Mitchell, James Erskine
South Pasadena, Calif., Wm. Carey Library, 1970, 184 p., p. 2.95
Tells the ninety-year story of the Associate Reformed Presbyterian Mission in Mexico, the trials and hardships as well as the bright side of the work. Eminently practical and helpful regarding the changing relationship of mission and church in the next decade.

Friends in Central America, Enyart, Paul C.
South Pasadena, Calif., Wm. Carey Library, 1970, 224 p., p. 3.45
An Analysis of the growth of one of the most virile, national evangelical churches in Central America, comparing its growth to other evangelical churches in Guatemala, Honduras, and El Salvador.

God's Miracles: Indonesian Church Growth, Smith, Ebbie C.
South Pasadena, Calif., Wm. Carey Library, 1970, 224 p., p. 3.45
The fascinating details of the penetration of Christianity into the Indonesian archipelago make for intensely interesting reading, as the anthropological context and the growth of the Christian movement are highlighted.

La Serpiente y la Paloma, Gaxiola, Manuel
South Pasadena, Calif., Wm. Carey Library, 1970, 200 p., p. 2.95
The impressive success story of the Apostolic Church of Mexico, (an indigenous denomination that never had the help of any foreign missionary), told by a professional scholar now the director of research for that church. (Spanish)

New Patterns for Discipling Hindus: The Next Step in Andhra Pradesh, India, Subbamma, B.V.
South Pasadena, Calif., Wm. Carey Library, 1970, 212 p., p. 3.45
Proposes the development of a Christian movement that is as well adapted culturally to the Hindu tradition as the present movement is to the Harijan tradition. Nothing could be more crucial for the future of 400 million Hindus in India today.

Peoples of Southwest Ethiopia, Tippett, Alan R.
South Pasadena, Calif., Wm. Carey Library, 1970, 304 p.
A recent, penetrating evaulation by a professional anthropologist of the cultural complexities faced by Peace Corps workers and missionaries in a rapidly changing intersection of African states.

Profile for Victory: New Proposals for Missions in Zambia
Randall, Max Ward
South Pasadena, Calif., Wm. Carey Library, 1970, 224 p., p. 3.95
The author has anaylzed contemporary political, social, educational, and religious trends, which demand a re-examination of traditional missionary methods and the creation of daring new strategies...

The Protestant Movement in Bolivia, Wagner, C. Peter
South Pasadena, Calif., Wm. Carey Library, 1970, 264 p., p. 3.95
A cogent analysis of the various subcultures and the organizations working most effectively, including a striking evaluation of Bolivia's momentous Evangelism-in-Depth for other parts of the world.

The Protestant Movement in Italy: Its Progress, Problems, and Prospects, Hedlund, Roger
South Pasadena, Calif., Wm. Carey Library, 1970, 266 p., p. 3.95
A carefully wrought summary of preliminary data, perceptively develops issues faced by Evangelical Protestants in all Roman Catholic areas of Europe. Excellent graphs.

Taiwan: Mainline Versus Independent Church Growth, A Study in Contrasts, Swanson, Allen J.
South Pasadena, Calif., Wm. Carey Library, 1970, 216 p., p. 2.95
A provocative comparison between the older, historical Protestant churches in Taiwan and the new indigenous Chinese churches; suggests staggering implications for missions everywhere that intend to promote the development of truly indigenous expressions of Christianity.

PERIODICAL ARTICLES

Bibliotheca Sacra

Published by the Dallas Theological Seminary, John Wolvoord, ed., Dallas, Texas
Mission-Church Relationships, Peters, George, W., Vol. 125, 1968, pp. 205-215, 300-312.

Missionary Society as the Sending Agency, Peters, George W., Vol. 125, 1968, pp. 116-122.

Calvin Theological Journal

Published by Calvin Theological Seminary, Grand Rapids, Michigan.
The Great Debate in Missions, McGavran, Donald A. Vol. 5, 1970, pp. 163-179.

Christianity Today

Published bi-weekly by Christianity Today, Harold Lindsell, ed., Washington, D.C.
Crisis of Identity for Some Missionary Societies, McGavran, Donald A., Vol. 14, 1970, pp. 10-14.

Bangkok Conference Loosens the Western Grip, Bray, W.T., and Raffe, G.E., Vol. 13, 1969, pp. 51-52.

Confronting Other Religions, Henry, Carol F. Vol. 13, 1969, pp. 31-

Encouraging Missionary Movement in Asian Churches Hian, C. W., Vol. 13, 1969, pp. 9-12.

Missionary Doctors Seek New Roles, Pearson, F., Vol. 13, 1969, p. 38.

Missionary and Cultural Shock, Perri, B. Vol. 12, 1968, pp. 14, 15.

Missionary, Come Home?, Carter, P.H. Vol. 11, 1967, pp. 9-12.

Changing Face of Missions, Fife, H.W. Vol. 12, 1968, pp. 3-5.

Concordia Theological Monthly

Published by Concordia Theological Seminary, St. Louis, Missouri.
The Gospel and the Missionary Task of the Church, Miller, R.E., Vol. 40, 1969, pp. 465-481.

Fellowship and the Younger Sister Churches (editorial) Zorn, H.M., Vol. 40, 1969, pp. 264-266.

Dialogue
Published by Augsburg Publishing House (Lutheran)
Minneapolis, Minn.
Sent into the World (Study documents for the 5th
Lutheran World Federation, 5th Assembly, Port Alegri,
Brazil, July 14-24, 1970), Burtness, J.H.
Vol. 9, 1969, pp. 114-121.

Ecumenical Review
Published by World Council of Churches, Eugene Carson
Blake, ed., Geneva, Switzerland.
Spiritual Conflicts in a Changing African Society,
Pratt, S.A.J., Vol. 8, 1965, pp. 154-162.

Evangelical Missions Quarterly
Published by Missions Information Service Inc., James
Reapson, ed., Springfield, Pa.
Problems of Conversion in Recent Mission Thought,
Sharpe, E.J., Vol. 4, 1969, pp. 221-231.

African Congress on Evangelism Faces Issues Confronting
the Church, Bellamy, W., vol. 5, 1969, pp. 112-114.

New Testament Blue Print: Starting and Organizing Local
Churches Overseas, Gerber, Virgil, Vol. 6, 1969, pp. 28-3

The Missionary of the 70's, Peters, George W., Vol. 7,
1971, pp. 138-147.

Receiving Churches and Mission, Clarke, Dennis
Vol. 7, 1971, pp. 201-210.

E.M.Q. Vol. 7, Number 4, Summer - the entire issue
What Missionaries Can Learn from the Peace Corps
Moffitt, R., Vol. 5, 1969, pp. 34-38.

Foundations
Published by the American Baptist Historical Society,
Rochester, N.Y.
Social Change and Theological Resources, Snyder, T.R.
Vol. 12, 1969, pp. 308-313.

Frontier
Published by William B. Eerdmans, Grand Rapids, Mich.
Wanted Missionary - Pacific Island Style, Forman, C.W.
Vol. 12, 1969, pp. 267-273.

His
Published by Intervarsity Press, Downers Grove, Ill.
The Right to be Indian (Not American), Mayers, M.K.
Vol. 29, 1969, pp. 37-39.

International Reformed Bulletin
Published by the International Association for Reformed Faith and Action, Paul G. Schrotenber, ed., Grand Rapids, Michigan.
Challenge of the N.T., Coenen, Lothar, Nos. 20, 21, 22.

The Christian Message to a Changing World, Schrotenber, Paul G.

International Review of Missions
Published by the Comission on World Mission and Evangelism of the World Council of Churches, New York.

The Problem of Indigenization in Nigeria, Ilegu, Edmand Vol. 49, 1960, pp. 167-182.

The Missionary Situation in South Africa; Some Reflections and Suggestions, Berthon, Alex L., Vol. 49, 1960, pp. 85-90

Indigenization and the Renaissance of Traditional Culture: A Comment on Vert Rossman's Article, Thomas, M.M. Vol. 52, 1963, pp. 191-194.

African Independent Church Movements, Hayward, Victor G.W. Vol. 52, 1963.

The Breaking in of the Future: The Problem of Indigenization and Cultural Synthesis, Rossman, Vern Vol. 52, 1963, pp. 129-143.

Indigenization in the African Church, Crane, William H. Vol. 53, 1964, pp. 408-422.

Asian Missions, Vol. 53, 1964, pp. 318-327.

Towards Church-Mission Integration in Germany, Müller-Krüger, Vol. 52, 1964, pp. 182-190.

The Church's Responsibility for the Missionaries it Receives, Kotto, Jean, Vol. 53, 1964, pp. 152-161.

'Devolved' Missionaries, Church Peace Corps or Prophet-Priests?, by a missionary, Vol. 55, 1966, pp. 213-220.

Laymen Abroad, Vol. 56, 1967, pp. 444-458.

Missionary Activity in Asia, Engel, Frank, Vol. 58, 1969, p. 308.

Missionary and Healing, Scheel, M., Vol. 53, 1964, pp. 265-271.

The Evangelistic Missionary's Role in Church Growth in Korea, Shearer, Roy E., Vol. 54, 1965, pp. 462-470.

Probing Missionary Inadequacies at the Popular Level, Tippet, Alan R., Vol. 49, 1960, pp. 411-414.

Consideration of the Integration of Church and Mission in Germany, Hoffman, G., Vol. 58, 1969, pp. 278-291.

The Missionary and His Task at Edinburgh and Today, Setiloane Vol. 59, 1970, pp. 55-66.

Roles of Foreign Missionaries and Missionary Organizations, vis-a-vis the Missions in the Six Continents, Kitagawa, D. Vol. 58, 1969, pp. 263-269.

The Ecumenical Sharing of Missionary Personnel Vol. 59, 1970, pp. 441-449.

Role of the European Expatriate in Asia (Reprint), Pormar, S.L. Vol. 59, 1970, pp. 450-460.

Role of the Church in Education Today, Somasckhar, R. M. Vol. 59, 1970, pp. 75-84

Background and Future Perspectives of Indian Missions, Lagerberg, H., Vol. 58, 1969, pp. 172-180.

Church Sponsored Development Efforts, Dickenson, R.D.N. Vol. 58, 1969, pp. 415-426.

Role of the Mission Agency from a World Confessional Body Perspective, Interview with Carl Johan Hillberg, Vol. 58, 1969, pp. 258-262.

Future Role of Western Missionary Bodies in the Christian World Mission, (reprint), Orchard, R.K., Vol. 58, 1969, pp. 258-262.

Integral Development; Reflections of a Conservative Evangelical from a Developing Country, Fernando, B.E. Vol. 58, 1969, pp. 408-414.

Missions after Vatican II: Problem and Positions, Syan, S.K., Vol. 59, 1970, pp. 414-426.

Priorities in Missions - Personnel or Programme?, Flatt, Donald C., Vol. 59, 1970, pp. 461-469.

Role of National Councils in Relation to Mission Agencies, Ralston, M.A.Z., Vol. 58, 1969, pp. 270-277.

Renewal in Missions - a Brazilian View, Sapsezian, A. Vol. 58, 1969, pp. 153-157.

Church Growth; a,Critique, Davies, J.G., Vol. 57, 1968, pp. 291-297.

The Mission of the Church in Today's World, Glazik, J., Vol. 53, 1967, pp. 316-329.

Church Growth, (the entire issue), Vol. 57, 1968, pp. 271-362.

Hindrances to Church Growth, Kessler, J.B.A. Vol. 57, 1968, pp. 298-303

Japanese Christian Quarterly
Published by Kyo Bun Kwan, Tokyo, Japan
English and Indigenization, Bayne, S.H., Vol. 34, 1968, pp. 123-127.

End of an Era; Further Thoughts on the Church and Mission, Powles, M. and Powles, C.H., Vol. 34, 1968, pp. 38-43.

The Christian Missionary in Japan - a Reply to Powles, Akogi, T., Vol. 33, 1967, pp. 3-6.
Missionary in Japan, a Continuing Discussion, Vol. 33, 1967, pp. 151-171

Role of Missionary, a Round Table Discussion, Draper, F.W., and others, Vol. 33, 1967, pp. 7-13.

Lexington Theological Quarterly
Published by Lexington Theological Seminary, Lexington, Kentucky.
The Third World First; the Relation of Theological Education to World Missions, Nottingham, W.J., Vol. 4, 1969, pp. 97-114.

Lutheran World
Published by Lutheran World, Geneva, Switzerland and Minneapolis, Minnesota
Positive Confrontation, Crisis in Mission (Geneva Diary) Ji, W.Y., Vol. 17, No. 4, 1970, pp. 356-361.

Revolution and Missions in the Third World, Gensichen, H.W., Vol. 16, No. 1, 1969, pp. 12-28.

Cross Currents in Missions (Report on a consultation of the L.W.F. Commission on World Mission), Kretzmann, M.L. Vol. 16, no. 4, 1969, pp. 354-357.

Mennonite Quarterly Review
Published by the Mennonite Historical Society, Goshen College, Goshen, Indiana
Mennonites of Brazil and the Question of Military Service 1920-1967, Minnich, R.H., vol. 43, 1969, pp. 299-321.

Moody Monthly
Published by Moody Bible Institute, Chicago, Illinois
What Lies Ahead in the 70's?, Kane, J.H.
Vol. 70, 1969, pp. 75-81.

A Pattern for Global Evangelism, Mooneyham, Stanley
Vol. 67, 1966, pp. 32-33.

Practical Anthropology
Published by Practical Anthropology, C. R. Taber, ed., Tarrytown, New York.
Changing Patterns of Missionary Service in Today's World (reprint), Stowe, D.M., Vol. 17, 1970, pp. 107-118.

Missionary, Wrecker, Builder, or Catalyst? (editorial) Taber, C.R., Vol. 17, 1970, pp. 145-152.

Dual Citizenship, Turnbull, S., Vol. 16, 1969, pp. 28-33.

Pith Helmet Attitude, Torgher, B.L., Vol. 14, 1967, pp. 186-189.

Whitey, Your Time is Running Out, Almquist, L.A.
Vol. 15, 1968, pp. 24-28.

Indigenous Background of Religion in Latin America, Wonderly, W.A., Vol. 14, 1967, pp. 241-248.

Church and Community Development in the Bolivian Jungle Hickin, John M., Vol. 18, 1971, pp. 72-81.

Reformed Bulletin of Missions
Published by the Orthodox Presbyterian Church, Philadelphia, Penn.
Strategy of Missions, Veenstrom, Rolf, Sept. 1967.

Mission School? Christian School? a Dialogue, V. 4, 5
July 1967.

Reformed Review
Published by Western Theological Seminary, Holland, Mich.
Renewal in Missions, Piet, J.H., Vol. 22, 1969, pp. 54-60.

Social Action
Published by Council for Christian Social Action of the United Church of Christ, New York
Church in Relation to National Development, Pornar, S.L.
Vol. 33, 1967, pp. 12-25.

South East Asia Journal of Theology
Published by the Theological Association of S.E. Asia, Singapore, Int. Colony
Whither Protestantism in Asia Today?, Song, C.S.
Vol. 11, 1970, pp. 66-76.

South-Western Journal of Theology
Published by Southwestern Baptist Theological Seminary, Fort Worth, Texas
Reflections on Mission Strategy, Culpepper, H.H. Vol. 12, 1970, pp. 29-41.

Evangelism and Social Involvement, Garrett, L.J. Vol. 12, 1970, pp. 51-62.

History of Mission Strategy, Beaver, R.P., Vol. 12, 1970, pp. 7-28.

The Springfielder
Published by Concordia Lutheran Seminary, Springfield, Illinois
The Church Overseas Speaks to the Church in America, Hintze, O.C., Vol. 31, 1967, pp. 8-21.

Thesis Theological Cassettes
Produced by T., T., C., Pittsburgh, Pennsylvania
Outlook for Tomorrow: Optimism in Missions, Winter, R.D., 1 No. 10, 1970.

Mission Possible? Africa? Marsh, C., 1 No. 7, 1970

Vision
Published by World Vision, Inc., Paul S. Rees, ed., Monrovia, California
Theological Education in Asia I: Cutting the Cord with the West, Clasper, Paul

#II: Making it Practical, Adeney, David H., Vol. 14, 1970, pp. 10-14.

Church Growth or Else, Vol. 12, 1966, pp. 12-13.

Zeitschrift für Missionswissenschaft und Religionswissenschaft
Published by Internationalen Instituts für missionsissenschaft und Religionswissenschaftliche Fershhungen, Münster Germany
From Mission to Church in Bugana, Hastings, A., Vol. 53, No. 3, 1969, pp. 206-228.

Other Papers and sources to consult:

Bibliography, A Decade of Evangelism-In-Depth in Latin America, compiled by Hans Kasdorf, Pacific College of Fresno, California, 1970
(A very complete Bibliography on Latin American Evangelism, 26 pages, mimeographed.)

Books on Islam and Islamic Countries - Books for Sale, published by the Fellowship of Faith, Ontario, Canada
(Ten pages memeographed.)

Church Growth and Human Resource Allocation, Miller, J. Melvin, Director South Asia Foundation, and Assoc. Professor of Economics and Management at Davis and Elkins College, Elkins, West Virginia.
(A Study Paper with Case Studies by the South East Asia Foundation.)

PULSE, Area editions for Latin America, Africa, Asia & Europe Published by the Evangelical Missions Information Service, Wheaton, Illinois.

Missionary News Service
Published by Evangelical Missionary Information Service, Wheaton, Illinois

The Mission's Relationship with the Church, Savage, Peter
(Paper prepared for the joint AEM/EUSA Field Conference)

Occasional Bulletin
Published by the Missionary Research Library, New York.
Revival in Missions? Some comments on current trends, Beaver, Robert Pierce, Vol. 6, No. 3, April 1965.

Selected Bibliography on Missions, an annotated Bibliography on Missions arranged by subjects, published by the Evangelical Foreign Mission Association, Washington, D.C.
(18 pages, mimeographed.)

These five books are now out of print, but have been printed and bound in one volume, CROSSROADS IN MISSION, published by the William Carey Library, South Pasadena, California, for the G L '71 Conference on Church/Mission Tension.

THESES

A complete list of Doctoral Dissertations and Masters Thesis on Missions and related subjects is published annually in the January or February issue of the Occasional Bulletin of the Missionary Research Library, 3041 Broadway, New York. N. Y. 10027.

Part 4

a sampling of early response

edited by Frank A. Ineson

ATTENDANCE SUMMARY

There were some 378 delegates in attendance at Green Lake '71 of the more than 400 who registered in advance. Of the attending delegates:

a. 72 were General Directors of missions (including 5 wives)

b. 143 were Associate Directors (including 7 wives)

c. 62 represented ministries overseas (including 1 wife)

d. 37 represented supporting agencies (including 6 wives)

e. 23 were pastors of home churches (including 1 wife)

f. 32 were educators

g. 9 were students

Some 61 of the Associate Directors have responsibility for direct relationships with the home churches in matters of deputation and personnel; 32 are Associate Directors with general responsibilities; 25 have responsibility for overseas ministries; 17 serve in administrative capacities; and 8 serve on mission boards.

Of those representing ministries overseas, 17 were national leaders; 15 were mission field leaders; and 30 were missionaries.

There were 122 missions and supporting agencies represented by these delegates: EFMA 43; IFMA 32; (with 4 duplicates between the two organizations); other missions 33; and supporting agencies 18.

There were 24 different Seminaries, Bible Institutes and Colleges represented by the 32 educators and 9 students. Pastors were present from 22 home churches.

LIST OF DELEGATES
GL'71 - Sept. 27-Oct. 1, 1971
Green Lake, Wisconsin

Hollis F. Abbott - World Gospel Mission
Evan Adams - Westmont College, Santa Barbara, California
Robert D. Anderson - South America Mission
Charles Anderson - Sudan Interior Mission
Vernon Anderson - Evangelical Free Church
Trevor Ardill - Sudan Interior Mission
Moses Ariye - Christian Nationals' Evangelism Commission, Nigeria
Philip Armstrong - Far Eastern Gospel Crusade
Patrick Arnold - West Indies Mission
Joe Arthur - Pentecostal Holiness Church
Milton Baker - Conservative Baptist Foreign Mission Society
Walter Baker - Unevangelized Fields Mission/Lancaster School of Bible
John Barcus - Gospel Missionary Union
G. Linwood Barney - Jaffray School of Mission
Ed Barram - Conservative Baptist Foreign Mission Society
Joseph Baucom - American Advent Mission Society
William D. Bell - North Africa Mission
Charles T. Bennett - Missionary Aviation Fellowship
Harold Berk - Missionary Aviation Fellowship
Don Berry - Missionary Aviation Fellowship
James Bertsche - Evangelical Mennonite Commission on Overseas Mission
G. Burton Biddulph - Oriental Missionary Society
Robert O. Bitner - Unevangelized Fields Mission
Dale W. Bjork - Board of Foreign Missions, Baptist General Conference
Kenneth R. Bliss - Society for Europes Evangelization
Richard G. Boss - Latin America Mission
Donald H. Bowen - General Missionary Board, Free Methodist Church
Louis T. Bowers, Sr. - Board of World Missions, Lutheran Church in America
A. S. Bowker - Universal Travel Service
Gerald Boyer - United World Mission
Ray Bradford - Northern Canada Evangelical Mission
Peter J. Brashler - Africa Inland Mission
Thomas Brewster - Evangelical Language Institutes for Missionaries
Mrs. Thomas Brewster - Evangelical Language Institutes for Missionaries
A. Glen Brown - Africa Evangelical Fellowship
Mrs. A. Glen Brown - Africa Evangelical Fellowship
Laurence Brown - Africa Inland Mission
Don C. Bruck - Japan Evangelical Mission
Don Brugmann - Greater Europe Mission
Richard Brunk - Vennard College, University Park, Iowa
Osborne Buchanan, Jr. - Child Evangelism Fellowship
Mark Budensiek - Evangelistic Faith Missions
Ray Buker, Jr. - Conservative Baptist Foreign Mission Society
Ray Buker, Sr. - Committee to Assist Missionary Education Overseas (CAMEO)
D. C. Bultema - Grace Mission, Inc.
Fred Burklin - Greater Europe Mission
Sam Burns - Sudan Interior Mission
Burnis H. Bushong - World Gospel Mission
Phill W. Butler - INTERCRISTO
Alan Button - Evangelical Union of South America
Elvio Canavesio - Pentecostal Holiness Church - World Missions Department
Rich Cannon - INTERCRISTO
Odd Carlsen - Evangelical Outreach

David J. Cho - Korea Evangelistic Inter-Mission Alliance
John C. Cho - Seoul Theological Seminary
Jack Christensen - United Baptist Church, Old Town, Maine
Dennis Clark - David C. Cook Foundation
Loren Clark - World Gospel Mission
Charles Claypool - Harvesters International
Ross M. Clemenger - Evangelical Union of South America
Arthur M. Climenhaga - Brethren in Christ Church
David E. Climenhaga - Brethren in Christ Missions
Edmund P. Clowney - Westminster Theological Seminary, Philadelphia, Pennsylvania
Elmore L. Clyde - General Missionary Bd. Free Methodist Church
Wade Coggins - Evangelical Foreign Missions Association
Mrs. Wade Coggins - Evangelical Foreign Missions Association
Bernard Collinson - North Africa Mission
Harold R. Cook - Moody Bible Institute, Chicago
Hubert Cook - Evangelical Union of South America
Mrs. Hubert Cook - Evangelical Union of South America
David L. Coots - Orinoco River Mission
W. C. Cornelius - Pentecostal Assemblies of Canada
James Cornelson - The Evangelical Alliance Mission
Wayne W. Courtney - Overseas Missionary Fellowship
Mrs. Loy A. Coward, Jr. - First Baptist Church of Van Nuys, Calif.
H. Robert Cowles - Christian and Missionary Alliance
Emmett Dean Cox - Church of the United Brethren in Christ, Board of Missions
George Cramer - Ramabai Mukti Mission
Raymond D. Creer - Baptist Mid-Missions
Ted Crewson - Missionary Church
William G. Crouch - Sudan Interior Mission
John Cumbers - Sudan Interior Mission
Norman L. Cummings - Overseas Crusades
William Currie - International Missions
Robert Dalke - West Indies Mission
W. Elwyn Davies - Bible Christian Union
Carl Davis - The Evangelical Alliance Mission
Charles E. Davis - Africa Inland Mission
Marshall E. Davis - International Missions
Raymond J. Davis - Sudan Interior Mission
Evelyn C. Davis - Sudan Interior Mission
Murray L. Dawson - Japan Evangelical Mission
Edward R. Dayton - MARC/World Vision International
Robert DeMoss - National Liberty Foundation
Peter Deyneka, Jr. - Slavic Gospel Association
Herman R. Dietsch - Liebenzell Mission of U.S.A.
Robert Dillon - Evangelical Free Church, Board of Overseas Missions
Arsenio Dominguez - Christian Nationals' Evangelism Commission, Philippines
George Doxsee- Christian Nationals' Evangelism Commission
Mrs. George Doxsee - Christian Nationals' Evangelism Commission
Wesley L. Duewel - Oriental Missionary Society
Ben Elson - Wycliffe Bible Translators
Ted W. Engstrom - World Vision Int'l
Arno W. Enns - Conservative Baptist Foreign Mission Society
Paul C. Enyart, Jr. - Friends Mission
Jake H. Epp - Mennonite Brethren Conference Missions/Services Offices
Paul Erdel - Missionary Church Association
Robert Erny - Oriental Missionary Society

Hector Espinoza - Instituto Evangelistico de Mexico
Robert P. Evans - Greater Europe Mission
Ronald L. Evans - Christian Literature Crusade
John M. Falkenberg - Bible Literature International
Horace L. Fenton, Jr. - Latin America Mission
Albert R. Fesmire - Battle Creek Bible Church / Independent Fundamental Churches of America
Allen Finley - Christian Nationals' Evangelism Commission
Mrs. Allen Finley - Christian Nationals' Evangelism Commission
P. Fredrick Fogle - Grace College and Seminary, Winona Lake, Indiana
M. I. Forsberg - Sudan Interior Mission
Walter Frank - Greater Europe Mission
E. L. Frederick - International Missions
Walter Fricke - Conservative Baptist Foreign Mission Society
Edwin L. Frizen, Jr. - Interdenominational Foreign Mission Association
Mrs. Edwin L. Frizen, Jr. - American Bible Society Women's Work
Thomas D. Fulghum - World Radio Missionary Fellowship (HCJB)
W. Harold Fuller - Sudan Interior Mission
H. S. Galloway - Church of the Nazarene
Mrs. H. S. Galloway - Church of the Nazarene
Phil Gammon - United Fellowship for Christian Service
Alden Gannett - Unevangelized Fields Mission
Mrs. Alden Gannett - Unevangelized Fields Mission
Vergil Gerber - Evangelical Missions Information Service
Mrs. Vergil Gerber - Evangelical Missions Information Service
John Gillespie - Arctic Missions
Mrs. John Gillespie - Arctic Missions
Cora E. Goble - Interdenominational Foreign Mission Association
Lud Golz - Pleasant Hill Community Church, Wheaton, Illinois
Walter Gomez - Mexican Mission Ministries
Mrs. Walter Gomez - Mexican Mission Ministries
Joseph Goossen - Evangelical Union of South America
David S. Gotaas - Moody Bible Institute, Chicago, Illinois
Dwight Gradin - Far Eastern Gospel Crusade/Missionary Internship
John Gration - Africa Inland Mission
Dallas S. Green - North Africa Mission
Don Gregory - The Evangelical Alliance Mission
Hal W. Guffey - International Students
Peter F. Gunther - Moody Literature Mission
Wesley Gustafson - Evangelical Free Church, Board of Overseas Missions
John Guthrie - Pentecostal Holiness Church World Missions Dept.
Delmer R. Guynes - General Council of Assemblies of God
Mrs. Delmer R. Guynes - General Council of Assemblies of God
Peter M. Hamm - Mennonite Brethren Bible College - Canada
G. Walter Hansen - Trinity Evangelical Divinity School
John Harder - Evangelical Union of South America
Robert B. Haslam - General Missionary Board, Free Methodist Church
Oliver W. Hasselblad - American Leprosy Missions
Ian M. Hay - Sudan Interior Mission
William Hays - Primitive Methodist International Mission Board
Mrs. William Hays - Primitive Methodist International Mission Board
George E. Hedberg - Home of Onesiphorus
Henry J. Heijermans - Worldwide European Fellowship
Ernest E. Heimbach - Overseas Missionary Fellowship
Marvin Hein - Mennonite Brethren
Glenda Hemme - Cottey College, Nevada, Missouri

E. R. Hemphill - Reformed Presbyterian Church, Board Foreign Missions
Olan Hendrix - American Sunday-School Union
Robert A. Henning - Reformed Presbyterian Church, Board Foreign Missions
Walter A. Henrichsen - Navigators
Ralph Hertzpung - The Evangelical Alliance Mission
Melvin L. Hodges - General Council of Assemblies of God
J. Philip Hogan - General Council of Assemblies of God
Phillip Hook - Dallas Theological Seminary
Thom Hopler - Africa Inland Mission
Jack Hough - South America Mission
David M. Howard - Inter-Varsity Christian Fellowship
Hobert Howard - Pentecostal Holiness Church World Missions Department
Philip G. Howard - Northern Canada Evangelical Mission
Mrs. Philip Howard - Northern Canada Evangelical Mission
Charles Hufstetler - Far Eastern Gospel Crusade
Orville Hunt - Grace Mission
Warner A. Hutchinson - American Bible Society
Stuart R. Imbach - Overseas Missionary Fellowship
Frank A. Ineson - MARC/World Vision International
M. Virgil Ingraham - Missionary Board of the Brethren Church
Edwin E. Jacques - Conservative Baptist Foreign Mission Society
Gladys M. Jasper - Evangelical Literature Overseas
A. Reid Jepson - Far East Broadcasting Company
Jim Johnson - Evangelical Literature Overseas
Arthur P. Johnston - St. Paul Bible College, St. Paul, Minneapolis
Leroy N. Johnston, Jr. - Christian and Missionary Alliance
Howard O. Jones - Billy Graham Evangelistic Ass'n
J. Herbert Kane - Trinity Evangelical Divinity School, Deerfield, Ill.
Richard Kantzer - Trinity Evangelical Divinity School, Deerfield, Ill.
Byang Kato - Evangelical Churches of West Africa
George R. Kennedy - Berean Mission
Bruce Ker - Western Conservative Baptist Seminary, Portland, Oregon
William W. Kerr - Christian and Missionary Alliance
Dale Kietzman - Wycliffe Bible Translators
Elmer Kilbourne - World Relief Commission/Oriental Missionary Society
Mrs. Elmer Kilbourne - World Relief Commission/Oriental Missionary Society
Samuel I. Kim - Korea Evangelistic Inter-Mission Alliance
Louis L. King - Christian and Missionary Alliance
Charles D. Kirkpatrick - General Missionary Board, Free Methodist Church
George C. Klein - Christian and Missionary Alliance
J. Raymond Knighton - Medical Assistance Programs
Mrs. J. Raymond Knighton - Medical Assistance Programs
Arthur W. Konrad - Central American Mission
Paul N. Kraybill - Eastern Mennonite Board of Missions
Delbert Kuehl - The Evangelical Alliance Mission
Raymond D. Kutz - INTERCRISTO
Don Lamberson - Bethel Bible Church, Evergreen Park, Illinois
Sidney Langford - Africa Inland Mission
John E. Langlois - World Evangelical Fellowship - TAP
R. J. Largent - Overseas Missionary Fellowship
Alfred Larson - Unevangelized Fields Mission
Donald N. Larson - Toronto Institute of Linguistics
LeRoy Larson - New Tribes Mission
George E. Ledden, Jr. - Far Eastern Gospel Crusade
Robert E. Lehnhart - Missionary Aviation Fellowship
Paul J. Lindell - World Mission Prayer League
C. Reuben Lindquist - Berean Mission

Henry Loewen - Mennonite Brethren Conference, Brazil
Kerry Lovering - Sudan Interior Mission
C. W. Lynn - Pentecostal Assemblies of Canada
DeWitt Lyon - The Evangelical Alliance Mission
Robert N. Lytle - Wesleyan Church
Joseph S. McCullough - Andes Evangelical Mission
J. Robertson McQuilkin - Columbia Bible College, Columbia, South Carolina
W. H. MacBain - Fellowship of Evangelical Baptists of Canada
Gordon MacDonald - First Baptist Church, Collinsville, Illinois
Hilkka Malaska - Olivet Nazarene College, Kankakee, Illinois
T. Grady Mangham, Jr. - Christian and Missionary Alliance
Jerry L. Mann - Trinity Evangelical Divinity School, Deerfield, Illinois
James Mannoia - General Missionary Board, Free Methodist Church
J. Murray Marshall - First Presbyterian Church, Flushing,N. Y.
Alvin Martin - Canadian Bible College/Canadian Theological College, Regina
Augustus Marwieh - Christian Nationals' Evangelism Commission, Liberia
Dick Matthews - Gospel Missionary Union
James E. Maxson - Sudan Interior Mission
Charles J. Mellis - Missionary Aviation Fellowship
Marjorie Metheral - Gospel Recordings
Juan Carlos Miranda - Missionary Board of the Brethren Church, Argentina
Bryant Mitchell - Open Bible Standard Missions
Mrs. Bryant Mitchell - Open Bible Standard Missions
Richard Moore - World Gospel Mission
Emmett B. Moorefield - Orinoco River Mission
Donald D. Moreland - Dover Baptist Church, Dover, N. H.
Lem Morgan - Overseas Christian Servicemen's Center
Vernon Mortenson - The Evangelical Alliance Mission
George A. Munzing - Trinity United Presbyterian Church, Santa Ana, California
Franklin O. Nelson - Board of Foreign Missions, Baptist General Conference
Carroll C. Ness - Africa Inland Mission
Anna Nixon - Friends Mission/Evangelical Fellowship of India
Claude Noel - Baptist Mission of Haiti
H. Wilbert Norton - Wheaton College Graduate School, Wheaton, Illinois
Glenn Ogren - Board of Foreign Missions, Baptist General Conference
Charles Olvey - Orinoco River Mission
Guy Owen - Free Will Baptist Foreign Missions Dept.
Peter Paget - International Christian Fellowship
Donald Palmer - Gospel Missionary Union
Elwin Palmer - Worldwide Evangelization Crusade
Virginia C. Patterson - Pioneer Girls
Dick Patty - Overseas Christian Servicemens' Centers
T. M. Paulson - World Missions to Children
Ed Payne - Christian Nationals' Evangelism Commission
Mrs. Ed Payne - Christian Nationals' Evangelism Commission
William R. Pencille - South America Mission
George Peters - Dallas Theological Seminary, Dallas, Texas
Donald G. Peterson - Wheaton College, Wheaton, Illinois
Don Phillips - Gospel Recordings
Dan Piatt - Final Advance of Scripture Translation (FAST)
Bernard L. H. Poole - Gospel Mission of South America
David L. Rambo - Canadian Bible College, Regina
James Reapsome - Evangelical Missions Quarterly
A. Brandt Reed - Africa Inland Mission
Robert B. Reekie - David C. Cook Foundation
Mrs. Robert Reekie - David C. Cook Foundation
R. J. Reinmiller - Gospel Missionary Union

Clarence Reimer - King's Garden
Jose Reinoso - World Radio Missionary Fellowship - HCJB, Ecuador
Dick Reiter - Trinity Evangelical Divinity School, Deerfield, Illinois
Walter Remple - Mennonite Brethren Conference
Robert F. Rice - Literacy & Evangelism
Joy Ridderhof - Gospel Recordings
Paul F. Robinson - Moody Bible Institute, Chicago, Illinois
J. Morris Rockness - Overseas Missionary Fellowship
Earl Roessler - The Evangelical Alliance Mission
Clell M. Rogers - Missionary Aviation Fellowship
Sam Rowen - Far Eastern Gospel Crusade/Missionary Internship
John D. Rowsey - Missionary Board of the Brethren Church
Eugene Rubingh - Christian Reformed Board of Foreign Missions
Andrew M. Rupp - Evangelical Mennonite Commission Overseas Missions
Keith Sarver - California Yearly Meeting of Friends Church
Mrs. June Sarver - United Society of Friends Women
Otto Sather - Slavic Gospel Association
R. Schilke - North American Baptist General Missionary Society
Edward G. Schuit - Africa Inland Mission
Earl Schultz - Youth for Christ
Ward Shantz - Missionary Church
Arni Shareski - Christian & Missionary Alliance
Paul W. Shea - Trinity Evangelical Divinity School, Deerfield, Illinois
Clarence Shelly - Global Outreach
Jacob R. Shenk - Brethren in Christ Missions
Jack Shepherd - Christian and Missionary Alliance
Reuben Short - Congo Inland Mission
Fred Shotwell - National Liberty Foundation
J. W. Skinner - Pentecostal Assemblies of Canada
Grant Sloss - Missionary Church
G. A. Small - Evangelical Purchasing Services
W. Dale Smith - Alfa Omega Publicidad, Mexico
W. Douglas Smith - Andes Evangelical Mission
David W. Snyder - South America Mission
Francis B. Sorley - Board of Foreign Missions, Baptist General Conference
Clarence E. Spencer - Missionary Service
Peter Spencer - Missionary Church, Jamaica
Douglas R. Spurlock - Wheaton College, Wheaton, Illinois
Peter Stam - Africa Inland Mission
Francis R. Steele - North Africa Mission
Warren Steward - Conservative Baptist Foreign Mission Society
David G. Stone - Africa Evangelical Fellowship
Harvey R. Stranske - Western Bible Institute, Denver, Colo.
John Stucky - Medical Assistance Programs
Mrs. John Stucky - Medical Assistance Programs
David L. Sunden - Africa Inland Mission/EUSA
Bill Tarter - International Missions
Clyde W. Taylor - Evangelical Foreign Missions Association
Mrs. Clyde W. Taylor - Evangelical Foreign Missions Association
William H. Taylor - Central American Mission
Tom Tazumi - Far Eastern Gospel Crusade
John Tebay - Calvary Church, Placentia, California
Perry A. Temple - Bible Literature International
A. G. Thiessen - International Christian Broadcasters
Mrs. A. G. Thiessen - International Christian Broadcasters
J. Allen Thompson - West Indies Mission
Orvin D. Thompson - Ebenezer Lutheran Brethren Church, Minneapolis, Minnesota

Walford Thompson - Men In Action, Caribbean
Frank C. Tichy, Jr. - Pastors' Resource Services
Gordon C. Timyan - Christian and Missionary Alliance
Charles A. Tipp - Ontario Bible College, Toronto
J. B. Toews - Mennonite Brethren Biblical Seminary, Fresno, California
Edwin Tomlinson - Sudan Interior Mission
William W. Tyler - Overseas Missionary Fellowship
B. E. Underwood - Pentecostal Holiness Church World Missions Dept.
Linden Unruh - Mexican Mission Ministries
Edward A. Van Baak - Christian Reformed Board of Foreign Missions
Abe C. Van Der Puy - World Radio Missionary Fellowship - HCJB
Henry Van Kluyve - Free Will Baptist Foreign Missions
Russel Van Vleet - Evangelical Mennonite Commission on Missions
Ernest Vatter - Conference of Evangelical Missions, Germany
C. Peter Wagner - Fuller Evangelistic Association
Pius Wakatama - Rhodesia Christian College, Rhodesia
Carl Walter - United World Mission
W. K. Warner - Christian College of Southern Africa
A. Gordon Watts - Overseas Missionary Fellowship
Stewart Weber - The Evangelical Alliance Mission
Warren Webster - Conservative Baptist Foreign Mission Society
Cyril F. Weller - Overseas Missionary Fellowship
Waldo J. Werning - Lutheran Church - Missouri Synod
Lester Westlund - Evangelical Free Church Board Overseas Missions
Norman Wetther - Conservative Baptist Home Mission Society
Howard A. Whaley - Moody Bible Institute, Chicago, Illinois
Allan Wiebe - Grace Bible Institute, Omaha, Nebraska
James Wiebe - Mennonite Brethren Conference
Vernon R. Wiebe - Mennonite Brethren Conference Missions/Services
Wesley L. Wildermuth - Oriental Missionary Society
Horace Williams - Worldwide Evangelization Crusade
Forrest Williams - Andes Evangelical Mission - pastor
C. E. Wilson - Christian Nationals' Evangelism Commission
Fred Wilson - Trinity Evangelical Divinity School
J. Reford Wilson - Free Will Baptist Foreign Missions Dept.
Richard Winchell - The Evangelical Alliance Mission
Ralph D. Winter - Fuller Theological Seminary, Pasadena, California
Bryce L. Winteregg - Evangelical Mennonite Church - Commission on Missions
Eugene A. Wittig - Oriental Missionary Society
Wayne W. Wright - Wesleyan Church
Donald Wunker - Unevangelized Fields Mission
Harold R. Wust - Church of the United Brethren
David Zehr - Greater Europe Mission
John W. Zielasko - Foreign Missionary Society of the Brethren Church
Enos Zimmerman - Greater Europe Mission

SUGGESTIONS FOR GROUP DISCUSSION LEADERS AND RECORDERS

I. OBJECTIVE

GL '71 has been structured to provide each delegate with the best possible circumstance for analyzing his own needs in M/C relations plotting a course of action to see that they are met. The purpose of the group discussions is twofold:

A. To assist each participant to identify and clarify his specific M/C relationship needs.

B. To provide ideas through interaction for him to take constructive action.

II. RELATIONSHIP TO REST OF THE PROGRAM

GL '71 is a workshop; what you get out of it will depend on the work you put in. Foundations and principles will be laid during the formal presentations. The panel will help to clarify, expound and relate these principles. Group discussions will wrestle with the specific areas of need attempting to find guidelines for constructive action. Hopefully the summation provided by the recorders and editorial committee will assist delegates in better understanding the areas of tension and developing new resources for individual action.

III. TOPICS

In order to isolate the issues delegates consider important, questionnaires were mailed to each person. Questionnaire #1 yielded the interests of the respondent together with over 200 tension areas. These were reduced to 72 specifics and sent to delegates for weighing. Two hundred and ten delegates responded to one or more questionnaires. The 11 topics chosen for discussion indicate concerns of first magnitude. Five topics have been assigned to two groups because of their importance or complexity.

IV. COMPOSITION

Groups have been formed using the criteria of primary interest and responsibility class. In addition persons from one organization have been distributed to differing groups. In so far as possible, overseas personnel, professors of missions, pastors, and students have been placed in each group. Those who have not had opportunity to respond to the questionnaires have been placed in groups discussing topics of interest mentioned by other members of their organization.

V. FUNCTION

During each session of your group you will attempt to work on specific M/C relationship needs related to your topic. These have been listed as "Some Significant Points of Tension." On Tuesday each group will discuss the issues relating to Home Church/Mission relationships and on Wednesday and Thursday National Church/Mission relationships. Spend the first 15 minutes clarifying the tension area and expanding the nature of the problem. Involve your group through specific questions and examples.

Then spend 30 minutes discussing solutions in the area of tension. For instance, ask several of your group to describe one example of progress in the past five years in this specific area. The goal is to obtain preventative as well as remedial help.

The last 15 minutes should be spent summarizing guidelines that can assist in solving the problem. This may include issues that must be solved if progress is to be made. The focus here is on ideas that can help us cope with the tension area. The recorders will turn the summaries over to the feedback committee.

VI. RECOMMENDATIONS

A. Create a spirit of openness through accepting people, their ideas and problems. Avoid an argumentative attitude and lead the group to wrestle with the problem from differing perspectives.

B. Don't let one person dominate the sessions, rather foster multiple participation. You may have to give some a specific time limit.

C. Stick to TOPIC though you may change the specific tension point. It is possible that you may finish the material suggested in two days. If so,feel free to move on to other related areas your group considers important.

D. Be sure the group produces specific guidelines for action. These do not necessarily have to represent a concensus. You're working toward a goal. Be sure it is reached.

J. Allen Thompson

GROUP	LOCATION	LEADER	RECORDER	GENERAL TOPIC	SOME SIGNIFICANT POINTS OF TENSION
A	John Peck Bldg. 13 Room A	Mortenson	Bennett	Transition to National Leadership (Non-denominational Missions)	1. Home church reluctant to donate money for distribution by national leaders. 2. Growing resentment on the part of the home church for bearing the cost of missions with the shift to national leadership. 3. Relinquishing initiative to national church and mission assuming supporting role. 4. The internationalizing of missions -- receiving countries become sending countries. 5. Relations between mission national workers and pastors.
B	John Peck Bldg. 13 Room D	Webster	Shareski	Transition to National Leadership (Denominational Missions)	
C	John Peck Bldg. 13 Room E	Baker	Schuit	Apathy Toward Evangelism Overseas (1)	1. Home church projects taking precedence over evangelism overseas. 2. Preference of national church for subsidy of institutions rather than evangelism. 3. Apathy & indifference of pastors toward foreign missions. 4. Lack of involvement & commitment of church members to foreign missions. 5. Pressures of ecumenicity, modernism and social action.
D	Garden Center (Administration Bldg.)	Ledden	Dillon	Apathy Toward Evangelism Overseas (2)	
E	Lower Kraft Bldg. 33	Davis	Winchell	Breakdown in Communications (Non-denominational missions)	1. Meagre understanding of cultural differences between home & field. 2. Unrealistic attitudes toward the missionary and his task. 3. Failure to provide information essential to parties concerned. 4. Difference of opinion regarding indigenous church principles. 5. Inadequate understanding of program and direction of the national church.
F	Brayton Case Bldg. 20 Room 3	Hogan	Enns	Breakdown in Communications (denominational missions)	

GROUP	LOCATION	LEADER	RECORDER	GENERAL TOPIC	SOME SIGNIFICANT POINTS OF TENSION
G	Mission Center Bldg.13A	Cummings	Tomlinson	Competition for Financial Resources (Non-denominational missions)	1. Competition for financial resources among missions. 2. Pressures for overseas funds at the expense of home projects. 3. Problems of shifting from subsidy to indigenous responsibility. 4. Shifting emphasis from institutions to evangelism and training programs. 5. Tendency for mission services and institutions to "outrank" national church.
H	Brayton Case Bldg.20 Room 4	Kirkpatrick	Ingraham	Competition for Financial Resources (Denominational missions)	
I	Brayton Case Bldg.20 Room 5	Stam	Bjork	Missionary/National Support (1)	1. Personal fund raising increasingly objectionable to missionaries. 2. Home churches increasingly reluctant to fill missionary meeting requests. 3. Discrepancy between living standard of missionaries and national workers. 4. Problems of shifting from subsidy to indigenous responsibility. 5. Relations between mission national workers and pastors.
J	Brayton Case Bldg.20 Room 6	Mellis	McCullough	Missionary/National Support (2)	
K	Brayton Case Bldg.20 Room 7	Larson	Mangham	Missionary Recruitment and Role	1. Failure of home church to take responsibility for recruiting. 2. Competition for personnel by home churches and missions. 3. Feelings of superiority on the part of missionaries. 4. Insensitivity to new missionary's need for pastoral care. 5. Lack of adequate attainment in language skills. 6. Degree of orientation training of missionaries for current problems.

GROUP	LOCATION	LEADER	RECORDER	GENERAL TOPIC	SOME SIGNIFICANT POINTS OF TENSION
L	Brayton Case Bldg.20 Room 8	Frank	Hurst	Mission Financial Policies	1. Short-term commitments preferred to long-term ones. 2. "Designated, personal gifts" versus "pooling" systems of fund handling. 3. Lack of trust toward nationals in distribution of finances. 4. Differences in financial emphasis on workers vs institutions.
M	Brayton Case Bldg.20 Room 9	Taylor	Wiebe	Lines of Authority	1. Continual struggle for personal involvement with missionaries. 2. Perception of missionary's loyalty to mission or to home church. 3. Ambivalence as to home church or mission being final authority for missionary. 4. Trend favoring small cell mission-sending groups vs usual mission. 5. Definition of missionary's role under authority of national church. 6. Unwillingness of leadership to relinquish control and position. 7. Degree of trust in assignments by board predominantly national. 8. Tendency of missionaries to act independently of mission home office.
N	Brayton Case Bldg.20 Room 10	Fricke	Bell	Mission Policy Making	1. Lack of participation in decision making of mission plans and policies. 2. Tendency of mission to "run its own show". 3. Inadequate representation of home churches on mission boards. 4. Mission as foreign agency in position of authority overseas. 5. Imposing of principles which go against the social/ethnic structures.

GROUP	LOCATION	LEADER	RECORDER	GENERAL TOPIC	SOME SIGNIFICANT POINTS OF TENSION
O	Brayton Case Bldg. 20 Room 11	Crouch	Anderson	Theological Differences	1. Detrimental separatist views held 2. Increasing scrutiny of mission doctrine and practice. 3. Lack of emphasis on sound theology in missions. 4. Doctrinal differences between home church and national church. 5. Theological positions which nullify search for middle ground. 6. Unbalanced emphasis leading to legalism. 7. Lack of appreciation of central emphasis in the New Testament.
P	Brayton Case Bldg.20 Room 12	Abbott	Conley	Organizational Alternatives	1. Multiplicity of missionary societies with resulting duplications. 2. Trend favoring small cell mission-sending groups vs usual mission. 3. Paternalistic oversight of national church affecting partnership. 4. Tensions in partnership when one or other not fully committed. 5. Political maneuvering from attempts to fuse national churches.

SUMMARY OF DISCUSSION GROUPS' FINDINGS - FACING UP TO REALITIES

INTRODUCTION

From the earliest stages of planning for GL '71, no one thought that the discussion groups, scheduled for each morning, would produce definitive solutions to the problems of church-mission tensions. Both the size of the problems and the size of the groups militated against the finding of easy answers to these vexing situations.

But this is not to downgrade the importance of the discussion sessions. Obviously, there had to be some place in the Green Lake schedule where the high ideals and lofty theories of the study papers were brought to bear on the situations which had made the holding of such a consultation a necessity. Further exploration and probing was called for, and this could only be done effectively in groups set up for that purpose.

The results of such discussions, limited by pressures of time and other factors, are therefore not "findings" in the usual sense of that word. Nor can they serve as the basis for an official "Green Lake Declaration." Yet this does not imply that the groups were not productive, or that there are no lasting results of their work. In presenting herewith a summary of these discussions we offer evidence of earnest grappling with important issues, by thoughtful servants of God, drawn together by a common passion for the work of the Lord. Such a statement of their concerns and convictions may serve us well in the days ahead, as we continue to seek God's solution to these knotty problems, and as we learn from each other that which God's grace and our experience have taught us about these things.

Horace L. Fenton, Jr.

(The summaries which follow are based on the brief notes turned over to the Feedback Committee daily by the Recorder of each Discussion Group. Some effort was made to avoid topic duplication and some relatively minor items were omitted in the interest of space.)

Compiled by Frank Ineson

TRANSITION TO NATIONAL LEADERSHIP

Group A - Nondenominational Missions
Leader: Mortenson; Recorder: Bennett

Group B - Denominational Missions
Leader: Webster; Recorder: Shareski

I. UNDERLYING ISSUES AFFECTING HOME CHURCH/MISSION RELATIONS

A. Modification of indigenous principle has resulted in justified financial involvement by missions in broader ministry of overseas churches even after independence and local self-support.

B. Home churches have not been adequately informed of these changes. Thus there is apparent difficulty in drawing out funds for projects of above type.

II. SUGGESTIONS FOR MISSIONS TO HELP DEAL WITH THE PROBLEM

A. Need to reappraise our methods. (Some members of group stated it as need to repent.)

1. To home churches for failure to fully inform them.

2. To overseas churches for using mission money as means to avoid their control.

3. But caution that home churches do not create other problems by bypassing missions and sending direct aid to individual nationals.

B. Need to better educate churches

1. Example given of a home church which gave its first 10% surplus above mission budget directly to a mission before they took on any more new missionaries.

2. Should find the key to education regarding missions and decision-making regarding giving money for missions in the home church. Maybe the missions committee is responsible but more often it is the pastor in non-denominational churches

3. Missions should not treat pastors and home churches as puppets, (i.e. push indigenous principles, then shift to need for subsidies.) Give them information and trust them to make intelligent decisions.

4. Some suggest emphasize support for missions, not just missionaries.

5. Encourage "feedback" from pastors of home churches and from youth.

I. DEFINITION OF PROBLEM OF RELINQUISHING INITIATIVE AND AUTHORITY TO NATIONALS

A. Initiative cannot really be relinquished but it can be stifled. Should better say inspire initiative.

B. Responsibility is better word than authority.

C. It is a fact that missionaries have stifled initiative, held on to leadership too long, etc.

D. Gradualism in the transfer of leadership to nationals without specific goals is vague and meaningless.

E. Tensions and crises develop when initiative and leadership are not transferred soon enough.

F. Cultural superiority complex and psychological need of missionary to play "role" of his professional specialty are greatest causes of reluctance to trust initiative and responsibility to nationals.

V. THE IDEAL - SUGGESTIONS FOR AVOIDING TENSIONS

A. Concept should be in the mind of the missionary before he begins his work (i.e. to trust nationals)

B. Encouragement of initiative should begin with the first convert.

C. Institutions and specialized ministries should include nationals early so as to avoid tensions at the time of complete transfer to nationals.

D. Missionary needs to pray for ability to trust nationals.

V. WHERE TENSIONS ALREADY EXIST BECAUSE OF PAST ERRORS

A. Bring in nationals to share leadership during transition period - don't suddenly dump it into their laps out of spite or fear.

B. Demand that missionaries set specific goals for transition of their ministries.

C. Do not wait for national leaders who can fill North American criteria. (For example, a national leader might not even be literate.)

D. Open repentance for past mistakes before nationals.

VI. THE INTERNATIONALIZING OF MISSIONS

A. Background - Sending missionaries to other countries is no longer a North American - Northern European show. Churches in third world countries are already sending out foreign missionaries and this will increase.

B. They often send them out under existing, western-based mission organizations. This is often an easy way to begin, but carries the stigma of being western and may duplicate our past mistakes.

C. Other third world churches now send out missionaries under their own sponsorship.

1. The disadvantage is a proliferation of agencies and they will have to repeat many of our own past mistakes.

2. Advantage is that it is theirs, carries no western stigma and they are free to be creative.

Group C - APATHY TOWARD OVERSEAS MINISTRIES

Non-denominational Missions
Leader: Baker; Recorder: Schuit

I. Many home church pastors and members appear to be ignorant of recent changes in the overseas missions situation and of the long-range goals of missions. Suggested solutions included:

A. Production of a joint EFMA/IFMA document that would make clear the present role of missions in today's world.

B. EMIS could be the voice of evangelical missions in providing:

1. Brochures on the totality of the thrust of missions.

2. Posters (especially designed for schools).

3. Spot announcements on Christian radio stations.

C. EMQ should have wider circulation with mission societies promoting it among pastors and missionary councils.

D. More effective use should be made of Christian journals in the presentation of significant mission reports.

II. Confusion exists due to conflicting reports by different mission representatives as to what is actually taking place. Too much literature from too many missions has contributed to this confusion. In order for this condition to be improved:

A. Missions must be more selective in the speakers which are sent out as their representatives and these need to be familiar with the general mission situation overseas.

B. Returning missionaries assigned to deputational activity must be made aware of the needs of audiences today and coached as to the type of presentation without in any way hindering the guidance of the Holy Spirit.

C. Fewer but better items of mission literature.

III. The shift of interest to home problems - racial tensions, poverty, war in Viet Nam - emphasizes the constant need to present to home churches the Biblical teaching relative to mission and their responsibility in world wide outreach.

IV. It was recognized that frustration brings apathy - the continual presentation of a "tell it as it is" type of message which dwells on the problems, defeats and negatives.

A. We need to be honest in our reporting to be sure, but an emphasis on the positive brings encouragement and enthusiasm.

B. Tell what God is actually doing overseas even though it includes the ministries of missions other than one's own.

V. Other practical suggestions for overcoming apathy were:

A. Hold one or two day seminars for local pastors where mission executives can share with them their burdens and problems and encourage them to become involved in missions.

B. Arrrange carefully planned visits to missions fields by pastors, laymen and students with opportunities to participate in overseas projects.

C. Mission executives and school administrators meet together to assure that curricula cover the Biblical position of the centrality of missions in the church.

D. Develop a dial-a-mission telephone ministry giving up-to-date reports.

Group D - APATHY TOWARD OVERSEAS MINISTRIES

Denominational Missions
Leader: Ledden; Recorder: Dillon

I. Discussion of this subject in a mere mission context is not valid. We are too mission oriented to see the true church at home and its total function.

   A. There has always been apathy in our churches at home toward evangelism overseas, to a greater or lesser degree. However, this is changing and improving with a greater involvement by our churches at home. People are more aware of people and responsive to their needs.

   B. Granted, apathy does exist in churches at home. However, there is new in many circles, and often outside the structured church, an awakening and concern in world-wide evangelism, at home and abroad.

   C. Personalization of needs and fulfillment have transferred our thinking from projects and institutions to people regardless of their location.

   D. The mission and the missionaries must bear with the church leadership the responsibility for the attitude of the church toward world evangelization

   E. Evangelism is a more acceptable term and program than in years gone by, thereby helping to erase the non-involvement by apathetic peoples.

II. How can missions relate to the home church?

   A. Missions seminars by missionaries and executives on Christian campuses.

   B. Seminars for pastors and local church mission boards. A subject for these could be "Missions Today", as well as principles and practices.

   C. Saturate campus with "mission days".

   D. Have a "missions' evangelist" staying in one church or area for four to eight days to follow through on all aspects of missions.

   E. The pastor is the key but his committees must be informed also.

   F. Seminars for the high school student relating him to the missionary and his cause.

G. The church, not just the pastor, must evaluate the candidate.

H. Give opportunity for the missionary to get acquainted by a stay of at least several days, with many people in the church.

I. Having meetings, small group concept, lends itself to communication between the missionary and church people.

J. Steer away from all of the problems of missions but balance them with blessings

K. Media is not getting the communication job done. It takes people relating to people.

L. Have the mission executive send a news cassette or have a telephone (amplified for congregation) conversation during the service.

M. Tours to mission fields, by pastors and laymen, help.

BREAKDOWN IN COMMUNICATIONS

Group E - Non-denominational Missions
Leader: Davis; Recorder: Winchell

Group F - Denominational Missions
Leader: Hogan; Recorder: Enns

I. There are communication gaps between the mission and the home church.

A. Recognizing that the pastor is the key to "lock or unlock" mission interest, how do we communicate to him the need for stimulus and development?

B. There is an unrealistic attitude (an erroneous concept) on the part of the home church toward the missionary and mission.

C. The missionary questions as to what his role is in stewardship education of the home church.

II. Guidelines for reducing the breakdown in communication with the home church.

A. Regarding the cultivation of interest and support on the part of the pastor, recognizing that one does not always find deep level identification with overseas missions:

1. Attempt to promote workshops, seminars, retreats, etc. which will include emphasis on the theology of missions.

2. Plan face to face meetings with individual pastors to share the burden, the news and the needs.

3. Encourage the pastor to at some time seek opportunity to go abroad and personally set foot on overseas locations.

4. Encourage seminaries and Christian schools to take care that there is a full emphasis on the theology of missions as a part of ecclesiology.

B. Relating to the cultivation of missions education in the home church.

1. Recognize that the missionary is generally the key to communicating a missionary vision.

   a. Use especially those missionaries who are good communicators.

   b. A missionary's skill in communicating may be improved through effective orientation and training.

2. The much maligned missionary prayer letter is a good communication tool if well prepared.

3. Recognize that a corp of concerned, informed laymen can do much to keep the missions interest afloat even if there is little pastoral encouragement, at least for a time.

4. If practical and financially feasible, encourage the exposure of young people, key leaders and pastors to actual experience in visiting fields abroad.

5. Recognize the need to recapture the missionary urgency within the home church. There is an "erosion of certainty".

6. Work for the recognition of and full importance of functioning missions committees.

7. Seek to employ all agencies in the task of building up missions education, i.e. publishing, Christian Education departments, etc.

8. Use the opportunity of visiting national (mature and experienced) to bring inspiration and information to the sending church.

9. The home church should become much more involved in following their own young people into their school and training experience.

COMPETITION FOR FINANCIAL RESOURCES

Group G - Non-denominational Missions
Leader: Cummings; Recorder: Tomlinson

Group H - Denominational Missions
Leader:Kirkpatrick; Recorder:Ingraham

I. HOME CHURCH/MISSION RELATIONSHIPS

A. Recognizing that there are social pressures here at home, programs should be initiated so as not to ignore needs but seek to maintain a balance to minister both at home and worldwide.

B. Competition between inter-denominational agencies, denominational missions and home churches require:

1. Relating support with joint service.

2. Seek openness among entities to recognize and respect individual needs.

C. Evaluation of ministries of independent missions to insure support of missions which reflect common objections within compatible theological framework.

D. Personalization of appeals for support must be related to missions program and strategy overseas but with allowance for individual spiritual gifts for service.

II. MISSION/NATIONAL CHURCH RELATIONSHIP

A. Circumstances within a country must determine the extent of participation with the national church.

B. Stage of development must determine the rate of declining support and personnel supply.

C. The problem of variation in national workers' support by different missions working in the same area requires concerted effort toward agreement, either locally or on the executive level, in order to avoid the spectre of "buying workers and congregations."

D. Teaching stewardship to local congregations essential from the very beginning to encourage maximum self outreach.

E. Care must be exercised to avoid depriving national churches the joy of new church planting and nurture through missions' offers for financial subsidies.

MISSIONARY/NATIONAL SUPPORT

Group I - Leader: Stam; Recorder: Bjork
Group J - Leader: Mellis; Recorder: McCullough

I. PROBLEM - Personal fund raising increasingly objectionable to missionaries, particularly candidates.

A. Some did not agree that this is true. They feel that personalized support has worked. It creates personal relationships and develops interest in the work by the donors.

B. The new generation of missionaries feel differently than those in the past. The prevailing mood is one of independency and hesitation to be under obligation to anyone. They object to what they classify as "begging" from churches in order that they might serve. They prefer that the mission care for the support from a centralized fund. They will choose to serve under boards where they will not have to raise support. The mobility of students often precludes a strong church relationship which would result in support backing.

C. The home church is a focal point in the matter of support. There is value in personal giving for the church and the individual. We must, as missions help protect churches from being overwhelmed with missionary speakers and candidates. There will always be some risk by churches in investing in students and in missionaries.

II. SOME SOLUTIONS - to problems of educating home constituency in switching from support of missionary to support of nationals.

A. Bring selected nationals here for deputation.

B. Support should not be direct to individuals abroad but through the administrating board or national,supervising agency on the field.

C. These support procedures must be based on clearly recognized and soundly administered STEWARDSHIP principles.

D. Must cling to personalized methods but administered as a stewardship trust.

III. Discrepancy between living standards of missionaries and national workers.

A. The discrepancy is rapidly lessening.

B. Cost of living standards are based on the area in which the missionary or national works and not from homeland standards.

C. Life style is tremendously important and affects the support level. The attitude of the worker in identifying with the people is a big factor. The general feeling was that we should take as little equipment as possible into other countries and that national food and products should be used.

IV. The support of national pastors.

A. In Latin America and perhaps other places as well it seems better that many pastors work, at least part time, to sustain themselves. This gives greater identification with the people to whom they minister.

B. Money from overseas alienates national workers from their people. It would be better for them to carry a tent-making, gift-receiving ministry.

C. Some churches in Chile have an apprentice type program of training pastors from the time of their conversion until they are fully supported by the church. They first give their testimony, then participate in open air meetings, then be responsible for the meetings, then minister to a group, etc. The work flourishes and this seems to produce good results up to the point of being in full time service with a growing church.

V. Some solutions to transition from mission subsidy to self-support.

A. Assist in selection of nationals who are trustworthy.

B. Use of area meetings which expose leaders who are under the subsidy scheme to have contact with and come under the influence of men who are under self support.

C. Employ long range planning, often including national base operations for building up agricultural projects, cooperatives, etc.

D. Seek out methods which will contribute to the economic base of the church people together with teaching of stewardship, tithing, accounting, etc.

VI. How can we teach <u>stewardship</u> in the field?

A. There was appreciation of Dr. King's suggestion regarding regional conferences which make for cross fertilization of idea and experience along this line.

B. There is the need for training key nationals in the philosophy and methods of proper accounting, reporting etc., such as a stewardship secretary for the national church.

Group K - MISSIONARY RECRUITMENT AND ROLE

Leader: Larsen; Recorder: Mangham

I. The failure of the home church to take larger responsibility for recruiting stems from a tendency of missions to require missionaries to relate to many churches and individuals.

II. The recruitment appeal using modern psychological reasons such as "make your contribution", "finding self-fulfillment", "doing my thing", and "what will this do for me?" is not challenging young people to a total commitment to Jesus Christ but leading them to short-term, peace corps type of commitments.

III. The need for greater emphasis on orientation training of missionaries to meet current problems resulted in suggestions that:

A. Not only the missionary but his wife and children be given orientation training.

B. Assessment be made of their adaptability and receptivity to cultural "shock".

C. Their linguistic ability be assessed using scientific measures available.

D. The church planting missionary be well grounded in principles avoiding dominance.

E. A year or more should be spent with a national family, apprenticeship training being provided by a qualified national leader.

IV. Every missionary has need for pastoral care - on the field and when home on furlough.

A. The pastor has a responsibility to minister to the missionary, by visiting with them, and listening, counseling.

B. Consideration should be given to developing cooperative relationship between missions working in a given area overseas whereby each year a qualified home church pastor could visit all missionaries in that area.

C. We expect far too much from the missionary on furlough. He usually needs spiritual refreshing - pastoral care.

Group L - MISSION FINANCIAL POLICY

Leader: Frank; Recorder: Guynes

I. Because short-term involvement is definitely "in", affecting mission societies to a greater degree than denominational missions, there is a need to study:

A. Cost accounting which takes into account initial investment, travel and support expenses in relation to a measure of results.

B. The behavior pattern of those who do not return as missionaries.

C. The possibility of enrolling second-career people.

D. The need of different areas of the world for different types of missionary involvement.

II. It was recognized that:

A. "Pooling" systems of fund handling held distinct administrative advantages for missions, enabling them to make equitable distribution among missionaries.

B. "Designated, personal gifts" held real motivational advantages in obtaining funds though missionaries varied appreciably in their deputational talents.

C. Some missions favored emphasis on "mission projects" rather than on personalized giving to missionaries but it was generally agreed that a combination of methods should be sought.

III. Though numerous missions have successfully entrusted fund handling to nationals, the following should be kept in focus:

A. The degree of maturity of the national church.

B. The amount of training in fund handling given to nationals concerned.

C. The general attitude of the national church toward handling their finances.

IV. It was suggested that:

A. In the disciplining and training process the matter of handling finances at all levels of local church development should be carefully included.

B. The maintenance of an attitude of "trust" in the national church on the part of missionaries would likely, in the long run, produce worthiness for it, including trust in the grace of God to accomplish what is needed.

C. The gifts of the Spirit which includes administrative enablements should be anticipated in the national church.

V. In considering differences in emphasis on financing workers vs institutions:

A. Often the national church is unable or unwilling to share equal responsibility with the mission.

B. There is a difference in the type of worker or ministry that should be helped (generally pastors should be supported by their congregations whereas special ministries might be assisted).

C. An economic imbalance could arise between workers' level of living and that of national Christians generally if support is derived from foreign sources.

D. Great concern should be had for the corrupting influence of financial assistance.

VI. Possible solutions in the matter of assistance lie in the area of:

A. Scholarships.

B. Revolving funds.

C. Matching funds.

D. Terminal assistance.

Certain institutions which contribute to evangelism or church planting should be considered more worthy of financial help, but all institutions should be evaluated regularly as to whether or not they are fulfilling their purpose for existence.

Group M - LINES OF AUTHORITY

Leader: Taylor; Recorder: Wiebe

I. A continual struggle for personal involvement with the missionaries by the home churches results in tension on the part of missions who assume that the home churches are seeking to bypass them. This takes several forms.

A. There is a growing tendency for individual pastors to send detailed questionnaires to missionaries whom they support fully or partially. (This may be done with a desire for greater involvement but is often done because of a hypersensitivity to doctrinal and/or ecumenical matters or to a desire for efficient use of their money.

B. Some churches do seem to want to control the missionary and his work, indicating a lack of trust in the mission concerned.

C. The missionary does indeed have a problem of loyalty to both mission and home church, expecially in the case of independent societies.

II. The home church and the mission should develop definite cooperative relationships to assure closer involvement of the former with missionaries supported while fully recognizing the autonomy of authority of the mission over the work of the missionary.

A. There should be a written, tacit agreement between home church and mission on the kinds of questions that may be submitted to the missionary.

B. The home church (not only the pastor), through an active, established group, should be involved in the processing of the missionary from the very beginning.

C. The number of home churches to which the missionary relates should be drastically reduced (both in the case of interdenominational mission with many supporters and for denominational missions with relations to many churches).

D. The mission should maintain a complete dossier on each missionary giving background, personnel information, and field reports, which may be shared with home churches when need arises.

III. The attitude of the missionary in his relationship with the national church has a great deal to do with developing tensions overseas.

IV. When there seems to be a problem developing between the missionary and the national church leaders, we suggest that:

A. The mission should wisely use good management principles of talking things over with the missionary and national church leaders.

B. The mission should not wait for either a "hands off" or a "hands on" attitude but one of "hands clasped", seeking those areas first where all can work together.

C. The mission should seek to prevent this problem developing through proper orientation and be prepared to provide pastoral counseling through pastors of home churches or through the field chairman.

V. To some extent traditional procedures have become obsolete in a youth culture whose mission outreach look more like communist cells and guerilla tactics than the present institutionalized church. This calls for frank admission that we do not know the answer to all questions and that we, too, are in the process of learning.

Group N - MISSION POLICY MAKING

Leader: Fricke; Recorder: Bell

I. There is validity to the accusation that an apparent tendency of some missions to "run their own show" exists and that this is due in part to:

A. Inadequate representation of home churches on mission boards.

B. Lack of participation of home churches in decision making of mission plans and policies. (However, it was generally agreed that it is impractical for home churches to be involved in the decision-making process of a mission because decisions must be made by those intimately connected with the work overseas. Rebuttal indicated that some felt that there should be a sharing of policy making in areas which affect the home church such as related to missionary recruitment, support, and pastoral care on the field.)

II. It was suggested that:

A. Missions need to do much more in the way of sharing information about their operational policies, personnel, and principles with the home churches.

B. Missionaries can serve as key people in the liason between missions and home churches, realizing that this necessitates an improved program of education of the missionaries themselves about mission policies.

C. Bible schools and seminaries should improve their process of educating all students in mission theory and practice.

III. There is a tendency upon the part of some national churches to look upon missions as foreign agencies operating in a position of authority overseas due to:

A. Growth of nationalism, instilling desire on part of national churches for independence similar to that obtained by their governments.

B. Move into a partnership relation referred to as of mutuality and equality.

C. Give the national churches a sense of belonging, participation, and teamwork in the work of the Lord.

D. Place more emphasis on a teaching ministry to our national brethren.

E. Create a climate of interaction and communication between the missionaries and the national churches.

Group O - THEOLOGICAL DIFFERENCES

Leader: Crouch; Recorder: Anderson

I. There are a number of focal points of tension between home churches and missions:

A. In an international mission (North American and European sending agencies) tensions are created by differing theological and cultural backgrounds among the personnel.

B. In interdenominational missions, a growing area of tension is "guilt by association" which often results in economic sanctions.

C. It was further stated that missions and missionaries tend to emphasize their theological differences which tend to draw lines of separation.

D. In denominations, tensions are often created because missionaries are of differing national or cultural origins.

II. The problem should be faced at the point of tension with:

A. Mission boards sharing information on the ministry of each of its missionaries with the sending churches (this suggestion met with opposition).

B. Missions communicating frankly concerning work on the field with the sending churches.

C. Missions encouraging pastors to visit field situations.

D. Missions showing flexibility and adaptability in accepting the views and proposed procedures of those of other national and cultural backgrounds.

E. Sending churches and missions accepting that viewpoint which most nearly meets the needs of the receiving church.

III. There are also points of tension over theological differences between missions and the receiving churches, largely over the question as to which agency is given Biblical authority to make decisions in overlapping areas such as outreach and evangelism.

IV. Suggestions for reducing mission/national church tensions over theological differences included:

A. A loving, understanding attitude would engender a cooperative spirit.

B. Lines of communication could be opened through consultation.

C. Unilateral action should be avoided.

D. The nature and doctrine of the church should be collectively studied.

E. Accepting the prerogative of the Holy Spirit to manifest His will through the mind of our national brethren.

F. The missionary is responsible for the initial indoctrination through Biblical teaching regarding baptism, eschatology, ecclesiology, etc.

G. The missionary should transfer his responsibilities to the national leaders as early as possible, determining with them what can be accepted from the receiving culture and what can not, using Scriptural criteria.

V. There has been an unbalanced emphasis on legalism within the national church regarding customs (dress, hair, etc.), rules for baptism, membership, etc. and that these problems stem from:

A. Cultural interpretation of Scripture.

B. Regulations which are supra-scriptural.

C. A negativistic missionary doctrination.

D. An age or generation gap at times.

VI. With reference to legalism it was suggested that:

A. A positive pattern in Christian ethics should be set by the missionary and his family.

B. The missionary and receiving church should together take a look at Scripture to see what it actually says about these matters - and willingly change as needed.

C. The individual missionary should bend and adapt so as not to offend.

D. The receiving church should have the right to set their own guidelines as they interpret Scripture.

Group P - ORGANIZATIONAL ALTERNATIVES

Leader: Abbott; Recorder: Jacques

I. The multiplicity of missionary societies causes tensions at home:

A. Because of greater competition for the missionary dollar. (Laymen, especially resent the resulting duplication and inefficiency.)

B. Because of greater competition for available missionary candidates. (Students become confused at the seemingly unreasonable proliferation of agencies. School administrators must place some limitation on the number of agencies invited to the school, which may breed student resentment.)

II. The proliferation of mission agencies is the natural counterpart of the proliferation of local churches in a community. New agencies do come into existence:

A. Because of a new vision.

B. Because of a strong personality.

C. Because of a doctrinal emphasis.

D. Because of a specialized ministry.

III. Because of the complexity of overseas work it was suggested that:

A. We would discourage local churches or groups from administering their own mission program overseas.

B. We would encourage them to cooperate with one or more established missions.

C. We recommend consideration of mergers of compatible agencies; (TEAM, FEGC, and GEM have each merged with another smaller mission.)

D. We emphasize cooperation at home in selected areas of responsibility, such as recruitment, transportation, joint headquarters complexes, joint use of data processing equipment, etc.

E. We demonstrate fellowship rather than competition, with occasional gatherings of mission leaders for fellowship, discussion, and prayer.

IV. Some of the tension between mission and the overseas church is caused by:

A. The overshadowing of the national church by a stronger, more affluent mission.

B. The paternalistic attitude of a mission which continues to make unilateral decisions affecting the national church.

V. To overcome the sense of overshadowing and of paternalism, missions should seriously consider lowering their profile overseas.

A. By voluntarily narrowing the gulf between the life-style of the missionary and that of the national Christian leaders.

B. By avoiding the use of imported equipment when the equivalent is available locally.

C. By transferring ownership and management of mission institutions to joint boards of governors on which national representation will become increasingly predominant.

D. By voluntarily initiating steps toward close cooperation with the national church organization <u>before</u> national church pressure may require it, recognizing that the process will change:

1. In a pioneer situation with no national church, the mission will be all in all.

2. As an emerging national church matures, it will become all in all.

3. During the intervening time period the proper pattern of mission-national church relationship may differ with culture and with stage of national church development.

NATIONAL CONSULTANTS PANEL

Hector Espinoza T.

In the first place, mention was made that the tensions that frequently occur between the sending and the receiving churches are often due to a lack of adequate communication. This dialogue would have been enhanced if the conference would have been held not at Green Lake but in different continents overseas, where the national church would then have had the chance to observe the missionary executives at work, trying to solve their problems.

Emphasis was also given to the need for immediate and intensive training of national leaders. The national consultants from the continent of Africa particularly felt that this area of specialized education for the national evangelical youth was not stressed enough during the sessions of the conference.

A very timely warning was heard regarding duplication of work by missionary agencies overseas, resulting in shallowness of the work in general. Also a strong recommendation was given that missionary executives should build their overseas structures in such a way that when the nationals become Christians the national church will not look as if they have simply taken over the white man's religion. Missionary agencies, on the other hand, should strive to implement the gifts of national Christians and seek in this way to edify the national body of Christ.

In reference to the nature of tensions in the foreign field, it was clearly pointed out that they are not only produced by missionaries as individuals, or by missionary structures, but that there also exist tensions within the national church between nationals, and often enough even between missionaries among themselves.

The panel expressed the need to have the sending church place a greater degree of confidence in the national church and the individual Christian. It is not rare that when nationals are not trustworthy in various areas of responsibility it has been due to the fact that they have looked into the lives of the missionaries and found them wanting.

In the area of relations to national churches it was felt that there should be a greater willingness on the part of mission executives to let go of the purse strings. Greater trust should be placed in the receiving church, so that while faithful stewardship of the funds allotted is required, the actual administration of finances provided by the sending church for once may be without the ever present hand of the American missionary.

Participants in the panel were: Walford Thompson (Trinidad), Byang Kato (West Africa), John Cho(Korea), Arsenio Domínguez (Philippines), Hector Espinoza (Mexico), and Claude Noel (Haiti) who moderated the entire session. All of the participants expressed gratitude for the privilege of having a part in the conference and of being present at a gathering of this nature.

FOR PASTOR DELEGATES - Gordon MacDonald

Recognizing the need of greater communication between sending churches and mission agencies, the following impressions are recorded and submitted in order that they might provoke a continuing dialogue among men who God has led and prepared to identify and solve problems. It is important to remember that the pastors regard these items as strictly impressions rather than formal criticisms, because we recognize that much has been done already on the part of some to bring these difficulties and tensions to solution.

1. We are concerned with what seems to be a pre-occupation on the part of mission leaders with overseas relationships and the surrender of the home church relationships to public relations personnel, not realizing that there is continuing theological and strategic significance between the ties between sending church and mission agency. We call for a re-examination on every level of consciousness of the relationship between sending church and mission agency.

2. We sense an absence of uniform understanding of the Biblical precedents for the sending church and mission relationship. We call upon mission leaders to join us in an even more aggressive search for Biblical wisdom concerning this relationship. We confess our lack of involvement on all levels of mission agency. We wish to know where we are at fault and what we can do to close the gap. There must be a new and refreshing search for a fuller understanding of this relationship.

3. We are alarmed at the continuing assumptions on the part of mission that the sending church understands the continued direction of mission, the meanings of many mission terms, the present concepts of mission strategy and the status of the worldwide overseas situation. Much information given to sending churches is based purely on financial implications, i.e., what will raise the greatest amount of money, what will give mission the best possible "face," and what will convince people to continue their enthusiasm. We call upon mission to be more descriptive, to be more honest in sharing the difficulties of needs of the overseas ministries.

4. We sense in our home churches a growing resentment against mission fund-raising due to the fact that missionaries and mission often give the impression that all they wish to get from us is our dollar. We believe that the lack of fervor for projects and missionary support is often due to a sense of being used in the past. We believe that more money would be available to responsible missions were there an attempt on the part of mission to inform us as to the strategic use of money in various projects, how the administration will work and what is the expected end result. We call upon mission to refresh their awareness that the lay constituency is becoming more business-minded, more investment-minded, and more pragmatic-minded. We call upon mis-

sion, therefore, to consider the fact that emotional appeals for money ought to be aided or augmented by sound business approaches in which the layity and pastors are informed of projects and missionary support in terms of business-like approaches.

5. We call upon missions to recognize the ignorance of the layity and pastors concerning the growing worldwide body of Christ, the national churches, their development and maturity. We believe that missions have not made us aware of the maturity of the overseas church and its leadership. We believe that there is a serious gap of knowledge of what believers are doing on other continents. We believe that there should be a greater attempt to link the overseas church with the North American churches in direct-line relationships. We are alarmed that with too great a frequence we only see national churchmen on fund-raising tours. We call for creative thinking as to how overseas pastors and teachers can come to North America and minister to us. We sadly recognize the need for our overseas brothers to become a sending church to our shores. We believe missions must accept part of the responsibility for making this possible.

6. We sense growing alarm over the internationalization of mission structures and funds. We call upon mission to recognize the growing sense of isolationism in the American mind, which is also having its effect in the American church. To instill confidence, we must be Biblically instructed as to the genius of turning over monies and properties to national churchmen and why we should be expected to send our monies to churches and groups whom we have never known.

7. We are alarmed at the proliferation of new mission organizations. We call upon missions to renew themselves in the quest for merger. While it can be historically demonstrated that there is health in "competition" and that there is growth of projects, personnel, and money given, this is by no means the only perspective or view to be taken. We ask for responsible approaches in the business of creating new organizations. We believe that evangelicals as a whole ought to take a stand on this issue and recognize the bewilderment and confusion of many sending churches as to where their monies should go, and who has the most significant strategy for the hour.

8. We are impressed with the deteriorating image of missions. We believe that some of the causes can be found in the suspicion with which laymen often regard missionaries. This suspicion is a result of the fact that the sending church often receives the impression that it is good only for money and nothing else. Because pastors often feel that missions are waiting for the opportunity to get behind their pastors and maintain direct contact with members, mission leaders ought to be continually reminded that pastors are faced with the responsibility of meeting a church budget and are often pressured by the personal pro-

jects of their members who have been contacted behind the scenes of the membership. We call upon missions to strengthen their sense of urgency in updating their missionaries as to the changing culture of America and the ways of communicating with the layity while on furlough.

9. We are impressed with the need for a greater pastoral-care relationship between sending church and missionary personnel. We call upon missions to re-examine the whole question of missionary-pastoral care and to devise creative ways in which pastors can have direct-line contacts with missionaries in aiding them in their spiritual and mental morale. We believe that pastors could be used on the mission field for short terms if missions would make reasonable requests of the churches (not the pastors) for loans of their pastoral personnel. Pastors could assist in individual counseling endeavors, retreats, and in research and development of new projects in overseas missions.

10. We call upon missions to recognize the pressures placed upon pastors to re-evaluate our commitment not only to foreign missions but to home missions. The growth of home missionary agencies for inner-city work, Christian social agencies, and work among minority groups has made our awareness of investment of Christian dollars much more acute. We confess with sadness the fact that a disproportionate amount of money is spent on church buildings and home personnel. We hope that the coming decade will see a change, and while we will set our financial house in order, we call upon missions to do the same.

11. We recognize the frustration of missions to approach the home church. Many pastors appear to be disinterested or inflexible, and often represent discouraging roadblocks to mission leaders burdened with the vastness of the world's needs. We sense that greater teaching needs to be done in our seminaries and Bible schools on the identity of legitimate mission and strategy.

12. We believe that missions can help churchmen become more acutely aware of the needs by being honest about the problems and successes. By taking us into your confidence, we believe that greater numbers of pastors and churches will join the worldwide church vision. Pastors feel that the initiative for these things belongs to the mission agencies. As you have been the church's conscience concerning the Great Commission and have been its implementing arm, so you must now be the church's conscience in calling it to a new awareness of its sense of life and mission here and abroad. We, therefore, urge more contacts on a personal level between sending churches and mission agencies. We call for seminars, conferences, and more significant writing in these lines. We too, believe that we stand on the threshold of some of the most exciting days in the history of the church. We are anxious to be a part of that change..

FOR EDUCATOR DELEGATES - Bruce Ker

There were 34 "educators" at GL '71, according to the "Input-Output" news sheet of Tuesday, September 28, 1971. I am confident that all were grateful for the privilege of being present at this historic milestone in Missions history. These educators did not meet as a homogeneous group, as did the pastors present, and our overseas brethren. Therefore what follows is not an official opinion of my colleagues, but purely personal perspective.

We professors of Missions represented a broad spectrum of the evangelical community in Canada and the U.S.A. We come from denominationally-related institutions as well as from independent and interdenominationally oriented schools. These schools were Bible Institutes, Bible Colleges, and Theological Seminaries. Repeated references to the role of our institutions in the missionary program of the church did not go unheeded by us. After all it is in our halls of learning that the training process proceeds for both our missionary candidates, who man the front lines in the regions beyond, and the missionary-minded pastors who should stand in meaningful partnership on the sending church front.

As I mull over in my mind the implications of GL '71 to our training institutions, four areas of mutual relationships stand out as needing prayerful and careful attention by all involved in fulfilling Christ's great Commission to His church.

1. A Prof's Relationship to Prospective Missionaries. A missions Prof should be able to maintain a close, warm personal touch with students with an avowed intent on serving the Lord Jesus Christ in another culture. These contacts through the period of training should reinforce the heavenly call. The missions Prof will also be alert to help guide other students seeking God's will for service toward a ministry overseas. To maintain these meaningful relationships with students the missions Prof should keep tuned in on the rapidly developing and changing missions scene, by attendance at conferences like GL '71, by regular trips to the fields, and by in-depth reading. The goal here is the continuing and growing supply of candidates for missions who are alert and abreast of the times.

2. A Prof's Relationship to Prospective Pastors. Probably most of our students will be going into some form of pastoral ministry in local American churches. In some cases this will be a valuable form of internship preparatory to overseas service. In most cases it will be for a life of pastoral vocation. Our influence upon these students must be significant for missions. We must motivate them to take an active and intelligent role in missions as pastors. This can be done in meaningful curricular offerings as well as in personal encouragement.

3. A Prof's Relationship to Mission Boards. I believe a mission Prof should keep himself right up on the latest developments in his denominational mission boards, or those interdenominational boards

with which he is aligned in some way. I also believe the mission boards could do a lot better in taking the missions Prof into their confidence; feeding him inside information; actively seekin his counsel on issues; perhaps even giving him a seat on the boar

4. Mission Boards Relationship with School Administrators. There were times at GL '71 when I felt that our Seminary and Bible Institute Presidents and Academic Deans should have been listening. Often the work of the church is made separate from the work of missions. Could our mission boards invite our Administrators to visit with them on their fields? Could these Administrators be invited to sit in on Mission Board meetings? And why not invite these Administrators to spiritually minister to the mission board members and also out on the fields to the missionaries in conference? If we could give to our Administrators a fresh vision of missions as they are - the policies, strategies, the challenges and problems - this would pay rich dividends in terms of better understanding and appreciation in our training institutions wher our pastors and missionaries are now being trained.

In conclusion, may I say that GL '71 really spoke to me to be increasingly sensitive to the God-ordained role I must play in the tota economy of God today in these multilateral relationships, each of which is vitally important to the Lord's work.

FOR STUDENT DELEGATES - Paul Shea

Although the student delegation never got together for a formal discussion concerning reactions to GL '71 and its issues, the following remarks and questions give an outline of a few of the most common thoughts of the group.

I. Church-Mission Tension Areas

A. Sending Church:

1. Historical and theological factors have developed a fault gap or even "dichotomy" mentality between home church and missions.

2. The situation calls for a new realization that mission is a vital function of the church, not a job it passes on to some handy organization.

3. The local church must have responsibility in recognizing gifted servants and sending them out into the work of mission.

4. Communications between church and mission should be such as to foster the understanding that this is one task for all.

5. The school (college, Bible school, Seminary, etc.) must be recognized as an important step in the training of servants for God's work. The school trains pastors and missionaries...here is where the barriers...the gap, could and should be broken down. Both church and mission should cooperate with the school in seeing to this.

6. A radical re-examination of use of money is needed. Will the rich in this world inherit the kingdom? What about $500,000 plants when brethren are in need overseas?

B. Mission:

1. Must see itself as part of the church or not exist...And must bring itself as close to the sending church as possible.

2. Each mission must clearly define its role and/or purpose in the light of...or more strongly on the firm foundation of Biblical Principles and directives.

3. Mission structures, relationships and policies must be examined and determined by Scriptural principles. Is the U.S.A., Big Business Image right?

4. Specific goals should be made for proper changes overseas.

5. Future candidates and recruits will respond to a mission with a well defined Biblical purpose and role; with specific goals that adapt to changing needs etc; and with specific recognition of their gifts and place for them to be exercised. (A job to do which fits into God's worldwide plan.)

C. Overseas Church:

1. There will be variation in structural arrangements in mission-church relationships overseas...but the process must go on.

2. No matter how the relationship is set up, there must be a oneness or unity in the calling of the church to reach the world.

3. Relationship of love and confidence is more important than structure. Poor structures have succeeded with it. The best of structures would fail without it.

4. The national church must be fully informed, trusted and listened to in these matters.

5. There is a need for real clarification as to who is the missionary? and who or what kind is allowed or needed? Does he only plant churches overseas, or does he also minister and build the church?

6. In these last days stress should be laid on the Headship of Christ worldwide...and the use of gifted saints from all parts of the world to all parts. Perhaps a new era when "sending" and "receiving" will no longer be needed is upon us.

II. Comments on GL '71 Itself

A. Heartwarming to witness cooperation and unity of missions leaders.

B. Glad to see the desire for self-examination and evaluation, although many came with definite, protective fences or circles around their existence. That is, it was taken for granted, it seemed, that mission organizations must still exist, but with necessary changes. Perhaps a more radical examination was needed.

C. Student reaction to small groups was mixed. Those which seemed most profitable were those where the central issues were raised and dealt with at the "expense" of quick lists of "solutions."

D. Recognize the need for the nationals to have a strong voice on these issues. Were they given an adequate enough hearing at GL '71? Missions must structure their handling of overseas situations with more national participation.

E. Frustration over the emphasis on the importance of Scriptural basis and theology of the church, yet a lack of determination to get into the problem and really search out the answers. See the need for practice in searching out the Scripture's teaching and applying it to specific situations. Perhaps each mission must again apply this on an individual basis. The theology of the church was the central issue in most of our thinking.

F. Appreciated prayer and spiritual emphasis, but also sense in some ways a need for real heartsearching...maybe revival is a key...maybe real repentence is needed.

OPERATION MIRROR

(Wrap-up session led by J. Allen Thompson)

Learning is a change of behaviour whether positive or negative. This week at Green Lake we have experienced growth. Some of these changes have occurred in:

1. New understandings

2. Changed attitudes

3. Enlarged information

4. Improved skills and coping strategies

In order for you to evaluate these changes in your experience take a sheet of paper and write down three or four specifics in one or more of the above categories. You may take five minutes for this exercise.

Now divide into saml1 groups of 10 or 15 people. Share with each other these specific areas of change. Don't analyze, debate, or judge their validity. Simply share them for the next 10 minutes.

STOP

Once again take your paper. In addition to intellectual changes, learning involves us in volitional acts. Write down two or three specific intentions you propose to carry out during the next few weeks as a result of this conference. Take about five minutes.

Regroup once again. Share your personal proposals and listen carefully to each other. You may do this for 10 or 15 minutes.

STOP

Please hand in your exercise sheets. Of course, this is optional. However, within six months I plan to return them to you as a reminder of your learning experience and as an incentive to resolve the obstacles that have hindered total fulfillment of your intentions.

Thank you very much.

Post Script

The involvement during this hour of self evaluation and sharing was exhilerating. Not only did individuals specifically recap their progress during the week, but they also took steps for immediate application. The sharing of these insights confirmed them in their own minds, and widened the total learning situation. For some this was the high point of the week. Remarked one, "I came with creative tension, and leave with creative intention."

SAMPLES OF EVALUATION

I. ATTITUDES:
   A. Give nationals more to say and receive more from them, and self out of the way for the Holy Spirit to work.
   B. I learned to put nationals into affairs of our mission, even though they may not be too much concerned.
   C. Let us join our works with other missions; in projects.

II. INTENTIONS:
   A. I intend to communicate better to sending churches, to our missionaries, and to our nationals.
   B. I want to strive (in the Lord) for better fellowships (Gal. 5:22 with Eph. 5:18b).
   C. More prayer and Bible study on Missions; then study about receiving and sending churches.
   D. Teach or train nationals to be missionaries also.

General Director of Non-denominational Mission

I. ATTITUDES:
   A. Trusting nationals to be of equal skills-even in unconscious comments.
   B. Possibility of giving superior attitude to others.
   C. Understanding the tremendous need of educating the church in what we are doing.
   D. Need for developing skills of nationals (but also in own congregations).
   E. Broader concept of the universal church and unity we should really work towards.

II. INTENTIONS:
   A. Check myself on this feeling of superiority.
   B. Train my people and help the mission board to see the need for training workers.
   C. By the grace of God seek to be evangelistic in my whole nature.
   D. Be occupied with the Lord's work and not so much office work. Let others assist me in this.
   E. Be definite in my planning so I accomplish these goals.
   F. When I go to the field give the nationals an opportunity to really express their feelings and be sensitive to them.

General Director of Denominational Mission

I. ATTITUDES:
   A. Does the link with the home church begin in the field?
   B. Field work - closer relations - dependence on national.
   C. Critical - watch for pride and know-it-all.
   D. Better understanding of how pastors feel about missions.
   E. Need for re-education of churches about basics of missionaries.

II. INTENTIONS:

A. Review and revise and implement fully new candidate procedure.

1. Work at close connection between candidate department and home church.
2. Not accept candidate until worked out in some satisfactory degree.

B. Try to communicate basis about my mission where people want to know about it.

Interdenominational Candidate Secretary

I. ATTITUDES:

A. Help in understanding that actions are more important than structure.

B. The results of structure in actual operations have helped to indicate directions in which we might go in the field in terms of how and where we should work together.

C. Deeper appreciation of the oneness of the Body of Christ.

D. I still have questions about the apostolic functions of missions.

E. Relations between persons must be on a level plain.

II. INTENTIONS:

A. Invite missionaries and nationals to meet and face - "What do we want to do?" "Do we want to work together?" "Should we be more closely related in how we function?" "How should we be related?"

B. Study further the content of dynamics. Specific acts to share Christ, personally and as organizations.

Associate Director of Denominational Mission

I. ATTITUDES:

A. Need of communicating more effectively with home churches. More articulate statement of goals, objectives, strategy, etc., for pastors, missionary committees of churches, etc.

B. Need of helping missionaries to better understanding and achievement in national relationships as well as work.

C. Administrators need of doing more soul-saving, ministering (outside area of our job) and being an example to others .

D. More cooperation with other missions and national churches on the field.

E. More partnership and quicker transfer to nationals.

II. INTENTIONS:

A. More time for persons, especially in witnessing and personal soul-saving work.

B. Letter to field and planning for job on field in relation to overall church building and growth, and build up of nationals.

Mission Field Leader

I. ATTITUDES:

A. Overseas pastors are losing patience with western mechanics and want greater demonstrations of real discipleship.

B. It was somewhat discouraging to sense that our missions give so much more emphasis to mechanics than to spiritual relationships, which our overseas brethren have pointed out as the root of the problem.

II. INTENTIONS:

A. Try to arrive ahead of meeting time long enough to share policy information, etc. with the pastor of the churches in which I speak.

B. Seek more spiritual fellowship with overseas colleagues.

C. Teach the church leaders more about the Biblical character of the church.

D. Give more emphasis to training materials.

Missionary

I. ATTITUDES:

A. Increased world concern.

B. A greater appreciation of the views of nationals.

C. A breakdown of barriers; value as well as danger of structured systems.

II. INTENTIONS:

A. More faithfully communicate missions "as they are" as well as "what they should be" from the standpoint of the sending church and the receiving church.

B. To improve the active fellowship which is missions, that hopefully every receiving church becomes a sending church.

Associate - Service Mission

A GREEN LAKE '71 AFFIRMATION

We, the delegates attending the Evangelical Missions Information Service-sponsored study conference on Mission-Church relationships, held at Green Lake, Wisconsin, September 27 - October 1, 1971 . . .

affirm . . .

. . . the continuing mandate upon the world-wide church to fulfill the Great Commission of Jesus Christ;

. . . our confidence in Jesus Christ, the head of the Body, to build His church, despite the imperfections in the human instruments;

. . . our reliance upon the Holy Spirit to provide the church gifts for ministry, to guide the church in form and outreach, and to call men to obedience to the Gospel;

and we confess . . .

. . . our failure to work more consistently toward the development of a fully responsible church at home and abroad;

. . . our tendency towards paternalism, authoritarianism and lack of trust in our relations with our Christian brethren;

. . . our slowness in building scriptural bridges of unity and fellowship between North American and overseas churches;

and we therefore urge mission societies . . .

. . . to discover forms of church-mission-church relationships that allow for the fullest scriptural expression of the missionary nature and purpose of the church;

. . . to share with their missionaries and their constituencies what is being done around the world to develop new patterns of church-mission-church relations;

. . . to evaluate their relations with home and overseas churches through fellowship and consultation in biblical and related studies;

. . . to foster reciprocal ministry between churches at home and overseas on the basis of mutual love, acceptance and oneness in Jesus Christ;

and we express thanksgiving and praise to God for . . .

. . . those men of God who came and ministered to us;

. . . the enabling presence of the Holy Spirit in times of prayer and discussion together;

. . . the joy of learning together in Christian fellowship;

. . . the new insights freely shared with us by our overseas brethren as well as the counsel and direction from North American pastors and professors.

. . . new facts and new hope upon which to develop, under God, our future relationships with the churches, through His grace and for His glory.

Green Lake, Wisconsin
October 1, 1971

Appendix

EVANGELICAL MISSIONS QUARTERLY SUMMER/1971

Churches need missions because modalities need sodalities

RALPH D. WINTER

Rev. Ralph D. Winter (B.S. Caltech, M.A. Columbia U., Ph.D. Cornell U., B.D. Princeton Theological Seminary) is associate professor of missions at the School of World Mission and Institute of Church Growth, Fuller Theological Seminary, Pasadena, Calif. He served two terms under the National Evangelical Presbyterian Church of Guatemala as a fraternal worker of the United Presbyterian Church in the U.S.A. He is author of Theological Education by Extension *and* The Twenty-Five Unbelievable Years, 1945-1969.

The concept of "the indigenous church" is widely emphasized today. But how much do we hear about the indigenous mission agency? The task of church planting is fairly well known. But what about the art and science of mission planting? We study the strong and weak points of different types of church policy. But where is there equivalent scholarly inquiry into the nature and structure of different types of missions? We may not have enough handbooks on how to start a church, but we have no handbooks at all on how to start a mission.

At a time when the nature of the *church* among the peoples of the world is extensively discussed, is the end of the vast world-wide *mission* apparatus so near and so inevitable that we do not really need to do more than politely ignore all this machinery as it properly and dutifully fades away? Are missions like colonialism or like hereditary monarchies? That is, are they

SUBSCRIPTION RATES: One year (four issues), $3.50; three years (12 issues), $9.00. Single copies, $1.00 each. Bulk rates to missionary societies on request. Address all subscription correspondence to Box 267, Springfield, Pa. 19064. Give old and new addresses. Allow two months for change of address.

lingering, anachronistic vestiges of an outmoded past which we must go beyond as soon as possible?

Even if we were to conclude that missions were in fact inherently objectionable, it is astonishing that there would not be more scholarly discussion of how the empire of the missions might best be dismantled. In such a case should we not at least try to head off the formation of new missions? Yet 145 new mission agencies have come into existence in the U.S.A. since 1945, as well as over a 100 or more in India. Fully half of all missionaries sent from the U.S.A. work for agencies that are not related to U.S. church governments in any direct way. These represent the fastest growing sector by far in missions today. Missions are not fading away, either at home or abroad.

Furthermore, all types of missions, for many different reasons, are now in a period of rethinking, restructuring, expanding, contracting, changing in ways unparalleled in history. Well-known is the example of the United Presbyterians who have tried to eliminate the colonial posture of the older mission in favor of a church-to-church relationship involving the mutual exchange of not "missionaries" but "fraternal workers." The head of another denominational board, Louis King (Christian and Missionary Alliance), is known for his clear-cut views on the nonintegration of church and mission. Still another approach is seen in the attempt by the Assemblies of God to give greater emphasis to their International Correspondence Institute, which is now not only moving beyond mere correspondence methodology to direct extension contact with students, but is also moving its headquarters outside of the U.S. in order to continue its mission in a helping yet nonpaternalistic relationship to non-Western national churches. It would almost seem that a denominational board is becoming a service mission. Another pattern is demonstrated by some international missions which are becoming multinational (like multinational business corporations, with no home office), others that were nearly multinational are becoming national, that is, unilateral again.

But all these details are not worth the effort of analysis if the category of the mission agencies is itself in question. Thus one reason for the apparent neglect of the subject is the strong feeling on the part of many that the *church* is the central and basic structure, whereas the *mission* is somehow secondary or perhaps merely a temporary aid in establishing churches: the scaffolding must come down when the building is done. But is this an adequate analogy?

No investigation of the proper present or permanent role of the mission agency can proceed very far, however, without going beyond the confusing variety of meanings possessed by the conventional terms *church* and *mission*. We can say, for example, that churches start churches, churches start missions, and that missions start churches, but do missions start missions? Churches, they say, *are* missions yet missions *are not* churches. The church has *a* mission, churches have missions and missions have churches. Churches are part of the church; are missions part of the church? Can we say that, as a seed gives up its life to a new plant, the mission must die when the church is born? At this point we must try to get at some underlying distinctions, even if we end up with two new terms.

At the risk of stating the obvious, one of the important characteristics of a church as contrasted to a Rotary Club, an Inter-Varsity chapter, a mission agency, a men's Bible class, or a Christian Businessmen's Committee, is that a church (whether Baptist or Episcopalian) includes whole families; membership in these other groups has some age or sex limitation.[1] Anthropologists call such fellowships *sodalities*.[2] The differences between *sodalities* we may call *sodal* differences. (Other structured groupings which have no age or sex limitations, such as churches, may then be called *modalities*; differences between them are *modal*.) Church governments, whose territorial bounds overlap those of other churches (as in the U.S.), ordinarily ignore or oppose those sodalities they do not themselves institute. In the case of the United Presbyterians, for example, the National Mariners organization could die and probably denominational officials would not weep too much. Even the United Presbyterian Women, as an organization, could blow away and not too many would notice – except for the millions of dollars which these women pour into the major denominational agencies each year.

On the whole Presbyterians have been more alert to the role

[1] Membership in a Baptist church does not extend to infants in a technical sense, but they are formally inducted by "dedication" and considered part of the church in a much more definite sense than are children who are related to members of Inter-Varsity groups, Rotary Clubs, women's associations, or even mission societies. Furthermore, a church does not retire you from membership at a certain age, as a mission society does. Finally, you can be a member of more than one nonchurchly fellowship, but people normally are not members simultaneously of more than one church.

[2] In Roman Catholic usage a sodality is generally a lay society for religious or charitable purposes. In our usage here the Catholic orders would also be sodalities.

of interdenominational sodalities than many other denominations, especially the newer, smaller groups. However, it is certainly fair to say that in general, interdenominational sodalities like the YMCA, the now defunct Student Volunteer Movement, Christian Endeavor, and even the American Bible Society have not been very precious in the eyes of denominational officials.

THE SODALITIES OF THE CHRISTIAN MISSION

When in 596 A.D. Gregory the Great as the Bishop of Rome sent Augustine to England, it was the case of a diocesan *modality* calling upon a Benedictine *sodality* to do a certain job. On their journey north through France, Augustine and his companions crossed the path of another distinguished missionary named Columban who had already gone from Ireland to work in Southeastern France. Both men were part of monastic fellowships. However, Augustine's ultimate mission was not merely to extend his own sodality, but to erect territorial organization under diocesan bishops, that is modalities. Columban, on the other hand, was extending merely the typical sodality of the Celtic form of Christianity. The most prominent structural feature of the Celtic Christian mode over the many centuries of its existence was not its rare or perhaps mainly absent diocesan structure but its selective, highly ascetic monastic fellowships, that is, its sodalities. The ability of the Celtic mode to survive as a vital faith without the help of modal structure is no doubt the main reason why the Celtic sodalities planted all over Europe typically clashed with the diocesan bishops on the continent: back home the Celtic sodalities did not have to contend with church structures.

This is an early example of the prominence of sodalities in the extension of the faith. Latourette confidently affirms that England was won mainly by the Celts, despite the almost entire absence of the modalities which today seem so essential to the Christian movement.[3] Nevertheless, these early events were a portent of coming conflicts between two inherently different structures, the modalities and the sodalities.

At the time of the Reformation, sodalities (the Catholic orders) were so powerful and so wealthy that they were a chief target of the new, nationalized churches both in England and on

[3] Latourette, *A History of the Expansion of Christianity*, Vol. II, (New York, N.Y., Harper and Brothers, 1938),

the continent. The international relations of the sodalities were also a threat to the new nationalism. Luther at first abolished both modalities and sodalities, but eventually Lutheranism restored a diocesan modal structure. However, for almost 300 years the Protestant movement had no effective mission sodalities. When they finally appeared, they were not created by the Protestant modalities, but sprang up spontaneously as "voluntary societies," that is, as sodalities. In the United States, however, two things happened within a few decades: (1) the resulting maze of voluntary societies gained astonishing momentum, and (2) the church governments began zealously soliciting and even demanding control over them.

In the United States, "state" churches transplanted from Europe to American soil found themselves with overlapping territories. Once they adjusted to this pluralism, they were called denominations. It is probable that only because these disestablished churches had a high proportion of committed people were they willing as modalities to give unified support to foreign missions. As a result, over a hundred years ago virtually all U.S. denominations joined the trend toward official boards of missions. These new boards provided denominations with new unity and their headquarters with new energy and purpose.

The first Baptist mission in the U.S. actually rallied a Baptist denomination into existence around the challenge to support it. Half of the Presbyterians, reacting in part against the nondistinctive polity of the interdenominational American Board of Commissioners for Foreign Missions, pulled away from those who were committed to cooperative mission and established an official Presbyterian Board of Foreign Missions.[4] However, of the hundreds of voluntary societies that had sprung up, only those that were church-planting were of special interest to the denominational governments. Others, like the YMCA and the American Bible Society, remained interdenominational, independent, and not so much opposed as neglected.

THE NEW SITUATION

Granted that in the early period in the U.S. church leaders

[4] There were 1221 ministers in the group that opposed the voluntary societies and 1200 in the group that was read out of the kingdom, some 400 of the latter being employed by the American Home Missionary Society, others by the American Board of Commissioners for Foreign Missions. Marsden, George M., *The Evangelical Mind and the New School Presbyterian Experience,* (New Haven and London, Yale University Press, 1970), p. 66.

came to feel strongly that church-planting should be done by church boards rather than by interdenominational missions. Such a stance is understandable where denominational distinctives are jealously guarded. Yet both then and now we find an amazingly large sector of missions supporters who honestly do not propose to perpetuate denominational distinctives in the foreign countries. In this sense the laity has often been ahead of church leaders. Unfortunately, the theological thinking that would undergird the concept of new, truly indigenous overseas denominations has only fairly recently become prominent, whereas the interdenominational mission, which by its nature cannot readily carry over denominational distinctives (and would therefore seem to be ideally suited to the development of indigenous churches), has long been frowned upon in denominational circles.

As a result, instead of moving back (or ahead?) to interdenominational autonomous agencies, the thought in some quarters today is the multi-denominational and if possible multinational (but church-related) agencies should be developed.[5] The idea behind this thinking is that if the church itself can continue to sponsor the mission, but now jointly with churches in other countries, the resulting mission effort will be less partial, less European and less colonial. Such agencies lack both the denominational distinctives that are now no longer cherished so much in high places, and they also lack the close relationship to the grass roots which is the hallmark of the voluntary society.

Modalities are characteristically impotent apart from careful maintenance of consensus, whether they are civil or ecclesiastical structures. Not all sodalities are prophetic, but prophetic influences will likely derive mainly from sodalities, not modalities. This is why prophets and politicians are very different breeds. The prophet launches out and his voluntary followers constitute potentially a sodality. Politicians, on the other hand, must watch the people who constitute the fixed, unchanging membership of their modality. The politician can only suggest what he hopes the majority will approve.

Speaking specifically of the church, then, it is notorious (but

[5] See Ralph D. Winter, "The New Missions and the Mission of the Church," *International Review of Mission*, Vol. LX, No. 237, Jan. 1971, pp. 89-100, where a middle ground is suggested between complete centralization and complete independence. Most European mission structures are in the middle ground.

not really scandalous, as some say) that the churches as *churches* have never in history cut a very impressive prophetic role, either at home or abroad. Many church leaders have been great souls, and prophetic at times. But, as with the hammer, they have worn themselves out on the anvil when they have not acknowledged and fostered the mobility and striking power of mission sodalities.

U.S. denominational leaders, we have noted, have not been outstandingly successful in their relationship to sodalities. They recall that the Methodist "connection" of the Methodist Church (originally a sodality) developed into a mode and then a separate modality. Presbyterians recall that an "alliance" of churches especially interested in missions broke away to form the separate modality of the Christian and Missionary Alliance, essentially a new denomination. Their caution is thus understandable, but their unusal remedy of mere opposition is questionable.

The state churches have learned to live with at least some mission sodalities. For example, the membership of the State Church of Norway is practically identical to the citizenry of the country itself. Yet, within a church of only 700,000 communicants, the three largest of the some 15 mission sodalities officially recognized by that church together support over 1,000 foreign missionaries. It seems inevitable that a single, centralized, denominational board cannot by itself fully express the vision and energy of the whole constituency of that denomination, especially as the tradition becomes older and more diverse internally. It is likely that the most creative structural changes for U.S. denominations in the near future will be in this area.

What is happening in the U.S. is paralleled by developments in the new national churches overseas. These new modalities may resent the continued presence of the mission sodalities that helped them into existence. In their lean newness they may also be slow to allow any kind of sodalities to form within their own membership. Many a national church, for example, is unfriendly to the development of either women's work or youth work. Yet a high proportion of the leadership in the Evangelical Presbyterian Church of Guatemala came out of a young people's sodality that never had much modal support. Ironically, now that those young people have grown up and have the reins of the church itself in their hands, they in turn frown on the development of a new young people's sodality!

Most crucial of all is the need for *mission* sodalities within the younger churches. Here the example of the U.S. denominations is no great help. However, where a "sending" church does have internal voluntary societies, as in the case of the Anglican church, they tend to appear in the foreign field as well. Two facts are not wholly unrelated: (1) the highest percentage of church membership of any large non-Western region of the world is found in Oceania; (2) there also is the outstanding record of islanders going to other islands as missionaries – over 1,000 are on a list recently compiled.[6] One of the key features of this outreach is the (Anglican) Melanesian Brotherhood, which is an indigenous voluntary society. This helps to explain why we may need only "fraternal workers" in church-to-church relationships, and yet still need missionaries in mission-to-mission relationships.

We cannot be content with church-to-church relationships, however, because of the massive, persistent call of those "two billion" who are beyond the reach of any existing Christian modalities, whether "older" or "younger" churches. We cannot overlook the new fact of our time – the younger church – that small beachhead on the shores of the vast, exploding non-Western population. But some agencies of mission are so enthralled by this new fact that they are busily modifying their "initiative" structure so as to focus nonpaternalistically and "responsively" upon the one sheep that has been found, rather than on the ninety-nine that are still lost.

The existence of a national church, here or there, merely proves that mission sodalities can be successful, not that they should be dismantled. Church-to-church "relations" are appropriate for those peoples within whose midst an active, evangelizing national church exists. But "missions" are no less appropriate for the vast ethnic groups in whose midst there is not yet any adequate national church, much less internal mission sodalities reaching out to undertake the specialized tasks of mission. Churches need missions, because modalities need sodalities. This fact has the gravest consequences for our fullest response in mission in this hour.

[6] See Charles W. Forman, "The Missionary Force of the Pacific Island Churches, *International Review of Mission,* Vol. LIX, No. 234, April 1970, p. 215.

Receiving churches and missions

DENNIS E. CLARK

Mr. Clark began his missionary career in India in 1940. He continues to travel extensively in the cause of missions as a member of the Bible and Medical Missionary Fellowship. He also serves the David C. Cook Foundation as a consultant in communications. His work has taken him to more than fifty countries, including those behind the Iron Curtain. This article is taken from his recent book, The Third World and Mission, *copyright © 1971 by Word, Inc., by kind permission of the publisher.*

Emergent and revitalized non-Christian religions threaten the churches of Asia like storm clouds on the horizon of the '70s, while in Africa, sunshine and bright skies suggest a decade of many open doors.

"They beat up two of our brothers and took away their tracts and literature. One died later of his injuries." A report from West Bengal, 1969.

"Christians are very fearful, and there is danger of their becoming an introverted ghetto like the other minority Christian communities in the Muslim world." Comment from West Pakistan, 1969.

"We can assign all the teachers we can get to religious education classes in the schools," report leaders in East Africa.

"Send us a French-speaking film producer so that we can accept the opportunity of TV programming," comes from Francophone Africa.

In Latin America, clouds and sunshine chase each other

across the sky. The fermenting revolutionary spirit **has**, if anything, emphasized the new freedom enjoyed by millions of Roman Catholics who now have access to the Bible. Kenneth S. Latourette called the period 1914-1960 "Vigor amidst Storm."[1] The name is equally applicable to churches in the Third World nations as we enter the '70s.

In addition to external pressures, Third World churches face two other interrelated problems: domestic dissension due to assumption of responsibility for their own affairs and repercussions from the influences of Western missionaries and fraternal workers.

Domestic dissensions are often tragically paraded before non-Christian magistrates, at great expense to the litigants.

"About the court case tomorrow," Munshi Prem Chand paused, "if the pastor and his party win – not that they will, mind you – we can appeal to the Supreme Court. The control of the church buildings meanwhile will no longer be in our hands."

The spokesman for his five clients cleared his throat: "Is there any hope the judge will let both parties use the church? We have spent a lot of money on witnesses; we could arrange a compromise."

Lawsuits, party strife, faction, and jockeying for the assets of church property have drained churches of spiritual power and evangelistic vigor.

The missionary beachhead of a hundred years ago soon consolidated into what became known as the compound. As cities have grown and real estate values increased, some mission properties are now worth millions of dollars. Some have been handed over to the national churches, but others are still run by missionaries as foreign bases on alien soil where foreign missionary families can live and rear their children in a protective cocoon of their own culture. Here the new arrival can unpack the half-dozen trunks and barrels of personal effects and foreign chattels, to be described to the locals by the ever-watchful houseboy. The soul need of exiles is fed by the concentration of automobiles, the chitchat and hum of a foreign base, but a great stumbling block to acceptance of missionary personnel by locals is created by its presence, as well as a temptation to avarice for the relatively poor local Christian colleague.

This center of missionary activity sees the comings and goings of would-be immigrants, scholarship seekers, client church leaders, and satellite workers who have learned the cliches and prayer forms to qualify as "our national worker."

The visiting foreign board members and other friends from home, the cables, mail, and magazines all point to the compound as the command post for a foreign enterprise. The social round, the discussion of servant problems, and the missionary weekly prayer meeting attended by twenty missionaries and two faithful nationals provide a busy life for those tied to the home. Over the rest we can draw a veil; but the problem is there, in 1970 in hundreds of Third World situations. As late as 1969, in a large city of Africa, at considerable expense, a complex of buildings was just being constructed which would be dominated from its inception by foreign missionary personnel.

First of all we must look at the disparity in living standards and *modus operandi* between foreigner and local. Though it is not so great in the metropolises of the Third World, the difference is very obvious in town and rural areas. There the employer-employee relationship between foreigner and paid worker is certain to hamper close ties of the spirit. Added to these factors is racial prejudice. In India during the '40s missionaries would place the national evangelist in the servants' quarters for the night but accept the visiting missionary as a house guest. In that era, native workers (as they were then called) were rarely invited into the mission house to talk, but were dealt with outside.

In the '60s this attitude still persisted in some parts of Africa. The young new missionary was received with special honors and quickly put in charge of some department. Locals were expected to show him deference, not because of his age and experience, but because he was a white missionary. Was it any wonder that this type of foreign missionary enterprise was viewed as colonial and that deep levels of intimacy and fellowship were inhibited by the affluence of the employer and by poor employee relationship? As these attitudes continue into the '70s, further resentment and reaction is bound to erupt.

One solution to this carry-over of the colonial era would be to dismantle all foreign mission compounds as well as to break up concentrations of foreign personnel having authority over the people who are being served. At the latest, 1975 could be set as the target date to implement this action. Concentrations of foreigners and the old type mission compound would be an anachronism by the end of the '70s.

The possible exception would be pioneer base camps serving very primitive areas. Maintaining schools for missionary children to enable them to qualify for their home university entrance may also be a valid reason for a foreign enclave, and one which can be rationally explained to local leaders. But such a base should be quite distinct in its function from all other mission activity. Existing property which can be used by responsible local Christian leadership can be transferred to the legal jurisdiction of that leadership. Other property can be sold and more modest accommodation rented among the people served.

In the Incarnation we see that God Himself voluntarily accepted the restrictions and limitations of being born into a carpenter's family in Nazareth. His identification was so real that, while remaining sinless, He was welcome at the table of publicans and sinners. Close identification with the peoples served is basic: living among them in as unobtrusive a style as health permits, reducing foreign chattels to the essentials for efficiency, and, finally, breaking free from the hardened chrysalis of mission compound walls.

CLIENT CHURCHES OR FREE?

Outside the mission circles, yet intersecting them at every point, are the receiving churches in varying stages of development. At one end of the spectrum there are those that are completely free, for example, the Baptist churches of Burma, the Pentecostal churches in Chile, and a number of churches affiliated with the Indonesian Council of Churches. In the middle are the client churches, technically autonomous, but under the influence of foreign missions or denominations, with extra-territorial controls. At the other end are churches, new and old, still under the direction of foreigners.

About Chile, Dr. John R. Kessler writes:

> Many of the Methodists never realized how strongly the Chileans felt that the missionaries had tried to prevent the free expression of the Holy Spirit. Chilean Pentecostalism owes its dual character of nationalism and spirituality to the Chilean reaction against every attempt to control the expression of the Spirit according to the insights of the foreign missionaries, coupled with an exuberant desire for the Spirit to express Himself freely in the local situation . . . The considered opinion even of those Methodists most able to appreciate the good points in the Pentecostal revival in Chile was that the movement was doomed to become a struggling sect which would probably collapse within a

few years under the weight of its own divisiveness. Instead, today the Pentecostal churches outnumber all others. 2

In Africa, Dr. David Barrett's careful research of 6,000 church groupings[3] reveals the longing of many African Christians to be themselves. Some groups, however, have overreacted in discarding Western accretions to the Christian faith and have gone beyond the point of a minimal Christian faith.

In Asia, a number of free churches, such as the Assemblies in India, are flourishing and supporting workers and programs. This development came through the ministry of Brother Bakht Singh Chabra.

It is a paradox that sending churches are urged to send and support missionaries for "the great need on the field," when the palavers and national prayer meetings reveal another picture.

"Oh, Lord," agonized one brother, "deliver us from the missionaries!"

"Oh, God," cried another, "break their pride and smash their palaces!"

Others pray more humbly: "Father, forgive them, for they know not what they do."

Western theological liberalism, like the ancient heresy of Arius, has spread to many of the faculty of the three hundred theologial seminaries and training centers of the Third World. But the vast majority of church leaders and most knowledgeable Christians still maintain the historic Christianity on which their churches were founded. They would subscribe without reservation to the Apostles' Creed, and they revere the Bible as the Word of God and final authority for faith and conduct.

When Third World church leaders travel to international conferences, they soon discover that many of their oppositie numbers are somehow different.

"I just stood up in Edinburgh and told them to their faces that they had lost their first love for the Lord," confided one Indian Presbyterian leader. "Why, many of them did not even believe Jesus was born of a virgin!"

Bishop Chandu Ray of Karachi, West Pakistan, who in 1969 assumed responsibility for the Coordinating Office for Asian Evangelism in Singapore, has on many occasions told his own experience as a young Hindu.

In Simla, perched 7,000 feet high in the Himalayas, I became a Christian. I had witnessed the miracle of a Christian missionary's eyesight being restored through prayer. I loved Jesus Christ. The Bible was living and real to me. Then I went to Bishops College, Calcutta, where much that I was taught destroyed my faith and first love for the Lord. It was much later, through a couple of godly women from New Zealand working as missionaries in Karachi, that I was restored to my early faith and joy in the Lord.

The divisive and disruptive effect of Western liberal theological thought continues into the '70s. If these liberals can be called the modern counterpart of the Sadducees, we have on the other hand the modern Pharisees, with their strong emphasis on separation which is just as disruptive to the growth of host churches. In fact, there is a question as to which is the greater of the two evils. Both of these streams from the West should be required to present their credentials before being given entree to Third World Churches.

"Your health documents please!" It was quite a day when the health officers of newly emerged nations checked on the documents of their former rulers at Passport Control.

"Sorry, sir, your smallpox vaccination is out of date."

"But, my dear man, there's not the slightest likelihood. . ."

"Sorry, sir, we'll have to put you in quarantine."

The innate courtesy, politeness, and accommodating character of Third World peoples, compounded by colonial repressions, and in the case of Christians, a long period of financial subservience, make it very difficult for receiving church leaders to introduce quarantine measures. But it is the only way to keep out the pox!

Paul's words to Timothy provide a biblical example of a similar situation in his day:

> Some, alas, have laid these simple weapons contemptuously aside, and, as far as their faith is concerned, have run their ships on the rocks. Hymenaeus and Alexander are men of this sort, and as a matter of fact I had to expel them from the Church to teach them not to blaspheme (1 Timothy 1:19).
>
> But steer clear of these un-Christian babblings, which in practice lead further and further away from Christian living. For their teachings are as dangerous as blood poisoning to the body, and spread like sepsis from a wound. Hymenaeus and Philetus are responsible for this sort of thing, and they are men who are palpable traitors to the truth, for they say that the resurrection has already occurred and, of course, badly upset some people's faith (2 Timothy 2:16-19, JBP).

Frank Strong felt his heart pounding. His head felt very light, with a floating sensation, as he walked from the car to the small room near the Bible school at La Paz.

"Senor Strong," – the question demanded concentration, he must listen – "tell us how you became a Christian." The oldest of the four Bolivian Indians put the question through the interpreter. The immense chests of these four men reminded Frank Strong that they were built for living 12,000 feet above sea level, and he was not. In fact, he felt very weak.

"At the age of sixteen . . ." and he began the story of his conversion, reflecting that he had not been cross-questioned like this very often in the past twenty-five years.

"Senor Strong, tell us what you believe about Jesus Christ, his birth, and his death," another of the elders spoke.

For twenty minutes the probing went on. Suddenly it was all over. A nodding of heads, shaking of hands, and cups of hot coffee.

"We would like you to speak to the students of our Bible school, and tonight in the church," the older man said as a smile crossed his face. Frank Strong mused, I thought this was what I came for!

"It's routine, Frank," his colleague said later. "They always check; they don't even take my word. They want to be sure you are sound in the faith!"

MISSIONS AND NATIONAL WORKERS

In the present climate of opinion in most Third World nations, is it credible to imagine nationals serving within the structure of Western missionary societies?

"Hello! Sage Britannia *(puppy dog of the British)!" said one Pakistani Muslim as he spat on the ground. "How much do you get paid for your job, uh?"*

"He'll always side with the missionaries," commented one pastor to the other as they watched the "national worker" drive off with the missionary in his car.

The national staff member of a foreign-controlled mission faces serious problems. Financed and directed by a society heavily dominated by Westerners and whose first loyalty is to foreign supporters, he owes extraterritorial loyalties to that society. Often the result of this situation is his alienation from local people. There are of course, always exceptions, but they are few. Missionary societies related to receiving churches do not face the same problem, because national personnel who operate from a church can do so in a more independent and dignified manner than can employees of a foreign society.

Christian leaders in Third World churches have become increasingly conscious of their responsibility to encourage evangelism beyond the borders of their nations, and to develop their own missions. Mr. Theodore Williams, an Indian, and secretary of the Indian Evangelical Mission, made this statement in his position paper given at the Singapore Congress on Evangelism, November, 1968:

> It is difficult for us to think of an Asian foreign missionary. People ask, 'Why should Asian churches send missionaries to other countries? Are there not enough unevangelized people in their own lands?' The question arises out of a misunderstanding of the nature of the church and its mission. The Great Commission is equally binding on all churches. The church at Antioch sent out Paul and Barnabas even though the whole of Syria was not yet evangelized.

The vitality of teams from Indonesia, the missionary program in Bolivia sponsored by Brazilian Baptist churches, and the itinerant preaching missions in East Africa by evangelists of the Revival Movement are indicative of a pattern likely to grow in the '70s.

It seems almost too late for Western societies to recruit the national because, with very few exceptions, the stigma of being labeled a "stooge" or "puppet" reduces usefulness. The more likely pattern of development will be the strengthening of existing missionary societies in Third World nations and proliferation of others. As national workers join these groups a partnership arrangement with Western societies in certain joint projects can then be worked out.

The Western concept of "hiring and firing" overlooks the deep feeling of Christians in the Third World and can only attract "hirelings" who will flee when the wolf comes. Despite the present climate of opinion, however, there is a scramble by many societies for "key nationals," and this harasses many receiving churches, preyed on by the "servant covetor." "Thou shalt not covet thy neighbor's manservant, nor his maidservant, nor his ox, nor his ass, nor anything that is thy neighbor's" is placed alongside "Thou shalt not kill. Thou shalt not commit adultery." This principle of respect for the rights of a neighbor is clear and precise. Christian leaders visiting Third World churches are unlikely to condone murder or adultery, yet in the scramble for "key nationals" they lay themselves wide open to the charge of coveting a neighbor's servant. In the Third World, money is a factor in buying one's way into the market. One such protagonist of action wrote: "Please find the best national around, and I will pay him double his present salary."

The Evangelical Fellowship of India has in its membership requirements the following clause which must be signed by all applicants:

> *Comity:* In our relations with other Christian bodies we hold that the love of Christ and the Scriptural teaching of mutual submission constrain us:
>
> 1. to respect the rights of other bodies in employment of workers, and the reception of church members;
> 2. to engage in mutual consultations under dispute; and
> 3. to take no final action on a unilateral basis without the approval of the Fellowship's negotiating committee.

Larger Western denominations walk a little more carefully, but the objective of drawing nationals into their orbit is clear. Free trips to North America, scholarships, aid, grants, and the flow of foreign visitors are all part and parcel of the approach to promote, plan, and develop Christian enterprise which will be directed and influenced by foreign Christians whose first loyalty is to an alien base, not the receiving churches in a host nation.

FINANCIAL CONSIDERATIONS

"Where will the money come from for the work of Christ in Third World nations?" is the question many ask. Money for national churches to maintain the expensive Western superstructures which have been erected will not be readily available. But then, are most of them necessary? Have some become idols which need to be destroyed?

In the great movings of the Spirit of God in Third World nations, foreign money did not play much part anyway. In the last decade, supported by the tithes of the Christians in the area, Protestant churches in Assam have multiplied rapidly.

"That pig is for the Lord," said one hillman, pointing to a snuffling porker nearly ready for market, "and those chickens also."

"Who supports this Bible school?" asked the visitor to a thriving Bible school in the Assam hills.

"The churches," came the answer. "They give part of their income to send their young people here for training."

Finance for grass-roots work and the food and clothing necessary for dedicated evangelists is often supplied by locals if they feel responsible and are not still suffering from a paternal handout of money.

In Gujarat, India, the Christian and Missionary Alliance churches passed through a testing period when the mission decided to terminate all foreign aid at the rate of 20 percent per annum over a five-year period. There was deep resentment in the hearts and minds of many pastors, until the day when the Reverend Chavan said: "This is a challenge to us, brothers; we must depend on the Lord and not on foreigners." Through his faith and leadership, the Spirit of God broke down the bitterness and resentment, and the churches experienced widespread spiritual revival as they faced for the first time their responsibility in tithing and giving to the work of the Lord.

Finances for local church work can be supplied in nearly all cases by local people, according to their standards of income and expenditure. The introduction of foreign funds for church work has a debilitating effect and weakens local initiative.

Finances for international and regional team ministries or consortiums involved in the communications media or for central training and research centers can be donated by the more affluent churches. If monies are pooled under accredited, responsible national and regional controls, they will be neutralized and can serve the whole area and the total Christian church. Such action, in contrast to the past era of colonial controls, would be a demonstration of the unity of the Body of Christ and an expression of real partnership.

This decade may well be critical in the history of missions. Many mission leaders are perplexed and looking for fresh direction – it could come out of the storm clouds like a rainbow, from the receiving churches of Asia, Africa, and Latin America, in the flush of their first love. If leaders of those churches will step forward with new initiative and declaration of purpose in the '70s, great changes could sweep over the whole foreign missionary enterprise.

[1]Kenneth S. Latourette, *A History of Christianity* (New York: Harper and Bros., 1953).

[2]*A Study of the Older Protestant Missions and Churches in Peru and Chile*, Oosterbaan and LeCointre N. V. (Goes, 1967), pp. 127, 130.

[3]David Barrett, *Schism and Renewal in Africa* (New York: Oxford University Press, 1968).

The evangel and nationalism

ARSENIO DOMINGUEZ

Mr. Dominguez is a graduate of Far Eastern Bible Institute and Seminary. He served for seven years as a tribal and rural missionary in the Philippines, an ordained minister in the Philippines, and as director of the Philippine Missionary Fellowship. In November, 1968, he became Philippine Director of Christian Nationals' Evangelism Commission, Inc., with offices at San Jose, Calif. At present he is on a two-year leave of absence from Philippine Missionary Institute and is enrolled as a student at Gordon-Conwell Theological Seminary, South Hamilton, Mass. This article is based on a paper Mr. Dominguez gave at the All Philippines Congress on Evangelism, May, 1970, in Manila.

The title suggests two fundamentals: the primacy of the evangel, and the propriety in asserting this primacy in the context of true, mature nationalism.

The evangel is the good news of Jesus Christ – his life, death, resurrection and coming again – and the necessity for every man to come to grips with Christ in order to be rightly related to himself and to his Creator. This article will concern itself with the second fundamental: the proposition that the speedy, spontaneous growth of the church in the Philippines can best be achieved in the spirit and context of true Filipino nationhood.

Mr. Leonides Virata, then Secretary of Commerce and Industry, speaking before the Far East American Council

Conference on Asia, Oct. 6, 1969 said: "We will continue to have principles and ideals, and we hope, many friends. But with them, we will hold on to the interest of our national self. In the field of foreign investment, or economic management as well as social reconstructuring, national interest shall be the overriding factor in our policies."[1]

Philippine nationalism is a "challenge to the scholar attempting to make comparisons in Southeast Asia . . . the only state to have had two recent colonial administrations: Spanish and American. And in the process the only state to have changed from the role of a government largely dominated by the clergy, which provided minimal opportunities for national self-expression, to the role of a power imbued with the philosophy of separation of church and state."[2]

We have lost our distinct self. But we are determined to find it. The student riots of early 1970 may yet carve a distinct, radical type of nationalism. This reaction will only plunge our country to a deeper step of self-interest, the type of which we, as a church, could do much to determine. If we miss the cue and thus make the wrong move, it may end in chaos and close the door for the evangel.

OUR RELIGIOUS HISTORY

The Roman Catholic priest did not just come to his own. "An interesting indication of this (of the second Council of Lima in 1591) may be noted in the rules and regulations drawn up by Governor Corcuera for the Seminary of San Felipe de Austria, which he founded in Manila in 1641. Rule 3 provides that the 'collegiates must be of pure race and have no mixture of Moorish or Jewish blood, to the fourth degree, and shall have no Negro or Bengal blood, or that of any similar nation, in their veins, or a fourth part of Filipino blood.' "[3]

Publicist Francisco Canamaque in the early nineteenth century wrote: "This lack (of Indian theologians, canonists, philosophers, moralists) is not due to (their) professors, for they were always picked men. What does this signify, if not that the deficiency is in the race, and not in the professors or the books?"[4] He concludes: "The indio priest is a real caricature. He is a caricature of the Spaniard, a caricature of the mestizo, a caricature of everybody. He is a patchwork of many things and is nothing."[5] This view gradually changed. In 1750 we are told that native priests had charge of 142 parishes and missions out of a total of 569.[6] But still when the revolution finally broke out the Filipino exiles in Spain had to issue a manifesto declaring their avowed intention that the "native clergy of the country would be those to direct and teach the people from every step of the hierarchy."[7] Archbishop Michael J. O'Doherty of Manila reported that the Spanish friars "neglected the Catholic principle that no church can rest upon a substantial basis unless it is manned by a native clergy."[8]

The evangelical movement fared better in its early beginnings. As early as 1908 the United Brethren Church aimed at good Filipino leadership in the church.[9] In the same breath in 1911 missionary Widdoes could write: "We are now in the midst of adjustments due to the second stage of the development of the Church. The responsibility for the local church has been largely shifted from the missionaries to the Filipino leaders."[10] A Tither's League was initiated by a Filipino leader, J. A. Abellera, and they established a Filipino Missionary Society shortly thereafter.[11] In the Decalogue formed in the Protestant Youth Convention of 1926, No. 11 states: "We believe in the Christian interpretation of nationalism. Therefore we hold that God has called the Filipino people to a high mission of service to humanity."[12] One is struck in a part of their 1928 Annual Report: "We (missionaries) are come as helpers to an indigenous church, which is already established here. We come as assistants to leaders who not only are our equals but excel us in their usefulness. As the work goes on, they must increase and we must decrease . . . No longer is the indigenous church in the Philippines a dream, it is a living, growing reality. There are many evidences of this fact. . ."[13]

Bishop James M. Thoburn of the Methodist Episcopal Church ordained Nicolas Zamora in Manila on March 10, 1900 as a deacon "to place an intelligent pastor over the Filipino converts, and thereby strengthen the brave company of those who had come out from the house of priestly bondage."[14] Zamora was ordained as the first pastor of Cervantes Church (now Knox Memorial) in 1903 and had a great teaching and evangelistic responsibility until February 28, 1909 when he announced he would form his own church. "It is the will of God for the Filipino nation that the Evangelical Church in the Philippines be established which will proclaim the Holy Scriptures through the leadership of our countrymen."[15] Zamora "had chafed under what he felt was the small voice

Filipinos were given in the actual policy-making decisions of the mission . . . (He) found himself in a church whose life was controlled by foreign funds and personnel. Strides were being made in self-leadership, but they were not fast enough for the Tondo independistas."[16] In this schism out of the 1,500 Methodists who joined Zamora "not a Bible woman, a deaconess, or a young person trained in the public schools and able to speak English . . . (was) drawn into the new organization."[17] Already the influence of the foreigner was weighing heavily on our nationalism. A new kind of *illustrados* were emerging, the difference being while the old kind was Spanish influence, now it was the American.[18]

WHAT NATIONALISM IS AND ISN'T

About seven years before the Zamora incident, during the schism of the Iglesia Independence Filipina from the Roman Catholic Church, Pedro Brillantes took possession of St. James Church in Bacarra, Ilocos Norte, and announced he was Bishop of the province. On the eve of his consecration he wrote a friend: "Without being dependent or independent (from Rome, that is), I am merely Filipino, Catholic, Apostolic and Divine, and for this reason I shall be consecrated *ritu divino et apostolica. . .*"[19]

I believe his words, "merely Filipino, Catholic, Apostolic and Divine," are the best definition of Filipino evangelical nationalism. For in becoming a nationalist we simply want to be Filipino. Nationalism is "the self-conscious assertion by a people of its own individuality in relation to other peoples."[20] It is the trait and characteristic of a people forged by traditions, geography and race. There is an element of patriotism there. Loving one's own country is a universal, natural characteristic. Renato Constantino's portrait of the late Don Claro M. Recto's "development proved that only the decolonized Filipino is a real Filipino" is one good way to put it.[21] A Filipino should be his own natural self. He has pride in it.

As a Filipino churchman I must recognize my oneness with the church of the world. No Christian is an island. Christ's church in the Philippines should be concerned with the mission and role of the whole church. The problems of evangelicals anywhere should be our problem. The church under persecution in other places is our concern. We are part and parcel of a truly ecumenical body in the different hues and colors of redeemed humanity. We have a world responsibility. We are catholic because we recognize our universal brotherhood as God's children in Christ – but catholic or universal without ceasing to be Filipino. We are proud to serve God according to our ways and culture.

Being Filipino should not mean becoming "anti-foreign." We should become anti-foreign when foreigners impose on us traits or characteristics all their own without considering our need or desire for them. An example of this is the assertion that the Filipinos "must adjust and accommodate themselves to our institutions, but we must not adjust our institutions to any features of their medievalism . . . It is not our mission to travel back through the centuries and meet an inferior civilization but to flood it with our better light, and when its iniquities are thus revealed, compel them to be promptly forsaken by entering upon this better way."[22] So wrote a religious leader in 1899. This should, of course, be viewed in the shadow of religio-political power that was just disentwining itself in the Philippines. It is a disdained form of colonialism.

But a missionary leader confirms that the Philippine church's "theology, worship and organization – all are duplications of American types, not always good duplication or duplications of the best in America. Churchmen in other Asian countries sometimes complain that the Protestant churches in the Philippines are not truly a part of the church in Asia, but are simply appendages or extensions of the churches in America, because of the dominating influence of a dependence on the United States."[23]

Observes an American theologian: "When a Filipino goes shopping he asks, 'Is this stateside or local made?' and buys foreign. That is his privilege, of course, and his decision is often enough justified. But seen more deeply, this shopping question manifests a wound. The 'stateside mentality' is a Filipino disease, and while it may flatter some Americans, it should alarm all concerned for the real welfare of the Philippine Republic. It is wrong to be ashamed of what one is. It is wrong for professionals to leave their own country in need and to seek more comfortable lives for themselves abroad."[24] By becoming mentally colonialized the Filipino has become artificial. In the words of a nineteenth century writer again, he is a "caricature." Possessing a culture of my own, however, does not mean a deliberate and wilful rejection of the good things in another nation's culture. I should welcome them and may even adapt some of them if they are proved workable in my own situation. But they should never colonialize me, nor make me an imitation of anybody. I must be myself.

Take the case of language. True, Filipinos are made up of many tongues and have all been instructed in schools in English. But there is a lingering misconception that our own tongue is inferior. Why should the ability to speak English be a status symbol? Unless, of course, we are prepared to admit that the flair for learning a language (which incidentally entails a good deal of memory work), is a sign of mental superiority. English has been tried to unify the nation and yet many of our countrymen just do not learn it. Many of our university graduates do not learn it well. Somebody so aptly said: "Our grandfathers spoke broken Spanish, now we speak broken English." True, in some modern branches of knowledge English is the best medium. But this is not altogether true in the church. The language hat can touch people's emotions, will and aspirations would be more effective there.

There is need to restructure our theology in a form the barrio folk can understand. Is it strange that the cults make headway in the text-proof catechetical method of teaching the Bible? If we can be understood in the barrio, it will not be so difficult to speak to the universities. For the concern of the latter is the welfare of the barrio man. There is a dire need of good evangelical literature written by Filipinos in our dialects; also for some written by Filipinos in English for the Philippines.

Some of our best melodies should be used in church music. The *kundiman* for one fascinates me. We need music that can capture the Filipino soul. True, most of what we call native folksongs were European songs brought here by the Spaniards. But we have adapted them through centuries of usage, and they have become distinctly Filipino. Let us have some of them for our churches.

It is time we examine our church polity. The Filipino is a man who wants to admire his leader. The *barangay* system of his past generation was led by a *cabeza* who had the respect of both the old and the young. Many will still give their lives for their political leaders. Church boards are hard to work in many of our churches. This is a set-up transplanted here by the missionaries. The pastor makes the decisions anyway, and the rest just follow.

WHERE LEADERSHIP SHOULD LIE

A Filipino leader told me that leadership in the church should be based on spiritual gifts rather than race. This sounds very spiritual, and biblical, since the church is a cosmopolitan community.

Let us face the facts about it. Many a naturally shy Filipino has been stifled in his God-given gifts. Normally a Filipino does not completely feel free among his foreigner-colleagues. The reasons for this could be because of Philippine history, education and social standing. The foreign missionary has money. The Filipino has none normally. After a time the Filipino could only suit his actions to please his foreigner-colleagues – to the bewilderment of some of his compatriots.

In the normal run only the Filipinos who have hobnobbed with foreigners in their study abroad discuss freely and frankly with foreign missionaries here. This has vexed the latter. They harbor the feeling that somehow study abroad has spoiled the Filipinos. The truth of the matter is that the Filipino only wants to show him and his countrymen that he is not inferior. He may also be in the process of extricating himself from foreign influence. He wants to show that he has not changed, that he has not become un-Filipino. He is in the process of being himself again. This accounts for much of the strain in our national-foreigner relationship.

A Filipino colleague has made some incisive observations. He said the vested interests of foreign mission groups have become an obsession with many of our foreign missionaries. To guard this they have offered a "packaged theology" to our Filipino leaders. This is done by suppressing liberal ideas that would cause our leaders to grow into full mature leadership. This is not done with their evangelical leaders in their own countries. This is a sign of insecurity on the part of some foreign missionaries. This has also stifled the gifts of some of our best leaders. To be evangelical does not mean being narrow and shallow; it means being discerning and deep.

Has the time arrived for the foreign missionary to leave? An American colleague observes: "The missionary relation to this problem is real. The missionary usually stays until he thinks the national churches where he serves are 'mature' enough in his estimation, financially and personally, to be able to sustain themselves when he leaves. Of course the moment of maturity, in the missionary's judgment, rarely arrives. The missionary, very often unwittingly and unwillingly, perpetuates by his very presence the problem: namely, the myth of Western superiority and Filipino inadequacy. The missionary is present in the Philippines precisely because the Filipino church claims to be unable to afford or to provide the goods or services which are available in the missionary. The missionary then, whether he realizes it or not, is a breathing monument to Filipino inability. And such monuments, it seems to me, need to be removed, not multiplied, in a developing nation."[25]

We cannot dispute the truth of this sense of inadequacy in the thinking of many Filipinos. Some of our churches can only maintain their "high class" membership because of their foreign missionary pastors. There is no doubt that foreigners can get a better hearing in many of our churches than the Filipino. In some sense this mentality has been allowed by the missionaries. Some of them have really thought of themselves as being indispensable. If this attitude is perpetuated by the missionary's presence, then he should be removed. Anything that stands in the way of a person's complete dependence on the Lord should be removed.

But the missionary's physical presence need not be removed if his role is to build up confidence in the Lord on the part of the Filipinos. Often, however, his paternalistic, authoritarian presence must be removed to accomplish this. In the final analysis the greater responsibility rests on the missionary, since he has the stronger personality.

Church institutions and programs still foreign-administered should be nationalized. The sooner the better. We have enough cues to force us to act soon before it is too late. This is right for the sake of Filipino dignity. It is right before the government and before youth and students who pulsate with actions for a new order and nationhood. The time is right in view of the radicals who would instigate this change sooner or later.

The Filipinos should not simply wait till the reigns of leadership and administration are handed over to them. They should be in a better position to gauge the current political climate of our country and, discerning the signs of the times, instigate this transfer. Of course, the process of transfer need not be fraught with misunderstanding and jealousies. There should be qualified Filipinos to take over. The Lord of the church will see to this. We cannot go on with the status quo. As a church we should be open for change, indeed initiate it, if that is the proper thing to do.

FOREIGN SUBSIDY

One perplexing matter is foreign aid. Strange, that the church, called in the vocation of the Master to minister and not be ministered unto, should find this so perplexing and complicated. The whole history of Philippine evangelical Christianity is replete with failures and frustrations is making her work self-supporting. Until now very few evangelical churches are truly self-supporting. "Although Filipinos are now generally at the head of the Protestant churches, these churches and their related institutions are still heavily dependent on support from the United States. Part of the reason is that a burdensome American pattern of organization, adopted by the early missionaries has been carried over. It is a pattern of organization and administration that the Philippine churches can ill afford. Many pastors are so poorly supported by their congregations (the average Methodist minister's salary is $23 a month) that they must supplement their income by other part-time employment. Inadequate stewardship is a major problem of all the churches, and there is need to rethink the pattern of pastoral service and support in the local churches."[26]

Perhaps the full-time pastorate system is an imported commodity not workable in the Philippines. In the Book of the Acts we see elders who worked on a normal life occupation while overseeing their local church. The Filipinos should devise some system of support for their ministers. In many cases, a part-time pastorate is the answer. In others, circuit ministers have worked just as well. Some pioneering ministers have supported their work partly through home industries, piggery, poultry-raising and gardening, where only a small part of their time is necessary to allow them to carry on an uninterrupted service in the ministry. The important thing is to discern the answer in each situation.

We are still faced with the question of finding support for our seminarians, their instructors, and others whose responsibilities require the whole of their time and efforts in the ministry. Christian organizations and functions cannot be discontinued. Aid is necessary. But aid has repercussions on the evangelical leadership. It is only natural and proper for the giver to be concerned about how his gifts are spent. This concern is often looked upon by the recipient as having "strings attached" to the gift. For in the end, the bigger the pocket-book, the bigger the say in the work. Consequently, the recipient thinks the donor paternalistic and the donor thinks the recipient ungrateful.

Furthermore, foreign-designed ministries are also appealing for support from our local churches. Their ads and gimmicks are far more convincing than the puny challenge the pastor gives. Filipinos as a whole are sensitive about asking for money for themselves. And so funds are siphoned from the churches.

The argument that the foreign-based institutions use the funds they receive here for the work here does not stand the test, for the simple reason that the programs they initiated are far beyond our churches' ability to maintain. The vicious cycle continues: we cannot be self-supporting, for our churches give to programs beyond them. We appeal abroad for programs that should be supported here.

What can be done in the face of such a problem? We can only give some guideposts. God has prospered certain peoples and sections of the world. It is part of their Christian obligation to give to those in need. Giving carries with it a duty to see that the money is used properly. But, after the gift is given, it is given. The donor's responsibility ceases there and the recipient's responsibility begins. It has come from his own heavenly Father.

Our churches should be taught that their first responsibility is to support Filipino pastors and missionaries. Their work may be unglamorous and less appealing – in terms of hands raised and letters received – but it makes for permanence.

A work in one part of the world should be the concern and responsibility of the church everywhere. It behooves the church in the Philippines to be prepared to send assistance abroad, not only prayers but money as well. This is part of our responsibility.

ROLE OF MISSIONARIES

The role of foreign missionaries is a very complex matter. But certainly in this day of ecumenicity it is a testimony to the unity and oneness of the church to have different races of men harmoniously working together for a common goal. It should be a demonstration of God's work in the midst of our chaotic racial tensions.

The church here needs specialists, especially in the areas of biblical translation and interpretation and related disciplines: archeology, original languages, biblical customs, etc. We also need men of world-wide vision who can sharpen our focus on the needs of the world at large. Pioneering missionary ministry here is still done by the foreigners. This is to our shame. When more than fifty percent of the world's population still has not heard of Christ's saving grace, we need all the missionary force available.

Nationalization of all missionary organizations should first be accomplished before the role of foreign missionaries can be put in its right perspective. The Filipino leadership should be able to determine the needs and to request the sending organizations to fill them. Should the qualifications and character of a particular missionary become questionable, the Filipino leadership should have the right to request his transfer. This will provide the right setting for a harmonious relationship.

If developing a national church were just a matter of mere pride in our culture and in our nation, then it would not be worth considering seriously. But what is at stake is not simply developing a church that we can boast is truly Filipino. What really is important is that we build a strong and distinctly national church, so that our compatriots throughout the nation can easily identify themselves with our churches as being truly Filipino. Only this way will we be able to reach our full potential for winning the unsaved of our country. A foreign-looking, foreign-sounding, foreign-dominated church will not appeal to those outside of Christ. But one that is both fully Christian and fully Filipino will.

Nationalization of our church and its related institutions would not mean anything if it were simply an end in itself. Nationalization should only be a means for the church to take a posture that is acceptable, or at least with as little prejudice as possible, to our *kababayan* (countrymen). Unless we allow ourselves to come under the scrutiny of the Word of God and be set afire by the Spirit of God for God's work, we will simply be like the proverbial politician who talks much about patriotism but allows himself to sink in corruption and to perpetuate his own vested interests.

God who has called us and made us what we are, and has ordained his work to be accomplished by poor flesh and blood, can use us just as we are, Filipinos who know how to give God their all and to serve him in their own way.

[1]Address by Leonides S. Virata, Secretary of Commerce and Industry, before the Far East American Council Conference on Asia, Waldorf Astoria, New York City, Oct. 6, 1969. Italics mine.

[2]*Religion and Nationalism in Southeast Asia* by Fred R. von der Mehden (The University of Wisconsin Press, Madison, 1963), p. ix.

[3]In BRPI, XLV, 175, quoted in "Development of the Native Clergy in the Philippines," by Horacio de la Costa, S.J., *Studies in Philippine Church History*, edited by Gerald H. Anderson (Cornell University Press, London, 1969), p. 75.

[4]E. Zamora, "Las corporaciones religiosa," in BRPI, XLVI, 348-49, *Ibid*. pp. 101.

[5]E. Retana, "Frailes y clerigos" (Madrid, 1890), p. 100, *Ibid*., pp. 99-100.

[6]Cf. Brou, "Notes", pp. 546-47, *Ibid*., p. 97.

[7]*Philippine Insurgent Records*, 1125.3, NA; "Las Memorias," *Ibid*., p. 226.

[8]"The Religious Situation in the Philippines," *American Ecclesiastical Review*, LXXIV (1926), 131-32, *ibid*., p. 102.

[9]*The Filipino Church* by Rev. Walter N. Roberts (The Foreign Missionary Review and The Women's Missionary Association, United Brethren in Christ, Dayton, Ohio, 1926), p. 35.

[10]*Ibid*., pp. 45, 46.

[11]*Ibid*., p. 49.

[12]*Ibid*., p. 138.

[13]*Ibid*., p. 129.

[14]*The Philippines and the Far East* by Homer C. Stunz (Cincinnati, 1904), G. H. Anderson, *op. cit*., p. 329.

[15]*Aklat Pang-Alaala sa Ika-50 Anibersario ng Iglesia Evangelical en las Islas Filipinas, 1909-1959* (Manila, 1959), p. 8, *Ibid*., p. 335.

[16]"Nicolas Zamora: Religious Nationalist," by Richard Deats, *Ibid*., p. 333.

[17]"Bishop Bashford in Manila," *World-wide Missions*, XXI, 7 (19-9), *Ibid*., p. 336.

[18]The *illustrados* were the elite class among revolutionary-period Filipinos who wanted to be like the colonials in their ways. For a fuller treatment of this see *The Making of a Filipino* by Renato Constantino (Malaya Book, Inc., Quezon City, 1969), pp. 5-22.

[19]*Religious Revolution in the Philippines*, Vol. I by Pedro S. de Achutegui, S.J. and Miguel A. Bernard, S.J. (Manila, 1960), p. 194.

[20]"Nationalism as an International Asset," by M. A. C. Warren, *International Review of Missions*, XLIV (Oct., 1955), 387, quoted in *Nationalism and Christianity in the Philippines* by Richard L. Deats (Southern Methodist University Press, Dallas, Texas, 1967), p. 3.

[21]*The Making of a Filipino* by Renato Constantino, *op. cit*., p. 296.

[22]"Facing the Twentieth Century: Our Country, Its Power and Peril," by Rev. James M. King, New York, 11899, p. 593, quoted in G. H. Anderson, *op. cit*., p. 157.

[23]*Christ and Crisis*, edited by G. H. Anderson, *op. cit*., p. 157.

[24]"The New Macedonian," F. Dale Bruner's unpublished address, California, 1969.

[25]*Ibid.*

[26]"Is There a National Church?" by Arsenio Dominguez, *Crusader Magazine*

What's happening in church-mission relations?

JAMES W. REAPSOME

Mr. Reapsome is managing editor of Evangelical Missions Quarterly *and a contributor to other publications. He also serves as president of the U.S. board of the Belgian Gospel Mission.*

Missions *are* doing something to nationalize the churches. A spot check by *Evangelical Missions Quarterly* reveals some interesting developments.

AFRICA

Kenya. The World Gospel Mission is restructuring mission-church relations so that all mission activities will be under the "umbrella" of the national church. The African moderator of the church will be the key administrative officer for the entire program, not the mission superintendent. All properties will be in the hands of the boards of governors for institutions, or the church.

Congo. The Board of Missions/Services of the Conference of Mennonite Brethren Churches of North America has made "some rather drastic strategy changes" including: negotiate withdrawal of financial support of institutions; strengthen the training of leadership in evangelism, church planting, and administration; negotiate financial grants with the church to replace missionaries with Congolese in the Bible school; provide a minimum program of social and economic development which will enhance the life of the church in its society; place the bookstores on a business basis and transfer to the church or to individuals; arrange for full government subsidy of the high school program.

The Evangelical Free Church of America is in the process of transferring the charter to the national church, the Evangelical Church of the Ubangi. The church is now totally independent.

Grace Mission has 110 "strictly indigenous" churches. They build their own churches, support their own pastors, and "are run by the nationals." The secretary and head of all the churches is a national. He and other national leaders are members of the Field Council and have a definite voice "in running the whole field."

Sierra Leone. The Wesleyan Church has begun the process for the registration and establishment of the Sierra Leone Wesleyan Church in place of the American Wesleyan Mission in Sierra Leone. The constitution has been drawn up and is being studied for approval.

The Sierra Leone Church of the United Brethren in Christ will assume full support of its conference expenditures in 1972. This has been accomplished by a partial reduction of funds from the U.S. over the past four years. The education secretary in charge of primary schools has been replaced by a young Sierra Leonean. The principals in charge of two secondary schools are Sierra Leoneans.

Central African Republic. The Foreign Missionary Society of the Brethren Church has begun steps to place mission properties and institutions in the name of the national church. Committees composed of Africans are encouraged to assume greater responsibility in the operation of hospitals, schools, and literature work.

Nigeria. The Sudan Interior Mission continues to nationalize the program of the education department. Three major institutions still have missionary principals; all the rest are nationalized. Plans call for the complete nationalization of school administrations within three years. In the medical department, the first of eight leprosaria has been turned over to a national administrator. Plans have been made for the complete nationalization of the Bible training ministry. A Nigerian vice principal has been appointed at Igbaja Seminary. The nationalization of the radio ministry has been implemented by the appointment of a Nigerian, Rev. David Olitayo, by the Evangelical Church of West Africa as radio pastor.

ASIA

India. The Evangelical Alliance Mission has amended its India Field Constitution and changed its name to The Evangelical Alliance Ministries Trust. This makes possible the inclusion of national leaders in the direction and operation of all field ministries. Under this arrangement nationals will be able to carry on all the present ministries if missionaries are withdrawn. Church properties will be held in the name of the trust. Local congregations can assume full control of such properties when requirements for leadership and finances are met.

The Assemblies of God held an All-India Conference on Evangelism at Bangalore to emphasize the responsibility of Indians to reach Indians for Jesus Christ. There has been "a new wave" of Indian evangelism since then.

The American Advent Mission Society established a national conference and placed nationals in key committees. Nationals were elected to take leadership positions in the conference; missionaries have begun to resign from certain committees. The national president will take full responsibility in 1972. The mission has begun to remit funds directly to the conference treasurer. A ten-year "pull back" program has begun, with one-tenth of mission-paid salaries to be withheld each year and assumed by the conference and the churches. A Trust Association has been formed to receive and supervise all properties. These are mostly church buildings, but eventually the Bible school, Christian education building and dispensaries will be turned over to the trust. A study is being made of the structure of the mission and its relation to the national conference. Probably a "parallel structure" will be instituted for the two organizations.

The Mennonite Brethren plan to withdraw all permanent missionaries by the end of 1972 in three equal annual stages. If necessary, a brief extension of medical services will be considered beyond 1972. Fellowship with the church in India will continue through periodic special ministries and Christian nurture. Financial grants with the church will be negotiated to meet specific needs.

All missionaries of the Ramabai Mukti Mission are under the supervision of Indians. The Indian pastor and the church board govern the church and direct the evangelistic outreach and the daily operations.

Churches of the International Christian Fellowship in the

Tamil and Telugu fields are "fully indigenous." The mission is giving assistance in organizing a national church conference.

The Ohio Yearly Meeting of Friends has made plans to have its hospital nationalized by an all-Indian staff. The Christian education arm of the Evangelical Fellowship of India is now in the hands of Indians.

Japan. The Japan Evangelical Mission has established a policy of complete financial independence by the national church. The church has been independent in organization and administration, but the mission has assisted with small subsidies for pastors working in pioneer areas. Under the new plan churches will be asked to give 10 percent of their undesignated offerings for these pastors.

Far Eastern Gospel Crusade has adopted a program for the transfer of responsibility from missionary to national pastor, and a sharing of responsibility for the economic and continued development of the group. There is a reciprocal relationship in which the pastors are asking the missionaries to help them in evangelistic outreach, and the missionaries are asking pastors for their counsel and pastoral ministry in the development of the church. The national church leadership is involved in the earliest planning for evangelistic thrusts in new areas. The churches are committed to see that evangelism results in the establishment of churches.

The Mennonite Brethren are negotiating for the transfer of their one-third interest in the Osaka Biblical Seminary to the national church. They also are working toward a reduction in missionary personnel and funds for the seminary. They hope to transfer missionaries to new areas for evangelism and church planting.

Korea. The 13,000-member Assemblies of God church in Seoul is building a $3,000,000 church building entirely with its own money.

The Evangelical Alliance Mission has directed its personnel away from "direct church planting" toward work with existing churches in a program of strengthening the local ministry and assisting local churches in their efforts to establish new congregations. Missionaries will no longer be the church planters and the church leaders, but assistants and helpers to the local churches.

Taiwan. The Ohio Yearly Meeting of Friends has put national pastors on the Missionary Council. The number is increasing each year. All churches are manned by national pastors. The churches are asked to assume all operating costs "as soon as they are able."

Overseas Crusades does not have its own churches, but has a team of U.S. and national personnel. The Taiwan advisory board of Chinese and one missionary meets monthly to review the ministry, to advise the Taiwan team, and to send recommendations to the U.S. A Chinese has been appointed field director. Both U.S. and national missionaries are responsible to him. He is a member of the mission's board of directors.

Philippines. Nationals have been appointed by Far Eastern Gospel Crusade to "high levels of responsibility" at Febias College of Bible. Missionaries are working with several independent church groups to encourage the emergence of national leadership.

The Evangelical Free Church of the Philippines, the national church body, was organized and made an independent group.

The Wesleyan Church missionary field superintendent was replaced by a Filipino. The new book of church government follows an indigenous policy. Approval was granted for holding the first provisional general conference. The first Filipino missionary family was sent to Indonesia. The national church began a project to establish a headquarters near Manila.

Hong Kong. The Free Methodist support of pastors is on a five-year program with a 20 percent cutback in subsidy. The chairmanship of the conference executive committee is to be rotated among nationals and one missionary.

LATIN AMERICA

Peru. The South America Mission has prepared the groundwork for the formation of a national church organization, to be the church counterpart of the mission, through whom and with whom the mission will work. A committee of seven – three Peruvians, two Indians, and two missionaries – has been appointed to prepare a draft of a constitution and to call a general assembly of all mission-associated churches as well as unaligned churches.

The Andes Evangelical Mission is associated with the Iglesia Evangelica Peruana, which is completely autonomous. The mission became associated officially with the church last year.

The Regions Beyond Missionary Union adopted a policy of

"strategic withdrawal." Missionaries will be withdrawn from the older, established church centers and will be redeployed to new, unevangelized areas. They will continue in service ministries: Bible institute and printing. Full administrative control of the Christian education program, radio work, youth work and the literacy program is to be turned over to the national church, together with the money formerly provided by and administered by the mission on these programs. The mission subsidy will be continued for another five years. This procedure, which is short of complete fusion, will allow the mission to continue its evangelistic mandate as a separate entity, while leaving the national church in full control of its own programs.

Guatemala, Honduras, El Salvador The churches which were a part of the Friends Mission of Central America (California Yearly Meeting) have been organized into an autonomous Yearly Meeting. Missionaries continue to cooperate with the new body.

The director of the Quiche Bible Institute, a cooperative work between the Primitive Methodist International Mission Board and the Presbyterian Church, U.S.A. is now a national. Nationals now control the Primitive Methodist national church conference. A national is directing the mission's hospital in Guatemala. Nationals are teaching literacy under the direction of the national conference.

Central American Mission churches in El Salvador were required to have their executive committee include at least 50 percent missionaries. Under a reform move, the constitution of the national church has been changed so that it has full voice in the selection of those who should represent the churches as members of the executive committee. Missionaries may still belong to the executive committee, but they are chosen by nationals, not imposed on them.

Mexico. Mexican Militant Mission has begun a program to achieve full support of national pastors by the churches.

The Mennonite Brethren plan to withdraw all permanent North American personnal.

Guyana. The Church of God continues partial support of its churches, but all funds are handled by nationals. Operating through a national council chosen by pastors, the national church directs all activities. A national will be appointed Supervisor. The mission feels that its work is progressing as well under complete nationalization as it did when U.S. personnel were there.

Jamaica. The Missionary Church in Jamaica elected its first black Jamaican as president. By-laws have been changed to encourage Jamaican leadership. The church is autonomous, but Jamaican delegates have often elected officers from among missionaries.

Venezuela. The Orinoco River Mission is studying a plan for the disposition of mission property, and for a new relation in which it would be "subservient" to the national church.

Chile. The national church organization of the Gospel Mission of South America is headed by a board of five Chileans and two missionaries, who are elected by the church convention. General fund money is turned over to nationals for building and evangelism projects. The heavily-subsidized Bible institute day residence program has been changed to an evening program, so nationals will more easily be able to maintain it.

Dominican Republic. The total work of the Commission on Overseas Missions of The Evangelical Mennonite Church is under the director of the national conference organization. Previously, some matters had been church-directed, other mission-directed. The home board lends missionary personnel to the national church.

All of the work of the West Indies Mission is under the national church, not only the assignment and evaluation of missionary personnel but also the designation of money. Missionary finance is handled individually through the home office.

Argentina. The administration and operation of the Russian Bible Institute of the Slavic Gospel Association is in the hands of national Slavic leaders and teachers. The school continues to receive a large portion of its financial support from the U.S.

Colombia. The Assemblies of God elected its first national superintendent. One missionary, elected by nationals, serves on the executive presbytery.

The Mennonite Brethren are working with the church to transfer missionaries to new areas of evangelism and church planting. The mission will discontinue operation of the high school, but will negotiate financial aid for the church to continue the school or to send students to other schools.

The South America Mission has drawn up a constitution which is being ratified by the national church. The result will be an association of churches with which and through which the mission can work.

Brazil. The Mennonite Brethren are negotiating with the national brotherhood for continued participation in cooperative evangelism and church planting. The mission will withdraw personnel from the Bible school by 1973. The theological extension program will be transferred to the church by 1972.

Fourteen Terena Indian churches of the South America Mission elected a committee of six nationals to draw up plans for a fellowship of Terena churches in South Mato Grasso. Subsequently, a general assembly will be convened for representatives from all of these churches.

In general. The Conservative Baptist Home Mission Society hopes eventually to internationalize its board so that it is not limited to U.S. citizens. In the work as a whole, there would be no position limited to U.S. citizens. The mission has assigned men from Jamaica, Cuba and Canada to work in the U.S. In Costa Rica, most of the missionaries are from other Central American countries.

The Latin America Mission, whose churches in Costa Rica and Colombia have previously been organized as independent associations, is working on plans for restructuring the mission "to root it more thoroughly in Latin America and enable it to become more fully an arm of the Latin American church, rather than a North American organization which offers services in Latin America."

JUST A COUPLE TENNIS PLAYERS

One day – in another country (Africa) – a USIS man shook his head and said, "This will be hard to believe, but as soon as these guys leave, all the press around here will call me up and say, 'Hey, what were those tennis players really doing here?' That's hard to believe, I know, but it'll happen, because that's what you get every time the U.S. has somebody in. It's that way almost everywhere. People just won't accept the fact that what they see on the surface is all there is. No matter how many times you tell them, people just won't trust you when you tell them, like, 'It's just a couple tennis players teaching the game.' I know, it's hard to believe." – *Sports Illustrated.*

The future role of western missions in the Muslim world, Africa, India and Asia - a concise survey

THE MUSLIM WORLD

The region being considered is both geographically and religiously near the heart of the Muslim world. It embraces, however, a number of different nations, races and varieties of religion and culture, so that it is impossible to make statements regarding the work of missionaries from the West that would be true in every situation.

In some, but not all, of these lands, there are ancient Christian churches, the histories of which go back more than 1500 years. Though they were surrounded and ruled over by Muslims for many centuries, these Christians were not overwhelmed or absorbed by Islam. However, because of their precarious position they usually made no effort to evangelize their Muslim and Jewish neighbors. Some of these lands in more recent times became colonies or mandates of Western nations, and in some instances many Europeans came to reside in them. For them Western-type churches were established, but usually the Christians from the West did not assist the native churches, or attempt to convert the non-Christians.

The first Protestant missions from the West were established in the Middle East early in the nineteenth century. The missionaries were seeking to obey Christ's command to make disciples of all nations. It was their hope that the Christian Armenians, Assyrians, Copts, Orthodox and members of the other ancient churches would, when instructed in the Bible and given new life by the Holy Spirit, become God's instrument for evangelizing all the peoples of Asia. Accordingly, they devoted themselves to the task of reviving the Christian minorities. It was not their purpose to divide these communities and create Protestant churches, but this was what happened. Those who accepted the evangelical teaching were often pushed out of the old churches, which on the whole resisted renewal, and they had no choice except to form the "evangelical" churches that exist in Turkey, Lebanon, Syria, Iraq, Egypt and elsewhere today.

Foreign missionaries continued to assist these small churches (which in several countries became large ones) by establishing schools and colleges for their young people, training their pastors, teachers and doctors, and keeping before the members their responsibility for making Christ known to the non-Christians. Some of these Christians became zealous and courageous evangelists to Jews and Muslims. But for the majority the walls of language, custom, belief, prejudice and fear that had existed for more than a thousand years were too high to scale, and too ponderous to move. Too often the "evangelical" churches did little more than the ancient churches had done to "seek and save the lost."

Because of the failure of the national Christians to evangelize, the foreign missionaries began to devote more of their time and effort to direct work for the non-Christians. They treated their sick in the mission hospitals; they educated their young people in the schools in which there were often more Muslims and Jews than Christians; they prepared and distributed Christian literature in the languages spoken by the Muslims; they carried on various kinds of social services, for the purpose of making the truth and love of Christ known both by deed and by word. Also, as the situation permitted, they made evangelistic journeys to towns and villages, and sometimes they were able to assist churches in conducting evangelistic services at which non-Christians were present, and to prepare converts for church membership.

Much of their evangelistic work, and the most effective part of it, was done in personal and friendly contacts with individuals. Wherever possible these efforts were related more or less closely to the evangelical churches, where any existed, though in some instances the churches resented the efforts of missionaries to convert Muslims and bring them into the membership of the church. However, in no land as the result of these efforts was the number of converts large. Today most of the members of the Protestant churches in the Middle East are from the ancient Christian races. The same is true of the Roman Catholic churches.

In recent years the situation in most of these countries has radically changed. There has been an upsurge of nationalism. In many of these lands Islam has been revived as an agent for developing national unity and strength. Foreign control and influence has been rejected or limited in various ways. In some countries the educational and medical institutions of the foreign missions have been taken over by, or largely controlled by, the national governments. In other places some of these institutions are being carried on by the national churches, with or without assistance from missionaries. In at least three of the countries the governments are now encouraging Western Christians to establish and administer important medical and educational projects. On the other hand, from several countries some or all of the Western missionaries have recently been expelled for political reasons. And to two of these lands no foreign missionaries have been admitted in modern times. These are lands in which the ancient churches do not exist. In the countries where Western missionaries are now residing, the problem of securing visas and residence permits is always present, and often becomes acute because of the political crises which frequently occur.

In view of all these things, what is the role of the Western missionary today in his relation to the churches, both old and new, in the Middle East? In some cases he may become a member of one of these churches, and perform his service as a pastor, evangelist, teacher, doctor, nurse, writer, etc., in and through the church, much as a national Christian would do. When the foreign worker has learned the language well, and won the confidence of the church, he will be able to render valuable service in teaching the gospel, in strengthening the evangelistic outreach of the church, in bringing guidance and encouragement to his brethren in the church, as well as in serving in the medical and educational institutions conducted by the church.

In other situations the missionary, while not a part of the ecclesiastical structure, is able to carry on his work in cooperation with the church, whether it be "evangelical" or "ancient." He may be invited to teach in a church school or seminary, and to assist in conferences or camps. In all countries there is urgent need for the preparation and distribution of up-to-date literature for both Christians and non-Christians, and qualified missionaries may share in this task. In some countries the opportunity for teaching the Bible through correspondence courses is very great. For example, one mission has during the past eight years distributed some 118,000 courses in North Africa alone. Missionaries are needed to help in carrying on this work. They are also needed in the radio ministry, which is becoming more and more important throughout the Middle East.

There is in most lands the need and opportunity for the promotion of literacy, in cooperation with both churches and governments. Missionaries may also play an important role in bringing closer together the many different churches and groups. They can become a vital link between the national Christians, who are often isolated from the Church universal, and their brethren in other parts of the world.

When William Carey went to India at the end of the eighteenth century he was forbidden to reside there as a missionary. So he became an indigo planter and a teacher in a secular insitution, and thus supported himself and his colleagues, and became one of the great founders of the Christian movement in Asia. Today in some places in the Middle East it is becoming necessary for Christian workers from other lands to follow Carey's example and find secular positions that will provide financial support, and also an opportunity for them to reside and serve Christ in areas closed to "missionaries."

In some countries Christian medical personnel are today being employed in government hospitals and medical schools, and educationalists are teaching in government and private colleges, or are giving private lessons in the English language to the many young people eager to perfect their English. It is reported that there is a man who is learning masonry in order to be able to reside in a country from which missionaries are being expelled. There are doubtless many positions in government, business and industry in the Middle East that are open to well-trained men and women from the West. Christians should take advantage of this opportunity to reside and share in Christ's work in these lands, in some parts of which no Christian church now exists. There is no place where a Christian whose heart is full of the love of Christ cannot influence others by friendship and prayer to follow his Master. Some of the "closed lands" are now in this way being opened to the gospel.

It is possible that in the providence of God the role of Western Christians in the evangelization of the Middle East will in the future be a decreasing one, and that he will give to missionaries from the Middle and Far East the privilege and responsibility of continuing and completing a task that has a yet been barely begun. However, as long as the door remains even partially open, we in the West must continue in faith, by every possible means and in the power of the Holy Spriit, the undertaking to which God called our fathers, namely, that of making Christ known to the people in the heartlands of the Islam.

– William McElwee Miller
Missionary of the Presbyterian Church in Iran, 1919-1962.

AFRICA

Since the day missionaries started to come to Africa, tremendous achievements have been made by their operations all over the continent. Numerous people have been won to Christ and trained for the Lord's service, either locally or nationally, and many churches have been established. Out of these churches have come individuals who are capable of rural and urban area evangelism. But the continent is so wide and needy that more evangelists are needed. Therefore, Western missionary societies should send more missionaries to train more nationals to preach the gospel and assist in other fields of Christian ministry.

Many nationals could become leaders if they had more training, but they are handicapped simply because of the lack of sound theological institutions and Christian schools. Western missionary societies could be of much blessing in the training of men and women who could adequately take their places in the greater Africa of tomorrow.

Training that cannot be obtained in Africa may be obtained in other countries, if funds are made available by the sending churches with the aid of the mission societies. Training of key people to take missionary posts is the major concern of governments today. Nationalization of posts is also the need and wish of the countries today.

Missionaries can be used to make available Christian literature on various levels for the hungry masses of people who like to read. There is a great ministry for literature in Nigeria today. Other secular and false cult publications are being sold almost everywhere on African streets. There is a great danger ahead of us if Christianity lags behind or fails to produce good Christian literature for the public to use.

There is also the ministry of the Word on the radio. These are the days when hundreds of people listen constantly to radio talks. Christian programs come now and then on the air, but there are not enough of them. There should be more support for the establishment of radio ministry in Nigeria.

As to organizational relationship, it is necessary that mission societies should be willing to identify themselves with the organized churches. Some do this by total identification and mixing together with the national Christian churches. These groups have every privilege that individual nationals have, but there are the other groups which feel they may lose their home church membership, so they cannot be full members of two churches at the same time. So they keep their membership with their homeland churches that send them to the mission field. However, whether the missionaries become full members, or associate members, the most important factor is that the missionary should love the national churches and show much interest in the church activities and support her programs. It is the missionary's interest that counts most. As mission and church organizations there should be one common aim in administration, support and the propagation of the gospel. Mission and church organizations should now be operating as collaborators in the Lord's vineyard.

Since this is a transition period in Africa, missionaries should be prepared to work under nationals, or as a subordinate to some less literate workers. The days of fear and feelings of inferiority are gradually passing away. If the mission and national church are to achieve anything, both should plan to work together. There are nationals who are much more experienced than foreign missionaires. Therefore, race and culture should not prevent a missionary from taking orders from his superior. National workers and pastors must seek the cooperation of the foreign missionaries. No program of the church should be conducted without the invitation and cooperation of the local missionaries.

The overseas or sending churches must bear in mind that general missionaries are still needed. Well-trained personnel will help in propagating the work and contributing to the building up of the nation. Sending churches need to encourage graduates, specially qualified individuals, and support them if they are called to serve in Africa. We need them, we have much use for them. But sending churches will help us more if they help nationals with their support, in order to produce men and women who will fill in for missionaries.

Missionaries are advised to adapt themselves to the culture of their area and not to condemn traditional practices outright.

One of the greatest needs of churches in Africa today is mass evangelism. Following this is the need for sound teaching of the Scriptures to fortify the Christians against the waves of Communism, false cults, and pagan teachings. Finance is one of the major needs in Africa. Poverty is still striking many individuals and countries. This is a handicap for the quick growth of the church. Where there is the possibility of helping nationals to tap the natural resources of their land in order to make money for the support of family, community and the Lord's work, this should be encouraged greatly. Total dependence on foreign assistance will not help as much as to be able to obtain this from one's own land.

There is the great need for evangelical bodies to unite. There has been separation and self-centeredness because of some differences in practice and worship that do not affect the fundamental doctrines of Christianity. There are criticisms from the outside and within that we are narrow-minded churches. It is time therefore for mission societies to support strongly the unity of evangelical bodies in Africa for the purpose of fostering the cause of Christianity in these last days. We need to mobilize our resources in order to survive and subdue the raging forces of the evil one. – Rev. Stephen J. Akangbe

President of the Evangelical Churches of West Africa (1,400 churches, 400,000 adherents) in Nigeria.

An interview with Rev. Samuel Odunaike, President of the Association of Evangelicals of Africa and Madagascar. Mr. Odunaike is Industrial Relations Officer for B. P. Nigeria, Ltd., Lagos, Nigeria. He was interviewed by W. H. Fuller.

Q. What do you feel should be the future role of western

missionary societies in regard to national churches in Africa?

A. In general, where churches have been established, I feel that churches will still very much value specialist services by missionaries for the next ten years. These will be necessary in such specialized fields as radio, training institutions, at certain levels, and evangelists with a definite ministry.

Q. What do you feel should be the organizational relationship of mission societies to national churches?

A. I have always felt that a missionary should become a member of the local church just like any other person. The missionary is basically a human being, a Christian, needing the fellowship of other Christians, and spiritual deepening which corporate fellowship provides. The discipline of being a church member is also good for the flesh. I feel this is the only right relationship for a missionary to the local church.

As far as organizational relationship is concerned between a mission society and the church, the ideal would be a submerging of mission and church. However, the ideal is *not* always feasible. Where missions confine themselves to specialist services as suggested, organizational problems are not likely to be as acute as at the moment, when some missionaries are actually carrying on church functions.

Q. What steps should be taken to fulfill these roles for the future?

A. There should be a decided move to phase out organizational control of churches by missions. The practice whereby missionaries still perform pastoral role in churches (notably in East Africa) should be progressively abandoned. There should be reorientation of missionary outlook by missions (old and new). Bible schools in Africa should include in their curriculum something on "the new dimension" of missions for the new generation. National churches should be reoriented in their outlook to see the evangelization of Africa as their primary responsibility, with missions lending a helping hand.

Q. What are the greatest needs of the churches in Africa?

A. I would list these in the following order: teaching in the Scriptures (with the resultant spiritual depth), evangelism, organization, finance, oneness with evangelicals elsewhere. One could be tempted to place finance higher on the scale, but I firmly believe that with sound biblical teaching, producing spiritual depth, finance will cease to be the perennial headache it is at the moment. I have never seen a New Testament church in want of the finance it needs to do God's work.

INDIA

(A) Since the attitude of the government is one of restricting the coming of "missionaries," the attitude of the western missionary societies should be more elastic and changeable regarding the structured definition of the term "missionary." The following suggestions come to mind:

1. *The missionary personnel.* The established concept that the missionary must be an ordained, and hence an established member of the ecclesiastical hierarchy, need not be true anymore. This concept was never true to the New Testament principles. The missionary of the future in India will be a lay person, with a deep sense of community with the church of Jesus Christ that exists as a witnessing-worshipping community not only in his home country but also in every country of the world. He will not witness in spite of his work, but he will witness within his total life, which definitely includes his daily work.

He may enter India as an expert representing a collaborating firm from a non-Indian nation (here, a Western country) to work with the collaborating firm that is Indian. He may come as a Peace Corps volunteer, knowing that he will share the life of the needy who need his know-how and his Christ. He may enter as an exchange scholar to live and work in an Indian university under a local or central government-sponsored scholarship in India.

The task of the Western missionary society will be to find such people and such opportunities, and to bring them together. The financial "burden" then will not be so much theirs. By the same token they may not be able to exercise unnecessary, sometimes irrelevent, authority over "their missionary." Technically qualified men like doctors, engineers, and teachers may band together and choose one spot in India under the guidance of the Holy Spirit, through the functioning usefulness of the Western missionary societies and their knowledge of mission needs. They then can divide the work on the "station" among themselves, so that no one member will have to stay in

India more than two or three months at a time. This plan will eliminate the red-tape and will allow each specialist to make his own living while he resides in the Western country for the rest of the year. At the same time, the "station" will be occupied throughout the year. The help and advice and continued counsel of the Indian churches is absolutely essential in this effort.

2. *The duration of a term.* This must be extremely flexible. This will be determined by the need of the specific type of entry permit. Short terms will be more and more workable and effective. This will help bring in new vitality from the home country to the Indian church, and from the Indian church to the home country.

3. *National church-missionary relationship.* This will no longer be one-sided. The lay missionary needs the national church as much as any Christian needs it. He is part of it and not a mere professional adviser. The national church needs him as she needs all other believers as her agency of expression.

(B) The Western missionary societies must be colearners with the national church as Christ continues to speak to both of them as one, i.e., his church in the Indian situation. There should be a partnership in obedience to the commission of Christ in this Indian situation, rather than to the dictates of men who may be tempted to safeguard the structure that gives them a present identity instead of the fulfilment of the purpose for which that structure was brought into existence. In this obedience there should be little thought of separating resources in time, talent or treasure in terms of "Indian" and "non-Indian." The response should be in terms of an organic wholeness rather than organizational calculations. When the church in India is pinched, the church in the U.S.A. or Canada must spontaneously cry, "Ouch, that hurts!" and vice-versa.

Such a oneness in obedience will be timely, will be relevant, and may demand types of action that may be considered too revolutionary in the understanding of the Western society. (Although under the present circumstances, I doubt if this will be true!). The church must once again begin to give the answers. She must scratch where the Indian society itches. Otherwise, she will be an agent of irritation rather than healing.

(C) The entire pattern that has been described thus far demands that the Western missionary societies lose themselves in the concern to fulfill the task of the church in India. They must be willing to transcend the denominational hang-ups. They should not be interested in fighting their theological wars on a foreign soil any more. We have had enough of that. The mood of the national church in India is one of regrouping for evangelical action: one Lord, one purpose, one kingdom.

– Rev. Samuel Kamaleson

Pastor, Emmanuel Methodist Church, Madras, India.

ASIA

1. Where a church is strong, the missionary societies from the West should withdraw all their personnel from the field. Only specialist workers such as those engaged in theological training and Bible teaching might be asked by the national church to remain.

2. Every effort must be made to train Asians for positions of leadership in the church. This will mean full freedom on the part of missionaries to allow Asian Christians to express their witness to Jesus Christ in the cultural pattern of their country and to restructure their church in a way that is practical to the national setting.

3. Finance on the field should not be in the hands of missions, especially if this relates to grants to national pastors' salaries, church projects and institutions. Asian Christians should be challenged to be self-supporting *and* contributing to the building of God's church on other continents. We become equals when we have the responsibility of giving to others.

4. Key Asian leaders could be sent abroad for training in post-graduate theological courses so that they could return to their countries to teach as theologians. Others might be sent for communications courses.

– Chua Wee Hian

Associate General Secretary, International Fellowship of Evangelical Students, Singapore.

MISSIONARY SUPPLIES NEEDED: . . . 3 packs Flashcubes, 6 rolls Instamatic slide film, 1 set king-size sheets (PERMA·PREST). – *From a U.S. church bulletin.*

The best reading on church-mission relations

DONALD G. PETERSON

Mr. Peterson is cataloger at Wheaton College, Wheaton, Ill. He is a graduate of Bethel Theological Seminary, St. Paul, Minn., Bethany College, Lindsborg, Kan. and has taken graduate studies at the University of Washington, Seattle; Western Illinois at Macomb, and Northern Illinois at DeKalb. An ordained minister for thirty-three years in the Baptist General Conference, he served the First Baptist Church of Geneva, Ill., 1965-1970. He was tne first President of the Board of Foreign Missions of the Baptist General Conference and a member of that board for fourteen years.

I asked mission executives, professors of missions, editors of mission magazines, publishers of Christian books, and the position paper writers and consultants for the 1971 Study Conference of Green Lake, Wis., to list, first, "the one crucial book" on the subject of church-mission tension, and second the next five books of importance on this subject.

While the response was not as great as I had hoped, one-fifth of those contacted did respond with a sufficient sampling to make the data valid. Nine responded without naming "one crucial book." Of the nine, three felt unable to recommend; three said that "in their mind there was no such 'one crucial book' "; another three indicated that in the absence of one such book, the best information was to be found in periodicals.

I will list here all the "most crucial books" nominated and those from the additional five books that had three or more recommendations.

"MOST CRUCIAL" BOOKS

Two books led all the others: *The Responsible Church and the Foreign Mission*, by Peter Beyerhaus and Henry Lefever (Grand Rapids: William Eerdmans, 1964) $1.95 (paper), and *The Third World and Mission*, by Dennis Clark (Waco, Texas: Word Books, 1970) $3.95.

The remainder of the "most crucial books" in alphabetical order by author follows:

Allen, Roland, *The Spontaneous Expansion of the Church and the Causes Which Hinder It* (Grand Rapids: Eerdmans, 1962). $1.95 (paper).

Bavinck, John H., *Introduction to the Science of Mission* (Philadelphia: Presbyterian and Reformed Press, 1960). $4.95.

Cogswell, James A., *Response: The Church in Mission to a World in Crisis* (Richmond: John Knox Press, 1970). $2.50 (paper).

Cook, Harold A., *An Introduction to Christian Missions* (Chicago: Moody Press, 1971). $4.95.

Davis, Raymond J., *Fire on the Mountain* (Grand Rapids: Zondervan, 1966). $3.95.

Glover, Robert H., *The Bible Basis of Missions* (Chicago: Moody, 1964). $3.95.

Hodges, Melvin, *Growing Young Churches* (Chicago: Moody, 1970). $1.25 (paper).

Horner, Norman, ed., *Protestant Crosscurrents in Mission: the Ecumenical-Conservative Encounter* (Nashville: Abingdon Press, 1968) $4.50.

Isais, Juan, *The Other Side of the Coin* (Grand Rapids: Eerdmans, 1966). $1.45 (paper).

McGavran, Donald A., ed., *Church Growth and Christian Mission* (New York: Harper and Row, 1965). $5.95.

McGavran, Donald A., *How Churches Grow* (New York: Friendship Press, 1966). $2.50 (paper).

McGavran, Donald A., *Understanding Church Growth* (Grand Rapids: Eerdmans, 1969). $7.95.

Matthews, George W., *Missionary Administrations* (Des Plaines, Ill.: Regular Baptist Press, 1970). $3.95.

A Moody Press Symposium, *Facing Facts in Modern Missions* (Chicago: Moody, 1963). Out of print.

Neill, Stephen, ed., *Concise Dictionary of the Christian World Mission*, Anderson, Gerald H. and Goodwin, John jt. eds. (Nashville: Abingdon, 1971). $10.50.

Nida, Eugene A., *Message and Mission: The Communication of Christian Faith* (New York: Harper and Row, 1960). $5.95.

Peters, George W., *Saturation Evangelism* (Grand Rapids: Zondervan, 1970). $3.45.

Pierce, Robert, *Emphasizing Missions in the Local Church* (Grand Rapids: Zondervan).

Schaeffer, Francis, *The Church at the End of the Twentieth Century* (Downers Grove, Ill.: Inter-Varsity Press, 1970). $3.95.

Street, T. Watson, *On the Growing Edge of the Church* (Richmond: John Knox).

Warren, Max, ed., *To Apply the Gospel, Selections from the Writings of Henry Venn* (Grand Rapids: Eerdmans, 1970). $7.95.

Winter, Ralph D., ed., *Theological Education by Extension* (South Pasadena, Calif.: William Carey Library, 1969). $7.95.

Winter, Ralph D., *Twenty-five Unbelievable Years 1945-1969* (South Pasadena: Carey, 1970). $1.95 (paper).

PERIODICALS

Since some indicated they thought that better material was to be found in periodicals, the following are included:

Peters, George W., "Mission-Church Relationships," I and II, Dallas, Texas, Dallas Theological Seminary, *Bibliotheca Sacra*, John Walvoord, ed. Vol. 125, No. 499, pp. 205-215, No. 500, pp. 300-312.

Flatt, Donald C., "Priorities in Missions – Personnel or Programme?", Geneva, Switzerland, Commission on World Missions and Evangelism of the W.C.C., *International Review of Mission*,Phillip Potter, ed., Vol. 59, 1970, pp. 461-469.

"The Christian Message to a Changing World," Grand Rapids, Michigan, International Association for Reformed Faith and Action, *International Reformed Bulletin*, Paul G. Schrotenber, ed., Number 35, October, 1968.

RECOMMENDED BOOKS

Space does not permit publishing the full list of additional five books recommended, but I include those that were mentioned three or more times (many of the first choices were also on the second list):

Allen, Roland, *Missionary Methods: St. Paul's or Ours?* (Grand Rapids: Eerdmans, 1962). $1.95.

Barrett, David, *Schism and Renewal in Africa: An Analysis of*

Six Thousand Contemporary Movements (London, Oxford University Press, 1968). $7.25.

Beaver, R. Pierce, *Missionary Between the Times* (New York, Doubleday, 1968). $5.95.

Cook, Harold R., *Missionary Life and Work* (Chicago: Moody, 1962). $5.95.

Lindsell, Harold, *An Evangelical Theology of Missions* (Grand Rapids: Zondervan, 1970). $2.45 (paper).

Lindsell, Harold, ed., *The Church's Worldwide Mission* (Waco: Word, 1966). $3.95.

Neill, Stephen, *The Unfinished Task* (London: Lutterworth, 1957). $2.10 (paper).

Read, William R.,*Latin American Church Growth* Monteroso, Victor and Johnson, Harmon jt. eds. (Grand Rapids: Eerdmans, 1969). $6.95.

Scherer, James A., *Missionary Go Home:A Reappraisal of the Christian World Mission* (Englewood Cliffs, N.J.: Prentice-Hall, 1964). $3.95.

An additional sixty-five books were listed among the five best books. They will be included in a complete bibliography that is in preparation for distribution at the Green Lake Study Conference.

Book Reviews

The Third World and Mission, by Dennis E. Clark. Waco, Texas: Word Books. 129 pp. $3.95.

Horace L. Fenton, Jr.

Only about one book out of every twenty-five I read genuinely excites me. Dennis Clark has written such a book. I have no hesitation in saying that I believe that every missionary, every mission executive, and every member of a mission board would profit greatly by reading it. And I would hope that many other concerned Christians would also read it; it would do them good and would greatly increase their understanding of the missionary situation today.

The author writes from a broad personal knowledge of the work of Christ in the Third World. He is no armchair expert, theorizing about conditions of which he has only academic knowledge. Instead, he grapples with the contemporary issues in missions, and, not content to engage in endless hand-wringing over them, he gives us practical suggestions about what we ought to be doing in the days ahead.

Clark's basic premise is that there will have to be some major changes in missionary thinking and in missionary structures, if missions are to survive the seventies and make a real impact for Christ on the world. According to him, we carry on our work in a context where the world situation is radically changed, and where "a Western missionary becomes very conscious of his vulnerability" (p. 28).

The author shows no reluctance to deal forthrightly with the sacred cows of the missionary enterprise. His approach is a hard-hitting one, and it may well stir up some violent reactions. So much the better! This may be just what we need to jar us out of insensitivity to some of the basic issues that cripple and compromise our witness abroad.

Specifically, Clark expresses concern over the actions and attitudes of both the home churches and the sending societies. He reminds us of the sub-biblical nature of much of our promotional program and of the motivations to which we appeal for missionary support. He is particularly burdened by the way "missionary giving is tied to the emotional appeal of 'the poor heathen far, far away.' As soon as a seasoned missionary or approved candidate wants to work only forty miles away from the sponsoring church, his support is dropped.

". . . During the '70's Christians in the sending churches of the Western world must be led from pre-colonial to post-colonial concepts and must return to the biblical pattern: 'every church in the world everywhere obligated to evangelize' (Matthew 13:38 [Phillips]). Churches happily supporting twenty missionaries 10,000 miles away would then consider also the inner-city ghettos ten miles from their place of worship. One practical way to bring about such a change in attitude would be for missionary societies to merge and diversify" (pp. 32, 33).

But it is obsolete mission structures that weigh especially upon Clark. He sees some value in bringing competent nationals into present-day missionary organizations, but at the same time he recognizes how hard it is for these nationals to find their place in organizations that basically, for all our claims to the contrary, are rooted in North America. To this end, he writes, "In the present climate of opinion in most Third World nations, is it credible to imagine nationals serving within the structure of Western missionary societies? . . .

"The national staff member of a foreign-controlled mission faces serious problems . . . It seems almost too late for Western societies to recruit the national because, with very few exceptions, the stigma of being labeled a 'stooge' or 'puppet' reduces usefulness. The more likely pattern of development will be the strengthening of existing missionary societies in Third World nations and proliferation of others . . . .

"The Western concept of 'hiring and firing' overlooks the deep feeling of Christians in the Third World and can only attract 'hirelings' who will flee when the wolf comes" (pp. 44,45).

The author is not unaware of financial problems that might arise under a changed structural setup, but he feels that these will be dealt with by (1) the elimination of unnecessary institutions, which reflect more the cultural background of the missionaries than they do the needs of the people; (2) increased giving on the part of the nationals themselves; and (3) a continuing flow of funds from the more affluent nations to those who have less.

In dealing with these problems he sees a strong need for receiving churches (in the Third World) to communicate their feelings and reactions to the sending churches in North America, and for the sending churches to trust the Holy Spirit to guide their brethren in the Third World in the use of funds which are channeled to them. He warns strongly against exporting the homeland problems of North America to the Third World, and sees us as missionaries frequently in danger of doing just this.

National leadership, the author insists, must be chosen by nationals and not handpicked by missionaries. He writes, "The foreign selection of individuals and the by-passing of national and accredited leadership has caused untold complications and problems to local Christians . . . . Many missionaries have been greatly humbled and spiritually enriched as they have served alongside national Christian leaders and watched the way they work " (pp. 91, 92).

Again the writer reminds us, "A main target in the '70's will be for Third World leaders to establish permanently and securely the principle that 'under God and led by His Spirit, we, His people, in this nation, will determine what is best for the evangelism of our peole, and how most effectively to ensure the development and strengthening of believers, so that they become fully involved as functioning members of Christ's body ' " (p. 94).

Clark says that we are plagued today by twentieth-century counterparts of both the Sadducees and the Pharisees. The former, in their present-day manifestation, are the theological liberals who have pressed their Bible-denying doctrines on the Third World. Today's Pharisees, he says, are the separatists who have insisted on imposing their unbiblical divisiveness on the mission fields of the world.

The author is not content to be critical. His suggestions as to what should be the objectives of missions during the next ten years (pp. 33, 34) are worthy of careful study and evaluation by every missionary society.

You won't agree with everything in the book, but where did we evangelicals get the idea, so tenaciously held by so many of us, that we had to agree with every position an author takes in order to profit by reading him? Clark will force you to reexamine your own positions, and this is surely a healthy thing for all of us. Moreover, his knowledge is so thorough, and his passion for the work of Christ so evident, that his positions are not lightly to be brushed aside.

Clark's book is to be one of the basic documents for the Green Lake Consultation, to be sponsored by the Interdenominational Foreign Mission Association and the Evangelical Foreign Missions Association next September. *The Third World and Mission* has much to say to the issues that will be discussed at that gathering. Our missions will do a better job in the days ahead if we take seriously what Dennis Clark has to say to us.

Dr. Fenton is general director of the Latin America Mission, Bogota, N.J.

Christianity and Comparative Religion, by J. N. D. Anderson. Downers Grove, Ill.: Inter-Varsity Press. 128 pp. $1.95.

William W. Bass

This is a short, useful summary of the comparative aspects of world religions. Reference is made to Islam, the writer's specialty, Hinduism, Zoroastrianism, Taoism, Shintoism, Judaism, and other religions, as they are compared with Christianity. The book would probably be more useful if side headings were used to make it easier to find specific aspects in which the reader would be interested. It is, however, very readable and a rather unique look at this phase of religion from an evangelical point of view. It is a rather rigorous consideration of the inherent thought patterns of the religions considered; it is a very honest treatment, and serves as a corrective to not only the syncretistic attitude of books in this area, but also to the rigorous position which sees no value at all in the other religions. The basic and straight-forward evaluation of the book is that, in terms of modern teaching and reading, it serves as a very valuable alternative in selecting the typical stack of paperbacks for a world religions course.

Actually, the extensive introduction is very penetrating and is worth the reading of the book. Taking a very hard perspective, Professor Anderson refuses to accept any form of syncretism because it does not allow for the peculiar saving act of God in Christ as expressed by the gospel. He denies that Christianity can be set within the general consideration of philosophy of religion or be expressed in the basic "wheel" philosophy of Eleade's timeless, motionless center, where all is peace. He sees clearly that Christianity must be interpreted historically, in terms of the imagery of the "road" – as a journey or pilgrimage. While he correctly holds syncretism and mysticism to be erroneous concepts, he refuses to interpret them uniformly as a Satanic delusion, a product of the unconscious mind, or as God-induced, but feels that one must discriminate very carefully, in that the elements of a given religion may have several sources. He encourages genuine and understanding dialogue between Christianity and other religions, without foregoing the uniqueness of Christ's death upon the cross or minimizing its importance. In this reviewer's opinion, the discussion is excellent, and constitutes a suitable basis for serious dialogue between evangelicals and others.

Understanding that the Israelites were saved on the basis of Christ's sacrifice alone, and not by their animal sacrifices, Professor Anderson holds that salvation may also be obtained for those who have not heard the gospel, provided that they recognize their need and throw themselves upon the mercy of God. While this may occur comparatively infrequently, it is not impossible that the heathen heart, being stimulated to a deep sense of need by the Holy Spirit, may repent and turn to God for mercy, and find it on the basis of Christ's atoning death, without understanding the basis of salvation. In their ignorance, through self-despair, they abandon themselves to God's mercy, after having been brought to that place of need by the Holy Spirit alone. The scriptural bases which Professor Anderson uses to lead to his conclusion are very secure; he presents it in such a way that it is not offensive and clearly represents his opinion only. He appeals to Ulrich Zwingli and G. Campbell Morgan to substantiate his view. Many evangelicals, of course, will take exception to this, but will also wish to grant the penetrating nature of the chapter.

Specific areas in which Christianity is contrasted to other religions are considered. Christ's atonement, in which the historical, decisive, redemptive, ultimate act of God for the world is manifested, is used to distinguish the Christian faith from all other religions. In this, the kingdom of God has come with power; no other religion boasts anything really even remotely comparable to the kerygma of the Apostolic Church. Professor Anderson sets in perspective the relationship between the present and the future in several of the religions, including Christianity, and also considers the role of the "Saviour" in the various religions. In comparing the idea of God, he emphasizes the basic early belief in a supreme God, who unfortunately gets neglected as the religion develops. There is a significant relationship between this highest God of the pagan religions and the God of Glory.

The book is useful by virtue of its brevity, suggestive bibliography, excellent perspective, and the honor which it gives to Christ and the Scriptures.

Dr. Bass teaches at Talbot Seminary, La Mirada, Calif.

Church Growth and the Word of God, by Alan R. Tippett. Grand Rapids, Mich.: William B. Eerdmans Publishing Co. 82 pp. $1.95 (paper).

David Howard

One of the most significant developments in the mission of the church in the past decade has been the emphasis on church growth. The entire world of missionary endeavor is deeply indebted to Dr. Donald McGavran and his colleagues for focusing our attention on a long neglected but vitally important principle that should underlie the outreach of the church. As one reads the rapidly growing volume of literature on this topic (both books and articles) the question often comes to mind, "What are the real biblical principles underlying this emphasis on church growth?" With a few notable exceptions, most of the writings have centered around the sociological, anthropological, and ecclesiastical aspects of church growth. They have emphasized the "what" and the "how." This has all been most stimulating and helpful, but the question of "why" keeps cropping up.

Now Dr. Alan Tippett, veteran missionary of the Fiji Islands and professor in the School of World Mission and Institute of Church Growth at Fuller Seminary, has undertaken the task of giving us a firm biblical basis for the "why" of church growth. Although brief, this book is packed with valuable exegetical material. The broad scope of church growth as a biblical concept is covered in chapter one. The biblical ideas of diffusion, growth (with a plethora of imagery in the Scriptures), numbering, obedience and responsibility, conversion and mission, and continuity are all treated in this one chapter. While it is not the author's intent to give a detailed exegesis of every passage he cites, he has certainly provided an abundance of material. For those who wish to pursue this topic more deeply he has dropped enough seed thoughts to keep an exegete busy for a long time to come.

In subsequent chapters the author treats the dynamics of church growth, problems of non-growth, the current situation, and the Christian hope as related to church growth.

The concept of multi-individual decisions, which underlies the whole idea of a "people movement," is shown to be prominent in both Old and New Testaments. This section alone (in chapter two) is worth the price of the book, as it deals with such a fundamental concept. For those who criticize an emphasis on results, Dr. Tippett shows the New Testament ideas of ingathering as depicted in such images as the steward, the farmer, the husbandman, and the fisherman.

The emphasis in some contemporary theology on a "churchless ministry" (the adequacy of merely being a Christian in the world without relating to an institution which is often attacked as dying) is met head on with Scripture. The New Testament teaching on the centrality of the church in the work of Jesus Christ on earth is clearly developed. It is also demonstrated that there is no place for a local church without outreach. "The congregation and its outreach stand or fall together" (p. 67).

Finally, the Christian hope as related to the church and its outreach is admirably expounded. The Old Testament hope was fulfilled in Christ. The New Testament hope is shown as moving, under the leadership of the Holy Spirit in his church, towards the final consummation in Christ. Again it is the church that becomes the center of God's activity on earth. Therefore, the growth of that church must be part of God's total plan and must become central in the concern of his people.

For any who have read the church growth literature and perhaps been disturbed at times with the question of "why," this refreshing and careful analysis of the biblical principles underlying the entire movement is a welcome addition. It is one of the most significant books yet to be published on this topic and should be studied carefully by all missionaries and mission leaders.

Mr. Howard is missionary director of Inter-Varsity Christian Fellowship, Madison, Wis.

To Apply the Gospel, Selections From the Writings of Henry Venn, edited by Max Warren. Grand Rapids, Mich.: William B. Eerdmans Publishing Co. 243 pp. $6.95.

Ralph Winter

One hundred years overdue, now at last Henry Venn's famous phrase, "the euthanasia of the mission," appears in its full context. Even in his own day Venn, general secretary of the Church Missionary Society, was widely and highly regarded as a keen and creative missions strategist. Now, one of his successors, Max Warren, an eminent mission statesman in this century, has done all mission leaders the great service of poring over thousands of pages of Venn's writings and pulling together choice excerpts that represent his central thinking. All of these are gathered together quite efficiently, and introduced with illuminating comments under the headings of "The Coming into Being of a Church," "The Calling and Work of a Missionary," "The Principles and Working of a Missionary Society," "A Voluntary Society and Its Relations with Ecclesiastical Authority," etc.

Even now – or *especially now* – the book wields a staggering punch. Here we see spread out idea after idea of the "latest" variety – *written well over a hundred years ago*! Here are "indigenous church principles," emphasis on "the formation of a national ministry." Here are the "three selfs" of "self-support, self-government, and self-propagation," etc.

Thus, an appalling question arises: if these ideas are not really recent, but were in fact widely circulated over a century ago, is it that they don't work or that they are very difficult to apply? I would rather believe that then, as now, relatively few missionaries study and reflect upon the strategy they are following. If this is the case, it is bad enough, but it is correctible! Perhaps this book itself will contribute significantly. It offers much to reflect upon that is still pertinent.

The book certainly clarifies the widely misunderstood phrase "the euthanasia of the mission." Apparently, it never was intended to refer to the end of a mission society but merely to gradual withdrawal from an established church in order to start anew in "the regions beyond." Where the idea in practice failed, it was not actually fairly or properly tried, according to Max Warren.

However, even in this very sound scheme for turning over authority to the national church, I find not the slightest suggestion that the emerging church would ever spawn anything like its own mission structure to peoples foreign to them. Here then we have a book constituting the most extensive exposition and defense of the voluntary society for mission, but the curious absence of even the tiniest suggestion that the younger churches themselves might need their own voluntary societies to fulfill the Great Commission.

Dr. Winter is associate professor of missions at the School of World Mission and Institute of Church Growth, Fuller Theological Seminary, Pasadena, Calif.

The Jesus Family in Communist China, by D. Vaughan Rees. Ft. Washington, Pa.: Christian Literature Crusade. 104 pp. 89 cents (paper).

Rev. Wesley L. Gustafson

This is a book of Christian and Communist facts. Even though it is not written for the purpose of strategy for missionary work, it is one of the finest on the subject.

The experiences of Dr. Rees, former China Inland Mission doctor, as he lived and worked with the "Jesus Family" in China under the Communists, date back to 1948-1951. Subsequent testimony bears out that many of this group have since sealed their witness in blood. Many others are in Communist prisons. Others are carrying on a faithful witness in China.

Obedience to the Scriptures is not only suggested as possible in Communist China, but illustrated profusely. We may hate to admit it, but many of their methods and organizational patterns far surpass what we often call biblical Christianity.

One may not agree with all the methods and means used. We may disagree with some of their doctrinal beliefs and practices. In spite of this, we have to admit that the "Jesus Family" is doing something no Western Church has succeeded in doing in Communist China – continue!

The "tent-making" practiced by this group while witnessing was very effective. It was an inspiration to the participants and awesome to the Communists.

One of the "observing" commisars of the Communist party said, "I have seen something I did not know existed in the world. This is what we Communists want to do; we won't do it in a hundred years."

A Communist observing the Christians working at a hospital asked, "How do you make the nurses take an interest in their work and love the children? How do you stop the nurses from stealing drugs?" The stock answer by the Christians was, "If they have the Lord Jesus in their hearts, then all these questions are solved."

The chapter on the indigenous church is profoundly simple. Why it takes us so long to catch on is hard to answer.

The "Jesus Family" approach to evangelism can be adapted anywhere in the world. Their type of Christianity is more than lipping phrases and turning to pat Scriptures. Their great impact was not just in telling about the Bible, Christ and the Christian life. The impact came through lives in vital touch with God the Holy Spirit.

Dr. Rees, after living with them a couple of years, summed it up by saying, "Why, all the Bible is true; I have only believed it in theory up till now."

Mr. Gustafson is Candidate and Orient Secretary, The Evangelical Free Church of America, Minneapolis, Minn.

Concise Dictionary of the Christian World Mission, edited by Stephen Neill, Gerald H. Anderson, and John Goodwin. Nashville: Abingdon Press, 1971. 682 pp. $10.50.

David Howard

"Only rarely is it possible for authors and editors to claim that they have done something that has never been done before. The editors of this dictionary, however, believe that this is a claim they are entitled to make." These are the opening words of the introduction and the claim is no doubt justified. Certainly the most up-to-date reference work on world missions, it is also the most comprehensive one volume available.

The extension of the Christian church from 1492 to the present is covered. Three types of articles appear: those dealing with *countries* of the world; *biographies* of leaders of every race and confession who have done something new and creative in missionary work; and *subjects*, ranging from acculturation to witchcraft. Arranged in alphabetical order, the articles include cross references and bibliographical material which will enhance further study.

More than two hundred contributors cooperated in the work. The names of many of these will be known to anyone familiar with contemporary literature on world mission. Names such as Beaver, Beyerhaus, Boer, Grubb, Hogg, Latourette, Newbigin, Nida, and Visser't Hooft are there. From IFMA and EFMA circles come contributors such as Goddard, Kane, Lindsell, McGavran, Mellis and Nelson. This has provided an unusually accurate and fair evaluation of most of the movements and subjects covered. The editors state that "each contributors has been free to express his own point of view; but in many cases it would be hard to guess from the contents of the article to which particular Christian confession the writer adheres."

While this is true in specifics, it is sometimes easy to guess the general viewpoint of the authors. It is only natural that any writer, whether related to conservative evangelical or ecumenically-oriented groups, should express his own understanding of the organization, person, country, or subject being treated.

The editors state that the publication in 1967 of *The Encyclopedia of Modern Christian Missions* edited by Burton L. Goddard and his colleagues at Gordon Divinity School, came too late to be consulted by most of the contributors to this dictionary. Some of the same material is covered, but the purposes of the two volumes are quite distinct. The former deals exclusively with the agencies involved in world missions, while this dictionary covers the whole scope of studies in the field of world missions. Thus, it is a valuable complement to the earlier encyclopedia.

The articles are concise and generally well written. The limitations of space (less than 700 pages to cover a vast field of study) have made selectivity indispensable. The editors are to be commended for their keen perception in choosing those subjects most vital to world missions. Evangelicals may be disappointed at times in looking for an article on their favorite missionary statesman (whose name may or may not appear), or their favorite topic. But usually they will find it treated. The article on "Evangelism" may seem inadequate to some, while the article on "Church Growth" (both by the editor, Stephen Neill) may prove more satisfactory. Occasional misprints are inevitable. (For example, World Vision is listed as having been founded by Bob Pierce in 1930 rather than 1950), but this is a hazard of the trade that will always be with us.

The editors state that "this dictionary is a work that can be read through with pleasure from cover to cover," and this reviewer is inclined to agree with them. Anyone who disciplines himself to undertake such a task will be richly rewarded with a comprehensive survey of world missions during the past five centuries. Any mission leader, regardless of his position, will want this outstanding reference work at his fingertips. This is a significant book, and the world of missions will long be in debt to the editors and contributors.

Student Power in World Evangelism, by David Howard. Downers Grove, Ill.: Inter-Varsity Press, 1970. 129 pp. $1.25 (paper).

James W. Reapsome

This was the "text" for Urbana '70, written by Inter-Varsity's missionary director, formerly a missionary in Costa Rica and Colombia. The "student" angle in missions constitutes the last two-thirds of the book. It is an illuminating historical survey. The first part is a biblical rationale for missions.

The historical section is about equally divided between the period from "the Haystack Prayer Meeting" (Williams College, 1806) to Moody's Mount Hermon student conference (1886), and the period from the founding of the Student Volunteer Movement (1888) to its ultimate demise and the rise of the Student Foreign Missions Fellowship (1936) and its merger with Inter-Varsity Christian Fellowship (1946).

Howard also discusses the current student generation ("critical, restless, honest, concerned") in relation to missions. There is an appendix, "Some Observations on the Charismatic Movement," which doesn't fit the theme of the book. A chapter on how mission boards might more effectively get in step with student concerns regarding missionary work in the '70's might have been more appropriate.

Howard's main thesis, however, is adequately proved: students have sparked revivals of missionary outreach in the past.

Mr. Reapsome is managing editor of Evangelical Missions Quarterly.

The Witnessing Church in a Changing World, by Dale and Alma Bjork. Evanston, Ill.: Harvest Publications. 120 pp. $1.95 (paper).

Vergil Gerber

Are the church and missions still live options in a so-called "post-Christian" era? Dale and Alma Bjork think so. They offer some straight-forward answers to the gnawing questions of the "now" generation. Is it really necessary to have the church in this twentieth century? Is the church relevant to the complex needs of a secularized society? Since the world in which we live is completely different from what it was a thousand or two thousand years ago, what is the church's mission today?

The authors write from a background of missionary service, first in China, later in Japan, plus years of administrative experience with the Baptist General Conference Board of Foreign Missions. Their book reflects broad reading and a unique sensitivity to the needs of today's jet-propelled, hate-filled society in revolt.

When and where did the idea of the church begin? The book lays the biblical foundations for her existence and witness. This is followed by panoramic flashbacks from her 1,900-year history – starting with the day of Pentecost and working through the modern missionary movement of the nineteenth century to the explosive decade of the 1970's.

The chapters which follow deal with the witnessing church in the midst of change – demographic, political, sociological, technological and religious. There are questions for discussion at the end of each. The climax is a descriptive image of the new kind of missionary needed

What the authors say is not startlingly new, but they do lay down in concise terms the *raison d'etre* for the missionary presence of the church. The book is an excellent guide for the use in youth meetings, Sunday school elective courses, lay institutes, and home study groups.

Mr. Gerber is executive director, Evangelical Missions Information Service, Wheaton, Ill.

Letter to the editor

Dear Sir,

Recently the article, "The Pastoral Care of Missionaries" (Fall, 1970) came to my attention. I am an evangelical Christian and also a counseling psychologist by profession. My family and I have taken a year's leave of absence from my position at the University of Nebraska and we are living in Tehran, Iran, where I am training counselors at the National Teachers University. Our purpose in being here is three-fold:

(1) We want to increase our understanding of missions and the problems of missionaries. (2) We are trying to provide support and assistance for the missionaries in any way we can. (3) We are trying to carry on a personal ministry to national students and to Americans living in the community.

During the last few years we have become increasingly aware of the personal problems and concerns among our missionary friends and acquaintances. Our personal experience certainly confirms the need as described in the article. As a Christian psychologist I have a real burden for the missionary and I am seeking the guidance of the Lord regarding a broader ministry in this area. If God has given some Christian pastors and psychologists special gifts and training in counseling, it seems only reasonable that the missionary should have access to these services without fear of condemnation from his colleagues.

My question for your readers is how can these services best be provided for missionaries? Personal and family counseling? Summer family conferences? Consultative services to mission boards? Child guidance services? Psychologists' participation in missionary conferences? Consultative services to missionaries via letters?

While here in Tehran I have conducted a series of classes in counseling for missionaries, and have also conducted a mini-family conference in which we dealt with such topics as the Christian family, the sexual relationship in marriage, the Christian responsibility in child-rearing, problem children in Christian homes, and so on. These topics seem to be of real help to the missionaries here. Is this the kind of thing that should be duplicated elsewhere or provided for missionaries on furlough?

If these questions could be answered by the missionaries, then those of us who are trained in counseling would be in a better position to know how our services might be offered. This is not intended to be an advertisement. I am concerned that missionaries have access to the services they need. I'm sure I am only one of the many Christian psychologists who would welcome a broadened ministry in this area. Possibly some of your readers can provide us with some guidance in this area.

Earl O. Wilson, Ph.D., 20 Sarabandi, Yusufabad, Tehran, Iran (after July 31, 1600 S. 44th, Lincoln, Neb. 68506).